Items should be returned on or before the last date shown below. Items not already requested by other borrowers may be renewed in person, in writing or by telephone. To renew, please quote the number on the barcode label. To renew online a PIN is required. This can be requested at your local library.
Renew online @ **www.dublincitypubliclibraries.ie**
Fines charged for overdue items will include postage incurred in recovery. Damage to or loss of items will be charged to the borrower.

Leabharlanna Poiblí Chathair Bhaile Átha Cliath
Dublin City Public Libraries

 Comhairle Cathrach
Bhaile Átha Cliath
Dublin City Council

Date Due	Date Due	Date Due
- 6 JAN 2018		

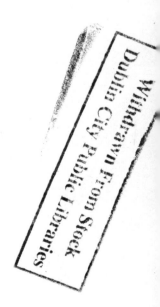

YOUNG IRELAND AND THE WRITING OF IRISH HISTORY

JAMES QUINN

UNIVERSITY COLLEGE DUBLIN PRESS

PREAS CHOLÁISTE OLLSCOILE BHAILE ÁTHA CLIATH

2015

First published 2015
by University College Dublin Press
UCD Humanities Institute, Room H103
Belfield,
Dublin 4
Ireland
www.ucdpress.ie

ISBN 978-1-906359-88-1 pb

CIP data available from the British Library

*The right of James Quinn to be identified as the
author of this work has been asserted by him*

Typeset in Scotland in Adobe Caslon and
Bodoni Oldstyle by Ryan Shiels
Text Design by Lyn Davies
Printed in England on acid-free paper by
CPI Antony Rowe, Chippenham, Wilts.

Contents

—

Acknowledgements

—

I have incurred many debts of both a professional and personal nature in writing this book. I would like to thank the staff of all the libraries and archives that I used, with a special mention to the staff of the library of the Royal Irish Academy, especially Siobhán Fitzpatrick, Bernadette Cunningham, Petra Schnabel, Sophie Evans and Amy Hughes, who were invariably pleasant and helpful and greatly assisted my work.

I wish to thank my colleagues on the Dictionary of Irish Biography project, James McGuire, Linde Lunney, Larry White, Patrick Maume, Turlough O'Riordan and Terry Clavin for creating such a pleasant and stimulating work environment. I owe a particular debt to James, who with characteristic generosity took on much more than his fair share of the work of the DIB to allow me to pursue my research interests. I would also like to thank Vincent Morley for bringing my attention to some research materials that I might have otherwise missed, and Roisín Higgins, for very kindly allowing me to see a draft of her work on reading rooms before it was published.

I wish to thank Noelle Moran of UCD Press for her efficiency and unflagging enthusiasm, and for making the publishing of a book just about as painless as it can be. Noelle also suggested some useful changes to the text, which have undoubtedly improved it.

Early drafts of the book were read by friends and colleagues such as Bernadette Cunningham, Patrick Maume, James McGuire, Kate Bateman and Manuela Ceretta. All these fine scholars made valuable suggestions and corrections for which I am very grateful. Any remaining errors are of course all my own work.

I am very grateful for the support of my family, especially my father Joseph, who in his own understated way was always a supportive presence, and helped to move things along with his interest and encouragement. Special thanks are due to my brother Paul for the use of his cottage in the quiet surroundings of Achill Island, where I did the initial reading for the book. My dear friend Eimear Nic Lochlainn also provided a pleasant refuge in her Glasgow home, and much congenial company in the Scottish Highlands and elsewhere.

Finally, I owe a special debt to Louise for her kindness, patience, good humour and understanding.

JAMES QUINN
March, 2015

INTRODUCTION

—

In 1842 a small group of Irish nationalists, who would later be known as Young Ireland, founded the *Nation* newspaper. They saw their mission as awakening the Irish people to the fact that they were an historic nation that should determine its own future. Ireland, they insisted, had a proud history, which told of sufferings bravely endured, resistance that had never faltered, and a national spirit that had never been crushed. However, since Ireland's history had mostly been written by its conquerors, the true record of her past had been misrepresented, leading the *Nation* to proclaim that 'The history of Ireland has not yet been written'.[1] Rectifying this was one of their most pressing tasks, to which they devoted much of their labour. This work seeks to examine why Young Ireland attached such importance to the writing of history, how it went about writing that history, and what impact their historical writings had.

The name 'Young Ireland' itself was coined by Daniel Owen Madden in his *Ireland and its Rulers since 1829* (1843). Madden saw strong similarities between the young men who produced the *Nation* and the elitist and nationalistic group of English Tories known as 'Young England', which included Benjamin Disraeli and Lord John Manners. For many years, most of the *Nation* writers refused to recognise the name, denying that they formed a separate party within the Repeal Association, but over time they came to accept it.[2] Unhappy with Daniel O'Connell's cautious leadership of the association, they believed the name Young Ireland captured the freshness and vitality they had brought to the nationalist movement, and it is the name by which they have gone down in Irish history. It was though a loose label and has been applied to many who would have undoubtedly rejected it. In his comprehensive biographical collection, *The Young Irelanders* (1944), T. F. O'Sullivan included all those who wrote for the *Nation*, regardless of their political views, with the result that the work included many marginal contributors to the paper and several who did not share the nationalist aspirations of Davis and Duffy. In this work I have generally used the term for the small group of like-minded nationalists who were regular contributors to the original *Nation* between the founding of the paper in 1842 and its suppression in 1848. In terms of the writing of Irish history, the most significant of these were Thomas Davis, Charles Gavan Duffy, John Mitchel, Thomas D'Arcy McGee, Charles Patrick Meehan and Thomas MacNevin.

Young Ireland embarked on its educational campaign at a propitious time, attempting to capitalise on the success of the temperance movement of the late 1830s. Believing that a sober people was eager for improvement and instruction, they sought to provide them with accessible reading matter that would nurture and fortify their national feelings. Rising levels of popular literacy provided further opportunities. By the early 1840s the first cohorts of those educated under the new national system of primary education (founded in 1831) were coming to adulthood. Nationalists welcomed this advance in literacy, but were concerned that the government were using the schools as a means of promoting Anglicisation. The authorities too were aware that history was capable of stirring up powerful emotions and took pains to ensure that the national school curriculum contained nothing that might encourage a sense of historical grievance. The writers of the *Nation* therefore saw it as their patriotic duty to give the Irish people the 'national' education that the British government had deliberately prevented them from receiving. To this end, they encouraged the establishment of reading rooms stocked with nationalist literature to supplement or supplant official educational initiatives.

The Young Irelanders also sought to take advantage of the growing interest and advances in Irish antiquarian studies that had occurred in the previous decade. New institutions such as the Irish Archaeological Society and the Celtic Society were founded, old ones such as the Royal Dublin Society and the Royal Irish Academy reinvigorated, and opportunities for research opened up by the work of the Irish Ordnance Survey. In Ireland, as elsewhere in Europe, there was a growing interest in the distant past and the Middle Ages, and a fascination with Ireland's picturesque archaeological remains. To satisfy and encourage this interest, the *Nation* set about promoting and popularising the pioneering work of a new generation of antiquarian scholars such as George Petrie, John O'Donovan and Eugene O'Curry.

Most contemporary European nationalists had a deep interest in history, believing that a knowledge of the past gave a people the title deeds to nationality, their existence as a distinct nation validated by the trials and triumphs of previous generations. This was particularly so for subject nationalities in multi-ethnic empires, who maintained that their imperial masters had deliberately obliterated their history to deny their claims to independent statehood. History was of particular importance for those who believed themselves wronged, and was central to stoking the mixture of pride and grievance that propelled nationalist movements across Europe. For Irish nationalists, it took on an additional importance. Religion and language, two of the most powerful components of national identity elsewhere, divided in Ireland rather than united, leading the Young Irelanders to stress their country's culture and history as powerful national unifiers.

Although they had few direct links with European nationalists, Davis and his colleagues generally identified with the Germanic romantic nationalism rooted in folk tradition that was then prevalent in much of Europe, and was explicitly acknowledged in the *Nation*'s motto: 'To foster a public opinion in Ireland and make it racy of the soil.' They were the first Irish nationalists to base their claim for self-determination primarily on cultural and historic arguments. A half century earlier the United Irishmen had formulated a nationalism that owed much to the progressive ideals of the Enlightenment and stressed the advance of humanity towards a universal future of liberty and fraternity. They usually dismissed the past as a collection of ancient and irrelevant quarrels, motivated by outmoded sectarian hatreds, and saw it as a troublesome burden to be shed rather than a heritage to be celebrated.[3]

Nineteenth-century nationalism was essentially historicist in character, arguing that the world was made up of distinct national communities with their own unique character and history.[4] Young Ireland saw their work as challenging the taunts and misrepresentations of hostile historians who had made the Irish look on their past with shame rather than pride. Such historians regularly contrasted the purpose and grandeur of English history, in which a coherent series of events led inexorably to domestic liberty and imperial glory, with the chaotic squabbling of Irish history: 'Our bravery they have called turbulence, our resistance rebellion, our virtue barbarity. . . . This must be undone before we can be a nation'.[5] The Young Irelanders therefore sought not just to reclaim the past, but to redeem it: to impose a pattern on the various incidents, disruptions and contradictions of Irish history, showing that it had as much purpose and coherence as that of any other country, and that its disparate struggles were all part of a sustained and noble campaign to resist foreign conquest and recover Ireland's independence. Their writings were vivid and partisan: scholarly detachment in relation to the Irish past was viewed at best as a form of academic self-indulgence and at worst as moral cowardice.[6] Young Ireland wrote history to nourish collective memory and reinforce allegiances and obligations to the nation, so that the Irish would see themselves as a distinct people rooted in the struggles and sacrifices of the past and insist that they should govern their own destiny.

The *Nation* lamented that before its publication 'all the world could not produce a people so ignorant of their own history' as Ireland, and dedicated itself to creating a nation of active and informed citizens, well-versed in the knowledge of their country's past.[7] It also argued that the study of history could enlighten opponents. Orangemen were encouraged to emulate the

Repeal Association and add reading rooms to their lodges, where they would learn that they had been ill-served by England's policy of divide and rule.[8] Young Ireland appealed to the Presbyterians of Ulster to remember the historic role they had played in asserting Ireland's rights with the Volunteers and the United Irishmen. Duffy included Orange songs in his *Ballad Poetry of Ireland* on the basis that

> they echo faithfully the sentiments of a strong, vehement and indomitable body of Irishmen, who may come to battle for their country better than they ever battled for their prejudices or their bigotries. At all events, to know what they love and believe is a precious knowledge.[9]

The Young Irelanders valued passion and imagination in their writings over objectivity and scholarly precision, and in most cases their knowledge of history was rather basic.[10] But they knew enough to be effective propagandists, and in a clear and coherent narrative of Ireland's past, they emphasised dramatic and picturesque events, lauding heroes and condemning villains, and aimed to enthral and inspire readers rather than just inform them.[11] Regarding history primarily as a literary and rhetorical enterprise that should engage the reader's emotions, Davis argued that

> exact dates, subtle plots, minute connexions and motives . . . are not the highest ends of history. To hallow or accurse the scenes of glory and honour, or of shame and sorrow; to give the imagination the arms, and homes, and senates, and battles of other days; to rouse and soften, and strengthen and enlarge us with the passions of great periods; to lead us into love of self-denial, of justice, of beauty, of valour, of generous life and proud death; and to set up in our souls the memory of great men, who shall then be as models and judges of our actions.[12]

He and his colleagues drew much of their inspiration from contemporary romantic writers such as Thomas Carlyle, Jules Michelet and Augustin Thierry. They attempted to emulate their vividness and engagement and had only contempt for those such as David Hume and Henry Hallam whom they dubbed 'philosophic historians', claiming that they peddled a complacent and spurious objectivity that cloaked sympathy for the oppressor and condescension towards the oppressed.[13]

Focusing on the dramatic and the inspirational, Young Ireland paid particular attention to military history – social history was generally ignored and economic history rarely went beyond denunciations of English attempts to stifle the development of the Irish economy. Much of the history being written elsewhere in Europe also emphasised great battles and heroes, but the

Young Irelanders attached a special importance to proving that the Irish were as brave as (if not braver) than other nations. The Victorian age placed a particular value on physical courage and martial prowess as an indicator of moral worth. Britain, it was argued, ruled a vast empire because its virile character and military might had enabled it to overcome inferior races. Influenced by Carlylean notions of hero worship, the Young Irelanders were intent on proving that the Irish were no less manly than their conquerors, and often focused on the deeds of charismatic warriors such as Hugh O'Neill, Owen Roe O'Neill and Patrick Sarsfield, creating semi-mythic figures who inspired later generations. When domestic history was not suitably heroic, notably during the years of Protestant oppression and Catholic quiescence that characterised the first three quarters of the eighteenth century, the Young Irelanders shifted the focus abroad, to the valiant deeds of the Wild Geese. French victories in which Irish Brigades were prominent such as Fontenoy and Cremona were lauded as victories for Ireland achieved by soldiers who remained loyal to their homeland and fought Ireland's battles on foreign soil.

Despairing at the cost, quality and anti-national bias of history books available to the public, in 1845 Davis and Charles Gavan Duffy launched the 'Library of Ireland', a series of works by different authors intended to provide Ireland with a national literature in history, poetry and fiction. Written in a lively and accessible style and focusing on some of the most dramatic events in Irish history, the series was an immediate success and gained a wide readership. It was the first time since the seventeenth century that a group of like-minded Irishmen had tried to write their country's history as a collective endeavour. Although covering a wide range of different subjects, their works were linked together by unifying themes, especially by the portrayal of Irish history as a continuous and heroic struggle against foreign domination. One of the most effective ways of doing this was with historical verse, which the *Nation* discovered was 'the most powerful of all possible auxiliaries in the work of spreading a knowledge of history among a people'.[14] The Library of Ireland published several collections of stirring historical ballads, most notably the best-selling *Spirit of the Nation*, which became Young Ireland's most enduring contribution to nationalist literature.

In using newspapers and cheap mass-produced books to propagate Irish history, Young Ireland can be seen as a classic example of Benedict Anderson's theory of nineteenth-century nationalism's use of print capitalism to create a mass solidarity that formed the basis of a new nationally based 'imagined community'.[15] This was a community that stretched back into the past and forward into the future, in which a knowledge of the glories and sacrifices of previous generations was crucial in creating the bonds of obligation and solidarity that bound it together. It required the creation of a coherent narrative of struggle and resistance that pointed the way to the future and the community's eventual realisation as an independent nation. Past failures to throw off the yoke of conquest were seen not as a matter of shame but as evidence of an undying spirit that could never be quenched. In one of his best-known essays Davis had proclaimed:

> This country of ours is no sandbank, thrown up by some recent caprice of earth. It is an ancient land, honoured in the archives of civilisation, traceable into antiquity by its piety, its valour and its sufferings. Every great European race has sent its stream to the river of the Irish mind. Long wars, vast organisations, subtle codes, beacon crimes, leading virtues, and self-mighty men, were here. If we live influenced by wind and sun and tree, and not by the passions and deeds of the past, we are a thriftless and hopeless people.[16]

While the Young Irelanders liked to portray themselves as pioneers in the writing of Irish history, their writings were not particularly original.[17] Lacking the time or inclination to engage in extensive primary research, they drew heavily on existing secondary works, especially those of eighteenth and early nineteenth-century historians such as MacGeoghegan, Curry, Leland, Plowden and Taaffe, filtering these accounts through the lens of their own romantic nationalism. The popularity of their writings owed much to the fact that their main themes of oppression and resistance were already deeply ingrained in popular memory. Ordinary people were not as ignorant of their history as the *Nation* claimed, but had often picked up a rudimentary knowledge in the home or hedge school. History books were generally scarce and expensive before the 1840s, but the deficiency was made up by a rich oral and manuscript-based vernacular culture.[18] The works of Young Ireland reinforced rather than replaced this popular interpretation, confirming and supplementing folk memories of dispossession, persecution and heroic struggle, and contributed to the conservative nature of nationalist historiography for decades to come. When in the 1890s a group of nationalists attempted to renew the work of Young Ireland by publishing a 'New Irish Library', their works largely repeated the formulae laid down by Young Ireland half a century earlier.[19]

Young Ireland's emphasis on culture and history differed from Daniel O'Connell's more populist and pragmatic politics, and added to tensions in the Repeal Association. Although they were cautious about openly espousing republican ideology, Young Ireland's programme to create virtuous and informed citizens who were proud of the heroism and sacrifices of their forebears owed much to the ideals of classical civic republicanism. Their belief that history was made primarily by warrior heroes and that, in the right circumstances, national independence was worth some bloodshed, put them on a collision course with O'Connell, who in July 1846 tried to bring matters to a head by forcing all members of the Repeal Association to condemn violence as a means of achieving political change. For four years the Young Irelanders had celebrated past efforts to win Ireland's freedom by the sword and, believing they could not repudiate the tradition of armed resistance without sacrificing their integrity, they seceded from the Association.

The rupture in the Repeal Association came about at a time when most Irish people had more serious concerns. In 1846 the potato crop failed for the second consecutive year and deaths from famine and disease began to mount. The *Nation* continued its propagandist and educational initiatives, but by 1847 more urgent concerns such as promoting famine relief and tenant right took precedence. The writing of history was further relegated in the revolutionary year of 1848 when the prospect of achieving Irish independence through armed action seemed possible. However, while the times were not conducive to the writing of history, an awareness of history strongly influenced Young Ireland's actions during these months. As the government cracked down on seditious protests and began arresting Young Irelanders, the movement's leaders believed that they had to strike to preserve their honour and keep faith with the tradition of gallant resistance they had championed in the *Nation*. From his prison cell Duffy, who only months before had been committing the organisation to a strictly constitutional policy, wrote that

> We fight, because the honour, the interest, the necessity, the very existence of this ancient nation depends upon our valour and devotion at this hour. If we cower, if we flinch, if we falter, the hopes are gone for which our fathers' fathers gave their life's blood. Gone in the stench of dishonour and infamy that will cling to it for ever.[20]

A sense of historical duty proved, however, to be an insufficient basis for an insurrection. The Young Irelanders had no military experience and few arms, were opposed by the Catholic church and reliant on a population demoralised by three years of hunger and disease. Their attempt at rebellion was ineffectual and collapsed in days. But far from damaging their reputations, the events of 1848 helped to secure them, and they were praised by later nationalists for having asserted in arms Ireland's right to independence. Their own writings contributed to this, with accounts by Michael Doheny, Charles Gavan Duffy and John Mitchel portraying the Young Irelanders as selfless and courageous idealists who kept the spirit of Irish nationality alive. Duffy's histories were widely read and often treated as the definitive accounts of an impartial eye-witness, his polemical intentions well cloaked by his measured judgements and moderate tone. His interpretation was supplemented by Mitchel's more openly polemical *Last Conquest of Ireland (Perhaps)*. Mitchel claimed that far from being a natural disaster, the Famine was an act of genocide by the British government which had taken advantage of the social disruption caused by the potato blight to conduct a deliberate campaign of extermination. It differed from earlier attempts at extermination in its methods and rhetoric, but its results were even more destructive than the brutal campaigns of the sixteenth and seventeenth century.[21]

Young Ireland's efforts to write history that served immediate political ends resulted in the creation of an interpretation that was strongly present-centred, doctrinaire and determinist, in which complexities, contradictions and discontinuities were ironed out into a grand narrative of heroic resistance. While history written with such an overtly polemical purpose inevitably invites challenge by later scholars, there is no denying its persuasive power and its importance in creating national solidarity. After 1848 growing prosperity and literacy ensured that print culture would play an ever greater role in creating an awareness of Ireland as an historic and distinct nation. Young Ireland followers founded newspapers that attempted to carry on the work of the *Nation*, and in exile, members of the original group – such as John Mitchel and Thomas D'Arcy McGee – continued to write lengthy national narratives which were among the most widely read Irish histories of the nineteenth century.[22] Nationalist journalists such as A. M. and T. D. Sullivan, and movements such as Sinn Féin, recognised the galvanising effect of historical writings, and their publications often repeated or distilled the historical writings of Young Ireland.

There were two distinct phases in the Young Ireland history-writing project: the publications of the *Nation* and the Library of Ireland in the 1840s, and the accounts of their own times and narrative histories of Ireland that were published after the collapse of the movement in 1848. In the latter phase history and contemporary comment were often combined: Duffy prefaced his work on the Young Ireland movement with a concise history of Ireland from the earliest times that emphasised the continuity of Ireland's struggle, while Mitchel concluded his *History of Ireland since the Treaty of Limerick* (1868) with the account of the 1840s he had first published as the *Last Conquest*. The Young Irelanders were well aware that writing about the past helped to shape events as well as record them, and managed to establish themselves as both chroniclers of and participants in Ireland's history.

The term Young Ireland enjoyed a new currency in the 1880s as young idealists turned away from the political and agrarian goals pursued by con-stitutional politicians and towards the cultural and historic roots of Irish nationalism. Activists such as William Rooney proclaimed Davis's writings as their gospel and formed Young Ireland societies to promote their historical legacy. Nationalists disillusioned with contemporary politics such as John

O'Leary, Arthur Griffith and W. B. Yeats were drawn into these societies in which the Young Irelanders were lauded as teachers and prophets. Young Ireland history books and poetry anthologies formed the core of the collections in nationalist reading rooms and were widely read by the generation that carried out the revolution of 1916–21. As the country became more radicalised in the early decades of the twentieth century, there was a growing demand for their writings, and new editions of their work provided much of the historical inspiration for the Irish revolution. The pervasive influence of Young Ireland teachings meant that for nationalists at least no major re-writing of Irish history was required in the decades after independence. Their historical ballads remained popular, and in schoolbooks and works of popular history their historical interpretation hardened into an orthodoxy that helped consolidate the standing of the new state.

No major work has been published solely on Young Ireland's writing of Irish history, but the topic has had some treatment. Séamas Ó Néill has examined Thomas Davis's history-writing efforts in a short article in Irish published in an official publication to commemorate the centenary of Davis's death in 1945, and the same work also featured an article on the Library of Ireland by P. S. O'Hegarty.[23] Richard Davis's general history of the Young Ireland movement mentions their efforts at history writing only briefly, but recent biographies of Thomas Davis and Thomas D'Arcy McGee have included detailed treatment of their historical writings.[24] Other writers such as David Dwan, Malcolm Brown, Joep Leerssen, Sean Ryder, R. F. Foster and Patrick Maume have also made valuable contributions to the topic by examining the long term influence of their historical writings and their contribution to nationalist ideology.[25]

In Chapter one of this work I examine the part played by history in the beginnings of the Young Ireland movement and the foundation of the *Nation*, and the impetus given to this by developments in education and the temperance movement. Chapter two looks at their reading of history, examining the historical and antiquarian sources from which they gleaned their knowledge, and the influence of contemporary romantic historians such as Thomas Carlyle and Augustin Thierry. The early writings of Young Ireland, especially the *Nation* and the Library of Ireland, form the subject of Chapter three, with particular attention paid to their use of verse as a vehicle for the writing of history. Chapter four examines what the Young Irelanders hoped to achieve by writing history and the uses to which they put their writings, in particular their efforts to use history to create a unified national consciousness. The way in which their view of history caused them to act, and contributed to their differences with Daniel O'Connell and their decision to take up arms in 1848 forms the main theme of Chapter five. Chapter six deals with the efforts of leading Young Irelanders after 1848 to write the history of their own times and the extent to which their view of the struggles with O'Connell, the Famine and the insurrection of 1848 influenced subsequent nationalist historiography. In Chapter seven I examine the continuities in the Young Ireland history-writing project, and how their work was carried on by like-minded nationalists who came after them. Chapter eight looks at the legacy of their historical writings: their followers and critics, how they influenced subsequent Irish nationalists, especially the generation that carried out the revolution of 1916–21, and how their work had an important bearing on the teaching of history in Irish schools for much of the twentieth century. Many of those who wrote or influenced the writing of nineteenth-century Irish history are now rather obscure figures, so in order to avoid weighing down the text with biographical detail I have included a separate section of biographical notes at the end.

ONE

LAYING THE FOUNDATIONS

THE 'NATION', EDUCATION AND TEMPERANCE

—

On 26 June 1840 Thomas Davis, a 25-year-old Protestant graduate, delivered the presidential address to the College Historical Society in Trinity College Dublin. In a speech marked by his characteristic earnestness and idealism, he strongly criticised the college's teaching, deploring its concentration on classical studies and its neglect of modern subjects. His address, entitled 'The utility of debating societies in remedying the defects of a university education', argued that Trinity's students were so crammed with material about the ancient world that they were ignorant of the most basic modern history, especially that of their own country. To remedy this, he suggested the founding of an 'Irish Lyceum' to cultivate the study of the Irish language, literature and history, and stressed the importance of learning truly 'national history', which he defined as that written by Irishmen for Irishmen. Most histories of Ireland, he maintained, had been written by hostile strangers who had misrepresented Ireland's past, and he exhorted the young Irishmen present to challenge their falsifications whenever possible.[1]

Davis argued that ignorance of Irish history was deeply damaging to Ireland's sense of itself, since all great nations should be able to recall the deeds and honour of their heroes and martyrs. 'The national mind,' he claimed, 'should be filled to overflowing with such thoughts. They are more enriching than mines of gold . . . The history of a nation is the birth-right of her sons.' He insisted that knowledge of Ireland's history was particularly important because her trials and misfortunes had come about not by chance, but to prepare her for a historic destiny in which she would rise 'with a purity and brightness beyond other nations'.[2] Arguing that there was much in Irish history to inspire pride – her military prowess in ancient times, the cultural achievements of her clergy and scholars and 'her gallant and romantic struggles, against Dane, and Saxon and Norman' – he reminded his audience that 'gentlemen, you have a country . . . the country of our birth, our education, of our recollections, ancestral, personal, national; the country of our loves, our friendships, our hopes; *our* country', and encouraged them to prove themselves worthy of it.[3]

Davis was supported in his views by other members of the College Historical Society such as Thomas Wallis, Torrens McCullagh, John Blake Dillon and Thomas MacNevin.[4] The latter two were representative of a generation of prosperous middle-class Catholics who had reached adulthood in the 1830s and had been educated at Trinity (about 10 per cent of its students were Catholic) or in English or continental colleges. According to a contemporary, these young men 'laughed at the pretensions of Protestant ascendancy', and believed themselves equal in every way to their Protestant counterparts.[5] Allied to liberal Protestants in Trinity, they established a small but influential nationalist grouping that challenged the dominant unionist ethos of the college. MacNevin, the son of a solicitor from Galway, had preceded Davis as auditor and president of the Historical Society and had delivered an address that encouraged his audience to study history that went beyond a superficial knowledge of dynasties and battles to examine the customs and soul of their own land to prepare them for coming days when 'all the genius, all the patriotism, all the feeling of Ireland, will be summoned to her aid in struggles great'.[6] Dillon, from a prosperous farming and shopkeeping family in Co. Roscommon, was described as a young man who 'united a lofty enthusiasm with great lucidity of intellect and an unvarying candour'.[7] The following year, he was elected president of the Historical Society and his presidential address on 'Patriotism' echoed that of Davis, emphasising the duty owed to one's country after 'long centuries of trial and affliction' and invoking the glories of the past:

> It is sweet to look back upon those times when our country was great and free. It is sweet to muse amidst moss-grown ruins, the memorials of her pride. It is sweet to read of the valour of her sons in their unequal struggles with the invader; to contrast their high-souled gallantry with the little arts and the ruffian fraud by which their ruin was effected. It is sweet to gaze upon the flag that waved above their heads in battle; it is sweet to hope that it shall wave again.[8]

Looking back on the origins of Young Ireland, Davis identified the College Historical Society and the Institute of Historical Study, a sister society founded by Dublin law students, as the cradle of the movement.[9] His address, which was published by the College Historical Society later that year, was effectively Young Ireland's founding manifesto. It brimmed with the kind of hortatory rhetoric that would become synonymous with the movement and introduced the main themes that would appear again and again in their historical writings: Irishmen should study their country's history, appreciate her sufferings, learn from her mistakes, take pride in her achievements, honour her heroes, and use them as an inspiration to work for Ireland.[10]

The addresses to the College Historical Society of 1840–1 were delivered at a time when Ireland's national distinctiveness had become a live political issue. In the early 1830s Daniel O'Connell had agitated for the repeal of the union with Britain and the re-establishment of an independent Irish parliament, but from 1835 had rowed back on demands for self-government in exchange for a more sympathetic administration in Dublin Castle and reforms in municipal government, poor relief and the tithe system. However, these reforms delivered less than he had hoped and, believing that his Whig allies would soon lose power, in April 1840 he founded the Loyal National Repeal Association to renew the campaign for full repeal of the act of union, a step warmly welcomed by Trinity's cadre of nationally minded students.

Wider social and economic changes also encouraged Young Ireland to take a greater interest in the past. Britain's dynamic capitalist economy threatened to sweep aside traditional manufacturing and agricultural practices, while Benthamite-inspired utilitarian reforms in education, policing, local government and poor relief led the state to play an ever greater part in Irish life. There was a general awareness of living in a time of rapid change and of an ever greater gap opening up between past and present. The Young Irelanders were fierce critics of the anti-historical thrust of 'Benthamism' and industrial capitalism, claiming that the memories, customs and traditions that linked them to earlier generations were being lost in the headlong rush towards mechanisation and materialism. They saw capitalism as a new and insidious form of Anglicisation that threatened what was left of Ireland's economic and cultural independence, and were convinced that it was more important than ever that their countrymen should know of the sacrifices and achievements of their ancestors.[11]

The Young Irelanders immersed themselves in Irish history. On a tour of Ulster in August 1845 they visited the little church at Dungannon where the Volunteer Convention of 1782 had adopted resolutions in favour of legislative independence and the relaxation of the penal laws, and were dismayed to see that it was not marked by a memorial to acknowledge the historic events that had occurred there. They travelled on to the estate of Lord Charlemont, founder of the Volunteer movement, and walked across the fields of Benburb, where in 1646 Owen Roe O'Neill had won his greatest victory. They visited the graves of St Patrick and the United Irishman Thomas Russell in Downpatrick, and were appalled at the shameful neglect of the grave of the national saint, which had no monument, railing or cross. All of these places fed their enthusiasm for Ireland's past, and their determination that the achievements of Ireland's great men should not go unnoticed.[12]

To this end, members of the College Historical Society regularly contributed historical articles to various Dublin magazines and newspapers. Davis wrote for a new liberal Dublin magazine, the *Citizen*, founded in 1839 by his Trinity friend William Torrens McCullagh, and taken over and relaunched in 1842 as the *Dublin Monthly Magazine* by William Elliot Hudson, a lawyer and scholar of national sympathies.[13] Most of Davis's contributions were historical, such as 'Udalism and feudalism', a history of land tenure in Europe with special reference to Ireland, and historical articles on India and Afghanistan. He also wrote articles on Irish historical topics such as Henry Grattan and the parliament summoned by James II in Dublin in 1689, and composed some patriotic verse that prefigured his poetic contributions to the *Nation*.[14]

In April 1841 Davis and Dillon joined O'Connell's Repeal Association, and were immediately appointed to its general committee. From February to July 1841 Davis and Dillon worked on the *Morning Register*, a staunchly Catholic and hitherto rather dull newspaper published in Dublin by Michael Staunton, a moderate repealer. They enlivened it with a strong national tone, but soon tensions arose between their youthful exuberance and Staunton's caution, and they quit after a few months.[15]

While working for the *Register*, Davis and Dillon met Charles Gavan Duffy, a 25-year-old Catholic from Co. Monaghan who worked as editor of the pro-Catholic *Belfast Vindicator*. They were impressed by his business-like approach and practical experience, and he in turn admired their commitment and idealism.[16] Like them he too was strongly interested in Ireland's history, but as an Ulster Catholic he admitted to being motivated by a strongly personal sense of historical grievance. He recalled his school days at a Presbyterian academy in Monaghan where he was force fed tales of papist atrocities and never allowed to forget that he belonged to a defeated race. Most of the history he learned was told to him by a local Catholic curate who told him of the oppressive effects of the penal laws, while others related the sufferings of Catholics during the 1798 Rebellion. Duffy recalled that 'my immature judgement was naturally inflamed with rage at these crimes; a rage which did not abate when I came to read history later and found the tragic story was substantially true'.[17] At the age of 18 he met Charles Teeling, a veteran of the United Irishmen, who inspired him with stories of 1798 and invited him to write for the Belfast *Northern Herald*. From that time on Duffy claimed

> my mind was largely occupied with speculations and reveries on Ireland. I read all the books I could buy or borrow on the history or condition of the country, and gradually came to understand the epic of Irish resistance to England, often defeated, often renewed, but never wholly relinquished.

He saw this resistance as an unbroken line stretching from 'St Lorcan to O'Connell' and he himself 'burned to strike a blow in that hereditary conflict'.[18]

Duffy had not enjoyed a university education but more than made up for it with shrewdness, drive and experience: after his apprenticeship on the *Northern Herald* he worked for Staunton's *Morning Register* as a sub-editor, before founding and editing the *Vindicator* in May 1839. Soon after meeting him Dillon suggested to Davis that 'a weekly paper conducted by that fellow would be an invaluable acquisition'.[19]

FOUNDING THE 'NATION'

On a visit to Dublin in the spring of 1842 Duffy, Davis and Dillon discussed setting up a new publication to invigorate the campaign for repeal. The latter pair were already intent on founding a pro-repeal newspaper, and had in mind something with the originality and vitality of London papers such as the *Examiner* or the *Spectator*.[20] There were intellectually lively periodicals being published in Ireland, notably the monthly *Dublin University Magazine* which often featured Irish literary and historical topics, but its general tone was strongly anti-repeal and anti-Catholic.[21] The *Dublin Review* (founded in 1836) examined topics of Irish interest from a moderate Catholic and nationalist stance, but its nationalism was rather oblique and its circulation small. The three young journalists believed that most other existing papers and periodicals, whether Tory, Whig or O'Connellite, carried little intellectual weight, and were convinced of the need for a lively and intelligent newspaper which would promote Irish nationality.[22]

Duffy's work on the *Belfast Vindicator* had supplied him with the necessary expertise and resources and he agreed to provide finance for the new publication and to move to Dublin and become its editor.[23] He also promised to bring in talented writers such as the poet James Clarence Mangan, the journalist Terence MacMahon Hughes who was already contributing to the *Vindicator*, and the writer and historian W. J. O'Neill Daunt, formerly private secretary to Daniel O'Connell. Davis was to enlist John Cornelius O'Callaghan, whose *Green Book*, a collection of nationalist poetry and historical sketches, had been published in 1841 and sold well, while Dillon would recruit John O'Hagan and John Pigot, two bright young men he knew from Trinity. The three originators met again in July for further discussions. Davis suggested that the paper should be called the *Nation* and be launched in the autumn.[24] Thus began what T. W. Moody called 'the most famous newspaper venture in Irish history'.[25]

In early October 1842 the paper's prospectus was issued. Written by Davis, it heralded the launch of the *Nation* as a new departure in Irish journalism, claiming that existing publications were 'shackled by old habits, old prejudices, and old divisions'. What was needed was a new paper to aid and organise the new movements going on amongst us; to make their growth deeper and more 'racy of the soil'; and above all, to direct the popular mind and the sympathies of educated men of all parties to the great end of Nationality . . . a Nationality which will not only raise our people from their poverty, by securing to them the blessings of a DOMESTIC LEGISLATURE but inflame and purify them with a lofty and heroic love of country . . . a Nationality which may come to be stamped on our manners, our literature, and our deeds, a Nationality which may embrace Protestant, Catholic, and Dissenter – Milesian and Cromwellian – the Irishman of a hundred generations and the stranger who is within our gates.[26]

The first issue of the *Nation* appeared on 15 October 1842. It contained an eclectic mixture of news, politics, history and poetry with articles by Davis, Dillon and Duffy, and verse by Mangan and O'Callaghan, and found a ready market. Despite the relatively expensive price of 6d., within hours it sold all 4,000 copies printed (double the amount of any other weekly Irish newspaper).[27] A weekly conference of its three originators decided on the paper's content, with Davis and Duffy writing most of the articles in the first year. Their work was complementary: Duffy's articles concentrated on the need for education, Dillon's dealt mainly with the land question, while Davis expounded the ideal of an historic nationality embracing all creeds and origins.[28] Intellectually, Davis was the dominant figure. While he had shown promise on previous publications, it was in his writings for the *Nation* that he truly blossomed. Although a rather shy and solemn young man, he was widely admired for his sincerity and integrity; he also had great determination, a voracious appetite for work and an ability to inspire those around him. Bringing an evangelical zeal to his propagation of Irish history, he read widely and corresponded with a host of scholars and contributors and by the early 1840s had acquired an impressive body of knowledge, building up a library of heavily annotated history books and political pamphlets and amassing extensive notes for various historical lectures and writings. He spent much of his time visiting historic sites, collecting stories, maps and documents and sketching ancient ruins and historic monuments, and channelled all this work into the *Nation*.[29] A colleague recalled how he used Irish history and legend 'to mould and animate nationality. Native art, valour, virtue and glory seemed to grow under his pen. All that had a tendency to elevate and ennoble he rescued from the past to infuse into the future'.[30]

By the autumn of 1843 the founders were being assisted by like-minded Trinity graduates such as Michael Joseph Barry, Denny Lane, Denis Florence MacCarthy, John Pigot, John O'Hagan and Thomas MacNevin. The *Nation*'s contributors formed a tightly knit group of friends, holding regular weekly suppers on Saturday evenings and excursions to places of historic interest on

Sundays. They thrashed out their ideas and differences in friendly discussion and argument: one later fondly recalled 'nights, winged with genial wit and cordial friendship . . . when the reckless gaiety of Irish temperament bore fullest sway'.[31]

The paper's combination of lively nationalist journalism and stirring patriotic verse proved popular with a public newly energised by O'Connell's repeal campaign and its circulation grew rapidly. According to the quarterly returns from the Custom House which showed the quantity of each newspaper printed, the stamps issued for the *Nation* exceeded 10,000 for each issue: 300 copies went to newsrooms and Teetotal Societies and were read by dozens; 1,100 copies went to repeal wardens (the association's local officers) and were read aloud at weekly meetings, reaching up to 100 persons each; 9,000 copies were sold by agents or went directly to subscribers, and many of these were handed around – each copy being read by an estimated 12 to 20 readers. Profits were considerable – around £2,000 a year – and were ploughed back into the paper and its distribution networks. The *Nation*'s staff were well paid, earning salaries of up to £500 a year, which gave them a financial independence matched by few others in the Repeal Association.[32]

According to Duffy, the weekly appearance of the *Nation* became an event in itself: 'Old men still describe the fever of impatience with which they waited for its weekly issue, and the delight with which they lingered over it.'[33] He claimed that in later years he met people from all walks of life: 'Methodist missionaries, British soldiers and judges, professors in Protestant and Catholic colleges, and even Orangemen who still recall the enthusiasm with which they read the *Nation*.' From his home town of Ballaghadereen in early 1843, Dillon wrote with astonishment that, despite the town's poverty, 23 copies of the paper were delivered there weekly. A subscriber wrote that 'My calendar for the week dates from the time the *Nation* arrives till the day I may hope for another *Nation*. I often walk three miles to the post office, to bring it home a few hours earlier than it would otherwise reach us'.[34] Many nationalists who grew up in the 1840s recalled the eager anticipation of waiting for the *Nation* and the inspirational thrill of its editorials, essays and ballads.[35] Its success was such that it firmly established the newspaper as a central pillar of all subsequent national movements.

EDUCATION AND TEMPERANCE

From the start the writers of the *Nation* saw their newspaper an instrument of moral reformation. They contended that centuries of subordination to England had led the Irish character to become 'false, cowardly and provincialised' and that it required strengthening through discipline and education.[36] The bans and restrictions on Catholic schools during the era of the penal laws made education a particularly contentious subject, with nationalists claiming that its denial to the mass of the population had been one of the most powerful instruments of subjugation.[37] The Young Irelanders' philosophy was summed up in the pithy slogan 'Educate that you may be free' and they warned that 'if the people do not persevere with a dogged and daily labour for knowledge and independence they will be slaves for generations'.[38]

The *Nation*'s educational crusade was assisted by the government's decision in 1831 to establish a national system of primary education to replace the existing mosaic of hedge and parish schools. The state's commitment to provide the building costs for new schools and the salaries of teachers encouraged a steady increase in the provision of primary education: there were 789 national schools in 1833; 1,978 in 1840; and 4,321 with 480,623 pupils in 1849.[39] The *Nation* applauded this progress as an important step in creating a literate and self-reliant people capable of governing themselves. It also welcomed the fact that children of different religions would be educated together, observing that the spread of a uniform system of education 'makes the peasantry and townsman share in one purpose, gives common facts and propensities to Ulster and Munster . . . and binds the native-born of every sect and blood into one family'.[40]

However, the *Nation* also found much to criticise in the new system, complaining of woeful underfunding and the poor qualifications and pay of teachers (the average basic salary of a national school teacher was £12 a year).[41] It argued that the term 'national school' was a misnomer and that the education provided was in fact 'anti-national': state-funded schools ignored Irish literature, history and geography; the Irish language was not taught at all, and indeed was actively discouraged in some places.[42]

The exclusion of Irish history from the curriculum was deliberate. The government recognised the power of education to mould young minds, and the teaching of the national schools was intended to create loyal and orderly subjects. The Board of Commissioners appointed to supervise the system claimed that the unregulated teaching of history in hedge schools in the past had helped to stoke ancient grievances, and it took measures to 'suppress all reading matter that did not specifically encourage piety, morality and industry'. Convinced that it was impossible to teach a version of Irish history that would be acceptable to both Protestants and Catholics, the authorities believed that it was better to avoid a subject that would only serve to open old wounds and sharpen sectarian animosity.[43]

The Board identified the difficulty in obtaining suitable textbooks as one of the great weaknesses of hedge and parish schools: in the past teachers had tended to use whatever reading matter was at hand and this often included almanacs, devotional literature, medieval romances and melodramatic tales of raparees and highwaymen.[44] To fill this gap and avoid the propagation of any potentially subversive ideas, the Board produced a series of graded textbooks, appropriate to the age and abilities of pupils, which proved popular with teachers and became widely used throughout the British empire.[45] The *Nation*, however, was unhappy at their assimilative and imperial character and denounced them as 'lying compendiums . . . poisonous to the last degree'. It complained that 'a boy leaves school filled with Greek, Roman and English facts, and most of them false facts, and profoundly ignorant of what it behoves him to know – the constitutional and general history of his own country'.[46] Given the absence of Irish history, it was seen as rather sinister that the pupil learned some English history 'as though England naturally succeeds to Greece and Rome, and takes their glory by inheritance. He is taught to link together in his mind the fame of Greece and Rome and England. He hears nothing of her crimes and oppressions – he is not taught to abhor her cruelties and perfidies'. When Ireland was mentioned, it was as 'a semi-civilised and barbarous province – engaged almost entirely in fierce rebellion, or sunk in moody submission . . . Not a word does he there read of noble struggles for freedom – of gallant efforts, brilliant success, or defeat as glorious'.[47] The result was that there were pupils and even teachers in national schools 'who had never heard of Tara, Clontarf, Limerick or Dungannon; to whom the O'Nials and Sarsfields, the Swifts and Sternes, the Grattans and Barrys, our generals, statesmen, authors, orators and artists, were alike and utterly unknown!'[48]

The *Nation* accused the Board of adopting 'a system of instruction devised by a master for those whom he seeks to make useful slaves'.[49] It noted that of the eleven members of the Board of Commissioners only one – the veteran barrister Robert Holmes – was sympathetic to Irish nationalism.[50] His colleagues were 'dry, ungenial men, ignorant of our history, in love with English literature and character, imperialists to the core', and were denounced 'for turning Irish history out of doors; and . . . for the painful skill with which they have cut from every work in their schools the recognition of the literature, antiquities and state of Ireland'.[51]

Nationalists contrasted the national schools unfavourably with the hedge schools that preceded them. The latter, they claimed, 'kept up something of the romance, history and music of the country' and 'were quite free from any assimilatory, imperial or mixed educational notions, and did aid in keeping alive a soul of nationality under the ribs of proscription and persecution'.[52] The absence of a set curriculum in the hedge schools allowed for more Irish material to be taught, especially when the teacher had an interest in Irish history and folklore, and patriotic teachers could foster national sympathies by inspiring their pupils with vivid and dramatic accounts of Irish history.[53]

Some believed that the national spirit of the hedge schools was being carried on in a more orderly and disciplined manner by the Christian Brothers. The Brothers had been founded in Waterford in 1802 by Edmund Rice to provide education for poor boys, and gained a reputation for providing thorough instruction with a strong national flavour. By 1847 the order was growing steadily, with 93 schools in Ireland and Britain, educating 15,000 students. The strong Catholic character of the Brothers' schools set them apart from the national schools and made their ethos incompatible with the state-supported system. The Christian Brothers used their own textbooks which, unlike those of the Board of Commissioners, emphasised Ireland's distinctiveness, and they made a point of teaching Irish history to their pupils, stressing the courage and constancy of Ireland's struggle against English rule.[54] After a visit to the Christian Brothers' school in North Richmond Street, Dublin, a deputation from the *Nation* noted that the Brothers were 'the very reverse of the National System ... In their class books, in their verbal teaching, in the spirit of their whole system, they infuse everything that can make their pupils proud and fond of their country, as well as attached to religion'. Their texts were highly commended for impressing on their pupils a devotion to faith and fatherland and for being culled mainly from the works of Irish and Catholic writers, including the Young Irelanders' own *Spirit of the Nation*.[55] The *Nation* commended the 'silent patriotism' of the Brothers and concluded that 'a race reared up upon such intellectual food, so strong and healthy should be good men and good citizens'.[56]

The Young Irelanders were well aware, however, that the Christian Brothers alone could not make up the deficiencies in Irish education, and saw this as their principal mission. In private Davis was sceptical of the effect of the Repeal Association's political agitation, regarding much of it as empty speechifying and impotent posturing, and regarded education as 'the only moral force in which I have any faith'.[57] He argued that the denial of education had been a deliberate policy adopted by the government to keep the Irish poor and ignorant: 'first, by laws prohibiting education, then by refusing provision for it; next by perverting it into an engine of bigotry; and now by giving it in a stunted, partial, anti-national way.' He claimed that the writings of the *Nation* had finally begun to change this and right the wrongs of the national system by 'teach[ing] the people to know themselves and their history'.[58]

As a further stimulus to its educational mission, Young Ireland sought to capitalise on the educational initiatives already taken by the temperance movement, which had grown rapidly in Ireland during the late 1830s under the leadership of the Capuchin friar, Fr Theobald Mathew. Mathew argued that the root cause of Ireland's poverty and backwardness was drunkenness, and that no social improvement was possible until this vice was curbed. His campaign to encourage moderation or abstention was an enormous success: from 1839 to 1842 the annual consumption of alcohol fell by half and excessive drinking became less and less socially acceptable.[59] Charles Gavan Duffy was a close associate of Mathew and saw temperance as a crucial step on the road to national regeneration. He believed that the vice of drunkenness would have to be replaced with the virtues of self-help and education and encouraged Mathew to excite 'a thirst for knowledge', suggesting that temperance meeting rooms should be used as lecture halls and reading rooms to provide members with an alternative to socialising in public houses.[60] Mathew arranged for the printing and distribution of suitable books and pamphlets, and although he insisted that works of political and religious controversy be excluded from temperance halls, this was difficult to enforce in practice, and his encouragement of reading opened the way for political instruction.[61]

Like Duffy, most nationalists believed that temperance had an important contribution to make to Ireland's moral improvement, and the impressive order and discipline shown at the great repeal meetings of 1843 owed much to Mathew's success. Although temperance facilitated the organisation of his mass political meetings, Daniel O'Connell never fully embraced the movement, harbouring reservations about its fervent evangelical character.[62] In contrast the Young Irelanders took up the temperance cause with enthusiasm, valuing sobriety as the foundation of a responsible and self-reliant people. For Davis drunkenness was 'the saturnalia of slaves', and he maintained that 'Irish temperance is the first fruit of deep-sown hope, the offering of incipient freedom'.[63]

Linking popular education to the temperance movement allowed the Young Irelanders to build on ardour and foundations that were already in place.[64] When it was proposed that Fr Mathew be commemorated by a national memorial, Duffy suggested that the most suitable memorial would be to use any available funds to transform temperance societies into 'the clubs, the adult schools, the lecture rooms, the parish parliaments of a sober people', and nurture an informed and disciplined patriotism.[65] Davis hoped that the attractions of learning would cause young men to shun 'cards, tobacco, dissipation, and more fatal laziness'.[66] To throw off such vices, it was essential that places be set aside for careful reading and sober discussion. Properly appointed reading rooms would provide a space not just for reading, but for the debate and fellowship that were central to creating an educated citizenry.[67]

During his incarceration in Richmond prison in 1844 with O'Connell and others convicted of conspiracy, Duffy drew up proposals to expand the Repeal Association's educational programme.[68] There were already 300 repeal reading rooms in existence, and the plan was to increase their number tenfold and make them centres of organisation and instruction.[69] O'Connell's lieutenant

Thomas Ray was charged with the task, assisted by Davis and Duffy, and the *Nation* undertook to provide the rooms with periodicals, books and maps, while the Repeal Association would supply them with the reports of its parliamentary committee and works on Irish topography and statistics.[70]

Young Ireland's educational project was largely shaped by the intention to teach subjects excluded from the national schools and, as few Young Irelanders had the ability or inclination to teach the Irish language, the teaching of Irish history dominated their educational efforts. In his efforts to make the Repeal Association the 'schoolmaster of the people of Ireland', Davis advised that works of history above all should be procured for its reading rooms: he recommended pro-Catholic histories such as James MacGeoghegan's *History of Ireland* (1758–63), Francis Plowden's *An Historical Review of the State of Ireland* (1803) and Denis Taaffe's *An Impartial History of Ireland* (1809–11). In addition he advised that they should procure more recent polemical works such as *A Collection of Speeches Spoken by Daniel O'Connell and Sheil on Subjects Connected with the Catholic Question* (1828), John Cornelius O'Callaghan's *Green Book* (1841) and Daniel O'Connell's *Memoir of Ireland* (1843). Other essential works were Thomas Moore's *Melodies* (1807–34) and *Captain Rock* (1824), along with some of the works of the English journalist and reformer William Cobbett and the *Reports of the National Association*.[71] He recommended that reading be supplemented by regular lectures, noting that if 'one strong-minded and earnest man' would apply himself for six months to learn the outlines of Irish history, he could then pass on his knowledge to his fellows, who could then 'take up a more detailed history of particular epochs, wars and revolutions. In this way a vast amount of knowledge might be acquired in a single undissipated year. And who can tell the rich reward of that year's labour?'[72]

Davis called for reading rooms to be transformed into national spaces, decorated with 'prints of as many great Irishmen and events as you can get'.[73] They could also perform an important function in safeguarding Ireland's heritage by collecting locally available manuscripts and books and surveys of historical interest to preserve them from loss. He envisaged a national network of reading rooms acting as focal points for the exchange of knowledge and opinions between members which would 'inform and strengthen them into liberty'.[74] He claimed that working men had raised their sights above idle amusements and were now demanding

> mutual co-operation for intellectual purposes; conversation on books; lectures on literary matters . . . familiar communication of ideas on the history of their country . . . A people instructed, familiar with the facts of their history, their own

social state and its defects – knowing something of the history of other countries, and
the relative advantages and disadvantages of different governments – are surely more
likely to attain their ends, than a mere ignorant, passionate, impulsive multitude.[75]

A people hungry for instruction was Davis's ideal rather than the reality.
He was uncomfortably aware that not everyone shared the *Nation*'s
enthusiasm for education. Many temperance and repeal clubs preferred to
devote their time and money to music and marching bands rather than books.
Reading rooms were generally confined to large towns, and were rarely found
in villages and rural districts.[76] Even when they existed the *Nation* complained
that many were badly run and poorly stocked with books. On a tour of inspec-
tion in Cork, one Young Irelander was struck by the 'melancholy spectacle' of
empty shelves.[77] Most of these problems stemmed from lack of finance and
the indifference of the Repeal Association's leadership. O'Connell allowed a
small portion of the repeal rent to fund reading rooms but saw no need for
their encouragement or regulation by the association, and valued them more
for organisational and fund-raising purposes than for education.[78] An exas-
perated Davis wrote to Duffy,

> For God's sake get O'Connell to undertake, or to allow others, to undertake, a
> plenipotentiary mission to establish repeal reading rooms and to give them books
> and good advice. Damn the ignorance of the people – but for that we should be
> lords of our own future; without that, much is insecure.[79]

In an implicit rebuke to O'Connell's stated policy of achieving of repeal
through peace and perseverance, the *Nation* claimed that without an educated
people, 'Peace is cowardice and Perseverance idiocy.'[80]
Such differences grew ever wider as the Repeal Association debated its
options after the proclamation of the Clontarf meeting in 1843 and O'Connell's
imprisonment in 1844. O'Connell's tepid support for their educational crusade
frustrated and angered the Young Irelanders, some of whom suspected that he
was happier to lead an ignorant and unquestioning multitude than an informed
and independent people. Since the Repeal Association refused to become the
'schoolmaster of the people of Ireland', Young Ireland decided that it would
have to assume the role itself, and it was a schoolmaster that was, above all,
intent on teaching history.

TWO

READING HISTORY

—

The Young Irelanders strongly promoted the reading of history as an essential part of their educational mission, but they were often sharply critical of the works available to Irish readers. The *Nation* claimed that popular ignorance of Ireland's history stemmed primarily from the lack of availability of suitable books and noted that most were either 'dear or bad; and sometimes they are both'.[1] In its efforts to write Ireland's history from a nationalist standpoint, the *Nation* often claimed that it was working an untilled field, but this was hardly the case. The *Nation* tended to exaggerate popular ignorance of Irish history (and its part in remedying that ignorance), and rarely acknowledged that much Irish history had already been written and had done much to shape popular attitudes. Donal McCartney, for example, suggests that the national spirit mobilised by Daniel O'Connell in the 1820s and 1830s had already been 'aroused by the popularisation of historical ideas which acted as a germinating force on Irish politics'.[2]

It was less the case that the history of Ireland had not yet been written, than that little of it had been written that met the contemporary requirements of Young Ireland. In a review of the historical literature available before the *Nation* began its work, Charles Gavan Duffy found little to praise. Geoffrey Keating's widely-read *Foras Feasa ar Éirinn* (*c.* 1634) was loftily dismissed as 'dull fable relieved by some glimmering of traditional truth'; Thomas Leland's *History of Ireland* (1773) was 'prejudiced and meagre, relieved by such stinted fairness as a professor of Trinity College and viceregal chaplain in the reign of George III might venture to exhibit'; Francis Plowden's *Historical Review of the State of Ireland* (1803) was 'Leland rewritten, compressed, liberalised, and supplemented by original documents'; John Lawless's *Compendium of the History of Ireland* (1814) was 'a rhetorical pamphlet of no weight or authority'; Thomas Moore's *History of Ireland* (1835–46) was 'overloaded with worthless antiquarian essays'; Daniel O'Connell's *Memoir on Ireland* (1843) was 'a skilful brief of the case against England' but lacked the depth and resonance of real history.[3]

Duffy's opinions should be regarded with some caution. Writing in the late 1870s, he was intent on establishing Young Ireland's reputation as a new and invigorating force in Irish nationalism: the more he disparaged the writings available before Young Ireland began its work, the more he highlighted the movement's achievement in producing popular and accessible historical works. But even in the 1840s, writers in the *Nation* were often harsh in their assessments of earlier historians, judging their work in the light of their own brand of nineteenth-century nationalism, and ignoring the context in which it was written. They were, for example, critical of the work of the eighteenth-century Catholic historian John Curry, who in his *Historical Memoirs of the Irish Rebellion in the Year 1641* (1758) and *Historical and Critical Review of the Civil Wars in Ireland* (1775) had challenged the anti-Catholic prejudices of Protestant historians. Curry, a founding member of the Catholic Committee, had written his works to highlight the injustice of the penal laws and advocate their repeal. However Curry's anxiety to reassure Protestants that Catholics were not the ignorant bigots of ultra-Protestant propaganda, but responsible citizens who could be trusted with freedom and political power, occasionally led him into fulsome declarations of Catholic loyalty to the crown. Nineteenth-century nationalists winced at such reassurances: John Mitchel was contemptuous of Curry's protestations of loyalty, while C. P. Meehan was scathing about his 'whining tone'.[4]

Although the *Nation* complained of the history books available to the Irish public, it nonetheless accepted that 'the boldest aggregation of facts is better than the present ignorance' and, while waiting for a suitable survey of Irish history to be written, cautiously recommended works such as Denis Taaffe's *An Impartial History of Ireland* (1809–11) or, failing that, the work of the pro-Catholic Francis Plowden or liberal Protestant Thomas Leland.[5] The eighteenth-century history that Young Ireland held in highest regard was James MacGeoghegan's *History of Ireland* (1758–63), originally written in French by an Irish-born Catholic priest who was chaplain to the Irish Brigade, and first published in an English translation by the former United Irishman Patrick O'Kelly in Dublin in 1831–2 (at Davis's suggestion a new edition was published by James Duffy in 1844).[6] Charles Gavan Duffy described it as 'a faithful and honest book', while Davis observed that by publishing his work in France, MacGeoghegan was free from English censorship, and came nearer than any other author to producing a truthful and accurate picture of eighteenth-century Ireland, noting that 'for the student, it is the best in the world. He is graphic, easy and Irish'.[7]

REVIEWING CONTEMPORARY AUTHORS

The *Nation* devoted considerable space to reviewing the work of contemporary historians, especially those sympathetic to Irish national aspirations.[8] It welcomed all work that was written in a national spirit, such as Daniel O'Connell's *A Memoir on Ireland, Native and Saxon* (1843), in which O'Connell denounced English and Protestant crimes in Ireland, and glorified the religious fidelity and steadfast resistance of Irish Catholics down the ages. English rule, he argued, had not only been characterised by cruelty, treachery and corruption in the past but 'much of that spirit of the worst days still survives'. O'Connell substantiated his claims with long quotations from English and Protestant authors such as Fynes Morrison, Sir John Davies and Thomas Leland, claiming that even the writings of the oppressor showed the justness of Ireland's case, and concluded that such a catalogue of misgovernment could only be put right by repeal of the act of union and the restoration of the Irish parliament.[9]

Coming from the pen of O'Connell, such a work carried great authority among Irish nationalists. It contained little with which Young Ireland could disagree, but nonetheless highlighted some of the differences in the way in which they and O'Connell viewed the past. Davis commended the work for its clear and concise layout, but considered it 'miserable in style'.[10] O'Connell's approach was a largely legalistic one, using history to make and prove specific points, such as highlighting instances of English brutality or exposing the corrupt means used by the British government to pass the act of union. He had dedicated his work to Queen Victoria, that she should know 'how much the Irish have suffered from English misrule' and understand that the disaffection of her subjects stemmed from centuries of oppression. To the Young Irelanders, however, such an approach seemed rather narrow and restrictive. They took a broader and more ambitious view, believing that history was more than just a polemical tool but had the power to create and sustain a nation's sense of itself. While they too could complain of past oppression, they were usually careful to balance grievances with accounts of battles won or brave fights against the odds that would make Irish hearts swell with pride and illustrate that Ireland's past was more than a depressing litany of defeats and suffering.

Other recently-published works recommended by the *Nation* were Jonah Barrington's *Rise and Fall of the Irish Nation* (1833) (a new edition was published by James Duffy in 1843), John Cornelius O'Callaghan's *Green Book* (1841), William J. O'Neill Daunt's *A Catechism of the History of Ireland, Ancient and Modern* (1844) and R. R. Madden's *The Lives and Times of the United Irishmen* (1842).[11] In the case of Barrington, a notoriously duplicitous eighteenth-century MP and founding member of the Orange Order, readers were cautioned that they could not 'believe all that he has written, nor approve of all that he has done' but assured that his *Rise and Fall* was an instance of 'a corrupt man writing a good book'.[12] Barrington's emphasis on Ireland's social and cultural vibrancy during the 18 years of Ireland's legislative independence and his revelations of the extensive corruption involved in passing the union with Britain were regarded as powerful arguments in favour of the restoration of an Irish parliament.[13]

John Cornelius O'Callaghan was a veteran repealer and one of the earliest contributors to the *Nation*. He was widely read and an indefatigable historical researcher, although even the Young Irelanders found tiresome his habit of incessantly declaiming about Irish history in a booming voice.[14] In 1841 he published *The Green Book, or Gleanings from the Writing Desk of a Literary Agitator*, a miscellaneous collection of his writings dedicated to the Irish people to defend 'their natural right to religious freedom and legislative independence' and to vindicate 'the national military character from English and Anglo-Irish aggression and calumny'. Its main purpose was to prove that the Irish lacked nothing in courage or military skill compared with other nations. Through an eclectic mixture of ballads, poems, literary extracts, historical quotations and epigrams, it detailed the many occasions in which Irishmen had fought bravely at home and abroad, particularly during the Williamite Wars and the continental campaigns of the Wild Geese. It was immensely popular, and its main theme of martial success as a vindication of the Irish character was regularly taken up by the *Nation* which lauded O'Callaghan's work as 'a prodigy of labour, originality and patriotism'.[15]

Similarly welcomed was *A Catechism of the History of Ireland* by the O'Connellite man-of-letters William J. O'Neill Daunt. Written in a simple question-and-answer format for those who knew little of Irish history, it was intended primarily for use in schools to counter

> the deceptive character of those quasi-historical abstracts which are put into the hands of our youth and which are calculated to create in their minds a contempt for their own brave and gallant Celtic forefathers'.[16] *The Nation* noted that 'a study so long neglected must be approached by degrees; and perhaps nothing could be done for a beginning better than a small, cheap, and universally accessible book such as this.[17]

R. R. Madden's *The Lives and Times of the United Irishmen* (1842) was praised for providing detailed accounts of the heroism and virtue of recent Irish patriots. It argued that the United Irishmen were not the dangerous incendiaries that their enemies had painted them but moderate and noble patriots who provided models for the nationalists of the present day to emulate. Madden's denunciation of the corruption and injustice of the British administration in Ireland, which he claimed had left the United Irishmen with no choice but to take up arms, became one of the recurrent themes of Young Ireland history. Next to the memoirs of Wolfe Tone, Madden's work was recommended by Davis as 'the most instructive book on that boldest attempt ever made to unite Irishmen and liberate Ireland'.[18]

While the *Nation* regarded the work of nationalist writers such as O'Callaghan, O'Neill Daunt and Madden as valuable supplements to its own efforts, it was sharply critical of writers (especially Irish writers) who defended England's record in Ireland or claimed that the Irish were unfit for independence. Robert Montgomery Martin's *Ireland Before and After the Union* (1843) was attacked for distorting Irish history in the manner of ultra-Protestant polemicists such as Sir John Temple or Sir Richard Musgrave and 'sneering at our antiquity [and] trying to make our history absurd and our character infamous . . . by an anthology of all the English pamphleteers have said against us'.[19] John Mitchel had particularly harsh words for the Church of Ireland clergyman James Wills, author of *Lives of Illustrious Irishmen* (6 vols, 1839–47), which had included derogatory assessments of several Irish patriots, including Wolfe Tone. Such writers were accused of carrying on the work of hostile foreign commentators who had misrepresented Ireland's history down the ages. Wills's work was dismissed as 'the basest, and most heartless, and most lying [memoir] we have ever met. Neither is this history. Mr Wills, in his philosophic dissertations is a twaddling nincompoop'.[20]

Thomas Moore's *History of Ireland* (1835–46) was another work found wanting by the *Nation*'s reviewer, who dismissed it as 'superficial . . . wanting in research, topography, and condensation [*sic*]'. Moore was judged to be insufficiently condemnatory of England's record in Ireland, and was criticised for ending his work before the Reformation, and so ignoring the turbulent centuries that succeeded it and had done so much to form the Irish nation.[21] That such a work should be written by the author of some of Ireland's most patriotic poetry was seen as particularly indefensible:

> Here a poet, a man sensitive to all the fine feeling of the human heart, a man who understands nationality – who has sung the glory of freedom through the earth, dares in the face of god and the world, to lie to and belie his native land . . . The rebel, says Mr Moore, has seldom a chronicler. May he never have the like of *him* again.[22]

Intent on popularising Irish history, the *Nation*'s writers considered it more important that historical works be lively and inspiring rather than comprehensively researched. In fact they argued that too great a concentration on tedious documentary evidence robbed history of its drama and exhilaration. Reviewing R. R. Madden's *The Connexion Between the Kingdom of Ireland and the Crown of England* (1845) the *Nation* was not impressed by its dry approach, contrasting it unfavourably with the vivid and engaged history he had written on the United Irishmen, and noting that 'we place but little value on such documentary evidence . . . Those who take the statute book for a history commit a grievous error; and they who believe that charters, letters patent, court rolls etc are anything but the mummies of old lies and interred subterfuges, labour under a delusion still more grievous'. The reviewer maintained that 'we had rather think on Sarsfield holding up his blood to heaven as an atonement for his country, than rummage through all the musty records of chancery – the legal quirks and subterfuges of justice – the lying letters patent and treacherous treaties that are monumental of English justice in Ireland'.[23]

YOUNG IRELAND AND THE ANTIQUARIAN REVIVAL

The Young Ireland conception of history as a rhetorical exercise that valued vivid and inspiring writing over detailed research and scholarly objectivity set their work apart from a new generation of Irish antiquarian scholars whose increasingly professional research was helping to illuminate the past. However, the Young Irelanders sought to harness and popularise such scholarly work in their efforts to promote a greater awareness of Irish history: Davis maintained that 'however Irish liberty may be won, the silent labours of the annalist and the antiquarian are essential to give to nationality anything of dignity or consistency'.[24] Among those he had foremost in mind were scholars such as George Petrie, Caesar Otway, John O'Donovan and Eugene O'Curry who had revolutionised Irish antiquarian studies. The energetic and versatile Petrie, a topographical and landscape artist, antiquarian, archaeologist, and collector of Irish music, was the driving force behind Ireland's antiquarian revival, helping to found new institutions such as the Irish Archaeological Society, and reinvigorate old ones such as the Dublin Society and the Royal Irish Academy.[25] From the 1820s he began to challenge the speculative scholarship that had hitherto dominated antiquarian studies, declaring that his aim was to study the past scientifically, to supplant or supplement previous inadequate or flawed studies and to establish 'the history of Ireland on the firm basis of truth'.[26] Lamenting that interpretations of Irish history had been distorted by political and religious prejudices, he sought to establish a middle ground between 'fabulists' who had overstated the glory of ancient Ireland, and hostile critics who had denied the existence of any civilisation in Ireland before the coming of the Normans and whose history was little more than 'libellous stories which mock and ridicule the Irish'.[27] Petrie was motivated by both scholarly and patriotic considerations: his approach was described by his biographer as one which 'placed historic truth before the country, awakened no angry passions . . . and while it laboured for the moral and intellectual advancement of the people dear to it, inculcated the respect of order and law'.[28]

Petrie brought his work to a popular audience with public lectures and the publication in 1832 of the *Dublin Penny Journal*, an illustrated weekly, and the first significant cultural nationalist periodical to be published in Ireland. Inspired by the success of the *English Penny Magazine*, Petrie and Caesar Otway started the paper to cater for Irish tastes, proclaiming its devotion to 'the history, biography, poetry, antiquities, natural history, legends and traditions of the country, and . . . moral improvement of the country'.[29] Petrie acted as editor for its first year and contributed many of its best articles. Among the other contributors were John O'Donovan and writers who would later be associated with the *Nation* such as the priest and historian Fr Charles Patrick Meehan and the poet James Clarence Mangan. The *Penny Journal* disavowed religious and political controversy and its historical articles dealt mostly with the remote past, its focus on ancient and medieval history chiming with the romantic tastes of the 1830s. It sought to instil in Irish readers an awareness of their cultural heritage by giving them a sound knowledge of Ireland's history and archaeological remains, claiming that the former was all but forgotten, and that the latter was crumbling away through neglect.[30]

The Young Irelanders claimed Petrie as an inspiration and the *Nation* praised him for combining 'the heart of a patriot [with] the learning and candour of a great antiquary'.[31] His 1832 essay on the origin and use of round towers brought a new level of scholarship to Irish antiquarianism. By carefully marshalling archaeological and philological evidence, Petrie refuted claims of the pagan origin of the towers argued by scholars such as Charles Vallancey and William Betham, concluding that they were built by Christian monks as belfries. His *The Ecclesiastical Architecture of Ireland, Anterior to the Anglo-Norman Invasion, Comprising an Essay on the Origin and Uses of the Round Towers of Ireland* (1845) was described by the *Nation* as the best of all the recently-published books on Irish history.[32] Such scholarly works would, the *Nation* claimed, provide ample material for Irishmen to challenge assertions that 'that we have no annals but those of violence, rapine and discord'.[33] Petrie was also much praised for his reinvigoration of the Royal Irish Academy: until he became involved, the *Nation* claimed that the Academy 'consisted of half a dozen men [who] valued truth moderately, and fame extravagantly . . . its publications were waste paper, its museums some dirty drawers'.[34] But thanks to Petrie's efforts, it could now boast of a superb collection of Bronze Age and Iron Age artefacts, and one of the best collections of Celtic manuscripts in all of Europe.

Petrie was also much admired for his valuable work on the Irish ordnance survey, to which he had devoted several years of his life. As well as producing a series of detailed maps of the entire country between 1825 and 1841, the project gave an immense boost to Irish antiquarian studies by planning to publish a comprehensive memoir of each county containing a full account of its topography, ancient place names, antiquities, local customs and social conditions. In addition to Petrie, the survey employed distinguished Gaelic scholars such as John O'Donovan and Eugene O'Curry for many years, and the experience they gained on the survey formed the bedrock for much of their later work. Only one memoir – for County Derry – was actually completed, but the preparatory work undertaken for other counties formed an invaluable record. Appreciating the wider implications of the survey, and the zeal and commitment of those involved, Davis praised it as 'an educational and political force which would help to awaken the national consciousness' of all Irishmen.[35]

The intensive research and writing of the memoirs was, however, a time-consuming and expensive process and, after the publication of the first, the Treasury baulked at providing funds for others. Financial economy seems to have been the main motive, but there were also those at the Treasury who believed that digging into the Irish past could revive old grievances of expropriation and add to the already formidable well of agrarian discontent.[36] After the report of an official commission set up in June 1843, the government agreed to sanction the production of the utilitarian sections of the memoirs (geology and productive economy) but decided that those dealing with history and antiquities did not justify the expense involved and would be discontinued.[37] The decision was strongly criticised by the *Nation* as a deliberate step to cut off the Irish people from their history and traditions, and the lesson was drawn that only an independent Irish government would be prepared to see through such projects of national importance.[38]

The *Nation* also claimed that only an Irish government would take adequate steps to prevent the destruction and neglect of Ireland's architectural heritage. For Davis neolithic graves, Iron Age hillforts, and Christian monasteries and high crosses were all precious evidence of a rich and enduring civilisation, and it pained him that each passing year saw more crosses, tombs, cairns, abbeys and castles destroyed.[39] He complained of the deplorable state of important Irish medieval sites, noting that the ruined chapels at Mellifont and Glendalough were being used to house farm animals. He was particularly outraged by proposals to run a road through the neolithic tomb at Newgrange, and appealed to the patriotism of all Irishmen to prevent such destruction. Such contempt for national monuments was, he claimed, the inevitable pernicious result of Ireland being ruled by those who had no respect for her past.[40]

One of the Young Irelanders' most fervent hopes was that a shared pride in Ireland's culture and historic traditions could play a part in helping to reconcile nationalist and unionist.[41] Noting that men of different politics and religion worked together harmoniously in studying the country's past, the *Nation* claimed that 'Cromwellian and Williamite were yielding to the sweet tradition of thraldom which made the old Norman settlers "more Irish than the Irish themselves"'.[42] The unionist *Dublin University Magazine* was praised for its increasing attention to Irish culture and antiquities and for the growth of an 'Irish feeling' in its pages.[43] An Irish Archaeological Society had been founded by Petrie and others in March 1840 and its efforts to interest the Irish aristocracy in the study of Ireland's past were seen as particularly significant.[44] Petrie, who combined support for the union with Great Britain with a deep love of Ireland's culture and heritage, argued that centuries of propaganda about Irish history, architecture, art, literature and music had 'almost entirely denationalised the higher classes', and saw it as a patriotic duty to reverse this trend. Interest in the Irish past paved the way for contact and friendships between leading Young Irelanders and unionists such as Isaac Butt, William Monsell, Samuel Ferguson, Joseph Sheridan Le Fanu, William Torrens McCullagh and William Wilde.[45]

The *Nation* was generally supportive of the Irish Archaeological Society and carried regular reports of its meetings and appreciative reviews of its publications.[46] Some nationalists, though, were critical of the society, claiming its membership was too exclusive, its admission fees too high, and its publications aimed at specialist scholars rather than the general public. In December 1845 the *Nation* threw its weight behind the foundation of the more open and populist Celtic Society, which sought to 'preserve the evidences and landmarks of a distinct nationality by means of a more enlarged cultivation of the Language, History, Antiquities etc. of Ireland' and to make scholarly publications widely available.[47] Its officials included prominent figures of varying political persuasions such as Sir Aubrey de Vere, Isaac Butt, Sir Robert Kane, William Smith O'Brien and Daniel O'Connell, and its council had a strong Young Ireland representation, including Michael Joseph Barry, Charles Gavan Duffy, Thomas MacNevin and John Mitchel.[48] In the end its plans to open the world of Irish antiquities to the general public had limited success and its range of publications was disappointing: the most notable were *The Book of Rights* (1847) edited by John O'Donovan, an account of the privileges of the ancient kings of Ireland, and an edition of *Cambrensis Eversus* (1848–51) edited by Revd Matthew Kelly, a defence of the Irish nation from the

disparagement of the medieval Welsh clergyman Giraldus Cambrensis, originally written in the seventeenth century by the Catholic historian John Lynch.[49]

Although their aims and means often differed from those of the scholarly
antiquarians, the Young Irelanders were keen students of their work and sought
to associate themselves with their endeavours as much as possible. Lacking
the time and expertise for in-depth study of the past, they relied heavily on
scholars such as Petrie, O'Donovan, O'Curry and James Hardiman when
writing their own historical works. Davis, for example, asked O'Donovan's
advice on Irish standards and coats of arms for Mitchel's biography of Hugh
O'Neill, while O'Curry provided assistance to Duffy with translations from
the Irish for his *Ballad Poetry of Ireland* (1845) and wrote historical and cultural
notes for Michael Joseph Barry's second edition of his *Songs of Ireland* (1846).[50]
John O'Donovan's *Annals of the Four Masters* became a particularly important
source for the historians and balladeers of the *Nation*.[51] Reviewing the
prospectus of O'Donovan's work, the *Nation* observed that 'the streams from
the remote regions of history mix their wisdom and learning with the hot rain
of political passion and swell the mind of the country', and on publication it
was praised as 'the most authentic and characteristic record of those ages,
illustrated by one of the best Irish scholars that has appeared since the days of
the Four Masters themselves'.[52]

For all their praise of the work of O'Donovan and other professional
scholars, the Young Irelanders were ready to support almost anyone who contributed to popular knowledge about Ireland's history, so long as they buttressed
the view that there was much to be proud of in Ireland's past. Davis, for
example, defended the much-derided Irish antiquarians of the eighteenth
century such as Charles Vallancey, Sylvester O'Halloran and Joseph Cooper
Walker, claiming that they had accomplished much good:

> They called attention to the history and manners of our predecessors which we had
> forgotten. They gave a pedigree to nationhood, and created a faith that Ireland
> could and should be great again by magnifying what had been. They excited the
> noblest passions – veneration, love of glory, beauty and virtue . . . While we
> concede that Vallancey was a bad scholar, O'Halloran a credulous historian, and
> Walker a shallow antiquarian, we claim for them gratitude and attachment, and
> protest, once and for all, against the indiscriminate abuse of them now going in out
> educated circles.[53]

The *Nation* had few qualms about making use of historical works that fell
short of the standards set by the best Irish scholars. Before O'Donovan's
painstaking translation of the *Annals* was published, Owen Connellan had in
1846 produced his own translation of the *Annals of the Four Masters* from 1171

to 1616 AD (a version that was based on the work of Dr Charles O'Conor in the 1810s with its English revised by James Clarence Mangan). Connellan's primary concern was to publish quickly and cheaply, and he was much criticised for the slipshod nature of his scholarship: the waspish O'Donovan, for example, dismissed him as having 'as much brains as a hatching goose'.[54] In order to provide historical context Connellan had included extensive essay-long footnotes based on available secondary literature and, although many were of dubious accuracy and often tangentially related to the text of the annals, they provided useful introductions to students of early Irish history. Connellan's prioritising of quick and cheap publication was in keeping with Young Ireland's strategy and the *Nation* welcomed his work for its 'simple, strong, and native' history and for providing an accessible source for the study of the middle ages (it sold for £1 10s., compared with £8 8s. for O'Donovan's three-volume 1848 edition).[55] Connellan was commended for popularising a vibrant history that English historians had dismissed or ignored, and providing evidence that the Irish in the middle ages were more civilised, more law-abiding, more devoted to song and music, and more comfortable in material terms than they had ever been since. This, the *Nation* claimed, was a period when Ireland enjoyed true civilisation rather than the spurious version promoted by Britain.[56] It added that 'there has not been published for many a year any book half so serviceable' as Connellan's *Annals* with its graphic illustration of 'the ways of this stormy, gentle, vehement, refined, splendid, and bloody race; a race well worth understanding instead of misunderstanding, especially by their own children; and whose history, whose moral, social and psychological developments, it is our duty to study, and to know thoroughly'.[57]

The clear polemical intentions of Young Ireland and their readiness to make use of second-rate scholarship to popularise Irish history created some tensions with professional scholars. Although Petrie, O'Donovan and O'Curry were personally friendly with some Young Irelanders, they avoided any political identification with the group and did not write for the *Nation*. Davis invited O'Donovan to write 'a volume of historical miscellanies' for the *Nation*'s Library of Ireland series, but he declined, preferring to devote his time to more scholarly work.[58] While scholars were wary of Young Ireland's simplistic view of Irish history and their subordination of scholarship to political propaganda, the Young Irelanders for their part were often frustrated by the failure of professionals to use their work to advance Ireland's claims to self-determination. In later life Charles Gavan Duffy recorded his contempt for 'the dilettante nationality' of the scholar who 'grew enthusiastic over the Cross of Cong, or a Jacobite song of the later bards, but was indifferent to the present sufferings or hopes of the people'.[59] (Significantly, the Cross of Cong had been acquired for the Royal Irish Academy by George Petrie).

PARALLELS AND INFLUENCES

Although the Young Irelanders were primarily concerned with Irish history, they also looked to the histories of other countries for inspiration and to draw parallels with Ireland's situation. Some of Davis's earliest historical writing in the *Dublin Monthly Magazine* was given over to foreign topics such as 'Who are the Afghans? And why should Irishmen fight with them?' and 'India – her own and another's'. The former was a concise account of the peoples of Afghanistan which praised their stubborn resistance to foreign invaders and advised Irishmen that they should not allow themselves to be used to suppress Afghan independence. The latter was a history of the British conquest of India from the arrival of the East India Company in 1601 to the decisive Anglo-Mahratta war of 1817–18, which implied analogies with the subjection of Ireland. It claimed that the entire British conquest of India was driven by greed and fraud under the pretence of bringing the benefits of civilisation and good government to a land of barbarous despotism.[60] Davis made clear that his intention was to reveal Britain's cruelty and hypocrisy since 'Reprobation of what is wrong is one of the unpopular duties which the historian is not at liberty to shun'.[61]

Ireland's struggle for independence was sometimes portrayed by the Young Irelanders as part of an international struggle by all oppressed European nations for freedom. If Ireland should win its freedom, wrote Davis, 'let not only Ireland but Poland, Italy and Hungary be glad . . . we are battling for Ireland; if we conquer, 'twill be for mankind'.[62] The *Nation* noted the need for Irishmen to write the 'histories of the rise and progress of other free nations'.[63] During the Polish insurrection of 1846, the sufferings and heroism of Polish history featured prominently in the paper, with the reminder that: 'It may be our case tomorrow'.[64] Scotland and Belgium were also cited as small nations that had suffered from the evils of foreign rule, with Belgium recently providing the example of a nation that had refused to be absorbed by another but had taken up arms to free itself from a more powerful neighbour.[65] Scotland, which featured regularly in the columns of the *Nation*, provided a different lesson, with the brave deeds of medieval Scottish heroes such as Robert de Bruce and William Wallace invoked to imply that Scots of the present day had betrayed their heritage of resistance and independence by accepting provincial status.[66] Under the union with England 'the Presbyterian, democratic and Celtic is ruled by the uncongenial spirit of aristocratic, Teutonic England', with the result that Scotland was now 'a province – a thing, the soulless serf of England. For sixty years after the union her sons were butchered and tortured; for seventy more corrupted and degraded'.[67]

The example of Canada, too, which was moving towards independence in the 1840s, was much cited. The situation was compared to Ireland in the 1780s, when a determined people had wrung its independence from an England weakened by foreign entanglements. The *Nation* asked 'Are we too few, too paltry, to attain liberation, when Canada is able to extort it?'[68] The history of the USA was also given some prominence – most notably in Michael Doheny's *History of the American Revolution* (1846) (the only volume of the Library of Ireland that dealt with a non-Irish subject). Doheny made much of the contribution of the Irish during the American War of Independence, and in passing made the observation that the Irish countryside was even more suited to guerrilla warfare than the American, while disclaiming any intention of encouraging such action. The contrast between the American and Irish situations was also drawn in the *Nation* article, 'How America became a nation.' It noted that before the revolution the American colony 'had but three million inhabitants, was almost unprovided with arms and ammunition and had not a single ship of war', but 'a straggling row of thinly-peopled colonies . . . are now a vast confederation of powerful states, prosperous, and proud, and self-reliant'. In a swipe at those who condemned the use of physical force to achieve Irish independence, the *Nation* concluded that 'by stout acts, and not by bragging speeches, nations have been made great, glorious and free'.[69]

While the Young Irelanders were willing to look beyond their own borders, most of the historical parallels they invoked were somewhat tenuous and dutiful. With some exceptions (such as Davis's work on India) they were not backed up by any substantial research and were based on a superficial reading of the history of the countries in question. Their relevance to the Irish situation was often contrived and rarely did such writings evince the passion that Young Irelanders devoted to the history of their own country.

The sentiments expressed in the *Nation* were generally of a kind with the liberal and romantic nationalism that had become a force throughout Europe by the 1840s. In their fascination with history and folk culture the Young Irelanders resembled contemporary continental intellectuals who sought to find the true essence and soul of their nation in the lore and traditions of the peasantry and the glories and trials of the past. These similarities and the name Young Ireland have sometimes led to their being seen as part of a wider movement of European nationalism inspired by Guiseppe Mazzini's Young Italy, founded in 1831 to harness Italian nationalist sentiment in the creation of a united Italian republic. The term 'Young Ireland', however, was initially applied to Davis and his followers as a mocking nickname and did not signify any direct connection with Mazzinian nationalism. Mazzini, in fact, was a critic rather than a supporter of Irish nationalism. He denied that Ireland was a separate nation, claiming that it lacked the fundamental characteristics of the nation such as its own language and distinct national customs, as well as the historic mission that set nations apart and enabled them to perform a particular duty in the service of mankind. Without these essential traits he believed that its agitation for independence was hollow and ill-conceived and that it should accept and make the best of its status as a province of Great Britain.[70]

However, while they had no direct links with other European nationalists, the efforts of Young Ireland to promote a nationalist agenda through the writing of history had strong parallels with what was happening elsewhere in Europe in the 1840s. Across the continent nationalist historians sought to preserve and synthesise the experiences of their people to arouse national awareness. As Eugene Kamenka has noted, 'historical consciousness formed the basis of all modern nationalism'.[71] Historians joined philologists and poets in laying the foundations for national awakenings and inaugurated a golden age of history writing. Great national histories, such as Friedrich G. Schlosser's eighteen-volume *General History of the German People* (1844–56), Thomas Babington Macaulay's five-volume *History of England* (1849–61) and Modesto Lafuente's thirty-volume *History of Spain* (1850–69), played central roles in shaping national historical consciousness in their respective countries.[72]

While the histories of larger and more established nations were often characterised by pride in their traditions and achievements, those of nations with unrealised aspirations to independence often dwelt on past grievances and challenged the complacent interpretations of their conquerors. The closest parallels to the work of the Young Irelanders can be seen in the efforts of nationalist journalists and academics in subject nations in central and eastern Europe, who strove to support their claims for autonomy by composing national narratives that emphasised the distinctiveness of their nations and their refusal to be absorbed by multi-national powers. To counter the denials and denigration of imperialist historians they wrote with pride of their nations' cultural and military achievements and how their national spirit had survived the vicissitudes of history. Foremost among such historians was František Palacký, whose *History of the Czech Nation in Bohemia and Moravia* (5 vols, 1836–67) was one of the great foundation texts of Czech nationalism, written in the hope that a greater awareness of centuries of Czech resistance to foreign invaders would restore a sense of national identity and advance the campaign for Czech independence. Palacký's endeavours were complemented by the rather less scholarly work of popularisers such as the Czech radical journalist-historian Zabid Vysokomytsky (1815–73) whose polemical history of

Bohemia, *The Conception of 1620 and its Results* (1849), was read widely and provided a popular starting point for Palacký's conception of Czech history as a millennium-long struggle against German oppression.[73]

Although the *Nation* occasionally reported on events in the Habsburg provinces, it was largely unaware of the writings of nationalist historians in these lands, who generally wrote in their own language for their own readers. When it expressed its admiration for foreign historians, it was generally for French writers such as Amable Barante, Jules Michelet and Augustin Thierry.[74] John Mitchel maintained that 'the greatest and most lasting nations have been the greatest and most lasting in their history' and that France above all had produced 'a well of story, pure and limpid as that which still reflects the ancient greatness of the pagan world'.[75] In his exhortations to prospective historians to take up the writing of Irish history, Davis strongly recommended as their model Thierry's *History of the Conquest of England by the Normans* (1825) (translated into English in its year of publication, and with further English editions in 1840 and 1841).[76] Davis was especially attracted to his empathy with history's victims. Thierry had attempted to puncture the complacency of British historiography and its French admirers by revealing the cruelty and ruthlessness that lay behind the Norman conquest of Britain and Ireland. He lauded the heroism of those who resisted and portrayed Ireland's history as the struggle of a brave and resourceful people to preserve their customs and traditions against the efforts of a brutal conqueror to obliterate them, describing centuries of Irish resistance as 'the most singular and noblest example ever furnished by any people in the world', and claimed that the frequent rebellions of the Irish were evidence of courage and nobility rather than lawlessness.[77] This unshakeable spirit he saw as present still in the songs and music of the people in which 'are recorded the sorrows of Ireland and the crimes of its oppressors' and argued that 'the bards and minstrels of Erin have become the archivists of their land'. Thierry's celebration of the resilience of Irish culture and his praise of Irish courage and nobility was seen as the best answer to the defamatory arguments of British historians such as Hume and Macaulay.[78]

Davis regarded Thierry's work as a vindication of the Irish struggle from one of the leading historians of the day. He was also taken with Thierry's lyrical and picturesque style and singled him out as the historian that all Irish nationalists should read, noting that 'there is more dramatic skill, more picturesque and coloured scenery, more distinct and characteristic grouping, and more lively faith to the look and spirit of the men and times and feelings of which he writes, in Thierry, than in any other historian that ever lived'.[79] The *Nation* hoped that someday Ireland might produce its own Thierry, a figure 'with the persevering labour and genius to master the numberless materials of our history, and out of the abundant chaos to create a true story of Ireland'.[80]

Unlike Thierry, Thomas Carlyle could not be said to have any sympathy for Ireland's struggle for independence, yet he probably influenced Young Ireland's writing of history even more than the Frenchman. Most of the Young Irelanders regarded his denunciation of modern society and his admiration for the heroes and achievements of the past as a prophetic voice crying out amidst the hypocrisy and materialism of the age. They read his works as a form of revelation and were thrilled to his celebration of heroic destiny and blood sacrifice.[81] As a young man, John Mitchel regarded Carlyle's *The French Revolution* (1837) as 'the profoundest book, and the most eloquent and fascinating history, that English literature ever produced'.[82] Mitchel praised him as 'our venerated and beloved preceptor at whose feet we have long studied and learned', and maintained that it was his reading of Carlyle that had inspired him to become 'a determined repealer and Irish nationalist'.[83] Charles Gavan Duffy, too, was a fervent disciple: he recalled that on reading Carlyle's *Miscellanies* for the first time 'his daring theories moved me like electric shocks'.[84]

However, although they were quick to acknowledge his influence, there was a marked ambivalence to Young Ireland views on Carlyle, which mirrored Carlyle's own ambivalence towards Ireland and Irish nationalism. In Carlyle's writings his recognition that Ireland had been abused and exploited by England jostles with his disgust at Irish poverty and contempt for Irish rebelliousness and, while he warmed to Young Ireland's sincerity and idealism, he found much of their politics naive and reckless.[85] He mocked their enthusiasm for Ireland's past, claiming that in the whole span of Irish history there was scarcely a single figure worth celebrating.[86] For their part, the Young Irelanders found so much to admire in Carlyle's critique of his age, that they were prepared to ignore his anti-Irish views or dismiss them as the product of ignorance. Jane Carlyle noted that when Duffy, Pigot and O'Hagan visited Carlyle's house in Chelsea in 1843, they came both to pay homage and to argue.[87] Duffy concluded that the Young Irelanders 'did not accept his specific opinions on almost any question, but his constant advocacy of veracity, integrity and valour touched the most generous of their sympathies . . . He did not teach them to think as he thought, but he confirmed their determination to think for themselves'.[88]

John Mitchel made essentially the same point when reviewing Carlyle's edition of *Oliver Cromwell's Letters and Speeches* (1845) for the *Nation*, admitting that he differed from Carlyle with 'reluctance and pain' and that no book he had read had ever troubled him so much. Mitchel's conflicting emotions derived partly from the fact that he disapproved more of Cromwell's nationality than his methods: like Carlyle he approved of Cromwell's determination and ruthlessness, praising him as a reminder of 'the indefeasible manhood of man'. But unlike Carlyle, who saw Cromwell as doing some good to Ireland, Mitchel regarded him as 'a curse to this unfortunate country . . . his whole mission and teaching here were a genuine gospel of the Devil'. While noting Carlyle's ability to inspire those with whom he differed, Mitchel upbraided him for his ignorance of Ireland and ended with a plea that 'our anti-Irish friend' should inform himself about Irish history or, failing that, let it alone and 'leave our history altogether to some Irish pen'.[89]

Despite such criticisms, Mitchel, and the other Young Irelanders were anxious to emulate Carlyle's ability to write vivid and engaging narrative history. Joep Leerssen has argued persuasively that Young Ireland identified so strongly with Carlyle because 'he expressed so powerfully a "sublime", conflict-based, un-British and uncomplacent view of history'.[90] Sharing Carlyle's contempt for disinterested scholarship and bland neutrality, the Young Irelanders believed that the writing of history should be driven by moral purpose, and that the historian should have no compunctions about praising or condemning as the situation warranted. Many (especially Mitchel and Thomas D'Arcy McGee) attempted to imitate his highly rhetorical prose style. Mitchel's first draft of *Aodh O'Neill* was swamped with overwrought Carlylean prose, some of which he eventually agreed to remove, although only with great reluctance.[91] Carlyle's influence on McGee's early work was also marked, with McGee's chastisement of Richard II in his biography of Art MacMurrough reading almost like a parody: 'For shame, for shame, son of Black Edward, to treat your noblest foe, as a wolfish felon, and not as he was, a chivalrous Christian prince, defending his undoubted inheritance by honourable strategy and just exercise of arms!'[92]

Carlyle was also important in providing Young Ireland with a mediated introduction to the German romantic idealism of Goethe and Fichte. It seems doubtful that Thomas Davis spent time in Germany as was once believed, but he was an assiduous reader of the *Dublin University Magazine* which regularly featured articles on German literature. These included reviews and commentaries on the work of writers such as Goethe, Schiller and Herder, and in his speech to the College Historical Society in 1840 Davis had quoted Lessing: 'Think wrongly if you will, but think for yourselves'.[93] The *Nation* too devoted significant space to German literature, with over eighty references between 1842 and 1848.[94] It was Goethe who observed that the best thing about history is 'the enthusiasm it arouses' and the importance attached to the past by writers such as himself, Lessing and Herder strongly influenced nineteenth-century nationalist discourse.[95] Herder believed that each nation possessed a character which made it unique and that the purpose of history was to discover the steps which had led to the formation of national character. He insisted that human civilisation depends not on the general and universal, but on particular and national characteristics, and that cultural assets such as language and folklore that distinguish one people from another should be carefully preserved.[96] His teachings convinced romantic nationalists that peoples were primarily bound together by the inner consciousness of sharing a common cultural heritage. Governments came and went, administrative rules were made and unmade, but society was an organic accretion of communal experience and past culture that endured. Those who sought the true character of their people would find it most authentically in the stories, myths, literature and traditions of the past.[97]

THREE

WRITING HISTORY

—

The *Nation* contended that 'the history of Ireland has not yet been written' and that Ireland could not claim to be a nation until this was done.[1] According to Davis, national morale was undermined by ignorance and historical misrepresentations, and a thorough knowledge of history was essential to inspire a people to realise their destiny as a united and independent nation. He had great faith in its effect, claiming 'it would clear up the grounds of our quarrels, and prepare reconciliation; it would *unconsciously* make us recognise the causes of our weakness; it would give us great examples of men and events, and materially influence our destiny'.[2] Writing Ireland's history was therefore a patriotic imperative, in which he was prepared to lead the way.

THE WRITINGS OF THOMAS DAVIS

Davis did not confine his efforts to the *Nation* but, seeking to reach as wide an audience as possible, contributed a series of articles to the *Dublin Monthly Magazine* in 1843 on the Irish parliament summoned by James II in 1689.[3] Mindful of unionist fears of repeal of the union with Britain, he was anxious to refute longstanding claims that James II's parliament had attempted to expropriate and oppress Irish Protestants, and that any assembly dominated by Irish Catholics could be expected to behave in the same way.[4] He saw the work as part of his broader attempt to counter the misrepresentation of Ireland's past and 'to rescue eminent men and worthy acts from calumnies which were founded on the ignorance and falsehoods of the Old Whigs, who never felt secure until they had destroyed the character as well as the liberty of Ireland . . . Never has any great deed been done here that the alien government did not, as soon as the facts became historical endeavour to blacken the honour of the statesmen, the wisdom of the legislators, or the valour of the soldiers who achieved it'.[5]

Far from it being an illegitimate or sectarian gathering as critics alleged, Davis argued that the 1689 parliament was the only Irish legislative assembly that had ever held a truly national authority and that it had acted with scrupulous fairness. Despite having legislated after a century of religious conflict and land transfers, it had passed no penal laws against Protestants nor attempted any sweeping expropriations, but merely sought to undo 'the Cromwellian robbery' by restoring the land to its rightful owners.[6] He praised it as a truly patriotic assembly intent on promoting national prosperity by such steps as forbidding the importation of foreign coal, providing for the recovery of waste lands, authorising measures to liberalise foreign trade and encouraging a domestic ship-building industry.[7] He warmly endorsed such protectionist policies and praised the parliament's educational initiatives, especially its legislative proposals to provide free schools of mathematics and navigation in Dublin, Belfast, Cork, Waterford, Limerick and Galway.[8] These measures, he implied, stood in sharp contrast to the shameful neglect of the Irish economy and Irish education shown by Westminster, and showed how an independent Irish parliament could foster domestic economic development.[9]

Davis stressed the 'Patriotic' nature of the 1689 parliament and attempted to link it with the achievement of legislative independence in 1782, declaring that 'the pedigree of our freedom is a century older than we thought'. He argued that its deliberations had provided the Patriots of 1782 'with principles and a precedent' and that Catholic parliamentarians of 1689 such as Sir Richard Nagle and Sir Stephen Rice should be revered in the Irish Patriot tradition alongside Protestants such as Henry Flood and Henry Grattan.[10] It ought to be seen as a unifying rather than a divisive event. Protestants could 'sympathise with the urgent patriotism and loyalty of the parliament, rather than dwell on its errors, or on the sufferings which civil war inflicted on their forefathers'. Both sides could join in deploring 'the falsehoods, corruption, and forgeries of English aristocrats, the imprudence of an English king, and the fickleness of the English people'.[11] In particular, Ulster Protestants should realise that they had gained nothing from William's victory but 'religious tyranny, mercantile oppression, and national ruin'.[12] The decision of the Williamite parliament to burn the acts and official documents of its Jacobite predecessor was, he implied, a deliberate effort to distort history and sow the seeds of division.[13]

In general, Davis's writings emphasised personalities, events and topics that could transcend confessional identification. Beginning in 1843 with his own work on the Patriot lawyer and MP John Philpot Curran, he launched a series of books on the orators of Ireland with historical introductions and edited versions of their speeches. He encouraged his Young Ireland colleagues to do likewise. His friend Daniel Owen Madden added a collection of the speeches of Henry Grattan, and Thomas MacNevin edited the speeches of Richard Lalor Shiel and an account of the state trials of the United Irishmen of 1798.[14] Such works were intended to reach out beyond supporters of repeal: Curran and Grattan were Protestant Patriots who supported Catholic emancipation and Shiel (a Catholic) was a whiggish supporter of O'Connell. All were renowned orators who engaged solely in constitutional politics, and even unionists who sometimes disagreed with what they said could admire the way they said it.

Davis's historical writings were, however, less effective than he had hoped. His scattered notes and ambitious plans put one in mind of an enthusiast, working with great energy but spreading himself over too great an area to make a significant contribution to historical research.[15] Having worked hard on the research for his articles on the 1689 parliament in the *Dublin Monthly Magazine* (at a time when he was also writing most of the *Nation*), he was disappointed at the poor response. This disappointment appears to have changed his approach to the writing of history, as most of his subsequent work consisted of popular biographies and stirring historical verse. The latter proved particularly popular with readers of the *Nation* and became Young Ireland's most effective and enduring contribution to the popularisation of Irish history.

HISTORY IN VERSE

Just as the *Nation* deplored the poor state of historical writing in Ireland, so it was critical of the quality of Irish ballads. It claimed Ireland was deficient in three crucial areas: 'national self-respect, knowledge of our own past, and *national* ballads'.[16] The comparison was often drawn with Scotland, whose ballads were seen to be an integral part of Scottish nationality, and the words of the Scottish patriot Andrew Fletcher were quoted approvingly: 'it is of little consequence who makes the laws of a country if the song-making be in proper hands'.[17] The *Nation* dedicated itself to the task of giving the Irish people better songs to sing, claiming that nothing could succeed until these had laid 'a fertile deposit in the public mind'.[18]

Raising the tone of Irish popular song accorded with Young Ireland's mission of national improvement. Just as the lack of national history allowed slurs and misrepresentations to flourish, so Duffy worried that the literary impressions of 'a people without native poetry . . . are liable to be caught from a foreign, a prejudiced, or a poisonous source'. Street ballads, he claimed, were either coarse and vulgar songs imported from England or clumsy compositions filled with the 'pedantry, pretension, and grossness' of hedge school masters.[19] In his *Songs of Ireland*, the Young Irelander Michael Joseph Barry explicitly rejected songs which are un-Irish in their character of language, and those miserable slang productions, which, representing the Irishman only as a blunderer, a bully, a fortune-hunter, or a drunkard, have done more than anything else to degrade him in the eyes of others and, far worse, to debase him in his own.[20]

The *Nation* was also critical of many traditional Irish songs, such as those collected by James Hardiman in his *Irish Minstrelsy* (1831) or Edward Walsh and John O'Daly in *Reliques of Irish Jacobite Poetry* (1844), for falling short of their national ideals. It claimed that 'their structure is irregular, their grief slavish and despairing, their joy reckless and bombastic, their religion bitter and sectarian, their politics Jacobite, and concealed by extravagant and tiresome allegory'.[21]

Before the Young Irelanders, the United Irishmen had also employed verse and song to propagate their message and some of their songs were still sung in the 1840s. (Despite his admiration for the United Irishmen, Davis regarded most of their songs as uninspired doggerel.)[22] More recently Thomas Moore had used Irish history as an inspiration for his verse and established himself as Ireland's national lyric poet.[23] Moore's *Irish Melodies*, consisting of 124 songs, was published in ten parts (1808–34), and his *National Airs* in six volumes (1818–28). Their sentimental and evocative lyrics, often lamenting the sorrows of an oppressed nation or recalling the tragic fates of ancient Irish heroes or United Irish leaders such as Lord Edward Fitzgerald or Robert Emmet, were skilfully matched with traditional airs collected by Edward Bunting in 1790s. Such compositions strongly appealed to contemporary tastes in Ireland and abroad, evoking sympathy for Ireland's troubled past and helping to create a new awareness of Irish grievances.

Young Ireland acknowledged Moore's achievement in popularising Irish traditional music and giving vent to an enduring expression of Irish national sentiment: he was the first Irish writer to feature in the *Nation*'s 'National Gallery of Irish Writers', and Michael Joseph Barry dedicated his *Songs of Ireland* to Moore as 'the national bard of Ireland'.[24] There was, however, some ambivalence in their attitudes: Davis praised Moore's 'expression of the softer feelings' and described him as 'immeasurably our greatest poet', but lamented that he 'does not speak the sterner passions, spoils some of his finest songs by pretty images, is too refined and subtle in his dialect, and too negligent of narrative'.[25] Davis believed him to be 'too delicate and subtle for the multitude. Rougher and bolder strains must make "the valleys sing" and the cabins rejoice'.[26] Some nationalists openly criticised Moore's work for its defeatist sense of resignation: one critic denounced his 'whining lamentation over our eternal fall, and miserable appeals to our masters to regard us with pity', while another quoted William Hazlitt's observation that 'if Moore's *Irish Melodies* with their drawing-room, lackadaisical patriotism, were really the melodies of the Irish nation, the people of Ireland deserved to be slaves forever'.[27] In many ways, the stirring refrains and pounding, martial rhythms of the *Nation*'s songs were an answer to Moore, an attempt to capture 'the rougher and bolder strains' so valued by Davis. Duffy boasted that the recurrent themes of death and despair in Moore's songs 'were the wail of a lost cause; while the songs of the *Nation* vibrated with the virile and passionate hopes of a new generation'.[28]

In order to avoid the sentimentality and fatalism attributed to Moore, Davis insisted that the songs of Young Ireland should have 'simple words, bold, strong imagery, plain, deep passions (love, patriotism, conciliation, glory, indignation, resolve), daring humour, broad narrative, high morals'.[29] He himself was the *Nation*'s most prolific writer of ballads, writing almost 50 over a period of three years. These were an eclectic mixture, with many devoted to recollecting historical events such as 'Lament for Owen Roe O'Neill' (19 Nov. 1842), 'The death of Sarsfield' (22 Apr. 1843), 'The Dungannon Convention' (18 May 1844), and 'The sack of Baltimore' (5 July 1845). Many celebrated Irish martial valour, such as 'O'Sullivan's return' (8 Apr. 1843), 'The battle of Limerick' (*Nation*, 21 Sept. 1844), 'Clare's dragoons' (5 Oct. 1844) and 'Fontenoy' (*Nation*, 3 Feb. 1844). The last was perhaps the classic of this genre, with its vivid recreation of the charge of the Irish Brigade which turned the tide of battle and won the day for France:

> Like lions leaping at a fold, when mad with hunger's pang
> Right up against the English line the Irish exiles sprang
> Bright was their steel, 'tis bloody now, their guns are filled with gore;
> Through shattered ranks, and severed files, and trampled flags they tore;

Davis also wrote national rallying cries such as 'The green above the red' (*Nation*, 12 Oct. 1844), 'The west's asleep' (22 July 1843) and, most famously, 'A nation once again' (*Nation*, 13 July 1844) in which readers were exhorted to live up to the glories of the past and dedicate themselves to achieving Ireland's freedom. Even poems that were ostensibly celebrations of Ireland's beauty, such as 'The rivers' (30 Mar. 1844), 'Glangariff [*sic*]', and 'My grave' (29 Oct. 1842): carried with them the implication that such a land was worthy of the best efforts of her sons and daughters and deserved to be a proud and independent nation rather than a cowering province. Love songs such as 'The lost path' (30 Mar. 1844), 'Annie dear' (10 Aug. 1844) and 'The bride of Mallow' (23 Dec. 1843) also had an inspirational nationalist purpose: they could be interpreted as aisling-inspired allegories in which Ireland is personified by a beautiful woman or as actual celebrations of the beauty and virtue of Irish women, to whom Irishmen must prove themselves by fulfilling their patriotic duty to their native land.

Davis's verse had many admirers. The unionist Samuel Ferguson claimed that it 'sounded the intellectual reveillé of a whole people' and that even 'the sternest opponents were captivated'.[30] Although Davis wrote primarily for propagandist effect – John Mitchel noted of Davis's work that '"literature", for the mere sake of literature, he almost despised . . . every sentence was a lever or a wedge'[31] – his poetic sensibility and facility with language succeeded in raising much of his verse above the level of nationalist doggerel, and he became the most popular and widely published of all the *Nation*'s poets. The *Celt*, a Young Ireland publication of the 1850s, praised him as 'a noble patriot and profound scholar' who had 'grasp[ed] the harp which Moore had laid aside, and with a strong purpose, waking the echoes of its strings'.[32]

Most members of the Young Ireland group wrote some historical verse, much of it in imitation of Davis's national rallying calls or celebrations of Irish valour. Among the more notable examples were Duffy's 'Faugh a ballagh' (29 Oct. 1842) and 'The song of Ulster (11 Mar. 1843), John Kells Ingram's 'The memory of the dead' (1 Apr. 1843), M. J. McCann's 'The Clanconnell war song' ('O'Donnell Aboo') (28 Jan. 1843), and John O'Hagan's 'Ourselves alone' (3 Dec. 1842) and 'The union' (22 Apr. 1843).

Some of the *Nation*'s most distinctive poetic voices were those of women, such as Ellen Mary Patrick Downing, who wrote under the name 'Mary' or 'EMPD'; Mary Kelly of Co. Galway who became widely known as 'Eva of the *Nation*'; and Jane Francesca Elgee (wife of the surgeon and scholar Sir William Wilde and mother of Oscar Wilde) who wrote under the name 'Speranza'.[33] The pithy and emotional nature of verse was regarded as more fitting to women than the laborious task of writing history. In their work the themes of love and devotion to Ireland predominated and, just like their male counterparts, they mined Irish history for inspiration in poems such as Mary Kelly's 'Our memories' (24 Apr. 1847) in which she recalls the heroes of Ireland's past and calls on the men of today to imitate them. Speranza became well known for her powerful verse, and her poem 'The stricken land' was one of the most bitter indictments of the inaction and incompetence of the authorities during the Famine. She continued to write in a similar vein throughout 1847–8, viewing the writing of militant verse as a kind of proxy war, arguing that 'strong nations fight, oppressed nations sing; and thus, not with armies and fleets, but with the passionate storm of lyric words have the Irish people kept up for centuries their ceaseless war against alien rule'.[34]

Duffy (and most later critics) gave first place among the *Nation*'s poets to James Clarence Mangan, noting that his 'war songs have the swing and the force of a battering-ram'.[35] However, although he wrote occasionally for the *Nation*, Mangan's relationship with Young Ireland was hesitant and sporadic, and he was never a central member of the group. According to Duffy, when he first met Mangan in the early 1840s 'he knew nothing of politics and cared nothing for them, and he averted his eyes from history as from a painful and humiliating spectacle'.[36] Socially he was ill at ease with the confident young men of the *Nation* and artistically he bridled at their formulaic attitudes to writing verse. He wrote an inaugural poem for the *Nation* in October 1842, but soon afterwards seems to have fallen out with Duffy and did not contribute regularly to the paper again until 1846. In that year the *Nation* published many of his best poems, including 'Siberia' (18 Apr. 1846), 'Dark Rosaleen' (30 May 1846), 'A vision of Connaught in the xiiith century' (11 July 1846), 'Sarsfield' (24 Oct. 1846), 'A cry for Ireland' (31 Oct. 1846) and 'The sorrows of Innisfail' (5 Dec. 1846), which projected a desolate and apocalyptic view of Irish history. Duffy made many attempts to persuade him to produce poems to order that conformed to Young Ireland nationalist ideals, but Mangan was too eccentric and wilful to subject himself to such discipline. He often frustrated Duffy by submitting playful or esoteric verse, and by refusing to adopt the didactic tone that characterised the *Nation*'s poems.[37] But there were periods when the mercurial Mangan identified strongly with the ideals of Young Ireland, and on one occasion he thanked Duffy for sending him two (unnamed) 'Histories of Ireland', commenting that 'they will furnish abundance of materials for the construction of the Irish historical romances'.[38] Mangan's natural talent and refusal to subordinate artistic to political considerations gave his work an enduring literary power, and his evocation of a suffering land in poems such as 'Dark Rosaleen', 'A vision of Connaught in the xiiith century' and 'Siberia' made a dramatic contribution to the nationalist perception of Ireland as a historically oppressed land whose wrongs cried out for vengeance.[39] Young Irelanders such as Duffy, Mitchel and Meehan were among the first to recognise the power of his poetry, and were foremost in promoting his work and memory.[40]

Much of the *Nation*'s verse was characterised by bombastic sentiment, facile rhyme and nationalist cliché, and later critics (notably W. B. Yeats) were scathing about its use as political propaganda. Such criticism often showed little understanding of the circumstances in which it was written and the purpose for which it was intended. The Young Irelanders regarded songs primarily as an effective means of propaganda, and soon discovered that the verse form allowed the writer to evade some of the constraints of history writing: it required little historical research or in-depth knowledge, could be written quickly, allowed greater licence in the use of provocative or militant language, and formed a crucial link with an earlier oral tradition that their writings had sought to supplement or even supplant. Set to stirring tunes, Young Ireland ballads were intended as the marching songs of an emerging nation, and made up in energy and passion what they lacked in literary merit. They particularly came alive in public performance, when they became both a public declaration of patriotism and an act of communal solidarity. The verse form succeeded in taking the learning of history away from the solitary act of reading and bringing it into family and social settings in which repeated performance confirmed and reinforced nationalist sentiments. Favourite songs and verses were passed on from generation to generation, becoming inextricably linked with memories of childhood, youth and home. Their reach extended to those who were not literate: as Roy Foster has noted, they had

> a resonance and appeal well beyond the printed word, as perhaps the most evocative form of popular culture in pre-literate societies . . . For those unable or unwilling to read either newspapers or books . . . the ballad managed to convey the essential features of the Irish past in just a couple of well-chosen verses.[41]

The most memorable Young Ireland songs such as 'A nation once again', 'The memory of the dead', and 'O'Donnell Aboo' propagated national pride more effectively than any other means, and became central to the way in which the Irish people interpreted their past.[42]

Davis fully appreciated the power of verse to teach history and planned to create a 'Ballad History of Ireland' – 'a string of ballads chronologically arranged, and illustrating the main events of Irish history, its characters, costumes, scenes, and passions'.[43] The intention was to link together all the glorious episodes in Ireland's past into a seamless narrative which could be continually enlivened by adding new ballads.[44] Such verse could easily be memorised by children and would lay the foundations of their historical knowledge, making Irish history 'familiar to the minds, pleasant to the ears, dear to the passions, and powerful over the taste and conduct of the Irish people in times to come'.[45] He believed that the ballad form was particularly suited to

> hallow or accurse the scenes of glory and honor, or of shame and sorrow; to give to the imagination the arms, and homes, and senates, and battles of other days; to rouse, and soften, and strengthen, and enlarge us with passions of great periods; to lead us into love of self-denial, of justice, of beauty, of valour, of generous life and proud death, and to set up in our souls the memory of great men, who shall then be as models and judges of our actions – these are the highest duties of history, and these are best taught by a Ballad History.[46]

Davis regarded a comprehensive ballad history as 'the greatest book (religion apart) that a country can possess' and lauded the part ballads had played in forging national sentiment in Scotland, Spain and Germany.[47] The proposed work began in the *Nation* on 18 January 1845 with a ballad on the battle of Clontarf of 1014; others on 'The battle of Callan AD 1261', 'The Coming of St Patrick' and the 'Battle of Credran AD 1257' followed. However, their quality did not match Davis's hopes and the series came to an abrupt end in May 1845.[48]

In keeping with Young Ireland's prose historical writings, most of the pieces in the ballad history series celebrated military victories. Such 'war songs' were a staple of the *Nation*, allowing the paper to express militant nationalist sentiment while avoiding the risk of prosecution by placing it in a historical setting. Davis saw them as a subtle and insidious form of propaganda that could appeal to the patriotic instincts of even political opponents.[49] However, Tories such as Isaac Butt, Joseph Sheridan Le Fanu and John Wilson Croker were deeply uneasy at the inflammatory language of much Young Ireland verse, and *The Times* of London commented,

> Let a man make his thoughts rhyme, and there is hardly any amount of treason and iniquity he may not utter . . . no sedition appears too daring to be spoken, no atrocity too great to be recommended with impunity . . . even [O'Connell's] mischievous exhortations are as nothing compared with the fervour of rebellion which breathes in every page of those verses, disguised . . . under the very penetrable mask of an allusion to other times. The writer seems to think his pen absolutely unfettered if he does put 1646 or 1782 at the head of his poem.[50]

In 1843 the most popular of these songs were collected and published as the *Spirit of the Nation*, in a cheap shilling edition. It was enormously popular, going into six editions in its year of publication. By 1877 it had gone through 50 Dublin editions, and was also published in Boston and New York; it remained in print for over 90 years with a 97th edition published in 1934.[51] Duffy claimed that more copies were sold than any other book published in Ireland since the union and that it was as important to Ireland as the poetry of Robert Burns to Scotland.[52] The *Spirit of the Nation* was followed by a number of other cheap pocket-sized collections, such as Duffy's *Ballad Poetry of Ireland* (1845), M. J. Barry's *Songs of Ireland* (1845), Thornton MacMahon's *Casket of Irish Pearls* (1846), and Denis Florence MacCarthy's *Book of Irish Ballads* (1846), all of which found their way into nationalist homes and reading rooms and formed the basis of a nationalist canon of popular Irish songs. Reviewing the work of the Young Irelanders, William J. O'Neill Daunt claimed that they had converted Irish history into 'verses glowing with a passionate fervour, that awakened into life every slumbering pulse of Irish patriotism'.[53]

The ballad form was endlessly versatile and its repetition of key themes and phrases made it a powerful means of propaganda. Duffy reckoned that these songs 'of singular vigour and dramatic power made the great men and great achievements of their race familiar to the people', and were worth more than 'a hundred speeches, or a wagon load of petitions. They echo the true, inner heartfelt feelings of the people'.[54] The dramatic and celebratory form of history favoured by Young Ireland lent itself better to verse than prose, and the strong emotions aroused by historical verse did much to shape Irish national consciousness. Although they owed more to Victorian conceptions of martial vigour than the tradition of Gaelic song, the very title the *Spirit of the Nation* implied that the soul of a people resided in these songs, and it is difficult to disagree with Davis's assessment that of all the *Nation*'s efforts to create a national literature 'the ballads and songs were our most unequivocal success'.[55]

HISTORICAL FICTION

For Davis, history, poetry and fiction were 'the three greatest branches of a national literature'.[56] He regarded them as complementary and believed that history, properly written, should have some of the passion of poetry and the drama of fiction. He argued that it was less important to record precise factual details than to convey the general spirit of Ireland's trials and triumphs, and that the historical novel offered the ideal vehicle to enter the past imaginatively and express moral truths about Irish history that could not be found in dry documents.[57] The model he had foremost in mind was Sir Walter Scott, described by the *Nation* as 'the greatest master that ever lived of historical divination'.[58] Scott's novels transformed the way in which Scottish history, and history in general, were viewed in the early nineteenth century, and Davis hoped that an Irish historical novelist might do the same for Ireland.[59] A keen collector of old ballads, stories, manuscripts and artefacts, Scott used his antiquarian learning to great effect, and his command of period detail and of the political, social and cultural background to his historical narratives made a vivid impression on readers all over Europe. During the nineteenth century romantic historians often strove to incorporate the imagination and empathy of the best historical novels into their work.[60] Historians such as Carlyle, Macaulay and Thierry acknowledged the influence of Scott's fiction on their own work: his novels, wrote Carlyle, have taught all men this truth, which looks like a truism, yet was unknown to the writers of history and others, till so taught: that the bygone ages of the world were actually filled by living men, not by protocols, state papers, controversies and abstractions of men.[61]

Nationalists throughout Europe admired the way in which Scott painted a vivid and compelling picture of the past, populating history with memorable characters and creating powerful images of Scottish nationhood which strongly asserted Scotland's cultural distinctiveness.[62]

Davis was an avid reader of historical novels and praised works such as John Banim's *Boyne Water* (1826) and Gerald Griffin's *Invasion* (1832) as striking examples of the way in which Irish history could be brought to life.[63] He also admired Thomas Moore's *Memoirs of Captain Rock* (1824), a work which skilfully melded together history and fiction by using an eponymous Whiteboy to relay to an English visitor an account of Ireland's past in which bad government produced an endless cycle of popular alienation and violent resistance. The *Nation* described it as a wise and witty attempt to engage the sympathy of English readers without sacrificing the honour and pride of its Irish ones, and recommended it should be stocked in all repeal reading rooms.[64]

Other than these, however, Davis claimed there were few Irish historical novels worth reading and criticised Irish writers for failing to make proper use of the dramatic materials they had to hand in the vast canvas of Irish history. Many were aimed at the English market, and often relayed through the eyes of English characters, baffled at the enduring animosities of Irish history. The *Nation* strongly disapproved of most of the Irish historical novels being published in the 1840s and condemned Irish writers such as Samuel Lover and Charles Lever for pandering to English prejudices by filling their novels with boisterous and drunken caricatures.[65] It constantly challenged writers to produce literature that would show Ireland to advantage rather than making it a laughing stock, and claimed that under its influence 'established writers of fiction, who seemed enslaved by party ties, or blinded by prejudice, came out of the mist, and learned to look on Ireland as she was'.[66] It noted that young Conservatives such as Isaac Butt and Joseph Sheridan Le Fanu were writing historical novels that conceded something of the justice of Catholic and nationalist claims, and even Lever's work had recently taken on a more national tone.[67] The *Nation* claimed too that William Carleton, whom it had once believed was lost to his country because of his anti-national views, 'had caught fire from the society of the young men, and renounced his bigotry forever'. Davis described Carleton as an 'historian' for his delineation of vanishing Irish types such as the Ribbonman, the poor scholar, the faction fighter, and the matchmaker, praising the vivid sketches of Irish characters in his *Habits and*

Character of the Peasantry (1845) and commended his *Valentine M'Clutchy* as 'a thunderbolt against the oppressive landlords'.[68] In three novels published in 1845 by the *Nation*'s Library of Ireland (the only novels published in the series) Carleton addressed some of the most pressing political and social themes of the day: *Rody the Rover* warned the peasantry of the dangers of being led astray by Ribbonism; *Parra Sastha* extolled the virtues of agricultural improvement, hard work and thrift; and *Art Maguire; or the Broken Pledge*, dedicated to Fr Theobald Mathew, was a cautionary tale of the evils of drink in which 'the hopefulness and self-respect of a temperate guided life – the blight of perjury and intemperance, become a part of our personal experience as thoroughly as if we had witnesses the scene'.[69]

These were among Carleton's most didactic works, in keeping with the self-improving ethic of Young Ireland, but they dealt with contemporary rather than historical themes. Despite Davis's exhortations, no Irish Scott emerged to take up his challenge and his hopes for inspiringly patriotic historical fiction were disappointed. Reviewing the work of Irish historical novelists in the 1850s, the Young-Ireland inspired *Celt* commented on their superficial research and failure to create credible characters and stories, and complained that 'a few pages in two or three of Scott's novels show a greater acquaintance and sympathy with Irish military biography than all has been written by Irishmen to illustrate the subject'.[70]

THE LIBRARY OF IRELAND

The lack of suitable Irish history books was one of Young Ireland's constant complaints. In a rallying call to nationalist writers Duffy announced 'we want half a dozen histories of Ireland. There is no one fit to be read . . . We want the evidence of a thousand intellects, being alive and active for the present and future welfare of our country . . . There is work for them all to root out the weeds of 700 years'.[71] Davis, who had steeped himself in Irish history since his graduation in 1836, was the Young Irelander best qualified to write such a work, and started out 'making a ground plan of his proposed history, estimating the space each era would require, putting previous studies in order, and seeking new materials wherever they were to be found'.[72] But there were so many other demands on his time that he despaired of finishing it, and early in 1844 admitted that 'I must either give up the notion of writing the history, or absolutely stop writing for the *Nation* during the spring . . . I am in a very sobered mood and feel doubts, serious doubts, of my ability to write the history at all'.[73]

In an attempt to attract talented young writers to the task, the Repeal Association (at the instigation of the Young Ireland group) offered a prize for a new concise survey of Irish history from the earliest times to the present. It encouraged all to compete, noting that 'some of the greatest works in existence were written rapidly, and many an old book-worm fails where a young book thrasher succeeds'.[74] Davis drew up a list of rules and guidelines for prospective historians, advising that the work should be written from original research, and claimed that Irish chronicles, annals and genealogies supplied authentic accounts of Ireland's history that were richer and more ancient than those of any other nation in western Europe.[75] He encouraged the historian to reveal

> the social condition of the peasantry, the townsmen, the middle-classes, the nobles, and the clergy (Christian or pagan) in each period – how they fed, dressed, armed and housed themselves. He must exhibit the nature of government, the manners, the administration of law, the state of useful and fine arts, of commerce, of foreign relations. He must let us see the decay and rise of great principles and conditions – till we look on a tottering sovereignty, a rising creed, an incipient war, as distinctly as, by turning to the highway, we can see the old man, the vigorous youth, or the infant child.[76]

He further stipulated that the historian must be devoid of 'bigotry of race or creed' and have 'a love for all sects, a philosophical eye to the merits and demerits of all, and a solemn and haughty impartiality in speaking of all'. To write history in this way 'will be a proud and illustrious deed . . . its first political effect would be enormous; it would be read by every class and side . . . it would people our streets and glens and castles and abbeys and coasts with a hundred generations besides our own'.[77]

Despite the offer of a prize, no suitable work was written, leading Davis and Duffy to conclude that charging a single author to produce a volume that covered the entire span of Irish history was not practicable and that the best approach would be to assign different topics to a team of writers who would each publish separate works.[78] Duffy had been struck by a series of cheap books published in England by the Society for the Diffusion of Useful Knowledge in the 1830s and 40s, and suggested that the *Nation* should undertake a similar venture. This led the paper to launch 'The Library of Ireland', a collection of popular works in history, poetry and fiction. The intention was to publish a volume a month which would eventually create a unified collection designed to

> enlarge the background of a nation's memory – to lead the feet of the student aright through the inward labyrinths of history – to cleanse great effigies of the

coats of calumny in which they have been long wrapped up – to make visible heroism, and piety and knowledge, as tenants of our island for many ages.[79]

In July 1845 the first volume in the series, Thomas MacNevin's *History of the Volunteers of 1782*, was published by James Duffy, a Dublin-based bookseller and publisher. Duffy had long experience in publishing cheap Catholic devotional literature. Among his first ventures into secular works were his re-publications of Jonah Barrington's *Rise and Fall of the Irish Nation* (1843) and Patrick O'Kelly's translation of James MacGeoghegan's *History of Ireland* (1844) which both sold well enough to convince him that there was a ready market for history. In the early 1840s he had invested heavily in new equipment such as steam-powered presses and stereotyping to reduce labour costs and undercut his competitors, and was the Irish printer best-equipped to produce large runs of cheap books. The Young Irelanders had initially printed the highly popular *Spirit of the Nation* from their own offices but were unable to keep up with demand and in 1843 turned to Duffy to make up the shortfall. From then on he was their publisher of choice and his ability to produce books quickly and cheaply was crucial to the successful dissemination of their literature.[80] Although primarily motivated by business concerns, Duffy appears to have been sympathetic to the Young Ireland project and in the face of production difficulties and declining sales in 1847 pledged himself to continue the Library of Ireland in the hope 'that a sound Irish literature may grow on Irish soil, and supply the intellectual wants of the Irish people; and that Irishmen of all classes may meet in the poetic, in the antiquarian, in the romantic, and in the historic literature of their common country'.[81] Duffy continued to publish history books until his death in 1871. Fittingly, the inscription over his grave in Glasnevin cemetery was written by the Young Ireland historian Fr C. P. Meehan: 'His devotional publications have instructed many unto salvation and the historical works he published have exalted the character of his native land, and saved its saints and heroes from oblivion'.[82]

Until the launch of the Library of Ireland, history books were generally prohibitively expensive, usually costing from £1 upwards, well beyond the means of most of the Irish population.[83] At a shilling a piece, the volumes of the Library of Ireland were rather more affordable. After MacNevin's *History of the Volunteers of 1782* (1845) came John Mitchel's *Life and Times of Aodh O'Neill, Prince of Ulster* (1845), MacNevin's *Confiscation of Ulster* (1846) and C. P. Meehan's *History of the Confederation of Kilkenny* (1846), all of which were written in a vivid accessible style and designed to appeal to as wide a readership as possible. In these works the Nine Years' War, the Plantation of Ulster, the Confederation of Kilkenny and the rise of the Volunteer movement were portrayed not as isolated historical events, but important episodes in the continuous struggle of 'the Irish people' against foreign rule and their efforts to assert their country's independence. In the *History of the Volunteers* MacNevin lauded the heroic character of the Volunteers and set out to tell the story of 'how trade and liberty were both acquired; by what arms, and by what men; by how much genius, courage, and fidelity a momentary glory was won for this country'. He praised their determination and moderation, the quality of their leaders, especially Henry Grattan, the toleration they extended to the Catholics and their willingness to confront the power of England to gain legislative independence.[84] In his *Confiscation of Ulster* MacNevin emphasised the bitter injustices that accompanied and followed the plantation of 1609 which were all the more galling because they 'came in the placid guise of law'. After decades of oppression Ulster finally exploded in rebellion in 1641, but he argued that this was not the sectarian massacre of ultra-Protestant propaganda, but the inevitable consequence of invasion and confiscation.[85] Meehan in the *History of the Confederation of Kilkenny* (1846) maintained that the founding of the Confederation in 1642 represented the 'transition from heart-breaking thraldom to bold and armed independence' and would have won permanent freedom for Ireland had it not been weakened by internal divisions.[86]

Heroic biographies such as Mitchel's *Aodh O'Neill* and Thomas D'Arcy McGee's *Life and Conquests of Art MacMurrogh* (1847) celebrated the deeds of these wily and brave commanders in Ireland's long and stubborn resistance to conquest. The series also republished older works, long out of print, such as Meehan's translations from Latin to English of the Dominican priest-historian Daniel O'Daly's *History of the Geraldines, Earls of Desmond, and the Persecution of the Irish Catholics* (1847) (originally published in Latin in 1655), and John Lynch's *The Portrait of a Pious Bishop: or The Life and Death of Most Revd Francis Kirwan, Bishop of Killala* (1848) (originally published in 1669). Republications also included *The Historical Works of the Rt Revd Nicholas French DD* (1846) edited by Samuel Henry Bindon, which included three political tracts by the seventeenth-century Catholic bishop of Ferns: *A Narrative of the Earl of Clarendon's Settlement and Sale of Ireland* (1668), *The Bleeding Iphigenia* (1674), and an attack on the Duke of Ormond, *The Unkinde Desertor of Loyall Men and True Frinds* [*sic*] (1676). Republishing seventeenth-century works made the point that the Library of Ireland was committed to the recovery of Ireland's history and was carrying on an important historiographical tradition that exposed English misrule in Ireland. The series also republished more recent works such as Thomas Davis's biography of John Philpot Curran (1846) and Edward Hay's *History of the Insurrection of 1798* (1847). There were also the three novels by William Carleton and various collections and several anthologies: Davis's *Essays* (1845) and *Poems* (1846), collections of song and poetry edited by Duffy (1845), M. J. Barry (1845), and D. F. McCarthy (1846), a prose collection by Thornton MacMahon (1846), *The Irish Writers of the Seventeenth Century* (1846) by D'Arcy McGee, and *The Poets and Dramatists of Ireland* (1846) by D. F. McCarthy.[87]

The Library of Ireland was an eclectic series, reflecting the rather ad hoc nature of the enterprise, and the end result was some way short of the collection of interlocking chapters on Irish history that Davis and Duffy had originally envisaged. Among volumes proposed and assigned to various writers but never published were 'The Military History of 1798' by M. J. Barry; 'A Life of Wolfe Tone' by Thomas Davis (stalled by Davis's death); 'History of "the Great Popish Rebellion" of 1641' by Charles Gavan Duffy; 'The History of Irish Manufactures' and 'The Constitutional History of the Irish Parliaments' by John Gray; 'Gallery of Irish writers (prior to the 17th century)' by Thomas D'Arcy McGee; 'Echoes of Foreign Song' by James Clarence Mangan; 'The Williamite Wars' and 'Orators of the Irish Parliament' by Thomas Francis Meagher; 'The Life of Owen Roe O'Neill' by John Mitchel; 'The Irish Lawyers of the Seventeenth Century' by Sir Colman O'Loghlen; 'Lives of the Irish Philosophers' by Daniel Owen Madden; and 'The Penal Days' and 'Biographies of the United Irishmen' by Thomas Devin Reilly; 'The Life and Times of Sarsfield' remained unassigned.[88] The most important determinants of publication seem to have been the abilities and professional commitments of the commissioned writers rather than the themes of the works themselves. Some prospective contributors – Meagher and Devin Reilly being the most notable examples – were talented orators but found it difficult to knuckle down to writing a major work. Time seems to have been a scarce commodity for most of these young men. Even the indefatigable Davis despaired of ever finishing his biography of Wolfe Tone, noting that 'between the *Nation*, and the bigots, and the quantity of exercise needed to keep me in health, there is small chance of my writing at all for the series'.[89] Some of the works begun in late 1846 and 1847 were overtaken by the social catastrophe of the Great Famine and the more pressing political concerns that followed in its wake. The fact that so many proposed books were not completed meant there were significant thematic and chronological gaps in a series that was meant to span the full range of Irish history.

The works published by the Library of Ireland were rarely based on extensive original research. Its writers worked to tight publishing deadlines, and had little time for in-depth scholarly investigation. Research was also often made more difficult by the scattered nature of Irish historical sources and the reluctance of the holders of archives to allow public access, and primary sources were used sparingly.[90] In his *Aodh O'Neill* (one of the better researched works of the series), John Mitchel made good use of a manuscript translation by Edward O'Reilly of 'The Life of Red Hugh O'Donnell' held in the Royal Irish Academy, and also used contemporary sources such as William Camden's *History of Elizabeth* (1615–25), George Carew's *Pacata Hibernia* (1633), and Fynes Moryson's *An History of Ireland from the Year 1599 to 1603* (1735). Similarly, the scholarly Fr C. P. Meehan used the Rinuccini Correspondence and the Thorpe Correspondence held in the Royal Dublin Society in his *History of the Confederation of Kilkenny*, but these were exceptions. While the *Nation* writers paid lip service to the notion of original research, they were more intent on telling the right story than consulting the right documents. Mostly they used existing published histories of Ireland as their main sources, with the surveys of Curry, MacGeoghegan, Leland, O'Halloran, Plowden and Taaffe providing their core information.[91]

Other than the *Nation*, the Young Irelanders regarded the Library of Ireland as their most important project.[92] Its sales exceeded all expectations – MacNevin's *History of the Volunteers of 1782* sold over 2,000 copies within weeks of publication. (The success of the Library of Ireland was such that it even spawned an imitation 'National Library of Ireland', a series of cheaper and more extreme nationalist works such as *The Rising in '98* and *The Mercenary Informers of '98* written by anonymously and published by James McCormick of Dublin.[93]) Davis held out great hopes for the Library of Ireland, contending that it allowed the Young Irelanders to do 'whatever we like with Ireland'.[94] Although these hopes were not fully realised – the series produced no classic work of history and was struggling to survive by 1847 – it was among the most successful nationalist publishing projects of the nineteenth century. Its afford-able and accessible volumes formed the basis of the historical and ballad collections in nationalist homes and reading rooms in Ireland for decades to come. Several of its works were immensely influential in their delineation of historic figures and events, and coloured readers' historical perceptions for many years afterwards. A. M. Sullivan, for example, claimed that it was Mitchel's biography of Hugh O'Neill that was primarily responsible for establishing O'Neill's historical reputation as a shrewd and far-sighted strategist:

> Mr Mitchel pictures the great Ulster chieftain to us as a patriot from the beginning; adroitly and dissemblingly biding his time, learning all that was to be learned in the camp of the enemy; looking far ahead into the future, and shaping his course from the start with fixed purpose towards the goal of national independence.[95]

In compiling a list of the '100 best Irish books' in 1886, the writer and critic R. Barry O'Brien included several historical works from the Library of Ireland, and credited the Young Irelanders with the first systematic effort to provide the Irish people with a popular literature.[96] O'Brien did not include any Young Ireland works in lists for the specialist scholar, but recommended several for the general student and the public, such as *The Spirit of the Nation*, Mitchel's *Aodh O'Neill*, Davis's *Essays* and *Poems*, Meehan's *Confederation of Kilkenny*, Mangan's *Poems*, and D'Arcy McGee's *Art MacMurrogh* and *Irish Writers of the 17th Century*.[97] The series proved even more enduring than Davis and Duffy had foreseen. A century after publication, the nationalist historian P. S. O'Hegarty singled out the Library of Ireland as 'indispensable to any proper collection of Irish books' and claimed that it was 'the father and inspirer of all Irish popular literature of the last century'.[98]

FOUR

THE USES OF HISTORY

—

THE IMPORTANCE OF HISTORY

The Young Irelanders' emphasis on the importance of history was a new development in Irish nationalism. Earlier movements, such as the United Irishmen who laid the foundations of modern Irish nationalism in the 1790s, had paid relatively little attention to history. Like most inspired by the new thinking of the Enlightenment, the United Irishmen prided themselves on looking to the future rather than the past. One of their founding documents announced

> we have thought little of our ancestors – much of our posterity. Are we forever to walk like beasts of prey over fields which these ancestors stained with blood? In looking back, we see nothing on the one part but savage force succeeded by savage policy; on the other, an unfortunate nation.[1]

Young Ireland, however, looked to the past with pride and regarded their country's history as a priceless inheritance. For them the past was not merely an arsenal of grievances to be ransacked for arguments against English rule (as it generally was for the pragmatically-minded O'Connell), but the central formative influence on the development of the Irish nation and its particular character. John Blake Dillon argued that

> this character has not been produced in a day, or in a year, or in a hundred years. Long centuries of trial and affliction have made it what it is. Its roots strike deep into antiquity, and its branches have been watered, from time to time, by the blood of the unfortunate brave.[2]

To Davis and his colleagues, the story of Ireland's past was no haphazard collection of events, but a coherent narrative that traced the evolution of a unique national community, and its efforts to defend its independence and cultural distinctiveness against a powerful conqueror.

John Mitchel noted of Davis that he largely despised literature for its own sake, and used it primarily as an educational tool.[3] It could be argued similarly that the Young Irelanders had little interest in history for its own sake, but valued it primarily for practical purposes. Like other Romantic nationalists, Young Ireland attributed an almost mystical power to 'History' (often capitalised in their publications). The *Nation* argued that 'If there be a thing dear to a nation as its liberty, it is the record of its existence. If there be a power restraining from evil, inciting to good . . . higher than earth, yet inferior to heaven, it is History. It compensates for death, enabling you to live eternally'.[4] Davis maintained that it was the duty of every repealer to inform himself about his country's past, asking 'Who can read of valour unsurpassed, of truth and faith preserved through torture and death, and not feel a better man? In going back to history, our purpose has been to elevate the heart of our country up to its destiny'.[5] In his address to the Dublin Institute of Historical Study in 1840, he maintained that a thorough knowledge of history provided the basis for all civic education:

> If you would influence the future, you must know the past . . . philosophy may be the compass, but history is the chart of the politician. Feeling and ambition urge us to study our native history. We have a land which produced famous men: we have a land in which great battles of body and mind have been fought . . . patriotism and piety have left their hallowing footprints. . . . The opinions of our predecessors are woven into our social state; their acts have determined our condition as surely as our thoughts and doings will influence the condition of posterity. Shall we breathe the native air of the preceding races . . . walk over their graves, and survey the monuments of their power, own the same blood, boast the same country, yet know not themselves?[6]

Above all, Young Ireland aimed to make historical memory a matter of pride rather than shame: Duffy claimed that for most Irish people their history 'was a story of disaster and defeat, from which they shrank. The cloud of 1798, and the Union, lay heavy upon it'.[7] Recalling his own childhood, he remembered suffering a strong sense of historical grievance but knew little of its origins and claimed that as a boy he had never so much as seen a history book on Ireland.[8]

It was this kind of ignorance, the *Nation* argued, that stood in the way of the Irish people realising their destiny. Ireland had become a province, not only because of the loss of her political independence, but because her people were ignorant of her history. Ignorance was the mark of the slave, while the freeman knew of the heroes and patriots who had gone before him and sought to live up to their ideals and sacrifices.[9] Although the Young Irelanders usually avoided using overt republican terminology for fear of offending O'Connell and moderate repealers, their programme drew heavily on the ideals of civic republicanism, with its emphasis on political education and engagement. Their aim was to transform ignorant and apathetic subjects into informed and active citizens, and teaching Ireland's history was central to this: liberty and learning went hand in hand.[10] The *Nation* claimed that its efforts had all but banished 'slavish provincialism' and that 'we are growing qualified for freemen . . . We are no longer quite ignorant of those who served our country long ago'.[11]

Davis believed that overturning centuries of neglect and falsification in the writing of Irish history was an essential first step in creating a true sense of nationhood. He maintained that the primary objective of all Irish literary exertion should be 'to furnish Irishmen the true history of their country . . . to create a new Ireland, or at least to wake in the hearts of Irishmen a new and informed patriotism'.[12] He contended that the patriotic Irishman was obliged to take an interest in history and that rather than 'blundering in foreign researches' Irish scholars should devote themselves to salvaging their own country's past: 'he who saves an air, a relic of antiquity, a tradition, an old custom, from loss . . . who gives or teaches a book on Ireland, or its literature or history instead of on England and the English . . . does an act which tends to prepare and secure self-government and prosperity'.[13]

To develop increased historical awareness the *Nation* strongly promoted works such as William Torrens McCullagh's *On the Use and Study of History* (1842). McCullagh was a liberal lawyer and social reformer who, although not a Young Irelander, had been friendly with Davis and Dillon during his days at Trinity. He had encouraged the growing interest in history with a series of lectures delivered at the Mechanics' Institute in the Royal Exchange in Dublin, and used these as the basis for his book. McCullagh's book did not specifically promote a nationalist interpretation of history, but the Young Irelanders were convinced that any in-depth study of Ireland's history would support demands for Irish self-government, and McCullagh's claims that the main function of history was 'to cheer on the future by the experience of the past – to saw through the bars of our despair – to prophecy what nations may be, by picturing what nations have been' chimed closely with their own views.[14]

Davis believed that strong feelings of nationality and historical awareness went hand in hand and that 'if Ireland were in national health, her history would be familiar by books, pictures, statuary, and music, to every cabin and workshop in the land'.[15] As well as writing, he saw the visual arts as an important means to bring the past to life. He called for Irish painters to devote themselves to Irish historical subjects to evoke the dramatic scenes of Irish history, and suggested particular events that would lend themselves to visual representation, such as the first landing of the Celts in Ireland, courageous scenes of the 1798 Rebellion and the unfurling of the Irish flags of a national fleet.[16] Such scenes, he claimed, would make wonderful subjects for artists, and properly reproduced, would put flesh on the bones of dry factual accounts:

> People think of our history as a set of political facts, not as the lives and deaths of men clad in skins, and armour, and silk bounding with strength and beauty, flushed with love, wrinkled with age, full of chivalrous ambition.

Images such as 'the Druid in his grove – the monk in his abbey . . . the martyr in his endurance – the hero in his triumph – his passing triumph' would 'represent Ireland in all her periods – Ireland imaginative, as well as actual and historical'.[17]

Young Ireland also insisted that Ireland should have monuments to celebrate her past. Duffy complained that 'Ireland has no public monuments of any kind except such as commemorate her defeat and degradation . . . there is no pillar on the shores of Clontarf, or the memorable banks of the Blackwater . . . the holy triumphs of '82 and '29, won by Irishmen and for Irishmen, are commemorated nowhere'.[18] This again was evidence of the insidious undermining of nationality that resulted from foreign rule. Instead of commemorating her own heroes, Ireland celebrated those of her conqueror. Monuments to Nelson and Wellington dominated Dublin's skyline, while there were none to Sarsfield, Hugh O'Neill or Robert Emmet.[19] Without any representation in local or national government it was beyond the scope of Young Ireland to commission structures that would suitably commemorate Ireland's heroes, but it was determined that if a national pantheon could not be built in stone just yet, it would be built in people's minds.

The *Nation* attributed much of the blame for ignorance of the Irish past to national schools that neglected the teaching of Irish history, and Irish publishers who were unwilling to publish anything about Ireland.[20] But the main culprit was 'England' and the contempt and condescension of her historians who had tried to 'efface the history of the Irish race'.[21] Unable and unwilling to read the ancient records of Ireland, they had denied the existence of a rich and cultured civilisation, exaggerated her defeats and ignored her achievements. The *Nation* claimed that English archives containing documents of Irish relevance were deliberately closed to Irish researchers to prevent them from uncovering the truth about their past.[22] This enabled English writers to claim that Ireland had no history (or at least no history worth recounting), with the result that 'the glorious deeds, the victories, the battles, the institutions, laws, and chivalry of Ireland have been lied away, and the only impression left upon men's minds of the varied annals of our country is one of turbulent rebellion, fickleness, and barbarism'.[23] In reply to an article in the *Spectator* that dismissed Ireland's past as 'a dreary sameness of slavery, varied now and then by fierce flashes of rebellion, but by no picturesque succession of historical incidents', the *Nation* countered that 'written or unwritten, history survives wherever man has made, in perpetuity, his dwelling. In half-remembered songs, in dim traditions, in the features of external nature itself, it may be read by the seeing eye and the understanding mind'.[24] Davis maintained that a nation with a glorious past must not allow its enemies 'to lie or sneer it away', and that although Ireland's history had yet to be written, 'we know that we have the great acts, the details, and the inducements to write, print, bind and publish such a history'.[25]

From Giraldus Cambrensis ('our first imported libeller') in the twelfth century onwards, the *Nation*, echoing the arguments that Geoffrey Keating had used in his famous historiographical preface to *Foras Feasa ar Éirinn*, claimed that English writers and historians such as Edmund Spenser, Richard Stanihurst, William Camden, Fynes Moryson and Sir John Davies had denigrated the Irish in order to justify the oppressive policies of their political masters.[26] The *Nation* singled out Sir John Temple's *History of the Irish Rebellion* (1646), with its lurid accusations of the cruelties committed by the native Irish in 1641, as the most libellous of all such works, and argued that the events of 1641 had been distorted to create a mythology of sectarian massacre, which had been endlessly propagated by Protestant writers. In his *Confiscation of Ulster* Thomas MacNevin described the 1641 rebellion as 'the terrible but natural progeny' of the plantations of Munster and Ulster. Far from being a 'popish uprising' as it had been termed by English writers from Milton to Macaulay, it was 'a war by a nation of injured men against robbers who had driven them from the inheritance of their fathers, and usurped their places'. MacNevin maintained that in such a conflict it was difficult to say which side had been the aggressor but when he recalled the 'inordinate and savage cruelty' shown by the English in Ireland, 'their habitual disregard of life and all its ties, their murders, their burnings, their infanticides and woman killings, I fully and entirely believe that it was by them first that war was turned into a butchery'.[27] This became the standard nationalist interpretation of 1641: the killings of Protestant settlers were seen as regrettable but squarely placed in the broader context of the oppression, bloodshed and chaos of the period.[28]

In contrast to the dismal picture drawn by so many English historians, Young Ireland popularised an inspiring and glorious version of the Irish past. The tenacity of resistance rather than the frequency of defeat was emphasised, as was the richness of Ireland's culture throughout the ages. In so far as the *Nation* propagated an origin tale, it was a vulgarised version of the eleventh-century *Lebor Gabála (Book of Invasions)* with successive waves of prehistoric invaders finally giving way to the Milesians or Gaels, who imposed their culture and mingled their blood with existing inhabitants. Even before the coming of Christianity, this ancient Gaelic civilisation of warriors and poets flourished in a land of chivalry and culture, governed by wise laws, which were respected by all.[29] The coming of Christianity built on the best parts of this civilisation to create a harmonious society in which Irish saints and scholars kept learning alive and spread Christianity abroad during the Dark Ages. Ireland was a prosperous and happy island – 'a Christian Greece, the nurse of science and civilisation'.[30] Such a land was a temptation to foreign predators, but although the Viking and Norman invasions were severe ordeals, they failed to extinguish Ireland's unique spirit. Scandinavians and Normans eventually succumbed to the beguiling influence of Gaelic ways and merged their blood with the native Irish. The willingness of foreigners to adopt Irish customs and language and become 'more Irish than the Irish themselves' was a favourite theme of Young Ireland, and an implicit reproach to contemporaries who despised or distanced themselves from Gaelic culture.[31]

It was only with the prolonged and stoutly resisted Tudor conquest of the sixteenth century, a conquest nationalists described as almost unparalleled in human history for its cruelty and ruthlessness, that English rule at last became a reality throughout the island. Even then the events of 1641 and 1689 showed that the indomitable spirit of the Irish was not crushed. Irish Catholics fought bravely at the Boyne, Aughrim and Limerick and, despite submitting on honourable terms, were betrayed and subjected to draconian penal laws which kept them in misery and slavery for most of the eighteenth century. With Catholics ground down, it was left to Protestant patriots such as Molyneux, Swift and Lucas to struggle against English domination and keep alive a sense of Irish separateness. Their efforts bloomed in the late 1770s when the Volunteers, led by patriots such as Grattan and Flood, managed to wrest legislative independence from London, and the beginnings were made in dismantling the penal code. The mini-golden age of 'Grattan's parliament' followed in which the wise legislation of a native parliament promoted prosperity and harmony, but this was brought to an end by a bloody rebellion fomented by England and her agents and used to frighten the Irish parliament into voting for its own extinction. With the Act of Union, Ireland became a mere province, and again entered a period of degradation and despair.

This familiar narrative was endlessly repeated in Young Ireland's writings. It stressed certain recurrent themes, among them that Ireland's sufferings were greater than those of any other country. The *Nation*'s writers claimed that Ireland's history was 'a museum of unique wrongs – a very menagerie of the monstrosities of tyranny and fraud; rife with insults and oppressions, calamities and plagues, in their nature, duration and intensity, unparalleled by the experience of any other people'.[32] English tyrants such as Grey, Sidney, Mountjoy and Cromwell were accused of engaging in campaigns of devastation and extermination comparable only to the barbarism of the Spanish conquistadors.[33] Contrary to what had happened elsewhere, the *Nation* claimed that the conquest of Ireland heralded an intensification rather than a relaxation of oppression, with the country deliberately reduced 'to the most miserable and degraded position of the nations of Europe, without liberty, without wealth, without power'.[34] The result was that most of Ireland's inhabitants were condemned to destitution, compounded by a relentless policy of religious persecution which reached its apogee with the penal laws: 'religion was their pretence, robbery their purpose. They crushed the Catholics with a code borrowed from Hell'.[35] Cruelty was compounded with duplicity: Irish leaders were invited to parley, only to be slain; treaties were broken; spies and informers were used at every possible opportunity. Even when the Irish were victorious in the field, they were eventually overcome by 'that combination of force and fraud and treachery, which has ever characterised the onward march of English power'.[36]

Oliver MacDonagh has noted that this emphasis on historic wrongs gave a timeless quality to the nationalist interpretation of history: the classic British view was one of beneficial development in which the tragedies of the past gave way to modern progress, but for Irish nationalists grievances such as Cromwell's massacres, the betrayal of Limerick and the penal laws were not mitigated by the passing of time.[37] Davis, in fact, saw this nurturing of grievance as one of the key uses of national history: so long as Ireland remembered her betrayals 'her conscience will smite her, and her pride irritate her' until she was driven to right these wrongs.[38] However, while the Young Irelanders sought to use the trauma of Irish history to productive effect, they recognised that dwelling on historical grievances had its dangers: readers could easily be demoralised with constant tales of defeat and suffering, and such a strategy risked creating a nation of sullen victims rather than self-respecting citizens. Young Ireland, therefore, sought to write history in such a way as to make clear that Ireland 'has ceased to wail . . . she begins to study the past – not to acquire a beggar's eloquence in petition, but a hero's wrath in strife'.[39] Young Ireland's writers were at pains to point out that the conquest of Ireland was incomplete and had been followed by centuries of courageous resistance.[40]

Thomas D'Arcy McGee claimed that until O'Neill's capitulation in 1603 it was more accurate to say that Ireland and England had been engaged in an inconclusive war, and the old slogan of 'seven centuries of English oppression' grossly overstated England's dominance.[41] MacNevin argued that Ireland was defeated only because a nation governed by warring chieftains was no match for a strong centralised state headed by a monarch, and that there was no shame in losing such a protracted struggle. Instead, it was 'a matter of national pride that so noble and unceasing a resistance could have been made, with such discordant materials'.[42] Most importantly, Young Ireland writers stressed that the spirit of the Irish people had never been fully extinguished and that this indestructible resolve formed a solid foundation for national independence.

The Young Irelanders wrote history as advocates for their country's cause (several of them had some legal training), with the practical intention of educating the Irish people about their past. Their writings were clear and didactic, repeating again and again the basic theme of courageous resistance to political and religious oppression. In so far as they had a philosophy of history, it was a strongly teleological one in which the Irish nation progressed inexorably towards freedom. Generally, however, they described events rather than analysed historical forces and prided themselves on writing simple narrative history that did not concern itself with philosophical matters.[43] For most Young Ireland writers the term 'philosophic history' was a pejorative one which they associated with the rationalist historians of the eighteenth century. They took their lead from their master, Augustin Thierry, who in an historical manifesto written in 1834 had declared war 'on the most vaunted historians of the philosophic school, because of their calculated dryness and their disdainful ignorance of national origins'.[44] Young Ireland writers believed that 'philosophic historians' had been too anxious to highlight the backwardness and barbarism of the past, and sought to distance themselves from an attitude of detachment and universalism they regarded as inimical to the creation of true national feeling. This led them to dismiss much of the previous century's history writing as dry and soulless, devoid of imagination and emotional sympathy with those who went before them.[45] John Cornelius O'Callaghan, for example, admitted to modelling his accounts of Irish military valour on the works French Romantic historians such as Barante and Thierry rather than the 'generalised mass of frigidly-narrated events, stripped of flesh and blood, and marbled into the comparatively hard, pallid, and eyeless image of what is styled "philosophical history"'.[46]

In contrast to Enlightenment historians who saw history as a progressive narrative in which the errors of earlier generations were gradually overcome, Romantic historians often argued that the past represented a more noble courageous and chivalrous era before man was corrupted by materialism and self-interested rationalism.[47] Romantics saw antiquity as the foundation for understanding the evolution of a nation's traditions, institutions and society, and argued that it deserved to be treated with respect rather than disdain. In addition to the general condescension they found in the work of 'philosophic historians', the Young Irelanders detected a particularly haughty attitude to the Irish. Voltaire's observation that Irish soldiers fought bravely everywhere except at home was endlessly quoted and regarded as a national slur.[48] In his work on the Ulster plantation Thomas MacNevin criticised British writers such as David Hume and Henry Hallam for their complacently anti-Irish views.[49]

Hume was particularly condemned for his lofty contempt for Catholicism and his portrayal of the Irish as barbarians blindly resisting the onward march of civilisation, and was singled out as 'the father of all the misrepresentations on Irish affairs with which English literature abounds'.[50]

The Young Irelander who came nearest to extolling an explicit philosophy of history was John Mitchel. Like his mentor Carlyle, Mitchel was contemptuous of the self-satisfied spirit of the Victorian age and believed that notions of moral or social progress were illusory.[51] He dismissed the grand historical narratives of the nineteenth century, such as Macaulay's *History of England*, as the self-congratulatory propaganda of complacent whiggery, with 'the true knack of administering reverential flattery to British civilization, British prowess, honour, enlightenment, and all that, especially to the great nineteenth century and its astounding civilisation'.[52] In contrast to Whig views of linear progress, Mitchel took a cyclical view of history, maintaining that the powerful would inevitably be brought to earth one day, and that their place would be taken by nations which were now weak or oppressed.[53] Mitchel, of course, was thinking primarily of the British empire, claiming that it had become so obsessed with making money that it was losing the warlike spirit that all powerful empires needed to survive, and was in terminal decline.[54] It was a consoling outlook: implacable forces of history were already undermining Britain's power, and Irish independence would eventually be built on its ruins.

VICTORIES AND HEROES

The historians of Young Ireland were anxious to show that the Irish had won victories as well as suffered defeats. The popular Irish view of history was, they believed, excessively marked by resignation and defeatism and failed to acknowledge that for many centuries 'Irish bravery, unaided, had a hundred times driven back the tide of robbery. . . . How many a battle won by native valour – how many a robber stratagem frustrated by native skill . . . of which we know scarcely anything as a people'.[55] Faced with overwhelming odds, the Irish had lost their share of battles but it was important for national self-esteem that people should know that 'Blackwater, Benburb, Limerick, Fontenoy and Gorey, are the points lighted by victory, and they are brighter in the surrounding darkness'.[56]

In an age when the standing of nations and races was often judged by their martial prowess, the Young Irelanders stressed the courage and fighting spirit of their countrymen. Not to do so risked being regarded as a weak and inferior race that deserved to be mastered and had no right to seek to govern itself. Young Ireland was uneasy with Daniel O'Connell's repudiation of the sword and his exclusive emphasis on moral force, which they saw as an attitude that undermined national morale and risked stigmatising Ireland as a country that was not prepared to fight for its freedom. According to John Mitchel, it was for this reason they wrote so openly of Ireland's victories and heroes, and added 'a proud and defiant military spirit' to the repeal agitation.[57] Annals and mythologies were mined for victories: the tales of legendary figures such as King Dathy, the 'Irish Trajan' who had died campaigning against the Romans in the Alps, were resurrected. Forgotten triumphs such as those of Domhall, king of Ireland, over an invading force of Saxons, Britons, Scots and Picts at Moyrath in 637, or the Jacobite victory at the battle of Dromore in March 1689 were added to Ireland's victory roll.[58] Well-known triumphs such as Brian Boru's victory at Clontarf in 1014 were portrayed as a simple battle of native Irish against foreign invader, and cried up as 'a victory of as great import in its age, as Godfrey's taking of Jerusalem, Don John's triumph at Lepanto, or Sobieski's success at Vienna'.[59]

This focus on great men and great deeds produced a heroic and inspirational interpretation of Irish history. When nationalists recalled reading the *Nation* or Library of Ireland in their youth, it was the celebration of Ireland's military valour that they remembered most vividly. A reading of history that sought to vindicate the Irish martial virtue was inevitably a history of conflict, with wars and battles, and heroes and martyrs providing the dominant motifs. The events of the late sixteenth and the seventeenth centuries provided the most suitable material, featuring the large set-piece battles and sieges that dominated contemporary history writing, and refuted the arguments of those who said that Ireland had no history other than petty tribal squabbles. Young Ireland writers gave particular attention to Ireland's desperate resistance in the seventeenth century, portraying it as a dramatic and heroic age 'which saw a gasping nation in her wildest throes . . . the convulsive vigour of her death-bed rising, and her final, fearful, quick collapse . . . ancient names swept from ancient places, and memories and language and gods buried together'.[60]

The period that followed was more problematic. To many nationalists, the eighteenth century appeared as a long winter of Protestant oppression and Catholic servility. Catholics generally had attempted to mitigate the effects of the penal laws through dissimulation and clever stratagems rather than outright resistance, and there were few heroic examples to inspire later generations. Young Ireland's response to this depressing picture was to shift the focus abroad and stress the extent to which the valour of Ireland's Wild Geese had been witnessed on battlefields across Europe. A victory such as Fontenoy (1745), when the charge of the Irish Brigade defeated an English army in the Low Countries, became even more celebrated than many of those won on home soil. Fontenoy was 'to Ireland a memory of unmixed pride . . . our exiles fought on that day . . . for glory, for vengeance, and for justice; and the God of battles vouchsafed to them abundant victory'.[61] Irish soldiers who served abroad were invariably seen in romantic and heroic terms. Young Ireland writers claimed that, in fighting for European powers against England, Irish military exiles saw themselves as fighting Ireland's battles (conveniently ignoring that many of them fought for powers allied with Britain), and stressed that their memories of Ireland and commitment to her cause never faded: Irish soldiers charged into battle to right Ireland's wrongs and gave their lives regretting that they had not died for Ireland.[62]

The nationalist cult of the Wild Geese owed a great deal to the Young Irelanders, whose histories and ballads did much to enshrine their actions in national memory. At Davis's suggestion a new edition of a *History of Ireland* by Fr James MacGeoghegan, who had been chaplain to the Irish Brigade in the 1740s and 50s, was published in Dublin in 1844, and the deeds of the brigade featured prominently in Davis's verse in the *Nation* such as 'The surprise of Cremona' (20 Apr. 1844), 'Clare's dragoons' (5 Oct. 1844), 'The death of Sarsfield' (22 Apr. 1843) and 'Fontenoy' (3 Feb. 1844). The works of John Cornelius O'Callaghan, one of the earliest contributors to the *Nation*, were largely devoted to the heroic acts of Irishmen fighting abroad and his researches eventually culminated in the eight volumes of the *History of the Irish Brigades in the Service of France* (1854–69) which definitively established the place of the Wild Geese in Irish nationalist historiography.[63]

There was nothing unusual about this: much of the history being written across Europe at the time extolled the military prowess of national heroes, but the writings of Young Ireland contained an insistence on Irish heroism that was more defensive than most, and were particularly anxious to refute the assertions of Voltaire and others that Irish troops fought well abroad, but badly at home. The central theme of O'Callaghan's *Green Book* (1841) was that Irishmen lacked nothing in courage, whether fighting in Ireland or elsewhere. To substantiate this he carefully itemised the number of men and the amount of money it took for William III's forces to prevail in the wars of 1689–91 as proof of the courage and military skill of his Jacobite opponents, and argued that it was primarily the indecision and timidity of James II rather than any weakness in his Irish troops that led to defeat at the Boyne.[64] The *Nation* claimed that O'Callaghan, with his skilful marshalling of evidence, 'not only called English history a liar, but proved it so.'[65]

In addition to extolling victories, the *Nation* was also given to lamenting the near misses of Irish history: Aughrim rather than the Boyne was portrayed as the decisive battle of the Williamite wars, and a desperately close-run affair, ultimately decided by the chance death of the Jacobite commander St Ruth. The *Nation* bemoaned those occasions when the Irish failed to capitalise fully on their victories and squandered advantageous positions because of lack of unity or foresight. Owen Roe O'Neill's failure to follow up his great victory at Benburb in 1646, for example, was put down to divisions in the Irish camp and the Machiavellian manoeuvring of the papal legate Archbishop Rinuccini.[66]

Lost opportunities had also occurred in more recent times: the one most deplored being the failure of the Volunteers to press for full independence in 1782 (although at the time this was never one of the aims of the predominantly Protestant Volunteers). It was not by chance that MacNevin's *History of the Volunteers of 1782* was the first publication in the *Nation*'s Library of Ireland series. Young Ireland revered the 'Revolution of 1782' above all historical events, and idealised the Volunteers as the virtuous citizen-soldiers of the Irish nation. They looked upon them as civic republicans *par excellence*, who elected their officers, debated their proposals in democratic conventions, and were determined to assert Ireland's constitutional and economic rights. Like the citizens of classical republics, they were not only politically informed and engaged, but trained in the use of arms, and had made clear to government that if they ignored the popular will, they did so at their peril. The agitation of this citizen militia, coupled with the efforts of their supporters in parliament, had wrung from the British government the right of Irishmen to legislate for themselves. The presence in some Volunteer corps of Catholics, and the prominent role played by the pro-emancipation Henry Grattan, permitted the event to be portrayed as a national rather than a sectional victory. It was a victory, moreover, won by the manly assertiveness of armed Irishmen, but without bloodshed. In all of this there was the implicit criticism of O'Connell's reliance on moral force alone: concessions would be won from the British government not by mass meetings, nor by wanton violence, but by an armed and disciplined national movement that would not shirk from using force if its demands were ignored. Recalling the Volunteer Convention in Dungannon in 1782, MacNevin claimed that it was an assembly unparalleled in Irish history: a citizen army fired by 'a thousand memories of glory or of suffering' which combined with

> the new ardour for liberty would have fired the soldiers of the land and made their arms invincible. . . . Had they adopted the precedents of their oppressor, and used their opportunities as she did hers, the empire of Great Britain had ceased in Ireland.[67]

Like many contemporary historians, Davis regarded history primarily as 'a series of pictures of great men and great scenes and great acts'.[68] Influenced by Carlylean notions of hero worship, the Young Irelanders attempted to show that Ireland, as much as any other country, had a national pantheon of inspirational figures.[69] 'The hero's name and the martyr's monument are the real tutors of the generous-souled youth, and in the land where these are not found, or being found, are not honoured, there devotion, and noble fortitude, and long abiding faith can never dwell'.[70] Arguing that a true knowledge of Ireland's past deeds was incompatible with national subservience, they sought to popularise the reputations of Ireland's heroes and martyrs, as the Scots had done with Bruce and Wallace and the Poles with Kosciusko.[71] Davis's ambition was said to be 'to rear a generation whose lives would be strengthened and ennobled by the knowledge that there had been great men of their race, and great actions done on the soil they trod . . . that they were heirs in name and fame to a litany of soldiers, scholars and ecclesiastics'.[72] A sharp contrast was drawn between the high ideals and noble virtues of the past and the cowardice and apathy of the present. Ireland's warrior heroes were portrayed as superior beings – their willingness to shed blood and sacrifice their own lives setting them apart from contemporary politicians. In his biography of the medieval warrior chief Art MacMurrough, Thomas D'Arcy McGee praised the heroic spirit that had persisted throughout the ages in Ireland's struggles for liberty, and pointedly asked where 'the manhood, the chivalry, the love of native land' that characterised Irish history were to be found today.[73]

The *Nation* lamented that not enough was known about Ireland's warrior heroes: few had been the subject of full-length biographies and it suggested that an Irish biographical dictionary written by Irish authors could help to fill the gap left by the absence of a suitable history of Ireland. Such a work would not fall entirely on one individual, but could be written by many different hands, and its 'influence on the young minds of Ireland of such a book would be incalculably great'.[74] However, the *Nation*'s resources did not match its ambitions and the project never got off the ground.

The desire to make the Irish people familiar with their victories and heroes was even seen in the new design of the membership card of the Repeal Association in March 1843.[75] Designed by John Cornelius O'Callaghan, it had the four great victories of Clontarf (1014), the Yellow Ford (1598), Benburb (1646), and Limerick (1691) on its corners. Another version of the card, proclaiming the association as the 'Volunteers of 1782 Revived' was inscribed with ten great Irishmen from the past, from the mythical high king and law-giver Ollamh Fodla up to statesmen of the recent past and present such as Flood, Grattan and O'Connell. Several of these were military figures: the legendary King Dathy, Brian Boru, Hugh O'Neill, Owen Roe O'Neill and Patrick Sarsfield.[76] Remembering this litany of heroes made the struggle for Ireland's independence 'not only a policy but a sacred duty. The men who had toiled and travailed for us in body or mind, though dead, should not be unhonoured. . . . let all the earnest and honest among the living join in the justification of all the brave and good among the dead'.[77]

Writing biographies that were worthy of military heroes was seen as particularly important. When Robert Tighe (1806–84?), a Whig barrister, volunteered to write the life of Patrick Sarsfield for the Library of Ireland, John Edward Pigot wrote to Duffy to object that 'Sarsfield requires bone, and such stuff as I fear [Tighe's] extreme gentlemanliness and refinement must have stripped him of . . . I think many better subjects can be assigned to him, and our soldiers kept for the sternest of us'.[78] Sarsfield was the Young Ireland military hero *par excellence* – dashing, daring, and loyal to Ireland to his dying breath. His heroic life and death became central to Ireland's national narrative and in the formulaic accounts published by nationalist newspapers throughout the nineteenth century, it seemed that an Irish soldier rarely gave up his life on a foreign field without echoing Sarsfield's dying words.[79]

CREATING A NATION

Young Ireland realised that without a knowledge of history the sense of belonging to a national community that has existed since time immemorial was impossible. Writing in 1978, T. W. Moody credited the literary ability and fervour of Young Ireland with the creation of a nationalist 'mythology' that told of 'an ancient Irish nation struggling for seven centuries to recover its independence from the domination of England'. Although the movement sang of 'A nation once again', this was in fact 'to be a new creation, a self-reliant, self-respecting community, in which all Irishmen, whatever their religion, class, or origin would have their place'.[80] Like others who sought the independence or unification of their homelands, the Young Irelanders wrote history to provide an aspiring nation-state with an historical lineage to justify its foundation. Their insistence that as an independent nation Ireland had flourished and was militarily powerful contradicted those who claimed that the Celt was incapable of self-government.

According to Duffy, they took up their work 'not as a cold, scientific analysis, but as a passionate search for light which might help them to understand their own race and country'.[81] Their writings emphasised an historical continuity that encouraged readers to identify with those who had gone before them, depicting a brave and resolute people maintaining their culture and traditions, guided by an indissoluble national spirit that had given them strength for centuries. They believed that this sense of historical continuity had waned in recent decades but with the *Nation*'s success in reminding people of the past:

'Ireland is changing the loose tradition of her wrongs into history and ballad . . . she will immortally remember her bondage, her struggles, her glories and her disasters. Till her suffering ceases that remembrance will rouse her passions and nerve her arm'.[82]

One of the prime lessons that Young Ireland drew from history was the importance of national unity, claiming that factiousness and dissension had undermined Ireland's claims to nationhood.[83] The *Nation* maintained that since such divisions had been fostered and encouraged by England, the study of history would clearly reveal how a policy of divide and rule had kept Ireland in a state of inferiority. Throughout the ages it had

> set the children of the one sky and soil at loggerheads . . . to split a nation into parts –
> to blind both by ignorance and calumny, lest they should know that they were
> brothers who fought . . . Prejudice of race, brutality of manners, religious bigotry,
> historical lies were all enlisted in the body-guard of tyranny.[84]

Irish nationalist historiography looked both to the past and the future: back to a long tradition of resistance and forwards to the achievement of independence, creating a continuum in which history and mission reinforced each other. The *Nation* argued that a sound knowledge of history was essential not just to achieve Irish independence, but to safeguard it. Davis warned his readers that 'If we attempt to govern ourselves without statesmanship – to be a nation without a knowledge of the country's history . . . we will fail'.[85] The Young Irelanders constantly stressed the power of history to teach by example and, as inexperienced politicians themselves, believed that a thorough knowledge of the past could endow them with insight and experience beyond their years.[86] Thomas MacNevin maintained that his *History of the Volunteers* was written with the purpose of relaying to his readers the 'instructive but igno-minious' account 'of their lost liberties and forfeited honour'. He hoped that by reading it 'they will learn to cherish the virtues by which freedom was acquired – and to avoid the intestine divisions, the want of high purpose, and the absence of self-reliance by which a corrupt body of patricians were allowed to sell their country to foreign despotism'.[87] If history was to be used as a tool for nation-building, then it was essential that it carried moral lessons applicable to their own day: the achievements of the Confederation of Kilkenny, the Patriot parliament of 1689 and 'Grattan's parliament' vindicated the contemporary Irish demand for independence by appealing to historical precedent and showed what Irishmen could do when they controlled their own destiny.[88]

In its use of newspapers and cheap mass-produced books to popularise this view of Irish history, Young Ireland can be seen as a prime example of Benedict Anderson's theory of the use of print-capitalism to create a new kind of shared experience and mass solidarity that formed the basis of nineteenth-century nationalism. This 'made it possible for rapidly growing numbers of people to think about themselves, and to relate to others, in profoundly new ways'. In particular, nationalist historians created a coherent narrative of their country's history that made people think of themselves as an 'imagined political community' that extended backwards and forwards into time.[89] The community imagined by Young Ireland had unique qualities of courage, self-sacrifice and resilience and was imagined primarily through its heroism at Benburb, Ballyneety and Fontenoy. Its deeds and heroes became as familiar to many readers as the events and personages of their own time. Youthful imaginations were fired with tales of vivid heroism and self-sacrifice and fantasied about emulating the heroes of the past and carving out their own place in this imagined community. The famous Dominican preacher and historian Fr Tom Burke recalled in his youth how

> Under the magic voices and pens of these men, every ancient glory of Ireland stood forth again. . . . I recollect with what startled enthusiasm I would arise from reading 'Davis's Poems'; and it would seem to me that before my young eyes I saw the dash of the Brigade at Fontenoy. It would seem as if my young ears were filled with the shout that resounded at the Yellow Ford and Benburb – the war cry of the Red Hand – 'Lam Dearg Abu' – as alien hosts were swept away, and like snow under the beams of the hot sun, melted before the Irish onset.[90]

RACE, LANGUAGE AND RELIGION

In their efforts to establish Ireland's national distinctiveness, the Young Irelanders stressed the Celtic origins of the Irish, noting that this ancient and noble race had their own rich language, literature and history, and throughout the Dark Ages had led Europe in learning, piety and virtue.[91] The Irish, they claimed, of all the Celtic nations were the purest inheritors of the culture and character of the Celts: the Irish alone 'seem destined to reproduce on earth a solitary Celtic nationalism . . . upon us and our descendants will sooner or later devolve the sole inheritance of that people which once covered western Europe, their literature, their poesy, their passion'.[92] As the son of a Welsh father and an Irish mother, Davis played up his own Celtic origins and proudly used the pseudonym 'The Celt' in his writings. Racial stereotyping was prominent in Victorian political discourse, and British commentators often discussed the Irish question as a clash between the opposing values and characteristics of the stolid Anglo-Saxon and the mercurial Celt.[93] Faced with the assumption of Anglo-Saxon moral superiority that often coloured English accounts, Young

Ireland countered by arguing the greater virtue of the Celt: 'the Saxon plots a vice where the Celt meditates a compliment . . . The gay, bold, joyous Irishman has no tendency to vice'.[94]

This, however, was dangerous ground and the Young Irelanders soon realised that using race as the basis of national identity risked perpetuating existing divisions. Davis's only criticism of the French historian Augustin Thierry was his 'too exclusive notice of the distinctions arising from race', and he concluded that Irishmen 'must sink the distinction of blood as well as sect'.[95] Descendants of the Danes, Normans and Saxons were reassured that they too were part of the Irish nation: Davis argued that 'Irish nationality must contain and represent the races of Ireland. It must not be Celtic, it must not be Saxon, it must be Irish'.[96] The fact that the Irish were a mixture of races was proclaimed as a source of strength, combining 'the fiery and fanciful Celt and the romantic Spaniard, strengthened by the stout Saxon and haughty with Norman blood'.[97] The *Nation* maintained that all these diverse racial elements were heirs to a common cultural and historical tradition that bonded them together into one nation, and denounced the differentiation between 'Saxon and Celt' as a 'pestilent and lying distinction between Irishmen . . . Sarsfield was a man of Saxon blood, so was Swift, so were Grattan, Tone, Flood, [and] Emmet'. Such racial distinctions, it claimed, were of interest only to the antiquarian scholar and had no place in creating an inclusive and modern Irish nation.[98]

If national identity could not be founded on race, what then could be used? Many European countries based their national consciousness on language and religion, both of which presented serious difficulties in an Irish context. Two different languages were spoken on the island, and many regarded Irish as a mark of poverty and backwardness. As the nineteenth century progressed English was increasingly valued for its economic and legal advantages and was the language of education in both Catholic and national schools. By the 1840s Irish had been in retreat for almost 200 years, and its decline had accelerated in recent decades and was spoken by probably less than half the population even before the Famine.[99]

Romantic nationalists throughout Europe attached particular importance to a nation's language as the expression of its soul, regarding it as 'a kind of coded history of the sufferings and joys of the nation', and believed that a people who lost their language lost with it their own unique spirit and identity.[100] Of the Young Irelanders, Davis, in particular, maintained that the Irish language was essential to national distinctiveness and conferred a sense of identity and rootedness on those who spoke it.[101] In one of his best known essays he argued

The language, which grows up with a people, is conformed to their organs, descriptive of their climate, constitution, and manners, mingled inseparably with their history and their soil, fitted beyond any other language to express their prevalent thoughts in the most natural and efficient way. To impose another language on such a people is to send their history adrift among the accidents of translation – 'tis to tear their identity from all places . . . and separate the people from their forefathers by a deep gulf . . . A people without a language of its own is only half a nation. A nation should guard its language more than its territories – 'tis a surer barrier, and more important frontier, than fortress or river . . . To lose your native tongue, and learn that of an alien, is the worst badge of conquest – it is the chain on the soul. To have lost entirely the national language is death; . . . the bulk of our history and poetry are written in Irish . . . shall we be content with ignorance or a translation of Irish?[102]

For Davis, it made little sense to teach the Irish people their history while neglecting their ancient language. He accepted that it was not possible immediately to re-introduce Irish into the schools and law courts of predominantly English-speaking districts, but argued that it should be encouraged and fostered in the schools of Irish-speaking districts in the west and from there gradually extended into neighbouring districts. In the meantime all Irishmen should be encouraged to cherish it as 'the vehicle of history, the wings of song, the soil of their genius, and a mark and guard of nationality'.[103]

But not all of his colleagues were of the same mind. The Cork-based Young Irelander Denny Lane did not think it feasible to preserve the Irish language as a living tongue and regarded it primarily as 'a historical monument of a great race'. He argued that a knowledge of English facilitated easier contact with Irish communities overseas, and conferred marked educational advantages in literature and science.[104] When Davis proposed to form a class to study Irish there were few takers and when, under the guidance of John O'Donovan, he insisted on the correct Irish spelling of native names and places in articles and songs for the *Nation*, he met resistance and occasional ridicule.[105] Thomas MacNevin dismissed his stand as linguistic pedantry that disrupted the melody and rhyme of the original verse. MacNevin believed that it was pointless to attempt to revive Irish, and also disparaged efforts to explore the recesses of ancient Irish history and other such 'pre-Adamite fictions', arguing instead that 'we must be cosmopolitan and deviate occasionally from our native bogs. We shall have a better chance of success by being less Irish'.[106]

With Davis's death in 1845, the Irish language lost its most passionate advocate on the *Nation*. The paper still paid lip-service to its importance, encouraging national schoolteachers to teach pupils Irish and to 'explain to them, its antiquity, its grandeur, its vehemence' and maintaining 'that a true Irishman speaking English has his soul in manacles'.[107] But most Young Irelanders settled for lauding Irish as a precious part of Ireland's cultural heritage, and trying to infuse their English writings with as much Irish spirit and character as possible. They used occasional Irish phrases in their verse, and included glossaries of Irish names, places, and phrases in new editions of the *Spirit of the Nation*.[108] A comprehensive revival of the language, though, was seen as impracticable, and no workable measures for protecting or spreading Irish were put in place. Most Young Irelanders saw little sense in propagating their message in a language that most of their readership did not understand and concluded that using Irish would impede rather than advance their educational project. Some such as Duffy claimed that while the *Nation*'s ballads were written in English, they were 'just as essentially Irish as if they were written in Gaelic' and that the Young Irelanders had managed 'to infuse the ancient and hereditary spirit of the country into all that is genuine of our modern poetry'.[109] The Irish people were to be given a sense that they were a distinctive historical community, but this would be done through English, and the writings of Young Ireland did much to establish English as the dominant language of Irish nationalism.[110] Irish language enthusiasts would later draw inspiration from Davis's passionate pro-Irish manifestoes, but the programmes and institutions they created owed little to the example of Young Ireland.

If language posed difficulties, then religion was an even greater source of dissension. The *Nation* recognised sectarianism as the most serious obstacle to its aim of creating a common nationality, and the coming together of repealer and unionist, Catholic and Protestant, was one of the most common themes in its editorials and ballads.[111] Young Ireland claimed that Protestants were the heirs of the Irish past every bit as much as Catholics: 'Their stories are twined with our history; their dust is Irish earth; and their memories are Ireland's for ever.'[112] In his addresses to Protestants, Davis oscillated between fraternal appeals and sharp reproaches:

> Poor deluded Irish Protestants! brave! fierce! impotent! You have denied the country for which a race of Protestant patriots – Molyneux, Swift, Lucas, Flood, Grattan, Tone – fought and spoke . . . You saw commerce extinguished, manufactures withered, your militia abolished, your parliament abolished . . . Are you men and bear it? Are you fools and cowards?[113]

Orangemen, in particular, were singled out for their misreading of Irish history, and their celebrations of past victories were dismissed as 'a barren pageant'.[114] While praising the courage and fighting spirit that Irish Protestants had shown throughout history, the *Nation* questioned what it had gained for them, arguing that William's victory was won by foreigners over Irishmen and had been followed by religious tyranny, mercantile oppression and national ruin. The flaunting of Orange symbols simply perpetuated a disunion that kept Ireland dependent and poor.[115] Once Orangemen began to read and reflect on their country's history, they would soon see where their true interests lay.[116] According to the *Nation*,

> No country in Europe has carried party spirit, antipathy of race and religious animosity, so far back into the past as we Irish have done. . . . If we are ever to get rid of this bad blood, it must be by means of enlarged knowledge – by means of truer insight and wider sympathies. In very truth, the wars and massacres, the forfeitures and robberies of three or four hundred years ago, are *not* a rational ground of hatred and strife at this day; and we should all confess as much if we would only look at our history steadily in the face.[117]

Young Ireland showed considerable optimism that Irish Protestants could be persuaded to reject the union and unite with their Catholic countrymen in pursuit of Irish self-government. Any signs of this were seized on eagerly. When those of different religions came together in antiquarian societies, the *Nation* proclaimed that the hatreds of the past were dead and that 'All men of cultivated minds are happy to forget their party politics in combining to spread a knowledge of our past history among Irishmen. The Archaeological Society includes more Tories than Repealers, and they work hand in hand in their patriotic and civilising labour'.[118]

The shortcomings of race, language and religion as foundations of nationality led the Young Irelanders to pin great hopes on history itself as Ireland's national unifier, but they were to find that an interest in Ireland's history and antiquities did not always signify or lead to nationalist sympathies. Protestant scholars studied Irish history on their own terms, with some such as Samuel Ferguson believing that national political history was best avoided since it only served to remind of past injustices and atrocities, and that scholars should instead concentrate on the 'particular and local . . . such as will enable us to know one another and the land we live in'.[119] Ferguson was perhaps the best example of Young Ireland's failure to use cultural arguments to persuade influential Protestants to support political independence. He had long championed the notion that Gaelic poetry and music were as much part of the inheritance of Irish Protestants as Irish Catholics.[120] Throughout the 1830s he contributed a series of tales drawn from Irish legend and history to the *Dublin University Magazine* and several of his poems featured in Duffy's best-selling *Ballad Poetry of Ireland* (1845). Ferguson was a close friend of Thomas Davis and after his death contributed an obituary article and poetic lament to the

Dublin University Magazine in February 1847. The following year, his anger at the government's inadequate response to the Famine led him to join the newly-formed Protestant Repeal Association, much to the delight of the *Nation*.[121] However, domestic responsibilities and Young Ireland's attempted insurrection in 1848 led him to retreat rapidly from nationalist politics, and for the rest of his life he attempted to reconcile a love for Ireland's history and culture with support for the union with Britain.[122] Ferguson was probably one of those that Duffy had in mind when he observed that their national sentiment was not 'of the kind that is fitted for the tough battle and the weary march to freedom'.[123] He concluded that for all Davis's efforts to persuade Protestant scholars to support national independence, 'he rarely succeeded in doing more than making them nationalists like Walter Scott or John Wilson, devoted to the literature and antiquities of their native country, but content with its subjection to England.'[124]

Some nationalists believed that the aspiration to unite Orange and Green merely showed Young Ireland's naivety. The O'Connellite W. J. O'Neill Daunt noted that 'Davis's jubilant hopes of an Orange accession to the national cause were premature. It is not easy to extirpate the inveterate anti-national venom that festers in the Orange heart'.[125] It was also the case that far from attracting Protestants, the *Nation*'s militantly nationalistic interpretation of history often alienated them. D. O. Madden, a Catholic convert to Protestantism, recorded that he found little appealing in a version of history that 'gloats over the recollection of past massacres . . . [and] thunders against the dead tyrants of former times'.[126]

In promoting the study of history as a panacea for Ireland's fractious past, the Young Irelanders underestimated the strength of historical divisions and the divisive effects of the writing of history itself. Their own histories mined the polemical works of Catholic historians such as Philip O'Sullivan Beare, John Curry and Sylvester O'Halloran and this sense of Catholic grievance often seeped into their own writings, producing a resentment of historic injustices that sat uneasily with calls for national unity.[127] Young Ireland learned that just like language and religion, history too could be a force for dissension. In exile in New York after the failed insurrection of 1848, a disillusioned John Blake Dillon concluded that Young Ireland's historical writings had provided 'not lessons for our future guidance, but . . . fuel to feed our animosities towards each other'. Far from bringing them together, Catholic and Protestant still brooded over the past and 'stood scowling at each other from the opposite banks of the Boyne'.[128]

FIVE

MAKING HISTORY

—

In addition to writing for the *Nation* and Library of Ireland, most Young Irelanders held prominent positions on the committees of the Repeal Association and were among its most active members in debating policies and producing reports.[1] Although strongly committed to the repeal of the act of union and the re-establishment of an Irish parliament, there were some significant differences between their approach and that of O'Connell. The Young Irelanders believed that previous repeal campaigns had been too exclusively political and that the association should advance on a broader cultural front, with the demand for self-government bolstered by a strong assertion of Ireland's cultural distinctiveness and historic traditions. This approach was motivated partly by a belief in the importance of history and culture, but also by a realisation that, compared to O'Connell, their own political influence was slight, and given their modest level of support within the Repeal Association they were more likely to gain a hearing by formulating their policy in historical and cultural terms. Moreover, O'Connell's general deprecation of violent rebellion left the way clear for Young Ireland to identify with the tradition of armed resistance, and use it to gain popularity and influence.

Young Ireland's interpretation of historic events did much to shape their immediate policies and objectives. Their intention was to convince people that the injustices of the present emanated from the grievances of the past and see themselves as part of a continuing struggle. As parliament debated a coercion bill designed to counter agrarian disturbances in March 1846, the *Nation* noted that 'tyranny perpetuates itself. The crimes of one generation become the apologies of another. The massacres of Mountjoy and the robberies of Strafford are the remote ancestors of the coercion bill of today'.[2] Young Ireland presented its claim for self-government as that of an historic nation seeking to regain its independence. Duffy maintained that 'long servitude' had left the Irish masses mired in ignorance, but hoped that the new generation, literate and sober, would prove receptive to a 'more informed and generous patriotism', which could be mobilised to encourage a more pressing demand for self-government.[3] To achieve this O'Connell's reliance on petitions and meetings was not enough. The work of the Repeal Association had to be supplemented by the efforts of a vigorous and imaginative press, which was capable of firing young minds with inspiring visions of 'the old historic island, the mother of soldiers and scholars, whose name was heard in the roar of onset on a thousand battlefields'. Such a press would, according to Duffy, inspire the youth to dream 'not of becoming repeal wardens, but of becoming martyrs and confessors'.[4]

O'Connell had announced that 1843 would be 'Repeal year' and stated his intention to summon a 'Council of Three Hundred' – a national assembly in-waiting – to prepare a bill for the repeal of the union. During the summer and autumn, agitation gathered momentum as massive demonstrations were held at sites with strong historical associations such as Limerick, Kells, Cashel, Kilkenny, Tara, Clontibret and Mullaghmast. The *Nation* rejoiced at these gatherings and played its part in stoking up the atmosphere, describing the crowds in military terms and drawing parallels with stirring historic events. In an editorial entitled 'The morality of war' Davis, while denying any intention to encourage violence, noted that the sword had played its part in Ireland's past struggles and praised the heroism and self-sacrifice of those who had fought against foreign rule down the ages.[5]

The campaign was to culminate in a great demonstration on 8 October 1843 at Clontarf on the outskirts of Dublin, the scene of Brian Boru's great victory over the Norsemen in 1014. The British government had until now allowed these rallies to proceed unhindered (much to the consternation of Irish unionists), but had watched with concern as the crowds swelled into the hundreds of thousands and O'Connell's rhetoric grew more inflamed. The prospect of a million people assembling near the capital was eventually deemed too great a risk and was prohibited by government proclamation on 7 October, with strong detachments of troops placed on the approach roads to Clontarf. Fearing the possibility of a violent confrontation and determined to stay within the law, O'Connell cancelled the demonstration.

A few days later, O'Connell and three of his lieutenants, his son John, the secretary of the Repeal Association, T. M. Ray, and the association's 'Head Pacificator', Tom Steele, as well as the editors of three pro-repeal newspapers, Richard Barrett of the *Pilot*, John Gray of the *Freeman's Journal* and Charles Gavan Duffy of the *Nation*, were arrested and charged with conspiracy. When they were tried some months later in January 1844, the attorney general noted the prominence given to battles such as Clontarf, Benburb and Limerick on the Repeal Association's membership card, and claimed that the card was 'framed and engraved with a view of raking up the animosities of by-gone faction – with a view of exciting hatred of the Saxon foreigner'.[6] Militant editorials from the *Nation* such as 'The morality of war' and several of its bellicose ballads were also offered as examples of the paper's seditious intentions.

On 30 May 1844 O'Connell and his fellow 'traversers' were convicted of sedition and sentenced to 12 months imprisonment at Richmond Bridewell. The Repeal Association closed ranks behind him and the Young Irelander William Smith O'Brien became its caretaker leader. O'Brien had joined the Repeal Association in October 1843 and, although not directly connected with the *Nation*, allied himself with Davis and his colleagues. The Young Irelanders were quick to appreciate the historical significance of their new recruit, who as the son of the baronet Sir Edward O'Brien of Cahirmoyle claimed descent from Brian Boru, presenting him as 'the representative of a house which for 20 generations had ruled territories, conducted negotiations and marshalled armies, and the lineal heir of a king still familiar to the memory of the nation after 800 years'.[7]

After judgement was passed, the *Nation* cautioned its readers not to lose hope and when the House of Lords reversed the decision in September 1844, the Young Irelanders and all other Irish nationalists celebrated exuberantly.[8] But once the cheering had died down, the question on everybody's lips was 'what next?' The government had shown that it would not be intimidated by demonstrations – no matter how imposing – and if it could derail the repeal by simply banning a meeting, O'Connell's strategy appeared bankrupt. The way was open for increasing dissension within the Repeal Association, led by the young men of the *Nation*.

Exploring a new approach, O'Connell made overtures towards federalists who advocated limited devolution for Ireland and on 12 October 1844 announced his willingness to accept a federal arrangement rather than outright repeal of the union. The *Nation* immediately repudiated O'Connell's move, claiming that federal government would continue the country's cultural subordination.[9] O'Connell backed off, but not without resentment at the *Nation*'s criticism, and the testiness of the disagreement was a sign of things to come.

Like O'Connell, the Young Irelanders too were reviewing their future strategy. Duffy later claimed that after Clontarf boasting and bombast were finally discredited and would have to be replaced by the steady and relentless work of education.[10] While in prison he had worked on a plan to promote the growth of reading rooms throughout the country and make them centres of learning and discussion.[11] In the period of reassessment that followed Clontarf, some Young Irelanders grew disillusioned with O'Connell's half-hearted support for such educational endeavours, believing that he was happier to bask in the devotion of quiescent followers than to lead a movement of informed citizens who might question his authority. Some even suspected that

O'Connell's relative lack of interest in popularising history stemmed from an unwillingness to recognise the achievements of Ireland's illustrious dead in case it distracted attention from himself: asked if O'Connell was jealous of the *Nation*, John Blake Dillon was said to have replied, 'Jealous of the *Nation* . . . Why he's jealous of Brian Boru!'[12]

In July 1844 Davis and others founded the '82 Club 'for the purpose of commemorating that glorious epoch, of doing honour to the memory of illustrious Irishmen and promoting the cause of Nationality'.[13] The club's name invoked the winning of legislative independence by Irish Patriots and Volunteers in 1782, and it held lavish dinners on the anniversary of the Volunteers' Declaration of Independence and other significant dates. It was primarily a Young Ireland initiative and its members, dressed in a military-style green and gold uniform, regarded themselves as the officer corps of Irish nationalism. With its patriotic toasts and eloquent speeches it imitated the political clubs of the eighteenth century and the contemporary French example of using banquets to conduct political debates which were then reported in the press. The intention was that the club would grow 'into a social league of political chieftains . . . to occupy every avenue of the public mind with the sentiments of freedom, and enlist the taste and honour of the country in the cause of nationality'. It would remind Irishmen of their proud heritage and 'encourage books on Ireland by Irishmen, Irish history, Irish poetry'.[14] The club enjoyed considerable popularity during 1845, making an impressive showing at several banquets at the Rotunda during the year. O'Connell was president, but never showed any enthusiasm for its meetings, which were sometimes the occasion for militant speeches that were not to his taste.[15]

INTERPRETING 1798

Since so much about the Irish past was contentious, speaking and writing about history had inevitable political consequences. Historical disputes carried on into current politics, and those of the recent past presented particular problems. The most contentious event in recent history was the bloody rebellion of 1798, the interpretation of which opened up the possibility of sharp divisions between O'Connell and Young Ireland. In his youth O'Connell had been sympathetic to the United Irishmen, and may have even joined the society, but mindful of the bloodshed and chaos he had witnessed while studying in France in the early 1790s, he had distanced himself from republicanism as rebellion approached, and in 1798 had served on the government side in the lawyer's yeomanry. Holding up the rebellion as a prime example of the folly of violent insurrection, he claimed that it had achieved nothing but bloodshed, repression and an upsurge in sectarianism and denounced its instigators as 'miscreants'.[16] In contrast, the Young Irelanders invoked the names of the United Irishmen with reverence. However, they knew that any explicit celebration of the 1798 Rebellion would open a breach with O'Connell, and approached the topic with caution.[17]

Young Ireland's usual approach was to contrast the nobility and idealism of the United Irishmen with the treachery and brutality of the British government and their allies. The *Nation* maintained that the very name of the United Irishmen had been misrepresented:

> 'United Irishmen' what a glorious name. How nobly sounds the title of brotherhood in any land! . . . And yet this name has been made a name of reproach. . . . The wicked conqueror imposed his opinions and his epithets with the same bayonet where with he enforced laws and exacted plunder.[18]

The *Nation* praised the efforts of Irish writers to put this right, citing R. R. Madden's work on the United Irishmen as proof that the society was 'a political association of our purest and ablest men' who had sought peaceful political reform until severe repression left them with no choice but to take up arms.[19] The *Nation*'s own writers generally avoided the topic and the paper's best-known treatment of the rebellion was the song 'The memory of the dead' by the Trinity College academic, John Kells Ingram, which was published anonymously in the *Nation* on 1 April 1843.[20] Rather than openly celebrating the rebellion, it scorned those who denounced or ignored it and praised the United men as brave patriots who had risen against intolerable oppression. Emphasising the character of the men of '98 rather than their actions, it chastised others for fearing to speak of '98, but only referred to the rebellion itself in a vague and rather evasive manner. (Even then, despite its caution, the poem was cited by the prosecution as evidence of the treasonable sympathies of the *Nation* when Duffy and others were tried on charges of seditious conspiracy in 1844.)[21]

Sean Ryder has noted that Young Ireland 'clearly aimed at de-sectarianising and de-republicanising the memory of the rebellion, recasting it in a more romantic, heroic, mythic mode that was politically flexible and more amenable to O'Connellite constitutionalism'.[22] Usually the *Nation* did this by celebrating the personal virtues and heroic deaths of individual United Irishmen such as Wolfe Tone. Davis claimed that

> a better ruler for Ireland than Theobald Wolfe Tone never lived. He was a man of unaffected, deep, plain patriotism – possessed of the highest political sagacity – of exact and comprehensive judgement . . . laborious in business, and gay and warm in heart . . . one of the greatest that Ireland ever produced.[23]

Largely through Davis's efforts a memorial stone was laid on Tone's grave at Bodenstown. Davis had intended to write a biography of Tone for the Library of Ireland, and had prepared some notes and discussed the project with his widow Matilda Tone in the months before his death.[24] Tone was also an inspirational figure for Mitchel, whose *History of Ireland* (1869) drew heavily and uncritically on Tone's memoirs, beginning a long tradition in nationalist historiography of treating Tone's writings as sacred scripture. Between them, Davis and Mitchel were crucial in establishing Tone's historical reputation as the father of Irish republicanism.[25]

In contrast to Tone's courage and openness, government figures such as Pitt and Castlereagh were condemned for their treachery in bringing about the union and Ireland's enslavement:

> The English government did bring on the insurrection of '98. Their base and deliberate breach of the treaty of '82, their government of Ireland by corruption . . . their destruction of the Volunteers, their refusal of religious liberty, their commercial oppression, their violation of the rights of armament and free discussion – in short their commission of every imaginable ruffianism in the executive, and of every crime that could be bought from the legislature were the remote causes of the insurrection.[26]

The *Nation* took every opportunity to remind its readers of the government's perfidy. In 1843 it gleefully revealed that John Warneford Armstrong, a militia officer who had feigned sympathy for the rebellion in order to betray the United Irish leaders Henry and John Sheares in 1798, was living openly at Ballycumber, King's County, and making no attempt to hide his past deeds.[27] This allowed the *Nation* to denounce the British government for its employment of spies, informers and agents provocateurs to provoke the rising, and claim that 'the government [and] not the United Irishmen were "the miscreants of '98"'.[28] Such denunciations were done with one eye on the past and the other on current politics: the argument that Britain's treatment of Ireland had always been devious and corrupt, and that any alliance with British politicians was a snare, was habitually employed by the *Nation* to discredit attempts by O'Connell to negotiate with English Whigs rather than continue to demand the immediate repeal of the union.[29]

Very occasionally, in order to portray itself as the organ of a vigorous and militant nationalism, the *Nation* cast ambivalence aside, and praised the fighting spirit shown by the men of Wexford. In a rare article on the rebellion Davis claimed that the county rose in '98 with little organisation against intolerable wrong and tho' it was finally beaten by superior forces, it taught its aristocracy and the government a lesson not easily forgotten . . . that popular anger could strike hard as well as sigh deeply . . . The red rain made Wexford's harvest grow.[30]

But such statements were few. Too close an identification with the rebellion risked alienating moderate repealers and unionists and branding Young Ireland as apologists for insurrection. For the most part the *Nation* took the safest course and avoided mentioning the rebellion, and could even argue that too much discussion of 1798 risked raking 'up the smouldering ashes of party discord'.[31] Although a number of new works on 1798 such as 'Biographies of the United Irishmen' by Thomas Devin Reilly and 'The Military History of 1798' by M. J. Barry were projected by the Library of Ireland, none were actually published, and the Library fell back on reprinting earlier works such as Edward Hay's *History of the Insurrection of 1798* (1803). It was far easier to publish an account by a moderate Catholic such as Hay which deplored sectarian violence and claimed that the rebels had been forced to take up arms in self-defence.

The 1798 Rebellion was too recent and too difficult a subject to receive sustained historical treatment by Young Ireland writers. It was not ignored but was generally subsumed into a wider anti-union polemic, showing the rebellion to be a trap into which the Irish fell and allowed the British government to stymie Ireland's progress towards independence. Differing interpretations of 1798 and the use of violence to effect political change were important, however, and prefigured the issue on which Young Ireland would eventually split from the Repeal Association. It was significant that when Mitchel sought to distance himself from the moderates of the Irish Confederation in 1848, he did so by adopting the name the *United Irishman* for his paper and openly espousing the separatist republican principles of the 1790s.[32]

THE SPLIT

Differences between O'Connell and Young Ireland emerged more pointedly over contemporary issues, especially university education. In order to open up university education to Catholics the government proposed in 1845 to create three new colleges in Belfast, Cork and Galway. The Young Irelanders approved of this new initiative, believing that increased access to further education would provide Ireland's youth with the knowledge and skills to contribute to their country's regeneration. In order to side-step the thorny issue of religious control, the colleges were to be free from religious tests and to have no theological faculties. The non-denominational nature of the colleges was welcomed by the *Nation* which hoped that by educating Irishmen of all persuasions together they would 'strengthen the soul of Ireland with knowledge, and knit the sects of Ireland in liberal and trusting friendship'.[33] The proposal was, however, criticised by some Catholic bishops and clergy, and O'Connell eventually joined with the more conservative bishops in condemning the putative institutions as 'Godless Colleges'.[34] On 26 May 1845 the issue was the result of a sharp disagreement between O'Connell and Davis at a Repeal Association meeting in Dublin, which reduced a distraught Davis to tears. At that meeting O'Connell drew a sharp line between the main body of the Repeal Association and Young Ireland, who he maintained were 'anxious to rule the destinies of this country'. Putting the young men firmly in their place, he noted that 'I am for Old Ireland . . . and I have some slight notion that Old Ireland will stand by me'.[35]

In the following months religious controversy began to seep into the meetings of the Repeal Association and articles appeared in O'Connellite newspapers accusing the *Nation* of anti-Catholic prejudices.[36] Increasingly, Davis believed that attendance at the association's Conciliation Hall was a waste of time, and instead threw himself into what he termed the *Nation*'s 'mind-making'.[37] During this time he fell ill with scarlet fever and after a brief illness died on 16 September 1845. His friends were shocked and grief-stricken, but decided that the best way to serve his memory was to continue to carry on his work.[38] John Blake Dillon, although seriously ill himself, took over his biography of Wolfe Tone, hoping to complete it while recuperating in Madeira.[39] John Pigot worked hard at his antiquarian pursuits to rescue ancient manuscripts and record traditional music as Davis had encouraged him to do.[40]

Davis's death was, however, a grievous blow to Young Ireland's history-writing project. He had been its main force and inspiration, planning and commissioning new works, and guiding and encouraging his fellow authors. Besides writing and editing several works himself, he was in the process of researching and writing several others. His personal papers show extensive notes on various historical topics and plans for history lectures and projects such as an Irish biographical dictionary, an absentee roll (a list of the owners of Irish estates who were non-resident), additional collections of poems and ballads, a history of the Cromwellian war, a military history of 1798, an illustrated history of Ireland, reprints of notable Irish historical pamphlets, and a series of short lives of illustrious Irishmen.[41] No other Young Irelander had his combination of learning, vision and drive, and the *Nation*'s most ambitious history-writing projects died with him.

Without Davis, Duffy despaired of keeping the *Nation* going, and sought additional help. In October 1845 he recruited John Mitchel as assistant editor and chief contributor of the *Nation*. Mitchel's *Life of Aodh O'Neill* had just been published by the Library of Ireland and had been well received, marking him out as a lively and spirited writer.[42] When Duffy was absent from the *Nation* (as he often was due to ill health), Mitchel assumed full editorial responsibilities, and his pungent articles introduced an increasingly combative note into the paper. In response to claims by Tory papers that the newly-built railways would provide an excellent means of transporting troops to curb any possible insurrection, Mitchel observed that railway defiles would make excellent ambush points and that the wood and iron used to lay tracks were ideal pike-making materials.[43] This led the authorities to prosecute Duffy (as the paper's proprietor) for sedition. Mitchel's assertion that resistance could be organised by repeal wardens also managed to offend O'Connell, who pointedly observed at a public meeting some weeks later that he had admired the *Nation* more 'in the time of the illustrious dead' than he did at present.[44]

In the summer of 1846 the differences between O'Connell and Young Ireland came to a head. After the prosecution of Duffy for Mitchel's railway article in June, O'Connell took the opportunity to propose that the Repeal Association sever all connections with newspapers, and publicly reassert its commitment solely to peaceful political agitation. Impatient at sniping from those he termed the 'juvenile orators' of Young Ireland, O'Connell was intent on challenging the *Nation*'s bellicose rhetoric and demonstrating that he was still in full control of the association. His actions were given additional urgency by the collapse of Peel's ministry and the accession to power of the Whigs on 30 June. In the preceding months O'Connell had stepped up co-operation with the Whigs in the House of Commons, and it seemed possible that he might now row back on repeal in return for a more benign administration in Dublin Castle and some official positions for his followers.

At a Repeal Association meeting on 13 July O'Connell moved two resolutions: the first committed the association to 'peaceable and legal means alone', the second to 'abhorring all attempts to improve and augment constitutional liberty by means of force, violence or bloodshed'. They were the subject of debate on that night and again two weeks later. At the time the question of physical force was very much an abstract one: no significant group advocated its use and the Young Irelanders had neither the intention nor the capacity to take up arms. As nobody was advocating violence in the present, the debate shifted to the question of whether physical force had ever been justifiable in the past. Thomas Francis Meagher claimed that history furnished many examples of when it had and famously refused to 'stigmatise the sword' that

had freed nations such as the Americans and Belgians from foreign domination. John Mitchel too was not prepared to accept a blanket condemnation
of violence which, he claimed, would condemn the Volunteers of '82, who had
taken up arms to assert their rights, the founding fathers of America, who
achieved their liberty through armed rebellion, and the United Irishmen of
1798. 'My father', Mitchel noted, 'was a United Irishman. The men of '98
thought liberty worth some blood-letting, and although they failed, it were
rather hard that one of their sons would now be thought unworthy to unite in
a peaceful struggle for the independence of his country, unless he will
proclaim that he "abhors" the memory of his own father'.[45]

The debate on the peace resolutions in July 1846 has sometimes been seen
in retrospect as an insignificant squabble at a time when Ireland was about to
experience the full horrors of famine, but it touched on matters of prime
importance for both sides. For O'Connell, it was an attempt to reassert his
control of the Repeal Association and reaffirm his lifelong commitment to
peaceful methods, while the Young Irelanders regarded the resolutions as a
repudiation of the martial tradition they had lauded for four years in the
Nation. The writing of Ireland's history was their battlefield, and they proved
their patriotism by refuting the libels of Ireland's enemies and celebrating the
warrior heroes of the past. Repudiating these views would, they believed, sacrifice their honour and integrity, and also limit their room for political manoeu-
vre. Meagher may have spoken of America and Belgium, but the sword he
refused to stigmatise was primarily an Irish sword. Duffy maintained that
accepting the resolutions meant 'presenting ourselves to our old, relentless,
hereditary enemy, bound hand and foot, by a renunciation for ever, under all
circumstances, of the last resource of oppressed nations'. Unwilling to con-
cede, the Young Irelanders walked out of the meeting and out of the Repeal
Association.[46]

Once they had seceded, the Young Irelanders decided to concentrate
their efforts on popular education and propaganda. The *Nation* advised its
followers that the press and reading rooms were the most powerful weapons
available to them and exhorted them to redouble their efforts: 'educate your
children in the National Schools and at home . . . Teach your sons the history,
the resources, the language, the rights of Ireland.'[47] Without a political
organisation of their own Smith O'Brien suggested that the Young Irelanders
should make up the deficit by forming a 'literary phalanx' to work for repeal.[48]
Many did so and 1846 was the most productive year in the Library of Ireland
series, with nine volumes published. In an attempt to diminish the *Nation*'s
influence, the Repeal Association tried to ban the paper from its reading
rooms, leaving it to complain that it was being 'cut off from schools of our own
foundation . . . shut out of our own People's Colleges'.[49] Aware of its limited

support, Young Ireland hoped to use its educational initiatives to create a cadre of informed citizens who would form its popular base and refuse to accept dictation from O'Connell. Dr Robert Cane from Kilkenny, a prominent repealer and friend of the Young Irelanders, wrote to Duffy in support, observing that the association must eventually change its course since 'the young men, the reading men, the tradesmen, clerks, young shopkeepers, &c, who have been educated in repeal reading rooms and fed upon the *Nation* . . . will be in a few years, the men of Ireland'.[50]

History became a weapon in contemporary disputes and within months of the secession, the *Nation* was already revising the historical record to play down O'Connell's achievement in winning Catholic emancipation. In an article entitled 'Popular fallacies about Irish history', Thomas D'Arcy McGee argued that the Catholic Relief Bill of 1793 which allowed Catholics to vote in parliamentary elections was a more significant measure in creating civic equality than the 'emancipation' achieved by O'Connell in 1829 and, far from being the leader of Irish Catholics for half a century (as some of his partisans claimed), O'Connell had only really become a figure of significance with the foundation of the Catholic Association in 1823. Before this, argued McGee, his contribution to Catholic emancipation had been less than figures such as Henry Grattan, John Keogh or Archbishop John Troy.[51] McGee's partisan article can be partly explained by the bitterness that remained after the secession, but it signalled what would become a recurrent theme in Young Ireland accounts of these years, namely the disparagement of O'Connell and his contribution to Irish history.

FAMINE AND REBELLION

By the time such articles were being written, however, millions of Irish people had more pressing concerns. The potato blight had reappeared in July 1846, and over the next couple of months the crop failed disastrously, creating the prospect of mass starvation for those dependent on potatoes. The government's relief measures had initially blunted the worst effects of the disaster through the early summer of 1846, but after two successive crop failures the meagre reserves of the Irish peasantry were exhausted and deaths from famine and fever mounted inexorably. In December 1846 an attempt was made to hold a conference to heal the divisions between Young Ireland and O'Connell to present a united front to the crisis, but neither side showed any real willingness to compromise and it failed. The following January the Young Ireland seceders decided to found their own organisation, the Irish Confederation, which would establish Confederate Clubs throughout the country. For the most part, these took root only in Dublin and other large towns and cities, attracting politically conscious artisans, clerks and students.[52]

The clubs (invariably named after historic figures such as Sarsfield, Swift, Grattan and Davis) were to be forums for debate and education.[53] Political agitation was to be accompanied by systematic study, especially of Irish history, which would teach readers 'to ponder over the story of our long torture and ruin, and to contrast their own state at this hour with the national condition of a land so gifted by God'.[54] However, the social disruption of the Famine did not lend itself to the kind of assiduous education and self-improvement advocated by the *Nation*, and Duffy noted that as conditions deteriorated pride and self-reliance were being eroded by fear and destitution.[55] Writing history in the midst of such a crisis often seemed pointless, with D'Arcy McGee observing that it was unthinkable that 'so many sincere men could not continue among their books while the country was falling daily more deeply into corruption and ruin'.[56] In response to a reader's query about the 'Ballad History of Ireland', the *Nation* replied

> Ballad Balderdash! Does he see no difference between last year and this? What man with a heart would sit down to write Ballad History while his country perishes? . . . We would rather hear of a great league of Irishmen of all creeds, confederated together in 1847, to give Ireland to the Irish, than all the victories since King Dathy. We are 'making history' this year, not writing it.[57]

In late 1847 there were plans to publish a volume of Mangan's translations in the Library of Ireland, but the publisher James Duffy advised that the Library should be wound up as there was no demand for books in such desperate times.[58] In the end the Library struggled on into the following year and produced a few more volumes before fizzling out. In a review of C. P. Meehan's edition of John Lynch's *Life and Death of Francis Kirwan* (1848) (the last volume to be published in the series), the *Nation* noted that the work 'reminds us of our literary designs abandoned for the sterner labour of politics', praising Meehan as the only figure who 'has continued the study and examination of our long unknown and disparaged Irish history, with uninterrupted ardour' and hoping that when the political turbulence of the present was over his fellow Young Irelanders could return to 'the special work for which they were fittest'.[59]

As the Famine became worse, the *Nation* devoted more attention to economic matters, and in April and May 1847 published the radical agrarian proposals of James Fintan Lalor, the crippled son of a prosperous Queen's County farmer and former O'Connellite MP.[60] For Lalor, notions of historical and cultural identity were dwarfed by the land question, which by 1847 had become a matter of life and death. He argued that since society had failed to perform its duty of providing food for its members it 'stands dissolved . . . and another requires to be constituted', and proposed a practical plan that would link agrarian grievances directly to the campaign for political independence and repeal the 'entire conquest of seven hundred years'.[61] When put before the Confederation, Lalor's proposals for a national rent strike were opposed by moderates such as Smith O'Brien and Duffy, but supported by Mitchel and other radicals. Debates in the Confederation were becoming more polarised and by autumn 1847 Mitchel was calling for a rent and rates strike and for the peasantry to keep their own cash crops and livestock. On a number of occasions his editorials in the *Nation* made thinly veiled calls for national insurrection.[62] Duffy began to censor his articles, claiming that they put the *Nation* at risk, and sharp differences emerged between the two in the Confederation. On 1 December Duffy produced proposals for a constitutional campaign to achieve repeal. It was endorsed by the Confederation's council, but Mitchel strongly dissented and, a week later, resigned from the *Nation*, claiming the paper 'has fallen into the merest old-womanly drivelling and snivelling, and the people are without a friend at the press'.[63]

Smith O'Brien was horrified by Mitchel's violent rhetoric, and drew up a series of resolutions, condemning armed insurrection and the refusal to pay rent and rates, and reiterating that the Confederation was committed to obtaining legislative independence for Ireland through the peaceful cooperation of all classes.[64] In early February 1848 the Confederation adopted O'Brien's resolutions, despite Mitchel's bitter opposition. Mitchel and his allies withdrew from its policy-making council, but remained members of the Confederation itself and continued to build up their support among the clubs.[65] As he could no longer use the *Nation* to propagate his views, Mitchel decided to set up a new weekly newspaper in Dublin with the assistance of his friends John Martin, Thomas Devin Reilly, Fr John Kenyon and James Clarence Mangan.[66]

The paper was called the *United Irishman*, and its masthead was Wolfe Tone's famous dictum that: 'if the men of property will not support us, they must fall; we can support ourselves by the aid of that numerous and respectable class of the community – the men of no property'. The first number was published on 12 February 1848 and immediately laid claim to Ireland's revolutionary tradition:

> That holy hatred of foreign dominion which nerved our noble predecessors fifty years ago for the dungeon, the field, or the gallows . . . still lives, thank God! and glows as hot and fierce as ever. To educate that holy hatred . . . I hereby devote the columns of the *United Irishman*.

Such sentiments had not been aired publicly in Ireland for half a century. The *United Irishman* eschewed the gradual educational ethos of the *Nation* – its cultural and historical content was slight, and it provided instruction mostly on skills such as barricade construction, pike drills and street fighting. Mitchel's timing was opportune, as within two weeks of publication the news arrived that political turmoil in France had led to a popular uprising in Paris and the overthrow of the French monarchy. Revolution spread across the continent and the political situation in Ireland was transformed. When the French declared a republic the *United Irishman* threw all reserve aside and proclaimed its republican credentials:

> Vive la republique! Yes! the only true form of government – the form which national liberty takes when it belongs to the people, and is not prostituted by a class, the Republic so worshipped by the United Irishmen of old . . . is won at last . . . And so we may have a Republic nearer home ere long: for in these events lies our fate.[67]

In the heightened atmosphere of 1848, differing historical interpretations took on strong political significance. Young Ireland's admiration for the legislative independence of 1782 gave way to a dismissal by radicals of the limited powers achieved. Mitchel denounced the constitution of 1782 as 'a humbug. It vanished in 18 years and I hope we may never see it again . . . whatever be the opinion of my brother Confederates, there shall be no rest for me until I see Ireland a free republic'.[68]

It was not just Mitchel who spoke in militant terms. As thrones toppled across Europe and revolutionary ideas gained currency, the *Nation* and moderate Young Irelanders became more outspoken. For those who thought in historical terms, history was on the side of revolution, and the independence of Ireland seemed there for the taking. Historical parallels were constantly invoked: the *Nation* observed that

> Never since Grattan fraternised with Keogh and Tone, did the country present circumstances so favourable for speedy success. Never since Carew turned south Munster into a desert without growing corn or living creature, did the necessities of the people so peremptorily demand a victory.[69]

In the early months of 1848 the Young Irelanders believed that the time was approaching when they would be called upon to emulate the heroic deeds of the past. In March the *Nation* published an editorial that spoke of Ireland as a country where liberty has maintained so gallant and so stubborn a battle . . . each generation offering up to death on the battlefield, or on the scaffold, or in forlorn exile, the best men of their race and time to the same black and bloody idol of foreign domination – shall that land alone stand like a dark shadow in the new sunshine of liberty?[70]

Anxious not to let the moment pass, the *Nation* proclaimed that indecision had always been the curse of Irish history: Hugh O'Neill, the Confederates of the 1640s, Patrick Sarsfield and the United Irishmen, had all lacked clear aims and had eventually been defeated; the Volunteers, on the other hand, had shown a determination to achieve a definite objective and had done so. The agitation for repeal, too, had been afflicted by a lack of clear thinking, and eventually had run aground. It hoped that the Famine might now spur those who remained in Ireland to seize independence without delay.[71]

In this highly-charged atmosphere old conventions were challenged and women began to play a greater role in the Young Ireland movement. Ellen Mary Patrick Downing ('Mary') despaired of the *Nation*'s moderation in 1848 and switched her allegiance to Mitchel's *United Irishman*, contributing an address 'To the women of Ireland' which called on them to put aside their aversion to bloodshed and allow their country to assert its rights in arms.[72] Young Ireland publications had generally taken a relatively cautious line towards female emancipation, arguing that women had every right to be interested in politics, but they should use their influence in the home rather than becoming openly involved in public life. The *Nation* strongly supported women's education, arguing that it would be 'a great, if not the greatest, means of effecting our national regeneration', and their knowledge could be passed on to their children.[73] They were exhorted to

Teach your sons the history, the resources, the language, the rights of Ireland . . . mothers of Ireland, we appeal to you. . . . Teach your sons they have a country to raise or ruin . . . Teach them to live for her and to die for her . . . So shall ye be the bringers forth of slaves no more, but the glorious mothers of a mighty people.[74]

However, Young Ireland was reluctant to go beyond such rhetoric. In May 1848 Duffy noted that he had received 'in a feminine hand, a most seditious proposal for the formation of a Ladies Society, to talk treason and defy the gagging act', and replied that 'the intention is excellent, but the plan is unnecessary . . . as for talking sedition, and acting on it, the men must do that'.[75] The pace of events, however, led women to play a more direct role than he had envisaged. By July 1848 most leading Young Irelanders had either been arrested or were preparing for insurrection and women such as Francesca Elgee and Margaret Callan took over the running of the *Nation* for its last weeks.[76]

In all of this, the Young Irelanders had a keen awareness of themselves as important historical actors, and with revolution in the air, they looked to history as their guide. Most of them had read Alphonse de Lamartine's *History of the Girondists* (1847–8) and readily identified with its leading figures: Smith O'Brien was their Lafayette, 'the gentleman of ancient lineage and generous nature'; John Blake Dillon 'the prudent, the steadfast Brissot'; John Martin was 'the honest, simple Mayor Bailly'; Duffy 'who organised the movement in his closet', was Carnot; and Mitchel was a latter-day Robespierre, 'the country lawyer, accepted as their chief by the Jacobins of Paris, because he was always more Jacobin than they.'[77]

Mitchel continued to proclaim his Jacobin-like beliefs in the *United Irishman* and was prosecuted on charges of treason-felony in May 1848. In a conscious effort to link his trial with the republican struggles of the past, he chose the eighty-two-year-old Robert Holmes, a former United Irishman and brother-in-law of Robert Emmet, as his defence counsel. After Holmes made a moving speech that placed Mitchel's actions in a tradition of historic resistance, Mitchel claimed that 'It caused me to think that my defeated life was at least one link in the unbroken chain of testimony borne by my country against foreign dominion; and with this consciousness I knew that my chains would weigh light'.[78] His speech from the dock was unrepentant and he self-consciously cast himself in the role of the historic national martyr.[79] Others too saw Mitchel in this historic light: the Celtic scholar John O'Donovan who had been contemptuous of Mitchel's calls for revolution, claiming that 'he had no party in this kingdom able to dethrone a cat', was won over by his bearing at his trial: 'I never believed him honest till the last day of his trial, but then saw clearly that he was a second Emmet'.[80]

Found guilty, Mitchel was sentenced to 14 years of transportation. The unexpected severity of the sentence helped to steel the resolve of the Confederate leaders who formally resolved upon a rising immediately after the harvest. To forestall any such efforts the government suspended habeas corpus on 25 July and began arresting leading Confederates. Smith O'Brien and others believed they had no choice but to take a stand, and stumbled into a disorganised insurrection. O'Brien's awareness of his heroic ancestry contributed to his belief that he had a historic role to play.[81] Inspecting the counties around Dublin before the rising, he travelled from Tara to Trim and observed that he 'could not visit the scene of so many historic events without much emotion. The memories and traditions of the royal Tara recalled the times when Ireland acknowledged no sway but that of her kings and chiefs'. The ruins of the formidable Trim Castle testified to the ferocity of the native Irish and led him to ask 'Is the spirit of that old Irish race extinct? Heirs of their soil, are we no longer heirs of their courage?'[82] But for all O'Brien's invocation of Ireland's heroic tradition, the attempted insurrection never gathered momentum and was defeated after a minor engagement with the Irish Constabulary at Ballingarry, County Tipperary, on 29 July. Most of the Confederate leaders were arrested or fled into exile. Brooding on the failure to gain mass support, O'Brien observed that

> abject and degraded are the sons of those who for centuries battled against English perfidy and rapine. But a nation never dies. . . . New generations will arise, and perhaps the proofs which we have given that there are still some who prefer death to servitude will reanimate and rekindle the fire of Irish manhood.[83]

Young Ireland's fascination with heroic history was clearly an important factor in their decision to take up arms, and also contributed to their adoption of inflexible or unrealistic political positions. As Gearóid Ó Tuathaigh has noted:

> They thought and spoke in heroic terms . . . Mixed with youthful idealism was a strong current of political naiveté; lofty earnestness often shaded into self-righteousness; the view from the heroic heights was often a trifle censorious of those on the lower plains of human fallibility.[84]

Having spent so much effort lauding Ireland's resistance to tyranny, the Young Irelanders were trapped by their own rhetoric. They believed they had no choice but to take up arms to vindicate their personal honour and demonstrate that the view of Irish history they had propagated for the past six years was more than just empty words. The nationalist politician Justin McCarthy believed that they were troubled

> by the thought that the public opinion of England might regard the whole Young Ireland movement as a poetic dream, the inspiration of poets and romanticists, and bearing with it no deep, determined resolution to make personal sacrifice for the Irish cause.[85]

In acting as they did, they were acutely aware that their actions would be judged by generations to come. At his trial for high treason in Clonmel, Meagher claimed 'the history of Ireland explains this crime, and justifies it'.[86]

Meagher, O'Brien and other leading Confederates were found guilty and sentenced to death, eventually commuted to transportation for life. The events of 1848 scattered the Young Irelanders and effectively marked the end of their efforts as a coherent group. Its leaders were imprisoned or in exile, and its newspapers prohibited. Some literary figures, such as William Carleton and Joseph Sheridan Le Fanu, who had associated with the *Nation* to pursue the Young Irelanders' educational objectives disassociated themselves after 1848 from earlier work that had been sympathetic to the nationalist cause.[87] Among the Young Irelanders themselves there was much soul searching and disillusionment, and a belief that the Irish people had failed to live up to the heroic image projected by the *Nation*. Some such as Michael Joseph Barry concluded that the Irish should give up the prospect of ever winning independence and reconcile themselves to union with Britain.[88] Reviewing their efforts to use history to stimulate national consciousness, a dispirited John Blake Dillon concluded that Ireland's history

> can hardly in truth be called the history of a nation. The glory that could be won in two or three battles is too small a thing for a nation to subsist upon. There is not one link that can bind the past of Ireland to its future. The old forms of society, the old laws, and the old language have perished irrecoverably. For these reasons I would, if I were Duffy, abandon this ground of Celtic nationality, and take my stand henceforth upon the rights of man.[89]

But most Young Irelanders were unrepentant and held to their original ideals. In New York Thomas D'Arcy McGee founded a newspaper, the *Nation*, to carry on the work of Young Ireland.[90] Duffy was one of the few leaders not to be convicted and after his release from prison in April 1849 he set about re-publishing the *Nation* in Dublin. The habeas corpus suspension act expired on 31 August 1849 and the *Nation* re-appeared the next day, although it never fully recaptured the vigour and influence it had in its heyday.[91] Its content was also different, eschewing the poetry and song that had been so prominent in the original paper: its second number announced that 'We have no desire to encourage this fashion of rhyme in our new series, but very much the contrary. The time demands very different work'.[92]

With the country still suffering from the after effects of famine, Duffy devoted himself to social and economic matters, particularly the land question. In August 1850 he was a founder of the Irish Tenant League which sought to harness the efforts of local tenant protection societies to achieve greater security of tenure for Irish farmers. The new paper reflected this change of strategy with coverage of agrarian matters and economic development largely supplanting the educational and historical articles of the old *Nation*. In a series of editorials, Duffy claimed that Ireland was prostrate and demoralised as never before, that talk of armed rebellion was idle nonsense, and that the priority for all patriotic Irishmen should be to resolve the land question.[93] A new approach was now required, one that concentrated on the struggle for survival that preoccupied most of the population, 'and as to the old harp, once so loud and bold, to keep striking it now, when its every string lies loose, were but dull music.'[94] In the years immediately after the Famine, writing of Ireland's distant past seemed out of tune with the times, and the turn to more practical issues was evident in nationalist provincial newspapers such as the *Kilkenny Journal*, the *Cork Examiner* and the *Limerick Reporter and Tipperary Vindicator* which had been influenced by Young Ireland's historical and cultural ideals.[95] This unrelenting focus on the land question helped the Tenant League to some political success in the early 1850s, but the government refused to legislate for tenant right and popular support for the campaign gradually ebbed away. It seemed that even the practical approach of agrarian politics had reached an impasse. Despairing of ever achieving political progress, in 1855 Duffy sold the *Nation* to A. M. Sullivan and emigrated to Australia, his farewell editorial famously concluding that there was 'no more hope for the Irish cause than for the corpse on the dissecting table'.[96]

SIX

THE HISTORY OF THEIR OWN TIMES

MEMOIRS, JOURNALS AND POLEMICS

—

If writing of Ireland's distant past seemed an irrelevant indulgence as Ireland attempted to recover from the devastation of the Famine, the same was not true of the more recent past. The Young Irelanders were determined that the recording and interpreting of their own times would not be left to enemies and critics, and much of their work from 1848 was devoted to explaining and justifying their own actions. After the collapse of their attempted rebellion, they were anxious to defend themselves from accusations that they were nothing more than rash and bungling insurrectionists. The first to attempt to do so in a work of contemporary history was Michael Doheny, a self-educated lawyer and regular contributor to the *Nation*, who in 1849 published *The Felon's Track*, an account of nationalist politics in the 1840s that culminated with a narrative of the insurrection of 1848. In July 1848 Doheny had tried to mobilise the peasantry in his native Tipperary, but with little success, and after the Rising's collapse he went on the run and eventually escaped to America. He claimed that his motivation in writing his account was to give 'a simple statement of all that occurred . . . that no disgrace attached to Ireland in her recent discomfiture'.[1]

In describing the campaign for repeal of the union, Doheny was highly critical of O'Connell's reliance on 'moral force' alone to effect political change. Maintaining that 'there can be no doubt of the tendency of Mr O'Connell's policy to demoralise, disgrace, enfeeble and corrupt the Irish people', he contended that his decision to back down at Clontarf sacrificed an auspicious opportunity to seize independence and that O'Connell's imprisonment from May to September 1844 finally broke his spirit; from this time onwards 'It was evident something within him had died'.[2] He traced the growing differences between O'Connell and Young Ireland over education and federalism, and restated the *Nation*'s argument that the main purpose of the peace resolutions of July 1846 was to expel Young Ireland from the Repeal Association because of their opposition to an alliance with the Whigs. From the time of the split Doheny portrayed O'Connell as duplicitous and vindictive, and his followers as venal thugs who attempted to deny free speech to the seceders. In contrast, the Young Irelanders were distinguished by their honesty and patriotism, and he claimed that when they founded the Irish Confederation in January 1847, it soon 'won the respect of every educated man in the land, however widely most of them of them may have differed from it in political faith'.[3]

Doheny strongly supported the decision to rise in July 1848, believing that Young Ireland had been left with no choice. He recalled that the prospect of taking up arms for his country's freedom overwhelmed him with 'the hope of satisfaction, or vengeance, if you will, for so many ages of guilty tyranny. The tears, the burning and blood of nearly 1,000 years seemed to letter the eastern sky'.[4] He defended the Young Ireland leaders from charges of cowardice and incompetence, claiming that it was not lack of courage but military inexperience and the opposition of the clergy that resulted in defeat, and argued that their military failure was mitigated by their brave and defiant bearing during their trials which won the admiration of their countrymen.[5]

The book ended with a lengthy account of Doheny's experiences on the run from one end of Munster to the other – 'the felon's track' of the title – in which he drew a parallel between his personal hardships and those of his country. Despite all that had happened Doheny believed the decision to rise had salvaged Ireland's honour and claimed that many of those involved had held onto their arms and were prepared to use them whenever a better opportunity presented itself.[6] *The Felon's Track* – aptly described as a 'mixture of political argument, social commentary and travelogue'[7] – found a receptive audience and was reprinted several times, making a significant contribution to the subsequent view of Young Ireland as idealistic and incorruptible patriots.

Personal experience played an even greater part in John Mitchel's *Jail Journal* published in 1854 (after being serialised in his New York paper the *Citizen* earlier that year). *Jail Journal* was an individual's response to transportation and imprisonment rather than a work of history, but was strongly influenced by his readings in Irish history. It owed much to the *Memoirs of Wolfe Tone* – a work Mitchel greatly admired – often mimicking Tone's lively and self-deprecatory style and playful use of literary quotations.[8] The account of his imprisonment was prefaced by a concise history of Ireland that ranged from the Jacobite defeat of 1691 to Mitchel's conviction for treason felony in May 1848, in which he noted that

The general history of a nation may fitly preface the personal memoranda of a solitary captive; for it was strictly and logically a consequence of the dreary story here epitomised, that I came to be a prisoner, and to sit writing and musing so many months in a lonely cell . . . My preface then will explain, at least to some readers, what was that motive spirit and passion which impelled a few Irishmen to brave such risks, and incur so dreadful penalties for the sake of but one chance of rousing their oppressed and degraded countrymen to an effort of manful resistance against their cruel and cunning enemy.[9]

Influenced by the contemporary romantic vogue for self-revelation, Mitchel identified his fate with the historic persecution of Ireland and called down hatred and vengeance on England. Without the books and resources to write his country's history, he wrote his own, imaginatively exploring the boundaries between personal and national history.[10] *Jail Journal* was governed by the same propagandist impulses that had inspired his earlier writing, but in this case it was he rather than Hugh O'Neill who was the main protagonist, and Mitchel's first-hand account of his life and sufferings gave it an even greater power and authenticity than his treatment of the distant past. In this work of personal history he descends to the depths of despair, and even contemplates suicide, but comes to see himself, like his country, as still unconquered, and resolves to go on. Brooding on reports that Ireland was tranquil after the events of 1848, he refused to believe that all their efforts had been in vain:

> Surely we have not been utterly losing our labour all these years past, with our *Nations*, and our Irish libraries, and ballads, and the rest of it . . . who can tell what a world of noble passion has been set aglow; what haughty aspirings for themselves and their native land; what infinite pity; what hot shame for their trampled country and the dishonoured name of their fathers.[11]

Besides acting as a historical record of his imprisonment, Mitchel used his journal as a therapeutic outlet: 'A vicious tirade discharged into this receptacle relieves me much . . . A good rant, like a canter on the back of a brisk horse, gives me an appetite for dinner.'[12] Thinking on his fate while in captivity reinforced his hostility to the British government, which he regarded as the embodiment of the hypocrisy of the age, hiding its ruthless exploitation of other nations beneath a cloak of benevolence. But, he maintained, that like all great empires, its very success contained the seeds of destruction. He derisively termed the British empire 'Carthage', a commercial empire grown so obsessed with making money that it was losing its martial vigour and becoming weaker by the day:

> British policy must drain the blood and suck the marrow of all the nations it can fasten its desperate claws upon: and by the very nature of a bankrupt concern sustaining itself on false credit, its exertions must grow more desperate, its exactions more ruthless day by day, until the mighty smash come.[13]

Mitchel wove into the narrative of his imprisonment a sharp commentary on recent and current affairs, and took the opportunity for much self-justification and score-settling. The prime target was Daniel O'Connell. With an irreverence designed to shock, Mitchel savaged him as

> Poor old Dan! – wonderful, mighty, jovial, and mean old man! with silver tongue and smile of witchery . . . lying tongue! Smile of treachery! Heart of unfathomable fraud! What a royal, yet vulgar soul! With the keen eye and potent swoop of a generous eagle of Cairn Tual – with the base servility of a hound, and the cold cruelty of a spider![14]

While O'Connell had been alive, and for a time after his death, the Young Irelanders had generally avoided attacking him personally, despite their bitter political differences in his latter years. They were aware of his great popularity and realised that any personal attacks would rebound heavily on them. But by 1854, and exiled from Ireland, Mitchel felt under no constraints and gave full rein to his antipathy. He was anxious to puncture the aura that still surrounded O'Connell, and his attack went much further than that of Doheny, deeply offending many moderate nationalists.

Invective was also aimed at former colleagues. After reading a newspaper report of Duffy's trial, Mitchel condemned his decision to offer a defence and call character witnesses as 'miserable grovelling'. He denounced Duffy's re-engagement in constitutional politics in the 1850s as a betrayal of the separatist cause: 'Thus blasphemes this traitor: thus snivels, rather this most pitiable sinner.'[15] Such attacks took their toll on Duffy's reputation. From the late 1850s onwards, there emerged a generation of younger nationalist journalists sympathetic to Fenianism, who identified with Mitchel's uncompromising militancy and regarded Duffy as a backslider who had betrayed Young Ireland's original ideals.[16] *Jail Journal* eventually proved to be Mitchel's most widely read and influential work, which the Fenian John O'Leary described as 'the best Irish book written in my time'.[17] Its popularity helped establish the prison memoir as one of the central works in the Irish nationalist canon, as subsequent Fenian prisoners such as Jeremiah O'Donovan Rossa, Michael Davitt, Thomas Clarke and many others kept diaries of their captivity that imitated Mitchel's work.[18]

The Last Conquest of Ireland (Perhaps) (1861), which originally appeared as a series of letters in the Knoxville newspaper the *Southern Citizen* in 1858–9, was a more explicitly historical work in which Mitchel attempted to place the Famine in historical context. He argued that it was not primarily a natural disaster but an opportunity exploited by the British government to crush

Ireland's demand for self-government once and for all. The Famine was portrayed as the latest in a series of English attempts to extinguish Irish resistance, and the most shameful episode in Ireland's long struggle. There was, he claimed, 'a certain mournful pride' in dwelling upon gallant Irish defeats in the time of Cromwell, William III and 1798, when Ireland's cause was

> stricken down in open battle, and blasted to pieces with shot and shell . . . but to describe how the spirit of a country has been broken and subdued by beggarly famine; how her national aspirations have been, not choked in her own blood, nobly shed upon the field, but strangled by red tape; how her life and soul have been ameliorated and civilised out of her; how she died of political economy, and was buried under tons of official stationery; this is a dreary task, which I wish some one else had undertaken.[19]

Mitchel began his account at the height of the repeal agitation in 1843. He emphasised the great power that O'Connell had over the Irish masses, and argued that he squandered it in meekly accepting the British government's proclamation of the Clontarf demonstration. The vituperation of *Jail Journal* was toned down, but O'Connell was still portrayed as a flawed figure who had sacrificed Ireland's prospects of self-government by adhering to a policy which allowed the government to suppress political discontent in the knowledge that no effective resistance would be offered. Mitchel denounced O'Connell's unwillingness to shed blood as a betrayal of Irish history and nationality. The Irish, he claimed, 'were an essentially military people' who believed that there was some substance to O'Connell's rhetoric: 'at one word from his mouth they would have marched upon Dublin from all the five ends of Ireland, and made short work with police and military barracks.'[20] But this was not to be as O'Connell had used his eloquence 'to emasculate a bold and chivalrous nation' and 'was therefore, next to the British government, the worst enemy that Ireland ever had, or rather the most fatal friend'.[21]

After Clontarf, Mitchel claimed that the British government, frightened by the realisation of the fragile nature of its control over Ireland, set about weakening the national movement. In an elaborate conspiracy theory, he claimed that the true function of the Devon Commission set up in 1843 to investigate the Irish land system was to undermine tenant right and draw up a blueprint for sweeping land clearances. This would enable small Irish holdings to be consolidated into large grain farms and cattle ranches to feed Britain's burgeoning population of industrial workers. The report of the Devon Commission became 'the Bible of British legislators and landlords; the death warrant of one million and a half of [*sic*] human beings, and the sentence of pauper banishment against full a million and a half more'.[22] In reality the

Devon Commission was a much more low-key affair: its report in 1845 admitted the beneficial effects of tenant right and recommended granting some additional protections to tenants. It spawned a modest bill that advocated compensating tenants for improvements, but this was eventually overtaken by the dislocation caused by the Famine and never became law. The vast amount of evidence that the commission had collected on the iniquities of the Irish land system did, however, eventually contribute to the land reforms of the 1870s and 1880s.

According to Mitchel, the failure of the potato crop provided a convenient opportunity for implementing the Devon Commission's blueprint, and the government's manipulation of workhouses and relief schemes helped to complete the work of hunger and disease in demoralising, uprooting and exterminating the Irish peasantry. This, he claimed, was all the more effective because it was done under a mask of social improvement. If repeal

> could not be crushed out by coercion, nor bought out by corruption, it might be starved out by famine. The thing was done by a process of 'relieving' and 'ameliorating'; for in the nineteenth century civilised governments always proceed upon the most benevolent of motives.[23]

A few years of famine served to thin the ranks of O'Connell's followers and the once vigorous agitation for repeal collapsed 'into a dismal and despairing cry for food'.[24]

Mitchel argued that the government's 'famine policy' was 'a machinery, deliberately devised and skilfully worked, for the entire subjugation of the island – the slaughter of a portion of its people and the pauperisation of the rest'.[25] This, he claimed, was a policy with historical precedents: he equated the actions of Lord Clarendon, lord lieutenant of Ireland during the Famine, with those of Mountjoy, lord deputy of Ireland (1600–3), who defeated Hugh O'Neill by means of a ruthless scorched earth policy. But whereas Mountjoy had used fire and sword to devastate the country, Clarendon had inflicted even greater devastation on the country by means of commissions and legislation.[26] The story of the Famine was that of 'an ancient nation stricken down by a war more ruthless and sanguinary than any Seven Years' War or Thirty Years' War that Europe ever saw'.[27] There were echoes here of Mitchel's *Life and Times of Aodh O'Neill*, written for the Library of Ireland in 1845, in which he had argued that the Elizabethan government had deliberately used starvation as a weapon of war. In this earlier work he noted that after Mountjoy's campaign in Ulster in 1602 unburied corpses littered a land devastated by famine and pestilence: in a portent of some of the scenes evoked in the *Last Conquest*, he quoted the accounts of Fynes Moryson, Mountjoy's private secretary, of ditches crammed with the dead, their mouths all coloured green, by eating nettles, docks and all things they could rend up above the ground . . . Three children, the eldest not above ten years old, all eating and gnawing with their teeth the entrails of their dead mother, on whose flesh they had fed for twenty days past.[28]

Mitchel's interpretation of the Famine was largely shared by his Young Ireland colleagues, but he was the only one of the group to address the subject at length. Although the Famine was the most important event that the Young Irelanders lived through, its magnitude bewildered and overwhelmed them, and left them unable to address the greatest catastrophe of their times. For a movement that had dedicated itself to raising Irish pride and self-respect, the widespread misery and degradation caused by the Famine seemed to invalidate much of their previous work. It was, as Clare O'Halloran has noted, 'hard to accommodate the famine within a framework that stressed the glories and continuities of Irish history.'[29] Mitchel, though, who viewed history primarily in terms of the rise and fall of individual states, refused to be downcast. He argued that although Ireland might appear to be prostrate, this latest attempt to conquer her had not in fact succeeded, but had sown a harvest of hate that would fuel a 'passionate aspiration for Irish nationhood' in years to come. It was this that allowed him to append the 'perhaps' to the book's title and to draw some consolation from the devastation he had witnessed: England's conquest was again only partial and had failed to quench Ireland's undying national spirit.[30]

Patrick Maume has argued that the *Last Conquest* was strongly influenced by being written in America, at a time when many Americans were concerned at the influx of impoverished Irish to their shores.[31] In order to challenge nativist portrayals of the Irish as indolent beggars, Mitchel detailed how the formidable alliance of an oppressive government and rapacious landlords had pauperised and demoralised the Irish masses. Writing for an audience who prided themselves on their readiness to defend their rights and livelihoods, he attempted to explain why the Irish had died in droves without offering serious resistance. O'Connell, with his insistence on moral force, was the main scapegoat, but Mitchel also carefully listed the legislation and state agencies – disarming acts, a large army, a strong, centralised police force, an established church, workhouses, national schools, a biased judiciary and packed juries – that were designed to keep the Irish in a state of submission. British government policy was not driven by concern for the governed, nor even by normal political circumstances and expediencies, but by a deliberate and systematic plan of extermination that had stripped the Irish of the means and will to resist. Laying bare these facts would, he hoped, explain the depth of Irish hatred for England which many Americans found so baffling.[32]

The extent to which Mitchel's American readers were convinced by his arguments remains an open question, but the *Last Conquest* certainly found a receptive readership among the Irish at home and abroad, and its thesis that the Famine was a deliberate act of genocide became an article of faith with many nationalists. The historian Patrick O'Farrell went so far as to claim that it was Mitchel who '"invented" the Great Irish Famine of 1845–9, that is gave it initially the place it has come to occupy in commonly perceived historical and imaginative understanding'.[33] The accusation that the Famine was engineered by the British government was not unique to Mitchel, but it was he who expressed the idea most vigorously and memorably. He argued that the Famine had occurred not in spite of Britain's economic progress, but *because* of it: Irish lives were deliberately sacrificed to fuel Britain's industrial revolution. His judgement that 'The Almighty indeed sent the potato blight, but the English created the Famine' was endlessly quoted by later nationalist commentators.[34] Despite the hyperbole, several of Mitchel's accusations hit home. Many who had reservations about his militant politics accepted his interpretation of the Famine without question.[35] The O'Connellite, W. J. O'Neill Daunt, recommended the *Last Conquest* as 'a detailed and faithful account of the horrors of that famine',[36] while P. S. O'Hegarty praised it for revealing

> the cunning and deliberation with which the whole Famine business was engineered, and the way in which England's huge scheme for finally fettering the country was devised and worked. And all with a vividness, a clarity, and a simplicity which make the book as easily to be understood as an elementary reading lesson.[37]

Mitchel's interpretation was taken up by several subsequent writers on the Famine, from John O'Rourke's *The History of the Great Irish Famine of 1847* (1874) to Tim Pat Coogan's *The Famine Plot: England's Role in Ireland's Greatest Tragedy* (2012), and had a notable influence on the tone and structure of Cecil Woodham-Smith's best-selling *The Great Hunger* (1962).[38] Moreover, some of the *Last Conquest*'s most striking phrases and images were appropriated and recycled in fictional accounts of the Famine by writers such as D. P. Conygham, Louis J. Walsh and Liam O'Flaherty, contributing further to the pervasive influence of Mitchel's work.[39]

The most comprehensive and detailed accounts of the Young Ireland movement were those published by Charles Gavan Duffy from 1880 onwards.[40] After emigrating to Australia in 1855, Duffy took up political life with some success in his new home and became premier of Victoria in 1871–2, was knighted for his services to the colony two years later and appointed speaker of the state assembly in 1876. Returning to Europe in 1879, he resisted offers to become involved in Irish politics, and devoted himself to writing. The insurrection of 1641 had long fascinated him and he planned to write a full account under the title 'The Rising of the North' which would deny that there had been widespread massacres of Protestant civilians and stress the provocation suffered by the native Irish prior to 1641.[41] However, he eventually decided to devote his efforts to writing a history of Young Ireland, maintaining that if he did not, 'no one else would, and the ideas and intentions of that movement would be forever misunderstood.'[42] Duffy believed that his central role in events best qualified him to write such a history, observing that 'For a generation I was a factor in whatever was done or projected in the public affairs of Ireland', and his experience, political responsibilities and ample time for reflection had given him a broad and informed perspective.[43] He believed that the era he had lived through contained many pertinent lessons for the current generation of Irish nationalist politicians and that writing its history 'was the best and last service I could render to Ireland'. He regarded himself as the custodian of the memory of Davis and of the Young Ireland movement generally: he held Davis's private papers and correspondence from many of his old colleagues, and had been entrusted with the records of the Irish Confederation.[44] Setting out to familiarise a new generation 'with the truthfulness, simplicity, and real moderation' of the Young Irelanders, he hoped that their example might invigorate and purify public life, claiming that in contemporary Irish politics 'the high principles of action which Davis preached are not only not practised, but apparently not remembered.'[45]

Duffy published two large volumes on the Young Ireland movement: *Young Ireland: A Fragment of Irish History 1840–45* (1880) and *Four Years of Irish History 1845–1849* (1883). Written over 30 years after the period described, they were as much an interpretation as a chronicle of events, carefully filtered through Duffy's subsequent experiences. His natural political moderation had been reinforced by his experiences as a constitutional politician in Australia, and by the incompetence of physical force Irish nationalism in the 1860s and 1870s. His proximity to events, moderate tone and studied modesty gave his accounts considerable authority. Written with a clarity and ease that make for compelling narrative history, his works were quarried by all the historians of Young Ireland who came after him, and became regarded as important primary sources. Their vivid pen pictures of colleagues still resonate today: John Mitchel, for example, was described as having

a face which was thoughtful and comely, though pensive blue eyes and masses of soft brown hair, a stray ringlet of which he had the habit of twining round his finger while he spoke, gave it perhaps too feminine a cast. He lived much alone, and . . . was silent and retiring, slow to speak and apt to deliver his opinion in a form which would be abrupt and dogmatic if it were not relieved by a pleasant smile.[46]

Duffy's writings were particularly influential in recording the relations between Young Ireland and O'Connell. Duffy claimed that a number of accounts already written on the split in the Repeal Association had been biased in favour of O'Connell, but that his version would 'write the rigid truth, as it was known at the time to adequately informed men, and as it will, I believe, be recognised in the end, in order that it may be a light and guide to other generations'.[47] He gave credit to O'Connell for his work in mobilising the Catholic populace and winning emancipation, but claimed that these achievements were dissipated by his failure to build on them and promote repeal of the union with sufficient vigour.[48] His criticism sometimes contained a sharp personal note: he conceded that O'Connell 'had constantly devoted great powers to a just cause', but 'from whatever moral or intellectual deficiency the habit sprang, he was undoubtedly careless of strict truth' and was 'not so free from self-seeking as Grattan or Washington'.[49] There were several other implied criticisms of O'Connell's character and tactics: his impatience with opposition, readiness to abuse opponents, tolerance of hangers-on, carelessness with accounting for funds, and his willingness to trade Irish self-government for places for his followers.[50] Commenting on Lord O'Hagan's eulogy on O'Connell on the occasion of the centenary of his birth in 1875, Duffy wrote

He was no more the generous, single-minded, unselfish hero of your prose idyll than he was the impostor ordinarily represented in *The Times* – but a strange compound of both. And unfortunately in his case . . . the evil consequences of his moral deficiencies are still in full vigour.[51]

W. E. H. Lecky noted that in Duffy's writings

O'Connell always appears as half-patriot, half-charlatan, a man of amazing abilities, sincerely devoted to his people and his creed, and in many respects in advance of his time, but untruthful, rapacious, unscrupulous, overbearing, very rarely acting through motives that were purely single-minded and disinterested.[52]

Duffy was strongly critical of O'Connell for basing his campaign on 'moral force' while also threatening resistance to English coercion, observing that 'men cannot have the benefit of two contradictory policies at the same time; and by adopting them alternately he forfeited the advantages of both'.[53]

The capitulation at Clontarf was seen as crucial: Duffy maintained that O'Connell's squandering of the opportunity to mount a successful challenge against British rule induced a legacy of national shame and that 'The abortive insurrection of '48, and the Fenian conspiracy which followed nearly 20 years later, were stimulated by a national pride wounded and humbled in 1843'.[54] Duffy's criticisms were all the more telling for their apparent restraint. In his 1965 biography of Daniel O'Connell, Angus MacIntyre described Duffy's *Young Ireland* as a 'classic account . . . [and] still indispensable'. Despite Duffy's 'subtly disguised' political prejudices, he considered it a work 'of absorbing interest, accurate, well-written and full of interesting character judgements'.[55]

Both Duffy and Doheny presented the history of the repeal movement after Clontarf as a struggle between the liberal Young Irelanders 'and a rather inept ultra-clerical group led by John O'Connell, with the Liberator an old and broken man dominated by his favourite son'.[56] They stressed the decline in O'Connell's mental powers, aggravated by the strain of his prolonged trial and imprisonment in 1844. Duffy's verdict that O'Connell was suffering from 'softening of the brain' from 1844 onwards was widely accepted by later writers and used to account for actions which seemed less sure-footed and more vindictive than in the past.[57] The accepted narrative became one in which O'Connell's diminishing vigour manifested itself in an increasing conservatism which aggravated tensions with the Young Irelanders on interdenominational education, federalism, and the Whig alliance; the waning of O'Connell's powers and his growing antipathy to Young Ireland were seen to be closely linked. O'Connell's insistence on the explicit renunciation of violence was simply a ruse to force his critics out of the Repeal Association. Duffy maintained that O'Connell had yielded to the persuasions of Irish Whigs close to the British government and agreed to abandon repeal in favour of reforms which would raise Ireland 'to a perfect equality with England'. Government places would then be given to Irishmen recommended by O'Connell and gradually the Protestant Ascendancy would be replaced by an administration dominated by Catholics. In order to accomplish this it was essential that O'Connell eliminate all internal opposition, and chief among them were the incorruptible Young Irelanders.[58]

According to Duffy, the Young Ireland group accepted O'Connell's manoeuvrings 'with a self-control rare in political history'.[59] He maintained that they made many efforts to heal the breach and even after the founding of the Irish Confederation in 1847 sought ways to re-unify Young and Old Ireland, but that their conciliatory efforts were rebuffed by O'Connell, who increasingly had fallen under the influence of small-minded lieutenants, especially his son John. Duffy's view of John O'Connell as an incompetent bigot became the accepted one in subsequent histories. It was John O'Connell who Duffy blamed primarily for the collapse of the Repeal movement after his father's death: 'his father began with a dozen followers and increased them to millions; he began with millions and reduced them to a score or a dozen.'[60]

In his account of the Famine, Duffy did not press the deliberate genocide theory as strongly as Mitchel, but claimed nonetheless that the British government bore much of the responsibility for the calamity. He too painted a vivid picture of Irish ports thronged with ships laden with food for export abroad while millions starved at home. Like Mitchel he was deeply concerned by the moral dimension of the Famine, claiming that the temperance, pride and self-reliance taught by the *Nation* had all been undermined. Doheny, Mitchel and Duffy were at one in arguing that O'Connell's rigid adherence to moral force undermined the campaign for Irish self-government and contributed to the Irish people's passive acceptance of hunger and degradation. Duffy claimed that of all the nations of Europe only the Irish would have accepted their fate so readily, beguiled as they were by O'Connell's exhortation 'to endure all with patience and submission'.[61]

Duffy's account was challenged by some twentieth-century historians. In his history of the Repeal movement Kevin B. Nowlan argued forcefully that O'Connell's actions and correspondence in all but the final months of his life show few signs of terminal decline.[62] Denis Gwynn maintained that O'Connell often showed generosity and tolerance to the Young Irelanders, even when their behaviour was marked by self-righteousness and inflexibility.[63] However by the time Gwynn wrote in 1949 a great deal of damage to O'Connell's reputation had already been done, and the judgements of his political opponents were often accepted as fact. The centenary of O'Connell's death in 1947 was a rather muted affair in which he was remembered primarily as a Catholic rather than a nationalist leader.[64] For some he remained 'a symbol of political imbecility and corruption'.[65] Such an estimation owed much to the popularity of Young Ireland accounts of these time and to the fact that O'Connell did not fit easily into Young Ireland's historical view. He was an innovative politician and organiser, whose combination of mass popular mobilisation and moral force politics had no precedent in Irish history. That one who commanded the allegiance of millions was steadfastly opposed to shedding a single drop of blood to win Ireland's independence was an altogether new concept that some nationalists struggled to comprehend.[66]

In *Four Years of Irish History*, his work on the later history of the Young Ireland movement, Duffy dealt with the various disagreements that convulsed the Young Ireland Irish Confederation in 1847–8. Just as his earlier book had put the Young Irelanders in the right in their disputes with O'Connell, so this put Duffy in the right in his disputes with fellow Young Irelanders. In particular, he took the opportunity to revisit his quarrels with John Mitchel, claiming that when writing for the *Nation*, 'Mitchel tried my patience sorely by defending negro slavery, and denouncing the emancipation of the Jews as an unpardonable sin', and that Duffy was often forced to censor his work.[67]

Such disagreements eventually led Mitchel to leave the *Nation*, but friction with Duffy continued in the Irish Confederation in the early months of 1848. With the Famine showing no sign of abating, Mitchel believed that if the Irish peasantry were to be exterminated, it was better for them to die fighting than endure ignominious death through starvation and disease, and proposed a campaign of refusing to pay rent and poor rates and forcible resistance to evictions that would bring the Irish countryside to boiling-point and eventually erupt in spontaneous insurrection.[68] This horrified Duffy and other moderates, who believed that the Confederation should continue to use legal and consti-tutional means to achieve self-government.[69] All the leading figures in the Confederation, including former allies such as Meagher, O'Gorman and Doheny, opposed Mitchel's policy. Adopting it, they maintained, would mean throwing away the support of landlords and the middle class merely to gain whatever fragment of the disaffected peasantry were prepared to defy their priests. Moreover, most of the peasantry were in no position to mount an insurrection but were (according to Doheny) 'sicklied, hungry, wasted, exiled, or in their graves'. Any insurrection would be localised and easily defeated, and blood would be shed in vain. The Confederation's support was mainly confined to the towns, and even there they were well outnumbered by O'Connellites. Mitchel's opponents maintained that he knew nothing of the peasantry, and they knew nothing of him: 'The people of Munster,' exclaimed Meagher, 'know as little of Mitchel as of Mahomet!'[70] Duffy, stung by some sharp criticisms from Mitchel, was particularly scathing. He claimed that the 'liberty of opinion' sought by Mitchel was 'liberty to ruin the national cause' and would result in 'chaos and destruction', while O'Gorman dismissed Mitchel and his allies as 'Infant Ireland'. To those who placed Mitchel on the same plane as Davis as a national leader, Duffy maintained that Davis

> was a statesman full of resources, circumspect, accustomed to look behind and before; [Mitchel] was simply a tribune of the people who passionately demanded the people's rights. Their animating motive was far from being identical; Davis loved Ireland, Mitchel hated England.[71]

Duffy's portrait of Mitchel as a reckless extremist was not universally accepted. Mitchel, after all, had written his own version of these events, and had his own partisans. By the time of Mitchel's death in 1875, only weeks after he had been elected MP for County Tipperary, he was regarded as an elder statesman of Irish nationalism who had suffered greatly for his beliefs. Duffy's attacks on him were seen by some as obsessive and spiteful, appearing as they did in a number of different works.[72] Many advanced nationalists greatly admired Mitchel for the depth of his hostility to British imperialism and were contemptuous of Duffy's moderation and political opportunism. Duffy had believed that exposing Mitchel's extremism would damage his reputation, but it was that very extremism that appealed to some readers. In the 1890s a new generation of radical nationalist journalists would taunt Duffy with the name of John Mitchel, preferring to see themselves as followers of the fiery rebel rather than the respectable statesman.[73]

Duffy's portrayal of other Young Ireland colleagues was generally sympathetic, praising both their political idealism and personal virtues:

> their intercourse . . . was familiar and cordial, free from priggery, and easily bubbling into badinage and laughter. So purifying is the passion of patriotism that I never saw one of these young men gravely exceed in wine, or heard one of them utter a coarsely licentious jest.[74]

Reluctant to criticise any of those who took part in the insurrection of July 1848 (especially William Smith O'Brien, to whom he was politically close), he regretted that more detailed preparations had not been made, but believed that after the suspension of habeas corpus taking up arms was the only honourable course open to the Confederation leaders. Even Duffy, however, felt compelled to play down the resulting insurrection as 'a poor, feeble, unprosperous essay; a mob of disorganised peasants in frieze coats suppressed by a handful of disciplined peasants in green jackets'.[75] Writing in the 1880s after a respectable political career, Duffy was anxious to distance himself from the insurrectionary tradition of Irish nationalism, which had largely been appropriated by American and Irish Fenians and violent splinter groups whose bombing campaigns and assassinations he strongly denounced. In describing the 1848 uprising he stressed the honour and chivalry of its leaders who confronted crown forces openly in the field, and claimed that the event was 'dignified and sublimed by the unflinching courage and devotion of the men engaged in it'.[76] He was determined that a failed rebellion should not detract from Young Ireland's reputation, noting that

> with rare exceptions they lived and died in their original convictions. We can now conceive that their first work was their wisest and best, and that Irish nationality would have fared better if there had never been a French Revolution of 1848. That

transaction arrested a work which was a necessary preliminary to social or political independence: the education of a people long depressed by poverty or injustice, in fair play, public spirit or manliness.[77]

Duffy insisted his work was 'not a panegyric on the Young Irelanders, but a narrative of the transactions in which they were chiefly concerned' and that he had 'described with complete unreserve the faults by which they failed and fell'.[78] But at all times he attributed the highest motives to his Young Ireland colleagues, and implied their moral superiority to O'Connell and his followers. He claimed they were thoroughly non-sectarian and incorruptible, sought no jobs or material rewards for their work, and were never prepared to barter Irish independence for political or personal gain. He noted that while 'O'Connell received an income from the people far beyond the official salary of the president of the American republic or the prime minister of any constitutional kingdom in Europe', Davis 'never accepted so much as a postage stamp from the repeal funds'.[79]

In 1890 Duffy added a major biography of Davis to his accounts of Young Ireland (he also published a short life of Davis in 1896).[80] His attitude towards Davis was one of simple hero worship: 'It never has been my good fortune to meet so noble a human creature; so variously gifted, unaffectedly just, generous and upright, so utterly without selfishness and without vanity; and I never expect to meet such another'.[81] This was the first substantial work to be published on Davis since his death in 1845, and its portrayal of an idealistic and self-sacrificing patriot revived interest in his writings and helped establish his reputation as a central figure in Irish nationalism, especially among those who promoted Irish-Ireland ideals in the 1890s.[82] Duffy wrote of these events with genuine personal modesty, and usually downplayed his own contribution.[83] He emerges from his books as a secondary player, but, as Kevin B. Nowlan suggests, 'He was certainly a much more active and controversial figure in the eighteen-forties than his own books suggest.'[84] His work was crucial in helping to establish Davis's reputation, and his own relative neglect owes is partly explained by the fact that he outlived all his Young Ireland contemporaries and no one did the same for him.

No accounts of this period written by an O'Connellite had anything like the same influence as Duffy's work. Richard Barrett's splenetic *History of the Irish Confederation* (1849) denounced the Young Ireland movement as irresponsible incendiaries and traitors to Irish nationalism, but had little enough impact in its own day and was soon forgotten. Most later nationalists took the Young Irelanders at their own estimate as noble patriots. Shane Leslie, in an essay on 'Irish Leaders' written in 1914, argued that the history of [Young Ireland's] failure is brighter in literature than the tale of O'Connell's triumphs. To read Duffy's *Young Ireland* and Mitchel's *Jail Journal* with draughts from the *Spirit of the Nation* is to relive the period. Without the Young Irelanders, Irish nationalism might not have survived the Famine.[85]

For P. S. O'Hegarty, the Young Irelanders were

> a group such as has not been seen in Ireland since, in quite the same brilliance, unselfishness, and generous-mindedness. They were interested in Goodness as a virtue, in Nobility of thought as well as of act, and all meanness, all littleness, were abhorrent to them. They were, above all, righteous men . . . essentially generous, fairminded, and good, hating cant, hating narrowness and intolerance, always speaking the truth, writing the truth, and acting the truth. They kept their knightly honour unstained. And they have since been a beacon light to every unselfish and generous soul in Ireland.[86]

Duffy's work also made strong claims for the long-term political influence of Young Ireland, particularly in laying the foundations for an effective Irish parliamentary party. According to Duffy, this was something to which O'Connell attached little importance, since he had achieved his greatest triumph – Catholic emancipation – by mobilising mass public opinion rather than working through parliament. He then tried to achieve repeal of the union in the same manner, by building up the Repeal Association, raising subscriptions and showing the great support he enjoyed through mass public demonstrations. Duffy maintained that during this time the Young Ireland group saw the need to establish a strong base in parliament, and after they broke away from O'Connell, Duffy prepared a report for the Irish Confederation calling for the creation of a disciplined Irish party to obstruct parliamentary business at Westminster to focus attention on Ireland's demands for self-government.[87]

On his release from prison in 1848, Duffy was determined to implement the plan to create a parliamentary party to provide leadership for nationalist Ireland.[88] His efforts contributed to the founding of an independent Irish party of 40 MPs that was allied with the newly founded Tenant League in the early 1850s, forming a novel conjunction of political and agrarian interests that appealed to supporters of tenant right in both north and south. It split in the mid-1850s after leading members accepted government office, but Duffy, its main strategist, claimed that it helped lay the foundations for the more effective Irish party that emerged in the 1870s and that the principles embodied in the land legislation of the 1880s were first set out by the Tenant League in 1850.[89]

His account of these events, *The League of North and South*, was published in 1886, the year in which the Irish Parliamentary Party led by Charles Stewart Parnell was at the height of its power and influence, and the book was dedicated to Justin McCarthy, one of Parnell's main lieutenants. Duffy argued that

> the present Irish party in more prosperous days have simply administered the principles, and executed the designs, devised by their predecessors in the midst of famine and disaster; that a single concession has not been won for the Irish people, or sought on their behalf, which may not be traced back to the labours of the men sent to parliament in 1852.[90]

While paying tribute to the effectiveness of the campaign for Home Rule in the 1880s, he felt obliged to remind McCarthy that 'you failed to win the ear of the North – you failed to unite the four provinces on a common platform as your predecessors did'.[91] Duffy claimed that one of the shortcomings of the politicians of the 1880s was their imperfect knowledge of the 'unwritten history of the last thirty years – a history which concerns them so nearly' and that Parnell was unaware that the policy of 'Independent Opposition was formulated by the Young Irelanders in contrast to the place-begging policy defended in Conciliation Hall; and was propounded anew as a more hopeful resource than Mr Mitchel's proposal of refusing to pay poor rate'.[92]

As with the Young Ireland historians of the 1840s, Duffy believed that it was his duty to defend his country's reputation and counter the arguments of anti-Irish historians. In 1872 the English historian James Anthony Froude published the first volume of his *The English in Ireland in the Eighteenth Century* (3 vols, 1872–4). Coming only two years after the launch of the Home Government Association by Isaac Butt, it adopted the traditional anti-Irish and anti-Catholic arguments of earlier historians and maintained that the Irish were incapable of self-government because of fundamental character flaws, and that the English, as a superior people, had the right to rule Ireland.[93] In countering Froude's prejudices, Duffy sought to appeal to 'the conscience of the best class of Englishmen' and to make them understand why so many Irish people were discontented under British rule. His moderation and calm tone (as well his knighthood) made his work all the more persuasive to English readers. The root causes of Irish discontent, he argued, were to be found in the country's history, and while he appreciated 'the loathing that sensitive Englishmen feel in descending into the catacombs of the Past, and handling the skeletons and cerements of historic crimes', he invited them 'to look at transactions which are not remote or ghastly, which happened in their own day, for which they cannot altogether evade a personal responsibility'.[94]

Duffy argued that the national policy of the Young Irelanders was 'the creation of remote causes and antecedent forces' and the English would never understand its 'extraordinary ascendancy over the public mind . . . till they have obtained some knowledge of the main facts of Irish history'.[95] He therefore proposed to preface his history of the Young Ireland movement with a short historical introduction that would 'touch only on events the consequences of which were still traceable in the habits and character of the people in the middle of the nineteenth century'.[96] The result was a chapter entitled 'A bird's eye view of Irish history', a short account of Irish history from the earliest times which summarised the history-writing of his Young Ireland colleagues. In a restrained but assertive manner, it catalogued the many injustices that Ireland had received at Britain's hands, and argued that it was little wonder that the Irish should seek to overthrow such an oppressive regime. Duffy's work was singled out by the old Fenian John O'Leary as the best of all rebuttals of Froude's charges, and helped rehabilitate his reputation with some separatist nationalists.[97] Thomas Clarke Luby for example, was a supporter of Mitchel and contemptuous of Duffy's knighthood and constitutional politics, but was impressed by the latter's histories, praising their 'Strong, robust, didactic English . . . freighted with deep thoughts, clear ideas and profound reasons'.[98]

By prefacing his work on Young Ireland with 'A bird's eye view of Irish history', Duffy managed to blend together the various personalised memoirs and accounts of his own times with the earlier Young Ireland history-writing project, producing a comprehensive view of Irish history in which Young Ireland both recorded and shaped events. Mitchel did the same by using the *Last Conquest of Ireland* as the final chapters of his *History of Ireland* (1869). Young Ireland used the writing of history to set themselves at the centre of events and claim their movement as the culmination of the nationalist forces that had preceded them. The works of Duffy, Mitchel and Doheny are far from a unified body of work and disagree on several fundamental points, but they have certain themes in common, notably the faults and errors of Daniel O'Connell, the callous indifference of the British government to the suffering of the Irish people during the Famine, and the idealistic self-sacrificing patriotism of the Young Irelanders. As the records of witnesses to and participants in the events they describe, these first-hand accounts carried considerable authority and were central in shaping nationalist perceptions of Ireland's most calamitous decade.

SEVEN

CONTINUITIES

FROM THE CELTIC UNION TO GRIFFITH'S 'BALLAD HISTORY'

—

HISTORY WRITING AFTER 1848

After the 1848 insurrection most of the Young Irelanders were in prison or in exile and the group ceased to exist as a functioning political entity. Their ideals, however, proved more resilient. For a time most nationalists were wary of openly expressing their aspirations for national independence, often confining themselves to drawing attention to pressing agrarian and economic issues, but by the early 1850s some were again using explicit cultural and historical arguments to advance the nationalist cause. Foremost among them was Dr Robert Cane of Kilkenny, a leading member of the Irish Confederation who, with Duffy's help, in October 1853 founded the Celtic Union, a nationalist literary society based in Kilkenny that sought to revive the spirit of Young Ireland. It announced that 'For years the voice of Nationality has been dumb in Ireland . . . Our ancient and pious ambition to restore our country to her forfeited place in the universe has almost ceased to find utterance'. The society proposed to cultivate 'a literature which concerns itself with the struggles and triumphs of our race' and to emulate the Library of Ireland by publishing

> Books and Tracts, dealing with historical, social, and industrial subjects, calculated to keep up the spirit, to stimulate the enterprise, and to inform the minds of our people . . . that the Union may become an extern teacher to perfect the education of our children, from which a knowledge of their own country is so habitually excluded.[1]

The works published by the Celtic Union were similar to the Young Ireland publications of the 1840s, including histories, collections of verse and historical novels such as the *History of the Invasion of Ireland by the Anglo-Normans* (1856) by Gerald Supple; *The History of the Williamite and Jacobite Wars in Ireland* (1859) by Robert Cane; *Alice: A Historical Romance of the Crusaders in Ireland* (1862) by J. T. Campion, and a collection of poetry,

Versicles (1856) by Thomas Irwin. The society acted as a lively forum for the discussion of Irish history and literature and prominent members included the nationalist writers William Kenealy, John Walsh, Robert Dwyer Joyce and Charles J. Kickham.[2] It produced a weekly magazine, the *Celt*, edited initially by Cane and after his death in 1858 by Campion, which appeared irregularly from August 1857 to November 1859. The *Celt* took its inspiration from the original *Nation*, announcing that its mission was 'To stir up past memories. To develop existing energies and resources, and to direct the national heart to pulsate with pride for the past and hope for the future'. It stressed the importance of Irish history to the nation's self-respect, arguing that 'the history of a nation is its second and higher life . . . [and] people whose achievements find no place in the annals of humanity class as a mere rabble'. While acknowledging the despondency that had settled on Ireland in the wake of the Famine, it sought to inspire its readers with the courage and endurance of past generations, announcing that 'not only does the history of this country remain to be written – it requires to be acted'.[3]

As the country recovered from the ravages of the Famine, increasing levels of prosperity and literacy created a growing market for books, newspapers and magazines. The removal of taxes on advertisements in 1853 and newspapers in 1855 gave a further stimulus to the print industry, and during the decade several new publications appeared. Although no single paper could lay claim to the influence exerted by the *Nation* in the 1840s, a broad range of nationalist newspapers repeated its formula of news, poetry, politics and history. In July 1858 the Young Ireland veteran John Edward Pigot and Denis Holland, a Cork-born journalist and follower of John Mitchel, founded the *Irishman: A Weekly Journal of Irish National Politics and Literature*. Holland claimed that a new paper was needed because the *Nation* (edited from 1858 by A. M. Sullivan) had departed from the spirit of Young Ireland by becoming politically timid and culturally conservative. The *Irishman* claimed that it would carry on the work of the original *Nation* and, quoting Davis, stated that its aim was to 'create a race of men full of a more intensely Irish character and knowledge'.[4]

In March 1859 M. J. McCann, author of some of the most stirring historical ballads in the *Nation* such as 'O'Donnell abu', launched the *Harp*, a monthly magazine published in Cork which combined Catholic and nationalist sympathies and featured articles on Irish history, antiquities and literature. In the manner of the *Nation*, it celebrated Irish military valour, notably with a serialised account of the Williamite wars written by McCann himself. However, it lasted only for a few months until October 1859. When McCann revived it in March 1863 as the *Irish Harp*, the same themes predominated: a series of long essays on 'Cromwell's Wars' claimed that the fanaticism of English Puritans exceeded that of Muslim zealots in the seventh century, noting that 'the Saracens were generally sincere – the Puritans still more generally were the rankest of hypocrites; while for remorseless cruelty, rapacity, and falsehood, the latter were incomparably more notorious than their eastern prototypes'.[5] Like McCann's earlier publication, the *Irish Harp* emphasised the historic persecution of Irish Catholics. It claimed that the history of Ireland since the Reformation

> has no parallel among human records . . . The scenes that ensued constitute a chapter of horrors which England may well wish to see blotted from the page of history; and it is no marvel that she should not wish it to be taught in Irish 'National schools'.[6]

The *Irish Harp* was a forcefully written publication, but it appeared irregularly and sold poorly, and finished after only four issues in February 1864.

Some of the *Nation*'s writers who had not been involved in the 1848 insurrection remained in Ireland afterwards and continued to write history. In the case of Fr C. P. Meehan, this involved turning away from Irish history to less controversial subjects. Meehan's involvement with Young Ireland had antagonised his clerical superiors, and after 1848 he devoted himself to his translation from the Italian of Marchese's *Lives of the Most Eminent Sculptors and Architects of the Order of St Dominic* (1852). It was only some decades later that he returned to the writing of Irish history, publishing *The Fate and Fortunes of Hugh O'Neill, Earl of Tyrone, and Rory O'Donel, Earl of Tyrconnel* (1868) (popularly known as 'The Flight of the Earls', with revised editions in 1870, 1872, 1877, and 1886), and *The Rise and Fall of the Irish Franciscan Monasteries* (1869) (revised editions 1870, 1872, 1877), in which he emphasised the heroism and sufferings of Irish Catholics down through the centuries. Meehan, whose work was generally based on more extensive research than most other popular history, also took the opportunity to amend and expand his earlier books, producing revised editions of *The Geraldines* (as *The Rise, Increase, and Exit of the Geraldines* (1878)), *The Confederation of Kilkenny* (1882), and Lynch's *Life of Kirwan* (1884). He also edited and published some of R. R. Madden's research and poetry as *Literary Remains of the United Irishmen* (1887). Duffy strongly praised his constancy and compared him to the great patriotic clerical scholars of the past who had devoted their lives to the study of Irish history.[7] Meehan's books were strongly Catholic and nationalist in tone, and leaned towards a stronger 'faith and fatherland' interpretation than most other Young Ireland writers. This tendency became more pronounced in nationalist history writing from the 1850s onwards as the non-sectarian idealism of Davis faded and neo-Young Ireland publications such as the *Celt*, the *Harp*, and the post-Duffy *Nation* openly proclaimed their Catholic sympathies.

Although Duffy was initially reluctant to include historical verse in the *Nation* after its re-launch in September 1849, it soon reappeared in the paper, and patriotic songs and ballads modelled on those of Young Ireland became a regular feature in other nationalist newspapers. The constant reprinting of Young Ireland ballad collections testified to a steady demand for historical verse. Duffy's *Ballad Poetry of Ireland* went through 39 editions between 1845 and 1866, and was reprinted frequently after that, and new editions of *The Spirit of the Nation* appeared every few years, bringing Young Ireland verse to generations of new readers (a 59th edition was published as late as 1934). Popular collections of verse, much of it historical, were issued by Young Irelanders such as John Savage (1850), Denis Florence MacCarthy (1850), John de Jean Frazer (1851), Elizabeth Willoughby Varian ('Finola') (1851) and Jane Francesca Elgee ('Speranza') (1864). Edward Hayes's comprehensive anthology *Ballads of Ireland* (1857) was dedicated to Charles Gavan Duffy, and its selection of historical ballads was dominated by the works of Young Ireland. These patriotic hymn-books became the most pervasive means of disseminating popular nationalist history and the most enduring legacy of Young Ireland. In his *Treasury of Irish Poetry* (1900), the poet and critic T. W. Rolleston claimed that 'The *Nation* poets inspired, almost recreated, Ireland; and their work still continues to inspire Irishmen all over the world with its nationalising spirit'.[8]

In 1857 the Irish Republican Brotherhood (which became better known under the name of its American wing, 'The Fenians') was founded. Many Fenians had been members of the Young Ireland Confederate clubs in the 1840s, but James Stephens, the main founder and driving force of the new organisation, was anxious to distance it from its Young Ireland origins. Stephens took a dim view of the Young Irelanders as revolutionists and believed that their fascination with literature had distracted them from the more important work of conspiracy and insurrection. He dismissed those who devoted themselves to 'creating an Irish national literature, schools of Irish art, and things of this sort' as 'dilettante patriots, perhaps the greatest fools of all'.[9] Although the Fenian newspaper the *Irish People* occasionally included historical articles, these were usually related to relatively recent events such as the rising of 1798, in which the courage and determination of the United Irishmen was contrasted with the half-heartedness of the Young Irelanders.[10] Committed to winning Irish independence through armed revolution, the paper expressed its contempt for those intent on 'smashing the Saxon foe to atoms in rhyme or prose'.[11]

There were, however, Fenians who took a different view to Stephens, believing that literature had its part to play in the national struggle, and the writing of historical ballads was taken up by Fenian writers such as John

Keegan Casey, John Francis O'Donnell, Michael Cavanagh and Stephen Joseph Meany. The very name 'Fenians' was coined by John O'Mahony, who had organised Confederate Clubs in south Tipperary in 1848 and had a deep interest in the Gaelic past, devoting many years of his life to producing an English translation of Keating's *Foras Feasa ar Éirinn* (1857) (with an introduction written by the Young Irelander Michael Doheny). Many prominent Fenians recorded that it was the *Nation* that first sparked their national enthusiasm.[12] John O'Leary recalled Davis as 'the fountain and origin' of his national feelings and maintained that 'If Young Ireland had failed and failed definitively in her revolutionary policy, she had certainly not failed in her educating and propagandist policy. The soul she had brought into Eire still stirred in many of us'.[13] O'Leary's views were echoed by other prominent Fenians such as John Devoy, Thomas Clarke Luby, William O'Brien and John Denvir. All attached great importance to their youthful reading in nationalist reading rooms and remembered being inspired by the works of Young Ireland: Devoy claimed that 'No weekly paper in Europe was equal to the old *Nation*'.[14] The industrious Luby wrote a number of significant historical works focusing on prominent figures in Irish history such as his *Illustrious Irishmen* (1878) or *The Story of Ireland's Struggle for Self-Government with the Lives and Times of her Great Leaders* (1893), and admitted to being inspired by Davis's 'glorious ideal of the way in which Irish story should be told'.[15] Some Fenians also sought to emulate Young Ireland's publishing schemes to provide cheap and accessible historical material. John Denvir started a printing and publishing business in Liverpool and from 1870 published the Penny Illustrated Irish Library series 'of biographies, stories, songs, and stirring episodes of Irish history' which proved very popular among the Irish community in Britain. Its publications included an account of the 1798 Rebellion, a life of Robert Emmet, a collection of street ballads, a life of John Mitchel and a short catechism of Irish history.[16]

The success of nationalist publishing ventures in the 1840s had convinced the publisher James Duffy that there was a lucrative market for history, and after 1848 he continued to publish cheap history books and ballad collections. In many cases he simply republished Library of Ireland bestsellers (especially *The Spirit of the Nation*), but he also offered nationalist writers an outlet for new works. He produced a series of magazines from the late 1840s onwards, such as the *Irish Catholic Magazine*, the *Fireside Magazine*, the *Hibernian Magazine* and the *Illustrated Dublin Journal* – all of which included articles on Irish history and antiquities, marked by patriotism and piety. Duffy had a keen eye for the public's tastes and was able to take advantage of a major distribution network with agents in Glasgow, Liverpool, Manchester, Birmingham and London – all places with significant Irish populations – and in 1869 established his own office in London.[17] The Glasgow publisher Cameron and Ferguson was also important. Founded in 1860 by the Belfast-born John Ferguson (whose conversion to Irish nationalism was strongly influenced by the writings of John Mitchel), it became a key publisher of significant works of Irish history by Young Irelanders and their disciples over the next 30 years, serving a growing Irish market in Great Britain and at home.[18]

HISTORY AND THE DIASPORA

Many nationalists despaired at the mass emigration from Ireland during and after the Famine, believing that such migrants would be lost forever, and that a falling population would sap the country's lifeblood and undermine her claims to nationhood. However, by creating substantial Irish communities across the globe, emigration helped make Irish nationalism an international force and fuelled the demand for Irish nationalist literature. The prejudice or feelings of alienation that immigrants often faced in their new lands encouraged them to look to their own national culture. Many took solace in Ireland's stories and songs, and pride in her long rich historical tradition. The journalist and land reformer Patrick Ford, who was born in Galway in 1837 but grew up in Boston, admitted that he knew little of Irish history until the anti-Irish and anti-Catholic prejudices he encountered in the 1850s inspired him to learn more of his origins.[19] For such immigrants nationalist reading rooms in foreign cities provided supportive spaces in which Irish books and newspapers were avidly read.[20] Irish-American publishers saw a ready market for Irish history, especially the popular works of Young Ireland. In Philadelphia Henry Carey re-published the entire Library of Ireland series; in Boston Patrick Donahoe published *The Spirit of the Nation* (1844) and T. F. Meagher's *Orations* (1856); in New York P. J. Kenedy published Mitchel's *Life of Aodh O'Neill* (1879) and Meehan's *The Fate and Fortunes of Hugh O'Neill* (1897), and Patrick Martin Haverty published a collection of Davis's *Poems* (1854), John O'Mahony's translation of Keating's *Foras Feasa ar Éirinn* as *The History of Ireland* (1857), Mitchel's *Memoir of Thomas Devin Reilly* (1857), the first collection of James Clarence Mangan's *Poems* (1859) and an edition of Mitchel's *Jail Journal* (1868).[21]

Exiled Young Irelanders who had contributed successfully to the Library of Ireland in the 1840s continued to write histories that told of the courage and fortitude of an ancient and proud people, and these too were published by Irish-American firms. Thomas D'Arcy McGee was especially prolific, writing such works as *A History of Irish Settlers in North America* (1851), *A History of the Attempts to Establish the Protestant Reformation in Ireland* (1853), and *A Popular History of Ireland, from the Earliest Times to the Emancipation of the Catholics*

(1863). *A History of Irish Settlers in North America* was the first major work on the Irish in America and detailed the heroic efforts of Irish immigrants in helping to establish and consolidate the American republic. McGee argued that the Irish had made a decisive contribution to America in business, politics and war and had been to the fore in spreading democracy and Catholicism throughout North America and in keeping British influence at bay. Predictably enough, his arguments were well received by the Irish-American community and the book sold well, going through six editions in four years. In keeping with the history written by the Young Irelanders, his work had a clear purpose: McGee openly stated that it was intended 'to encourage Irish Americans to emulate the example of their illustrious predecessors and seize the unprecedented opportunities that were opening up in the American North-West'.[22]

The *Protestant Reformation in Ireland* was written by McGee after his conversion to ultramontane Catholicism in the early 1850s and portrayed Irish history from the sixteenth century onwards as the story of a steadfast people who had struggled bravely against the persecution of foreign oppressors. Far from weakening their attachment to their faith, such persecution had strengthened it and made it an indissoluble element of their nationality. Throughout the ages it had been defended by heroes and martyrs such as Roger O'Moore, Owen Roe O'Neill and Oliver Plunkett, and their struggle had culminated in the achievement of Catholic emancipation in 1829.[23]

McGee's most comprehensive work was his *Popular History of Ireland* which, despite being written from a Catholic and nationalist point of view, eschewed some of the partisan extremes of his earlier work. Written primarily 'for the use and instruction of our countrymen and women in America', it recounted Irish resistance to foreign invaders from the beginnings of recorded time. It stressed the cultured, chivalrous and pious nature of Gaelic civilisation, its tenacity in the face of adversity, and its courage in defeat, noting that after the Williamite wars the Irish 'had wrung even from their adversaries the reputation of being "one of the most warlike of nations"'.[24] The story continued through the persecution of Catholics in the eighteenth century, the military outrages of the 1790s, and the treacherous means employed to pass the act of union. McGee added his own slant to the usual themes of nationalist history by praising Patriotic Whigs such as Henry Grattan and John Philpot Curran at the expense of separatist radicals like Wolfe Tone and, in line with his own political thinking at the time, his work shows a marked preference for the constitutionalist over the conspirator.[25] Like his *Protestant Reformation in Ireland* it ended with the achievement of Catholic emancipation and looked to a future without religious persecution or discrimination in which people of all faiths would work together. It proved a highly popular work in both Ireland and North America, going through several editions and becoming a standard nationalist account. The editor of the *Nation*, A. M. Sullivan, thought it 'the best history of Ireland yet written and the best likely to be written within the same compass in our time'.[26] It earned McGee election to the Royal Irish Academy in 1864 and his biographer considers it 'the crowning achievement of McGee's literary career'.[27]

John Mitchel added to the historical works of exiled Young Irelanders with *The History of Ireland from the Treaty of Limerick to the Present Time*, published in New York in 1868. He styled his work as a continuation of the Abbé James MacGeoghegan's *History of Ireland* (1758–63), one of the few general histories of Ireland that was well regarded by Young Ireland.[28] Mitchel claimed that he was carrying on MacGeoghegan's work, arguing that he would have wanted

> the dark record of the English atrocity in Ireland, which he left unfinished, to be daily brought down through all its subsequent scenes of horror and slaughter, which have been still more terrible after his day than they were before.[29]

He contended that his work was merely a factual history with 'very few opinions or theories put forward at all' since the simple presentation of the facts of the oppressions and devastations inflicted on Ireland since 1691 would leave readers in no doubt as to the justice of Ireland's cause.[30] He described the entire history of Ireland from the Treaty of Limerick onwards as 'one long and continual breach of this treaty', with the result that from 1691 the Catholics of Ireland effectively disappeared from political history and only emerged again with the formation of the Volunteers in the 1770s.[31] During this period the best of Ireland's youth, oppressed and humiliated at home, emigrated to fight for foreign powers and, with the cry 'Remember Limerick' on their lips, proved their valour in battle after battle. According to Mitchel, 'all these true Irishmen were lost to their own country, and were forced to shed their blood for the stranger . . . so that the remaining masses of abject people might be the more helpless in the hands of their enemies.'[32]

Mitchel brought his history up to his own day by incorporating the chapters of *The Last Conquest of Ireland (Perhaps)* to describe the condition of Ireland from 1843 to 1851 and place the Famine in a continuum of a century and a half of persecution and treachery. He argued that while in the past the English had attempted to exterminate the Irish with fire and sword, they now used political economy to starve them and uproot them from the land. Such relentless oppression led him to conclude that 'while England lives and flourishes, Ireland must die a daily death, and suffer an endless martyrdom; and that if Irishmen are ever to enjoy the rights of human beings, the British Empire must first perish'.[33]

Mitchel's history enjoyed considerable popularity. It linked together the grievances of past and present and offered a cogent explanation for Irish poverty and humiliation. Although it said little that was new, it said it with Mitchel's usual verve and outspokenness, arguing that English governments had pursued a consistent policy of perfidy and cruelty from the betrayal of Limerick to the attempted genocide of the Famine. As with other Young Ireland histories it emphasised the stubbornness of Irish resistance, asserting that having withstood England's latest diabolical attempt at extermination, the Irish people had again proved the resilience of their national spirit and were not without hope. Mitchel himself was dissatisfied with the book, having rushed it to make the publisher's deadline, but it had many admirers and played an important part in moulding the historical outlook of Irish nationalists.[34] W. E. H. Lecky noted that

> Mitchel's Irish history has had more effect on the popular mind than any other work – it is circulated everywhere at a low price and is to be found in most farm-houses and cottages. It is of course written in the most bitter anti-English spirit.[35]

Not surprisingly, separatist nationalists tended to prefer it to Lecky's work. P. S. O'Hegarty argued that it was far superior to Lecky's *Ireland in the Eighteenth Century* which was merely

> a history of the English garrison in Ireland . . . Mitchel's is the better history and the better book. It deals both with the Irish nation and the English garrison, never forgetting that it is a history of a nation and not the history of a colony, the history of a noble people in bondage, not the history of a slave civilization.[36]

Recalling the influences that had made him a separatist, an IRA officer of the War of Independence from County Mayo cited his father, a Fenian, who had Mitchel's *History of Ireland* 'off by heart'.[37]

The writing of history by Young Ireland exiles abroad was mostly the work of isolated individuals, and lacked the co-operation and collegiality that had marked the writing of the Library of Ireland. In 1847 McGee had dedicated his *Life of Art MacMurrogh* to Mitchel, but by the time they wrote their respective histories of Ireland, the two men were bitter enemies, and their political differences extended to their writings. While McGee identified with the Patriot-Whig tradition, Mitchel denounced Henry Grattan for his 'superstitious reverence' for constitutional agitation and the Irish parliament, claiming that if he had supported the United Irishmen 'he, with his powerful political following, could have given to that organisation a consistency and a power such as it never possessed, and might have made of Ninety-eight a greater Eighty-two'.[38] Mitchel identified his own radical wing of Young Ireland with the United Irishmen – 'the bravest and purest men whom Ireland ever produced' – noting that the execution of Thomas Russell in Downpatrick in 1803 marked 'the end of the United Irishmen – at least for that generation'.[39] Battles between constitutionalists and revolutionaries that had been fought out in the Irish Confederation in the early months of 1848 were afterwards carried on in the writing of history, with McGee identifying the struggle for Irish independence as a continuation of the Patriot campaign for legislative autonomy while Mitchel drew his inspiration from the separatist republicans who sought the violent overthrow of British rule in 1798.

In both cases, however, their decisions to write lengthy surveys of Irish history owed much to the Young Ireland project of the 1840s, especially to Thomas Davis's desire for an accessible nationalist history that told Ireland's story from the earliest times to the present.[40] The rapidly moving events of the 1840s were not conducive to the production of such a comprehensive work, but the time and distance provided by exile allowed both men the opportunity to realise Davis's wish. In doing so, they produced works of history that resonated strongly with Irish readers at home and abroad, and were of particular importance in shaping the identity of the Irish diaspora by constructing an interpretation of the past in which emigrants 'were the dispossessed exiles expelled from the homeland by the malevolent British government in Ireland'.[41]

FURTHER EDUCATION

Just like the *Nation* in the 1840s, nationalist newspapers continued to voice their concerns about the teaching of Irish children in state-sponsored schools. Holland's *Irishman* claimed that the British government was intent on eradicating Irish nationality by training 'our youth in treason to their country as well as to the Church of our ancestors'.[42] In particular, nationalists focused their misgivings at the system of state education by criticising the absence of Irish history from the school curriculum.[43] Claiming that Irish children were being encouraged to ignore and despise their own history, nationalists set about developing an alternative curriculum. Their periodicals often had sections devoted to younger readers and a number of magazines were specifically produced to provide the historical knowledge unavailable at school.[44] Typical of these was A. M. Sullivan's *Young Ireland: An Irish Magazine of Entertainment and Instruction*, a weekly illustrated publication which ran from 1875 to 1891 and featured dramatic stories from Irish history alongside exotic tales by Captain Mayne Reid and others. It treated Irish history as an adventure story, with exciting accounts of the victories of the Irish Brigade on the Continent or the heroic deeds of Sarsfield and Sergeant Custume during the Williamite wars.[45] Such publications also provided alternative reading to the mass of imported English comics celebrating the real and imaginary adventures of imperial heroes that nationalists saw as a corrupting influence on Irish youth.

As editor of the *Nation*, Sullivan saw himself as a guardian of the Young Ireland tradition and was intent on continuing its work.[46] He had considerable success in reaching a young readership with his best-selling *The Story of Ireland* (1867), a single-volume distillation of the history writing of the Young Irelanders that relied heavily on the work of McGee, Mitchel and Meehan. Joep Leerssen has noted that its format and style are strongly influenced by the advice given by Davis in the *Nation* on the writing and presentation of history, and that it presents 'an emotive, gripping, pictorial and literary version of "exciting history"' which promiscuously mixed myth and history and recycled earlier nationalist accounts.[47]

Sullivan's work was designed as an uplifting introduction to Irish history for young readers: he described his aim as 'to have a pleasant talk with them about Ireland, to tell its story, after the manner of simple storytellers'. Making a virtue of selectivity, he announced he would avoid confusing young minds

> with a mournful series of feuds, raids and slaughters, merely for the sake of noting them ... I desire to interest them in their country; to convince them that its history is no wild, dreary and uninviting monotony of internecine slaughter, but an entertaining and instructive narrative of stirring events, abounding with episodes thrilling, glorious and bountiful.[48]

As Roy Foster has noted, recounting Ireland's history as a story gave it structure, coherence and easily disgestible moral lessons.[49] To appeal to younger readers the style and presentation were lively and accessible, and it was well-illustrated and supplemented with dramatic historical verse from Davis, Mangan and others. *The Story of Ireland* attempted to give meaning to the diverse struggles of Irish history by arguing that they had all been part of a single unified effort: it concluded that

> other nations have bowed to the yoke of conquest and been wiped out from history ... but Ireland after centuries of suffering and sacrifice such as have tried no other nation in the world, has successfully, proudly, gloriously defended and retained her life, her faith, her nationality.

Because she had survived such trials her people were 'destined to receive the rich reward of such devotion, such constancy, such heroism' since 'an all-wise

Providence has sustained and preserved them for great purpose, for a glorious destiny'.[50] This interpretation of Irish history as a self-contained and coherent 'story' without contradictions or loose ends had enormous appeal. The *Story of Ireland* succeeded admirably in its efforts in making Irish history attractive to young readers: booksellers reported that children bought it with their own pocket money and Éamon de Valera remembered it as the first history book he had ever read.[51]

Between 1851 and 1911 the literacy rate in Ireland rose from 53 per cent to 88 per cent and the number of newspapers from 109 in 1853 to 230 in 1913, even though the population was declining.[52] Print culture became ever more important and reading rooms an integral part of nationalist and agrarian movements. During the 1880s numerous nationalist and literary societies were affiliated to the Parnellite Irish National Land League, and these were described as 'the true heirs-at-law of Thomas Davis's reading rooms of forty years ago'.[53] Even the reading rooms of non-political bodies such as mechanic's institutes, temperance clubs and religious societies usually included nationalist newspapers, history books and collections of patriotic verse. In 1883 a priest in charge of a Catholic Young Men's Society noted that its members read almost exclusively Irish history, poetry and biography, the prime subjects of Young Ireland's history-writing project.[54] A survey of the reading habits of the Catholic Young Men's Society in County Cork found that among the most popular works were Mitchel's *Jail Journal* (1854) and *History of Ireland* (1869), McGee's *Popular History of Ireland* (1867), Duffy's *Young Ireland* (1880) and *Four Years of Irish History* (1883), O'Callaghan's *History of the Irish Brigades* (1854), A. M. Sullivan's *Story of Ireland* (1867), and T. D. Sullivan's *Penny Readings for the Irish People* (1879), a selection of Young Ireland prose and verse.[55]

By the early 1880s the term 'Young Ireland' enjoyed a new vogue, being adopted by several nationalist literary societies.[56] John Dillon MP, son of the founder of the *Nation*, was elected president of the first such society in Dublin in April 1881, and advised its members that the best way to advance the national cause was to immerse themselves in their own history.[57] The Young Ireland societies were anxious to remind people that there was more to Irish nationalism than the parliamentary and agrarian agitations of the 1880s, and often contrasted the idealism and cultural vitality of Davis and his colleagues with the soulless materialism of contemporary constitutional politics. They attached great importance to teaching history to the younger generation, and encouraged them with incentives such as prizes for the best essays in Irish history in the hope that 'knowledge of our country's history, our country's song, will help to buoy every Irishman in their march for political independence'.[58] In June 1885 third place in the Young Ireland society's historical essay competition went to the fourteen-year-old Arthur Griffith, whose prize consisted of Mitchel's *History of Ireland* and *Jail Journal* and Duffy's *Ballad Poetry of Young Ireland*.[59]

In January 1885 the Fenian John O'Leary became president of the Young Ireland Society in Dublin and gave the inaugural address on the subject of 'Young Ireland: the Old and the New'. Praising the literary achievement of the Young Irelanders, he paid tribute to the inspiring effect of their ballads and histories and encouraged his audience to continue their work. In an address reminiscent of Davis's to the College Historical Society in 1840, he argued that a knowledge of history was central to Ireland's national well-being, claiming that the country needed more songs, histories, chronologies and national maps, and that all who loved Ireland should make it their business to mark the birthplaces and graves of national heroes to remind the current generation of their sacrifices for Ireland.[60]

It was through O'Leary that the young W. B. Yeats was introduced to the writings of Young Ireland. Yeats joined the Young Ireland Society in 1885 and his reading of Davis and Mitchel from O'Leary's vast library 'led him to reconsider the canons of national literature'.[61] Their works had a powerful influence on Yeats's young mind, and persuaded him for a time to try 'to see the world as Davis saw it'.[62] It was under the auspices of the Young Ireland Societies that *The Poems and Ballads of Young Ireland* was published in 1888. Dedicated to O'Leary and regarded as one of the founding texts of the literary revival, it featured work from young writers such as Yeats, Ellen O'Leary, John Todhunter, Katharine Tynan, Douglas Hyde and T. W. Rolleston, and included verse that celebrated Irish heroism and lamented the deaths of patriots in the prescribed Young Ireland manner.[63]

Yeats was a leading member of the Irish Literary Society, founded in London in 1892 to resume 'the long-neglected work of Young Ireland' and take up 'the unfinished schemes of 1842 and '45'. It proclaimed 'Dark Rosaleen' as its muse and expected from its members 'both the earnest effort and spirit of Young Irelandism'.[64] In 1892 Yeats proposed that it should reissue some of the classics of the Young Ireland 'Library of Ireland' such as *The Spirit of the Nation*, Duffy's *Ballad Poetry of Ireland* and Mitchel's *Aodh O'Neill* to introduce a new generation to their writings. He also suggested that the Society should publish a 'Ballad Chronicle' written by himself, and new works of history such as a life of Wolfe Tone by T. W. Rolleston and one of Patrick Sarsfield by Lady Wilde ('Speranza') – works that had been proposed but never published by the original Library of Ireland.[65] The initiative was to be called the 'New Irish Library' and, as in the original series, volumes were to sell for the affordable price of one shilling. They would be published every two months, with Yeats acting as managing editor. He assured O'Leary that the series would be accessible to the general reader and would preach 'sound national doctrine'.[66]

The venture gained widespread support and offers of help. Sir Charles Gavan Duffy, who still took a strong interest in Irish cultural and political matters, was particularly anxious to be involved in a venture so closely linked to his activities of the 1840s. In addresses to the Irish Literary Society in London in July 1892 and June 1893, Duffy spoke of the importance of national education and knowledge of the past in creating national awareness. Young Ireland, he announced, had managed to put in a place a body of writing that was a 'treasure to two generations of Irishmen', but its task was not yet completed.[67] In his history of Young Ireland he lamented that their work had been 'swallowed up by famine, emigration, and unsuccessful insurrection' and concluded that 'if the Irish race, instead of being Anglicised or Americanised, are to be developed in harmony with their nature, it is a work which must be begun anew, by another generation'.[68] Duffy lamented that many of the writings of Davis and Mangan were to be found only in old newspapers and periodicals or scattered among anthologies, and in neither case was there a comprehensive edition of their collected works. He stressed the need for the publication of popular writings such as

> picturesque biographies, which are history individualised, or vivid sketches of memorable eras, which are history vitalised. A dozen lives of representative Irishmen would teach more of the training and growth of Ireland than a library of annals and state papers. They would familiarise us with great men, whom the Celt loves better than systems or policies.

He maintained it was shameful that half a century after Davis had called for Irishmen to write their own history, the country still lacked suitable biographies of national heroes such as Roger O'Moore, Luke Wadding and Patrick Sarsfield.[69]

Duffy was intent on using the New Irish Library to continue the work of the original series and publish inspirational nationalist history. His first suggestion was to re-publish Davis's articles on the 1689 Parliament (originally published in the *Dublin Monthly Magazine* in 1843), which he thought had been unjustly neglected. This, however, was not to the liking of Yeats, whose main concern was that any new publications should be of outstanding literary value.[70] Yeats believed that Davis's work on the 1689 Parliament was 'informing' but 'dry' and of no literary distinction.[71] Duffy, though, eventually had his way, and contributed a lengthy introduction to Davis's work in which he denounced the complacency and arrogance of British historians for their failure to acknowledge the importance of Davis's research.[72] He was also convinced that Davis's articles had an important contribution to make to contemporary political debates. Gladstone had introduced his second Home Rule bill in the House of Commons in February 1893 and unionists were again faced with the prospect of Irish self-government; the second reading of the bill was greeted with riots in Belfast. Exactly half a century on from the 'Repeal year' of 1843, unionist opposition to Irish self-government focused on the long-standing claims that a Dublin parliament would mean the persecution of Protestants and economic ruin. Duffy hoped to use Davis's arguments to show that just as such fears had been exaggerated and without foundation in 1689 and 1843, so they were equally mistaken in 1893.

Although Davis's *Patriot Parliament* sold an impressive 10,000 copies, Yeats maintained that the decision to publish it as the first volume of the New Irish Library had cast a pall of dull worthiness over the entire series which ensured that it would never fire the public imagination.[73] In the end the venture produced only a few additional books such as John Todhunter's *Life of Patrick Sarsfield* (1895), J. F. Taylor's *Life of Owen Roe O'Neill* (1896), Standish James O'Grady's *The Bog of Stars: And Other Stories and Sketches of Elizabethan Ireland* (1893), a collection of stories that told of cruel English oppression and stout Irish resistance, Douglas Hyde's *The Story of Early Gaelic Literature* (1895), a refutation of those who claimed that early medieval Ireland had no literature of value, and an anthology of songs published in the *Nation* entitled *The New Spirit of the Nation* (1894). The last of these contained poetry published in the *Nation* after 1845, and included some of the paper's best pieces such as Mangan's 'Dark Rosaleen', McGee's 'The Celts' and Speranza's 'The Famine year'. It was edited by Martin MacDermott, a veteran of the Young Ireland movement and a contributor to the original *Nation*, who hoped that this new collection would help inform 'future generations of the part taken by Young Ireland in the great work, still to be completed, of building up a National Literature'.[74] The works of Todhunter and Taylor showed an especially close continuity with the Young Ireland tradition. Biographies of Sarsfield and O'Neill had been scheduled for publication in the original Library of Ireland in the 1840s (O'Neill had actually been assigned to John Mitchel), but neither was completed. They portrayed their subjects as heroic and charismatic figures and were avidly read by young nationalists in the 1890s, including the young Roger Casement.[75]

Arthur Griffith was another who saw himself as carrying on the work of Young Ireland. In 1899 he founded a new paper, the *United Irishman*, which saw itself as a successor to Mitchel's militant publication of 1848. In January 1904 he announced his intention of compiling in the *United Irishman* a 'Ballad History of Ireland' that would continue a project brought to a halt by Davis's early death. The writing of much additional historical verse since the 1840s, noted Griffith, now made it possible to compile a comprehensive ballad history which would trace the story of the development of the Irish nation from the earliest times to the present day. He began the series in pre-history, citing the mythology of the eleventh-century *Book of Invasions* to detail the various groups who had come to Ireland before the Celts. Like Davis he regarded historical precision as secondary to the creation of an engaging and inspiring narrative. In dealing with the pre-historic Milesian invasion, Griffith referred the reader to D'Arcy McGee's poem 'The Celts', noting that 'it is not quite accurate, but it is accurate enough for the purpose of a ballad history'.[76] Young Ireland writers such as McGee, Davis, Duffy, Mangan, D. F. MacCarthy, John O'Hagan, M. J. Barry, Dalton Williams, M. J. McCann, Jean de Jean Fraser, Francis Davis and Speranza featured prominently in the series, their work supplemented by dozens of other writers of varying national sympathies such as William Drennan, Thomas Moore, Samuel Ferguson, Arthur Gerald Geoghegan, Edward Walsh, Aubrey de Vere, George Sigerson, Robert Dwyer Joyce, P. J. McCall, Thomas Boyd, William Rooney, T. D. Sullivan and Ethna Carbery.

The series consisted of one or more pieces of verse (often quite lengthy) recounting historical events in roughly chronological order. The primary emphasis was on great figures and great deeds, especially on the battlefield. Each piece was accompanied by a prose commentary by Griffith which set the scene and outlined its significance in Irish history. Abiding themes were the disunity of the Irish in the face of their foes, and the failure to seize opportunities to inflict a decisive defeat on the invader.[77] The series lasted almost two years and concluded with the Fenian rising of 1867, on the basis that 'the subsequent history of Ireland is known to all – the agrarian agitation, the fall of Parnell and the growth of the national revival in which we are all engaged'.[78] Griffith's 'Ballad History' was a remarkable achievement, linking the verse writing of the original *Nation* with the neo-Young Irelanders it had inspired, and stands as an ambitious attempt to substantiate Duffy's claim that Irish history had 'the grandeur and continuity of an epic poem'.[79] Such initiatives by followers of Young Ireland extended the movement's influence long after most of its original members were dead, and contributed significantly to the importance and endurance of its legacy.

EIGHT

THE LEGACY OF YOUNG
IRELAND'S WRITINGS

—

DISCIPLES

Through the influence of bodies such as the Young Ireland societies and the Irish Literary Society, and the writings of figures such as A. M. Sullivan and Arthur Griffith, the ideals of Young Ireland became a central part of Irish nationalist cultural discourse from the late nineteenth century onwards. In a laudatory chapter on Young Ireland in his *New Ireland: Political Sketches and Personal Reminiscences* (1878), Sullivan claimed that the movement did more to awaken Irish national consciousness than any other and that 'we of today reap the fruits of their labours'.[1] In his *Ireland and Her Story* (1903), the historian and MP Justin McCarthy, who had come under the influence of Young Ireland while working on the *Cork Examiner* in 1847, described the founding of the *Nation* as an epoch-making event and maintained that after the collapse of the repeal movement the spirit of Irish nationalism was kept alive primarily by the literature of Young Ireland.[2]

In his efforts to create a nationalist canon, the writer R. Barry O'Brien published his *Best Hundred Irish Books* in 1886. His selection included Young Ireland publications such as *The Spirit of the Nation*, Duffy's *Bird's Eye View*, Mitchel's *Aodh O'Neill*, Davis's *Essays and Poems*, Meehan's *Confederation of Kilkenny*, Mangan's *Poems*, McGee's *Art McMurrogh*, *History of Ireland*, *Irish Settlers in America* and *Irish Writers of the 17th Century*, and he credited the group with the first systematic attempt to provide Irish readers with a popular nationalist literature.[3] O'Brien admitted that their historical work was often rushed and sometimes fell short in scholarly terms – 'They were not historians; they had not time to be historians' – but he commended their efforts 'to create an historical taste. They tried to teach the Irish people that they had a country with no ignoble past'.[4] O'Brien's selection gave rise to a lively debate, with additional Young Ireland works featuring in many readers' suggestions for Ireland's best books. One of O'Brien's correspondents, Dr John Healy, later the Catholic archbishop of Tuam and an important historian in his own right, praised the Young Irelanders for their work in acquainting ordinary people with their own history and claimed that were responsible for 'the most brilliant epoch in Irish literary history. There has been nothing like it before or since. Their genius stirred the soul of the entire nation, and moves it still'.[5]

The writings of Davis and his colleagues were eagerly read by a generation disillusioned with the bitter political quarrels that followed the Parnell split in 1890, their lofty ideals and celebration of past heroism proving far more appealing than the pettiness and vindictiveness of contemporary politics. The Irish-Irelander William Rooney was a particularly keen student of Davis and Mitchel. His prose and verse self-consciously imitated the work of Davis and like him he strongly advocated the creation of a uniquely Irish literature and its propagation by a nationally-oriented education system. In February 1893 he founded in Dublin the Celtic Literary Society, claiming its purpose was 'again attempting the work begun and left unfinished by Young Ireland'.[6]

The young Arthur Griffith was one of those who came under Rooney's influence, and he absorbed much of the latter's enthusiasm for the ideals of Young Ireland.[7] His newspapers such as the *United Irishman* (1899–1906) and *Sinn Féin* (1906–14) regularly featured articles on Irish history, language and topography, and acknowledged their debt to Young Ireland's educational philosophy. Griffith himself read history voraciously, using it primarily to furnish examples of England's unscrupulousness and insincerity, and to point the way to future policies of self-reliance.[8] Throughout his career he drew a strong parallel between Young Ireland's opposition to O'Connell's co-operation with the Whigs in the 1840s and his own condemnation of the Irish Parliamentary Party's readiness to side with the Liberals to gain Home Rule.[9]

The influence of the writings of the Young Irelanders in forming Griffith's nationalism is widely acknowledged.[10] Just as Rooney sought to imitate Davis's literary style, so Griffith sought to imitate Mitchel's, and he regarded the latter's *History of Ireland* as 'the very best book an Irishman could study'. Griffith was also an avid reader of the historical writings of other Young Irelanders, especially those of C. P. Meehan, such as: *The Confederation of Kilkenny, The Fate and Fortunes of Hugh O'Neill . . . and Rory O'Donel* (1868) and *The Rise and Fall of the Irish Franciscan Monasteries* (1869). He described these works as 'invaluable and deeply interesting books for Irish readers', noting that 'I have loved the Irish Franciscans since I first read Fr Meehan's sketch of those brave and faithful priests who were Irishmen, always, not Italians'.[11]

In 1898 Griffith, Rooney and other nationalists such as John O'Leary, Maud Gonne and W. B. Yeats took the initiative in commemorating the centenary of the 1798 Rebellion and used the opportunity to re-invigorate the tradition of militant nationalism by attempting to unite all shades of patriotic opinion behind the ideals of the United Irishmen. Griffith later claimed that this was the year when advanced nationalists, inspired by the idealism and heroism they associated with 1798, seriously began to think again of how to set about achieving Irish independence. Interest in Ireland's past was, however, not just confined to separatists.

Constitutional nationalists too were well aware of the importance of laying claim to Ireland's history so as not to be outdone in expressions of patriotic devotion by separatists and cultural revivalists. This was not simply tactical. No one raised in a literate nationalist environment from the 1840s onwards could have avoided Young Ireland's popular history and balladry and the national consciousness of many leading members of the Irish Party such as John Dillon, William Redmond and T. M. Healy had been deeply influenced by their writings, especially those of John Mitchel, and had a view of the Irish past that differed little from their separatist rivals.[12] Most constitutionalists opposed armed action as a matter of policy rather than principle, and to maintain their dominant position as the leaders of Irish nationalism, leaders of the rival Nationalist Party factions such as John Redmond and John Dillon fought hard to gain control of the various 1798 commemorative committees and public demonstrations. This often involved a difficult balancing act between the constitutional and physical force traditions. As they addressed large and enthusiastic crowds at events to commemorate the rebellion, mainstream politicians invoked the insurrectionary traditions of the past, while claiming that such methods were unsuited to the present, in which self-government could be achieved most effectively through parliamentary means.[13]

Those in the separatist camp were less constrained. They argued that Ireland was an ancient and historic nation that had undergone great trials and sufferings in pursuit of its freedom and therefore deserved complete independence rather than the piecemeal reforms and limited legislative autonomy sought by Home Rulers. Any attempt to compromise or negotiate on this demand they denounced as treason. If such independence could only be achieved by taking up arms in the manner of the heroes of the past then this was something at which no true patriot baulked. An article in the militantly republican newspaper *Irish Freedom* managed by Seán Mac Diarmada and edited by Bulmer Hobson in 1911 proclaimed that

> We stand for the Ireland which produced Hugh, Shane and Owen O'Neill, and O'Donnell the Red, and Roger O'More, and Tone and Emmet and Fitzgerald, and Mitchel and Davis and Stephens and Rooney. On their behalf . . . we repudiate all bargains or treaties concerning the rights of this nation. Concessions be damned, we want our country![14]

The Young Irelanders' use of literature and history for propagandist purposes resonated with the zealous generation that emerged out of the cultural revival. Reading, teaching and discussing Irish history were central activities in nationalist organisations, and the writings of Young Ireland held great appeal to those who saw the past in heroic and romantic terms. Patrick Sarsfield 'P. S.' O'Hegarty, whose works such as *The Indestructible Nation: A Survey of Irish History from the English Invasion* (1918), *The Victory of Sinn Féin* (1924) and *A History of Ireland under the Union* (1952), encapsulated the historical outlook of that generation. He praised the fact that they wrote

> almost entirely with propagandist intent, appealing to tradition, to history, to national pride, making ballads because they could not make laws. In poetry and prose they wrote to make the ordinary Irishman conscious of his history and traditions, to make him politically-minded out of pride in the knowledge of the historic past of his country, and they succeeded.[15]

Although their attempted insurrection in 1848 failed in a military sense, O'Hegarty argued that 'in the long run, they won. The written word remained. The principles of nationality expounded in the *Nation* were never again wholly obscured. They became an integral part of the Irish consciousness'.[16]

The writings and ballads of Young Ireland did much to create the vocabulary of Irish nationalism. Whenever nationalists needed a rallying cry it was usually to Young Ireland that they looked, their ballads yielding resonant slogans such as 'Ourselves alone', 'Who fears to speak of '98' and 'A nation once again'. When in November 1913 Eoin MacNeill called for the founding of an Irish Volunteer movement with an article in *An Claidheamh Soluis*, he used the slogan 'The north began', a phrase taken from Thomas Davis's 'Song of the Volunteers of 1782'.[17] The spirit and style of Young Ireland's historical ballads influenced figures as diverse as Alice Milligan, Thomas MacDonagh and Roger Casement.[18] Casement, who was enthused by the founding of the Volunteers and became one of their main organisers, wrote poems on the battle of Benburb and 'The triumph of Hugh O'Neill' in the manner of *Nation* poets such as Mangan and MacCarthy, and in 1914 published an article entitled 'The romance of Irish history' based on his reading of works such as O'Callaghan's *History of the Irish Brigades*, Mitchel's *Life of Aodh O'Neill* and *History of Ireland*, Taylor's *Life of Owen Roe O'Neill* and Todhunter's *Life of Patrick Sarsfield*.[19] Mitchel, as an Ulster Protestant nationalist who had stubbornly defied the British government, was a particular inspiration and as early as 1906 Casement had written: 'If God grants me life and purpose to end as I hope, I'll do some of the things John Mitchel left undone.'[20] Casement was not alone in such activities. Thomas MacNevin's *History of the Volunteers of*

1782 was recommended as an essential text for aspiring Volunteers by their newspaper.[21] Some Volunteers even made their own attempts to bring the past to life: Michael O'Hanrahan, a Gaelic Leaguer, journalist and vice-commandant of the 2nd battalion of the Dublin Brigade that occupied Jacob's biscuit factory during the 1916 Rising and was afterwards executed, wrote the melodramatic historical novels *A Swordsman of the Brigade* (1914), *When the Norman Came* (1918), and *Irish Heroines* (1917), based on a series of lectures he had given to Cumann na mBan in the winter of 1915–16.

In nationalist cultural and military circles a thorough knowledge of Irish history was seen as an affirmation of one's patriotism. Many saw themselves as acting in a long tradition of resistance and claimed that it was primarily their understanding of Irish history that motivated them to seek their country's independence. Very often this history was learned at home, or from nationally-minded schoolteachers (especially the Christian Brothers), but Young Ireland songs and books also played their part.[22] When interviewing IRA veterans from the War of Independence, the historians Peter Hart and Joost Augusteijn discovered that they predominantly derived their sense of nationality from works such as Sullivan's *Story of Ireland*, and Mitchel's *History of Ireland* and *Jail Journal* rather than from the contemporary separatist press of the Gaelic Revival.[23] One such veteran, Tom Barry, the renowned commander of the IRA's West Cork Brigade flying column, claimed that he had joined the British army in 1915 'because I knew no Irish history and had no national consciousness' but, inspired by the actions of the 1916 rebels, on his return to Ireland after the war he

> read avidly the stories of past Irish History: of Eoghan Ruadh, Patrick Sarsfield, John Mitchel, Wolfe Tone, Robert Emmet and the other Irish patriots who strove to end the British Conquest. I read the history of the corpses of the Famine, of the killings of Irishmen without mercy, the burnings, lootings, and the repeated attempts at the complete destruction of a weaker people. In all history there has never been so tragic a fate as that which Ireland had suffered at the hands of the English for those seven centuries.[24]

The 1916 Proclamation made clear its debt to Irish history, explicitly invoking 'the dead generations from which [Ireland] receives her old tradition of nationhood' in justification of armed action and placing the insurrection in a continuous tradition of resistance to conquest. For some, it was a long-standing sense of historical grievance that led them to take up arms that Easter, while for others, the Rising itself acted on latent historical memory. The young Ernie O'Malley, who had earlier scoffed at the Volunteers on their marches and parades, recalled how his heart swelled with pride on hearing

Volunteers singing 'Who fears to speak of '98' during Easter week. The Rising left him 'in a whirl', his mind 'jump[ing] from a snatch of song to a remembered page of economic history'. He noticed that in its aftermath 'something strange stirred in the people, some feeling long since buried, a sense of communion with the fighting dead generations, for the dead walked around again'.[25]

As a school teacher Patrick Pearse had done his best to lay the groundwork for such feelings. The prospectus of his school at St Enda's attached a particular importance to the teaching of Irish history 'to instil into the minds of the pupils an intimate and lively love of their fatherland'.[26] In an editorial in *An Claidheamh Soluis* in 1907 Pearse spoke of the necessity of combining the study of the Irish language and Irish history in order fully to appreciate both, and he himself read widely in Irish history and mythology.[27] The focus on warriors and heroes in Young Ireland's historical writings proved popular with a generation that had only recently discovered mythological heroic cycles of Cú Chulainn and Fionn Mac Cumhail through the works of Standish O'Grady and Lady Gregory, and contributed to a view of the past formed by an amalgam of myth, legend and history that portrayed the Irish from time immemorial as a heroic and martial race who would never rest easily under conquest. This outlook did not necessarily create simplistic aspirations to 'blood sacrifice', but it did bolster the notion that Irishmen had a duty to assert in arms their country's right to independence even if their chances of success were negligible – honourable defeat was infinitely preferable to apathy and cowardice and if blood needed to be shed to show their countrymen that they were in earnest, then this was a price they would pay willingly.[28]

Pearse's sense of history, in particular the notion that he owed a sacred debt to his nationalist predecessors, was a key influence in shaping his actions throughout his life. He defined patriotism as 'in large part a memory of heroic dead men and a striving to accomplish some task left unfinished by them'.[29] This concern with fulfilling one's duty to the past was most explicitly acknowledged in his pamphlets *Ghosts*, *The Separatist Idea*, *The Spiritual Nation* and *The Sovereign People* – all written in the months immediately before the 1916 Rising. Pearse observed that the demand for Irish independence 'has been made by every generation; that we of this generation receive it as a trust from our fathers; that we are bound by it; that we have not the right to alter it or abate it by one jot'.[30] In *Ghosts* Pearse made his most explicit acknowledgement of his debt to the Young Ireland tradition, describing Tone, Davis, Mitchel and Lalor – 'the four great nationalist evangelists' – as insistent 'ghosts' that haunted his imagination and cried out to be appeased.[31]

For separatists, the leading Young Irelanders, particularly Davis and Mitchel, became models to emulate: Davis's emphasis on cultural matters and the Irish language was much admired, as was Mitchel's fierce Anglophobia and uncompromising separatism. For many nationalist idealists the Young Irelanders became the exemplar of all that was good about Irish nationalism. Their emphasis on the spiritual essence of Irish nationality, revealed through their study of Ireland's past, had a profound effect on idealists who saw the past as heroic and noble in contrast to a corrupt and debased present in which idealism and self-sacrifice had been supplanted by venality and compromise. If Ireland's future was to match its past then this nobility and heroism would have to be recovered, and this could only be done by taking up arms and proving Irish courage and virtue once again.

CRITICS OF YOUNG IRELAND

In Ireland, as elsewhere, the late nineteenth century saw an increasing professionalisation of the writing of history, with a greater reliance on in-depth research and the use of primary sources. Leading Irish figures in this movement, such as the historians J. P. Prendergast, W. E. H. Lecky, and Richard Bagwell eschewed the nationalist and journalistic approach of Young Ireland and, wary of becoming embroiled in nationalist polemic, ignored their work for the most part and ploughed their own furrow. Lecky, though, had thought highly of the *Nation* of the 1840s, especially admiring the writings of Davis and Duffy (while heartily disliking those of Mitchel). A Trinity College contemporary of the late 1850s described him as 'saturated with the writings and poetry of the patriotic party' and a great admirer of John Kells Ingram, author of 'The Memory of the Dead', one of the *Nation*'s most memorable songs. As Irish nationalism became more militant and demotic with the rise of Fenianism in the 1860s, the Young Irelanders seemed reminiscent of a more chivalrous and romantic nationalism and, in order to distinguish his national sentiments from those of the Fenians, Lecky once described himself and Lady Wilde as the only living Young Irelanders. Like the writers of the *Nation*, Lecky believed in the literary value of history and was sceptical of the obsession of many contemporary historians with the classification and interpretation of original documents.[32] He praised Davis's work on the 1689 parliament, and his own account of this period owed something to Davis's interpretation. At times some of Lecky's judgements ran close to those of Young Ireland, most notably in their shared admiration for Henry Grattan and the Volunteer movement and their glorification of the years of 'Grattan's parliament' as a golden age of political liberty, cultural vitality and economic progress.[33]

But despite Lecky's admiration for Young Ireland's idealism and literary talent, their historical writings did not affect his work in any significant way.

He drew most of his influence from broader European currents of philosophy, sociology and history. His *Leaders of Public Opinion in Ireland* (1861) traced the development of 'nationality with loyalty' through the political careers of Swift, Flood, Grattan and O'Connell. Though far from uncritical of O'Connell, it gave a more sympathetic and rounded view of his career than Duffy or Mitchel. The studiously impartial tone and imperial sympathies of most of his work are sharply at odds with the polemical nationalism of Young Ireland. His view of Irish history as a series of 'perplexed, petty internal broils, often sustained by atrocious crimes, but turning on no large issue and leading to no clear or stable results' directly contradicted the Young Ireland view of Ireland's history as a noble and continuous struggle for national independence.[34]

The publication from the 1860s of scholarly works by Lecky and Prendergast threw into sharp contrast the hurried and hackneyed nature of much popular nationalist history. The historian R. Barry O'Brien deplored the lack of rigour and superficial research of many popular writers, especially their failure to substantiate their arguments by consulting original sources. He noted that 'Nothing strikes one more forcibly in looking through our historical literature than the absence of any attempt to be exact. Men spend the time in turning sentences which they ought to devote to verifying facts'. He claimed that this had resulted in the endless repetition of errors, half-truths, and vague generalisations.[35] Significantly, in the lists of history books recommended for the general reader in O'Brien's *Best Hundred Books in Irish*, almost half of the titles came from the Young Ireland school, but O'Brien failed to include even one of their works in reading lists intended for the serious student of Irish history.[36]

The writer and critic John Eglinton reacted more directly against the ubiquitous influence of Young Ireland on popular national literature. He attributed to Davis the creation of Ireland's 'only distinctive national literary tradition', but claimed that its nationalistic bias had stifled all other literary voices. He called for 'the de-Davisisation of Irish national literature', which he defined as

> the getting rid of the notion that in Ireland, a writer is to think, first and foremost, of interpreting the nationality of his country, and not simply the burden which he has to deliver. The expression of nationality, literature cannot fail to be; and the richer more varied and unexpected that expression the better.[37]

The young James Joyce also argued that Young Ireland had a deadening effect on Irish literature by being slavishly imitated by later nationalist writers. In a review of *The Poems and Ballads of William Rooney* (1902), Joyce dismissed Rooney's verse as having no spiritual and living energy, because they come from one in whom the spirit is in a manner dead, or at least in its own hell, a weary and foolish spirit, speaking of redemption and revenge, blaspheming against tyrants, and going forth, full of tears and curses, upon its infernal labours.[38]

Although Davis's essays and poems had helped spark his national sympathies, W. B. Yeats eventually came to see much of Young Ireland's work as shallow and chauvinistic. He disagreed strongly with their belief that literature was primarily a polemical tool subservient to politics, and condemned their historical writings as an attempt to turn the past into a simplified melodrama in which a virtuous Ireland was assailed by a villainous England.[39] As Roy Foster has noted, 'he became increasingly conscious through the 1890s that the Davisite style of balladry was uncomfortably near doggerel, and that his own literary mission was to move things to a more demanding plane'.[40] One of the main reasons he founded the Irish Literary Society in 1893 was to allow 'a new generation of critics and writers to denounce the propagandist verse and prose that had gone by the name of Irish literature'. He was therefore dismayed when Duffy joined the society with the intention of using it as a vehicle to continue the work of Young Ireland. Duffy's voluminous writings themselves he regarded as severely limited in vision and execution, noting that they had 'not one sentence which has any meaning when separated from its place in argument or narrative, not one distinguished because of its thought or music'.[41] Young Ireland, he argued, had sought to fill the minds of the young with simple slogans and images, whereas he sought to give his readers a richer and more complex view of the past. However, he soon found that 'The Irish people were not educated enough to accept images more profound, more true to human nature, than the schoolboy thoughts of Young Ireland'.[42]

The Young Ireland style of nationalist versifying could irritate even convinced nationalists. Eoin MacNeill warned of the dangers of 'lying in waiting for the latest piece of Gaelic lore dug out by the philologists, to dress it up in an alien garb, and turn it into third-rate English poetry'.[43] Douglas Hyde was concerned at the Anglicising effect of Young Ireland writers, and believed that a literature that aimed to foster Irish nationality in the English tongue could do more harm than good to the Irish people's sense of themselves. He praised Young Ireland's attempt to give Ireland a literature that raised national pride and awareness, but believed that by confining themselves to English they limited their reach to the urban Anglophone classes, and failed to engage the Irish-speaking peasantry. Their appeal, therefore, was partial and cut off from the vibrant folk-history and vernacular culture of much of the population.[44] D. P. Moran went further, claiming that the writings of Young

Ireland had contributed to the creation of a superficial patriotism divorced from any real understanding of Ireland's Gaelic past. He dismissed Young Ireland's 'jingling rhymes' and 'spirit-wearying flow of romances', claiming that 'they brought into life a mongrel thing which they called Irish literature in the English language. Literature in the English language is English literature and all the Duffys that were ever born could not make it anything else'.[45]

INDEPENDENCE AND AFTERMATH

The revolution that brought about Irish independence was one in which the printed word was crucial. A host of newspapers, pamphlets and books were published that stressed Ireland's national distinctiveness and argued the case for self-government. In the decade before independence the writings of Young Ireland provided much of the ideological sustenance of Irish nationalism and were widely re-printed. Arthur Griffith saw their work as central to the nationalist education of the wider public and promoted the re-publication of Young Ireland classics to make them available to a new generation. He edited or wrote prefaces for new editions of works such as Mitchel's *Jail Journal* (1913), Doheny's *The Felon's Track* (1914), *Thomas Davis: The Thinker and Teacher* (1916), *Meagher of the Sword: Speeches of Thomas Francis Meagher* (1916), and *James Fintan Lalor: Patriot and Political Essayist* (1918), and concluded that 'when the Irish read and reflect with Davis, their day of redemption will be at hand'.[46]

It is common for newly independent states to commission an origin legend to establish their historical lineage, but a strong sense of Ireland's destiny rooted in the struggles and sacrifices of the past was already well entrenched in Irish nationalist historiography, and independence heralded a strong degree of continuity in the writing of Irish history. The interpretation popularised by Young Ireland and taken up by Griffith and other separatist nationalists dominated historical perceptions after independence.[47] It became part of the official propaganda intended to consolidate the legitimacy of the new state, and hardened into an orthodoxy largely unchallenged by new research or fresh insights. Many still saw themselves as attempting to continue or complete the work of Young Ireland. In 1927 the Jesuit priest and librarian Stephen J. Brown produced his *Poetry of Irish History*, a comprehensive collection of Irish historical verse which he announced he had published to carry on the work of Thomas Davis.[48] For the centenary of Davis's death in 1945, the nationalist author and journalist M. J. McManus edited a collection of essays with a foreword by the president of Ireland, Seán T. Ó Ceallaigh, which claimed that no period of Irish history has produced a more remarkable group of men than the Young Irelanders . . . Theirs was a cleansing and a resurgent movement . . . they quickened the pulse of the nation; they re-awakened interest in Ireland's history, legends, traditions and antiquities, and they composed songs and ballads which kindled a new fire in the souls of a depressed people. It can with truth be claimed for them that they were the real fathers of the Sinn Féin that in our generation made the Ireland that we know.[49]

Before independence, nationalists had fought hard to have Irish history taught in schools. In response to their demands, the Board of National Education included some basic Irish history and geography in the curriculum from the 1870s onwards, although this was rarely enough to satisfy nationalists. Gradually, though, as the cultural revival of the 1890s took hold, the Board became more sympathetic to the teaching of Irish history, and in 1902, the resident commissioner, Dr W. J. M. Starkie, went so far as to denounce the anti-national bias of previous boards. Sustained pressure for the inclusion of Irish history on school courses eventually bore fruit when in 1908 the Board sanctioned history as a specific subject in its own right for national schools.[50] However, the actual teaching of history remained patchy, depending largely on the level of knowledge and interest of individual teachers. Until the achievement of independence many nationalists continued to argue that the Irish national school system was still implacably hostile to the development of Irish nationality.[51]

The achievement of independence provided the opportunity to reverse the policies of the past. Eoin MacNeill, the Irish Free State's first minister for education, had argued in an article written in 1911 that successive British governments had used the national schools

> to cut the Irish people off from their own past – to make them think that they were foundlings in the world, nobody's children – and thereby to destroy their self-respect and render them more easily handled like a set of broken paupers in a poorhouse.[52]

He was determined that the educational system of the new state would undo this damage.[53] The teaching of Irish history and the Irish language, regarded by many Irish-Irelanders as complementary subjects, was central to this endeavour. MacNeill maintained that 'ignorance of Irish history is the chief cause of the want of interest in the Irish language. To anyone who has not a feeling of Irish history or does not identify himself with Irish history, the learning of Irish is mere philology'.[54] Irish history was seen as providing the essential background to the language by reminding students of the struggles and sacrifices for its preservation over the centuries. It was also the case that teaching students the rudiments of Irish history through English was usually a considerably easier task than making them fluent in Irish.

Given the pervasiveness of Young Ireland writings in the first two decades of the century, their main themes had an obvious influence on history text-books and on the generation of Irish history teachers in the 1920s and 1930s. Notes for history teachers issued by the Department of Education in 1934 (two years after Fianna Fáil had come to power) could almost have been taken directly from the *Nation* 90 years earlier:

> In an Irish school in which history is properly taught, the pupils will learn that they are citizens of no mean country, that they belong to a race that has a noble tradition of heroism and persistent loyalty to ideals. In such a school no formal exhortation should be necessary to bring home to every pupil the worth of good faith, courage and endurance, and . . . that a race that has survived a millennium of grievous struggle and persecution must possess qualities that are a guarantee of a great future.[55]

The guidelines maintained that the best way of doing this was to arouse a child's interest in history

> through stories of the heroic or romantic exploits of the national heroes of legend and semi-history . . . the material must be presented in vivid and striking narrative, and appeal made to the child's love of the heroic, even at the risk sometimes of giving the impression that history is concerned absolutely with the deeds of great men and women.

The Department noted that 'In contrast with the men against whom they were pitted, the characters of Owen Roe O'Neill and Patrick Sarsfield stand out vividly' and advised that every school library should have their biographies (both of which were published by the New Irish Library in the 1890s). As well as Taylor's *Life of Owen Roe O'Neill* and Todhunter's *Life of Patrick Sarsfield*, texts recommended for further reading included *The Fate and Fortunes of the Earls of Tyrone and Tyrconnell* and *The Confederation of Kilkenny* by C. P. Meehan, *The Life of Aodh O'Neill* and *The Last Conquest of Ireland* by John Mitchel, J. C. O'Callaghan's *History of the Irish Brigades in France*, Duffy's *Life of Thomas Davis*, and Griffith's *Thomas Davis* and *Meagher of the Sword*. Teachers were also encouraged to procure one of the many available collections of Irish historical poems and ballads and to encourage their students to sing and recite them with 'spirit and vigour' since these 'not only crystallise historical knowledge but they make an emotional appeal to youth such as is beyond the power of prose'.[56]

Not all teachers of Irish history were happy with this, and some argued it was time to move on from the militarist and determinist simplicities of Young Ireland. The historian Edmund Curtis criticised the teaching of Irish history in schools for its lack of historical perspective and its excessive moralising. Curtis, professor of history at TCD (1914–43), had seen too many examination papers that were 'a gush of legend, rhetoric, passion or panegyric'. In 1925 he wrote that

> as far as written history is known, it is generally derived from popular works of the D'Arcy McGee and John Mitchel type of historian. This type makes the history of Ireland that of a virtuous, noble, intensely patriotic and deeply religious race, whose troubles have come entirely from foreigners . . . this form of national history, which served its turn in keeping up the self-esteem of the people in dark days, has now rather curdled on the national stomach.[57]

Writers such as Sean O'Faolain agreed, dismissing the Department of Education's publications as 'fairytale textbooks on history'.[58] Part of O'Faolain's challenge to Ireland's cultural orthodoxy was to produce new biographical studies of Daniel O'Connell (1938) and Hugh O'Neill (1942) that gave these figures a more complex and nuanced treatment than had the historians of Young Ireland. The desire to challenge the widespread public acceptance of a determinist nationalist narrative based mainly on polemical secondary sources contributed to the foundation by T. W. Moody and R. D. Edwards of *Irish Historical Studies* in 1938. The new journal sought to promote historical writing based on original sources that was sober and impartial in tone, and called for co-operation between the professional historian and the history teacher to disseminate the fruits of their research.[59]

The dominant influence of Young Ireland's interpretation diminished with the passing away of the state's founding fathers and 'with them passed away much of the canon of literary and political history that formed them, outmoded by the passage of time and the fall of the Union against which it defined itself'.[60] By the 1960s few academic historians regarded Irish history as the story of a uniquely courageous and protracted struggle against foreign oppression. Some saw it as their duty to demythologise the Irish past by questioning accepted notions of heroic struggle and national continuity, and in the process created an often sharp opposition between scholarly and popular views of Irish history.[61] Some teachers became concerned that the history being taught in class rooms did not sufficiently reflect the shift away from myth and propaganda achieved by professional historians: in 1966 a Fianna Fáil study group asked if the teaching of Irish history schools had over-emphasised 'sublime patriotism, self-sacrifice and unswerving commitment to noble ideals' – characteristics that had been at the core of the Young Ireland interpretation of history. Such opinions led to major syllabus reforms in the 1960s and 1970s and the introduction of a new series of textbooks that shifted the emphasis away from a militaristic interpretation of Irish history.[62]

The polemical and determinist nature of Young Ireland history writing had diminishing appeal to a new generation of readers who sought to question old orthodoxies and nationalist pieties, and the iconoclasm displayed by many historians from the late 1960s onwards was partly a reaction to the earlier nationalist emphasis on history as the deeds of great men. This in turn provoked a reaction. The historian, Brendan Bradshaw, argued that the attempt to dismantle the traditional version of Irish history risked depriving the public of a heroic and inspiring narrative that was central to their national identity and opened up an ever-widening gap between the interpretations of professional historians and those of the wider public. In a manner reminiscent of Davis, he called for modern historians to approach Irish history with imagination and empathy, that would make of it an essential form of national sustenance.[63]

Although Young Ireland's historical writings are now little read, their influence on national historical perceptions has had an enduring tenacity and persists in popularly-held views of Irish history: as Bradshaw has observed, 'the bitter reality, recalled in song and story, continues to haunt the popular memory.'[64] Many of their titles and slogans remain current and continue to shape the vocabulary of Irish nationalism. When in 1986 Martin Mansergh edited and published a voluminous collection of the statements and speeches of Charles J. Haughey, he entitled the work *The Spirit of the Nation*.[65]

The Young Irelanders produced no great historian nor any great work of history, but they still managed to create a compelling body of historical writings that inspired generations of nationalists. They did not originate the notion that Irish history was primarily a continuous and courageous struggle against foreign domination, but they propagated it with energy and imagination, and took advantage of advances in literacy and printing to reach a greater readership than any previous nationalist historians. Their interpretation of Irish history was a construction, but it was one constructed from familiar materials and resonated with their readers. Their writings did much to shape Irish communal memory, and helped convince generations of nationalists that they formed a distinct and historic community that was destined to make its own future. In this the young men of the *Nation* succeeded better than they could ever have expected.

Notes

INTRODUCTION

1   *Nation*, 7 Jan. 1843.

2   R. D. Edwards, 'The contribution of Young Ireland to the development of the national idea', in Séamus Pender (ed.), *Féilscríbhinn Torna: Essays and Studies Presented to Tadhg Ua Donnchadha* (Cork, 1947), p. 120.

3   See Kevin Whelan, 'The United Irishmen, the Enlightenment and popular culture', in D. Dickson, D. Keogh and K. Whelan (eds), *The United Irishmen: Republicanism, Radicalism and Rebellion* (Dublin, 1993), pp 269–96.

4   A. D. Smith, *Myths and Memories of the Nation* (Oxford, 1999), p. 29.

5   'Misrepresentations of history', *Nation*, 9 Dec. 1843.

6   Charles Gavan Duffy, *Thomas Davis: The Memoirs of an Irish Patriot* (London, 1890), pp 352–3.

7   'The present and the future', *Nation*, 21 Oct. 1843.

8   'Twelfth of August', *Nation*, 9 Aug. 1845.

9   Charles Gavan Duffy, *The Ballad Poetry of Ireland* (Dublin, 1874), p. 37.

10   Charles Gavan Duffy, *Young Ireland: A Fragment of Irish History 1840–1850* (London, 1880), p. 153.

11   'Sismondi on federalism', *Nation*, 2 Sept. 1843.

12   'A ballad history of Ireland', *Nation*, 30 Nov. 1844.

13   'Irish history', *Nation*, 18 May 1844; Thomas MacNevin, *The Confiscation of Ulster* (Dublin, 1847), p. 50.

14   *Nation*, 9 Sept. 1843.

15   Benedict Anderson, *Imagined Communities: Reflections on the Origins and Spread of Nationalism* (1983; revised ed. London, 2006), p 6, 36.

16   'The Library of Ireland', *Nation*, 28 June 1845.

17   'A year's work', *Nation*, 14 Oct. 1843.

18   Vincent Morley, 'Views of the past in Irish vernacular literature, 1650–1850', in T. C. W. Blanning and Hagen Schulze (eds), *Unity and Diversity in European Culture* (Oxford, 2006) (*Proceedings of the British Academy*, p. 134), pp 171–2.

19   See especially John Todhunter, *Life of Patrick Sarsfield* (London and Dublin, 1895) and J. F. Taylor's *Life of Owen Roe O'Neill* (London and Dublin, 1896).

20   'The toscin of Ireland', *Nation*, 29 July 1848.

21   John Mitchel, *The Last Conquest of Ireland (perhaps)* (Glasgow, 1861), p. 144.

22   Especially Thomas D'Arcy McGee, *A Popular History of Ireland* (New York, 1864); and John Mitchel, *The History of Ireland from the Treaty of Limerick to the Present Time* (New York, 1868); J. Pope-Hennessy, 'What do the Irish read?', *Nineteenth Century*, xv (Jan.–June 1884), pp 926–7.

23 Séamas Ó Néill, 'Tomás Dáibhis – staraithe', in M. J. MacManus (ed.), *Thomas Davis and Young Ireland* (Dublin, 1945), pp 114–15; P. S. O'Hegarty, 'The "Library of Ireland" 1845–1847', in ibid., pp 109–13.

24 Richard Davis, *The Young Ireland Movement* (Dublin, 1987), pp 237–41; Helen F. Mulvey, *Thomas Davis and Ireland: A Biographical Study* (Washington DC, 2003), pp 205–27; David A. Wilson, *Thomas D'Arcy McGee: Volume 1 Passion, Reason, and Politics 1825–1857* (Montreal and Kingston, 2008), pp 274–5, 307–9; and idem, *Thomas D'Arcy McGee: Volume 2: The Extreme Moderate 1857–1868* (Montreal & Kingston, 2011), pp 184–95. See also James Quinn, 'Thomas Davis and the Patriot Parliament of 1689', in James Kelly, John McCafferty and Charles Ivar McGrath (eds), *People, Politics and Power: Essays on Irish History 1660–1850 in Honour of James I. McGuire* (Dublin, 2009), pp 190–202.

25 David Dwan, *The Great Community: Culture and Nationalism in Ireland* (Dublin, 2008), pp 23, 31–9. Joep Leerssen, *Remembrance and Imagination; Patterns in the Historical and Literary Representation of Ireland in the Nineteenth Century* (Cork, 1996), pp 85–6; idem, 'Irish cultural nationalism – its European context', in Bruce Stewart (ed.), *Hearts and Minds: Irish Culture and Society under the Act of Union* (Gerrards Cross, 2002), p. 180; idem, *National Thought in Europe: A Cultural History* (Amsterdam, 2006), pp 124–5. Malcolm Brown, *The Politics of Irish Literature: From Thomas Davis to W. B. Yeats* (London, 1972). Sean Ryder, 'Speaking of '98: Young Ireland and republican memory', *Éire-Ireland*, 34:2 (1999), pp 51–69; idem, 'Young Ireland and the 1798 Rebellion', in L. M. Geary (ed.), *Rebellion and Remembrance in Modern Ireland* (Dublin, 2001), pp 135–47; and idem, '"With a heroic life and a governing mind": nineteenth-century Irish nationalist autobiography', in Liam Harte (ed.), *Modern Irish Autobiography: Self, Nation and Spirit* (Basingstoke, 2007), pp 14–31. R. F. Foster 'The story of Ireland', in idem, *The Irish Story: Telling Tales and Making it up in Ireland* (Oxford, 2002), pp 1–22; idem, 'The first romantics: Young Irelands between Catholic emancipation and the Famine', in idem, *Words Alone: Yeats and his Inheritances* (Oxford, 2011), pp 45–90. Patrick Maume, *The Long Gestation: Irish Nationalist Life, 1891–1918* (Dublin, 1999), p. 220; idem, 'Young Ireland, Arthur Griffith, and republican ideology: the question of continuity', *Éire-Ireland*, XXXIV, pt 2 (summer 1999), pp 155–74.

ONE

LAYING THE FOUNDATIONS: THE NATION, EDUCATION AND TEMPERANCE

1   *An Address Delivered Before the Historical Society, Dublin, June 26, 1840* (Dublin, 1840). It was later published in T. W. Rolleston (ed.), *Prose Writings of Thomas Davis* (London, 1890), pp 1–43, and in D. J. O'Donoghue (ed.), *Essays, Literary and Historical by Thomas Davis* (Dundalk, 1914) under the title 'The young Irishman of the middle classes', pp 1–51. It is subsequently cited here as O'Donoghue, *Davis Essays*.

2   O'Donoghue, *Davis Essays*, p. 34, 49.

3   Ibid., p. 50, 46.

4   John N. Molony, *A Soul Came into Ireland: Thomas Davis 1814–1845* (Dublin, 1995), p. 38; Helen F. Mulvey, *Thomas Davis and Ireland: A Biographical Study* (Washington DC, 2003), p. 36; T. W. Moody, *Thomas Davis, 1814–1845* (Dublin, 1945), p. 24.

5   Charles Gavan Duffy, *Young Ireland: A Fragment of Irish History* (London, 1880), p. 148.

6   Thomas MacNevin, *Address Delivered before the College Historical Society, Dublin* (Dublin, 1836), p. 30.

7   John O'Hagan, 'Thomas Davis', *Irish Monthly*, xix (Jan. 1891), p. 5.

8   Charles Gavan Duffy, *Thomas Davis: The Memoirs of an Irish Patriot, 1840–1846* (London, 1890), pp 68–9.

9   See 'On the origins of the *Nation*', Thomas Davis papers, NLI MS 3199, ff 4–5.

10   Brendan Ó Cathaoir, *John Blake Dillon: Young Irelander* (Dublin, 1990), pp 7–8.

11   David Dwan, *The Great Community: Culture and Nationalism in Ireland* (Dublin, 2008), pp 40–6.

12   Duffy, *Young Ireland*, p. 348.

13   Molony, *Thomas Davis* (1995), pp 45–54.

14   'The life and times of Henry Grattan', *The Citizen or Dublin Monthly Magazine* (Nov. 1839–May 1840), i, pp 154–65; (July–Dec. 1841), iv, pp 53–63, 145–51; India – her own and another's', ibid., i, pp 245–53, 418–33; (June–Dec. 1840), ii, pp 120–9, 325–36; (Jan.–June 1841) iii, pp 83–95; 'Who are the Afghans? ibid., (Jan.–June 1842), v, pp 439–52; 'The Irish parliament of James II', ibid., (Jan.–Apr. 1843), vii, pp 25–42, 75–90, 105–34, 170–201.

15   Michael Staunton to Davis, 24 July 1841 (RIA MS 12/P/15/18); 'Origin and writers of the *Nation*' (Duffy, *Young Ireland*, p. 526); see also Davis papers, NLI MS 3199.

16   Duffy, *Thomas Davis*, p. 71.

17   Charles Gavan Duffy, *My Life in Two Hemispheres* (2 vols, New York, 1898), pp 3, 7, 13–14,17–18.

18   Ibid., i, p. 20, 29.

19   Dillon to Davis, [1842?], RIA MS 12/P/15/2.

20   Duffy, *Thomas Davis*, p. 72 ; 'On the origins of the *Nation*', Davis papers, NLI 3199.

21   For a comprehensive study of the *Dublin University Magazine* see Wayne E. Hall, *Dialogue in the Margins: A Study of the* Dublin University Magazine (London, 2000); Duffy, *Thomas Davis* (1890), p. 55.

22   Barbara Hayley, 'Irish periodicals from the union to the *Nation*', *Anglo-Irish Studies*, ii (1976), pp 94–7; Duffy, *My Life*, i, p. 59.

23   Duffy, *Young Ireland*, p. 49.

24   'On the origins of the *Nation*', Davis papers, NLI 3199.

25   T. W. Moody, 'Thomas Davis and the Irish nation', *Hermathena*, ciii (1966), p. 12.

26   Prospectus for the *Nation*, Oct. 1842.

27   Duffy, *Thomas Davis*, p. 89; see also Brian Inglis, 'The press', in R. B. McDowell (ed.), *Social Life in Ireland* (Dublin, 1957), p. 110.

28   Duffy, *My Life*, i,p. 65.

29   Duffy, *Thomas Davis*, pp 160–1; John D. Noonan, 'The library of Thomas Davis', *Irish Book Lover*, v (Oct. 1913), pp 37–41. For the extent of Davis's historical knowledge and his wide-ranging plans for further research , see his notes in NLI Ms 3199, RIA Ms 12 P 15/15–17 and RIA Ms 12 P 16.

30   Michael Doheny, *The Felon's Track* (Dublin, 1918), pp 21–2.

31   John Mitchel, *The Last Conquest of Ireland (Perhaps)* (Glasgow, 1861), p. 151.

32   Duffy, *Young Ireland*, pp 387–8; Charles Gavan Duffy to R. R. Madden (Dublin Public Libraries (Gilbert Collection), Madden papers, MS 278).

33   Duffy, *Young Ireland*, pp 387–8.

34 Ibid., p. 185.

35 See, for example, John O'Leary, *Recollections of Fenians and Fenianism* (2 vols, London, 1896), I, pp 257–9; John Devoy, *Recollections of an Irish Rebel* (New York, 1929), p. 39, 290, 378; William O'Brien, *Recollections* (London, 1905), p. 56; John Denvir, *The Life Story of an Old Rebel* (Dublin, 1910), p. 37.

36 'Irish character', *Nation*, 3 Apr. 1847.

37 'Freedom's way', *Nation*, 30 Aug. 1845; Duffy, *Young Ireland*, p. 148.

38 *Nation*, 5 Oct. 1844; 'Irish policy', *Nation*, 15 June 1844.

39 Donald H. Akenson, *The Irish Education Experiment: The National System of Education in the Nineteenth Century* (London, 1970), p. 140.

40 'Growth of an Irish nation', *Nation*, 12 July 1845; 'Popular education', *Nation*, 27 July 1844; 'Report of the Commissioners of National Education – 1846, part 2', *Nation*, 3 Oct. 1846.

41 'Report of the Commissioners of National Education – 1846, part 2', *Nation*, 3 Oct. 1846.

42 'Education', *Nation*, 18 Feb. 1843.

43 Mary Castleyn, *A History of Literacy and Libraries in Ireland* (Dublin, 1984), pp 36–7.

44 Akenson, *Irish Education*, p. 51.

45 Ibid., p. 154.

46 'Education', *Nation*, 14 June 1845.

47 'Irish literature', *Nation*, 15 Mar. 1845.

48 'Education', *Nation*, 18 Feb. 1843.

49 'The schools of the Christian Brothers', *Nation*, 18 Dec. 1847.

50 'Report of the education commissioners – 1846, part 2', *Nation*, 28 Nov. 1846.

51 'Popular education', *Nation*, 27 July 1844.

52 'Education', *Nation*, 18 Feb. 1843; 'The schools of the Christian Brothers', *Nation*, 18 Dec. 1847.

53 L. M. Cullen, 'The cultural basis of Irish nationalism', in Rosalind Mitchison (ed.), *The Roots of Nationalism: Studies in Northern Europe* (Edinburgh, 1980), p. 101; Vincent Morley, 'Views of the past in Irish vernacular literature, 1650–1850', in T. C. W. Blanning and Hagen Schulze (eds), *Unity and Diversity in European Culture* (Oxford, 2006) (*Proceedings of the British Academy*, 134), p. 172.

54 Barry Coldrey, *Faith and Fatherland: The Christian Brothers and the Development of Irish Nationalism, 1828–1921* (Dublin, 1988), p. 9, 57.

55 'The schools of the Christian Brothers', *Nation*, 18 Dec. 1847.

56 'Review of Christian Brothers' *Modern Geography* and *Literary Class Book*', *Nation*, 16 Mar. 1844.

57 Thomas Davis to William Smith O'Brien [1844?] (Duffy, *Young Ireland*, pp 673–4).

58 'Educate that you may be free', *Nation*, 5 Oct. 1844; 'No redress – no inquiry', *Nation*, 15 July 1843.

59 Elizabeth Malcolm, *'Ireland Sober; Ireland Free': Drink and Temperance in Nineteenth-Century Ireland* (Dublin, 1986), pp 144–5.

60 Duffy, *Young Ireland*, pp 528–9.

61 Paul A. Townend, '"Academies of Nationality": the reading room and Irish national movements, 1838–1905', in Lawrence W. McBride (ed.), *Reading Irish Histories: Texts, Contexts and Memory in Modern Ireland* (Dublin, 2003), p. 23.

62 Colm Kerrigan, *Father Mathew and the Irish Temperance Movement 1838–1849* (Cork, 1992), pp 72–3, 109, 117.

63   *Nation*, 28 Jan. 1843.

64   Duffy, *Thomas Davis*, p. 348.

65   Duffy, *My Life*, 1, pp 66–7.

66   'Repeal reading rooms', *Nation*, 17 Aug. 1844.

67   Townend, 'Academies of Nationality', p. 21. On the importance of reading rooms see Roisín Higgins, 'The *Nation* reading rooms', in James H. Murphy (ed.), *The Oxford History of the Irish Book, vol. iv: The Irish Book in English 1800–1891* (Oxford, 2011), pp 262–73; and Marie-Louise Legg, 'Libraries' in ibid., pp 250–54.

68   'The *Nation* – Repeal reading rooms', *Nation*, 8 Aug. 1846.

69   Duffy, *Young Ireland*, pp 500–1.

70   'Repeal reading rooms', *Nation*, 17 Aug. 1844.

71   Ibid., 14 Dec. 1844.

72   'Freedom's way', *Nation*, 30 Aug. 1845.

73   'Popular projects', *Nation*, 15 Apr. 1843.

74   *Nation*, 12 Oct. 1844.

75   'Repeal reading rooms', *Nation*, 8 Feb. 1845.

76   Ibid., 19 Apr. 1845; 'Popular education', *Nation*, 26 Jul. 1845; 'The reading rooms', *Nation*, 11 Oct. 1845.

77   To Davis, Sept. 1844 (Duffy, *Young Ireland*, p. 571).

78   Duffy, *My Life*, 1, p. 68; Duffy to Davis, *c.* June 1844 (Duffy, *Young Ireland*, p. 238).

79   Davis to Duffy, [*c.* 24 Sept. 1844] (Duffy, *Young Ireland*, p. 569).

80   'Knowledge and conciliation', *Nation*, 24 Aug. 1844.

TWO

READING HISTORY: CONTEMPORARY AUTHORS,
ANTIQUARIANS AND FOREIGN INFLUENCES

1   'Irish history', *Nation*, 18 May 1844.

2   Donal McCartney, 'The writing of Irish history, 1800–1830', *Irish Historical Studies*, x, no. 40 (Sept. 1957), p. 62.

3   Charles Gavan Duffy, *Young Ireland: A Fragment of Irish History 1840–1850* (London, 1880), pp 663–5.

4   John Mitchel, *The Life and Times of Aodh O'Neill* (Dublin, 1845), p. 204n; C. P. Meehan, *The Confederation of Kilkenny* (Dublin, 1846), p. 143.

5   'Propagandism', *Nation*, 18 Sept. 1843.

6   Charles Gavan Duffy, *Thomas Davis: The Memoirs of an Irish Patriot* (London, 1890), p. 147.

7   Duffy, *Young Ireland*, p. 664; 'The history of Ireland', *Nation*, 11 Nov. 1843.

8   Barbara Hayley, 'Irish periodicals from the union to the *Nation*', *Anglo-Irish Studies*, ii (1976), p. 105.

9   'Review of O'Connell's *Memoir on Ireland*', *Nation*, 18 Feb. 1843; Daniel O'Connell, *A Memoir on Ireland, Native and Saxon* (Dublin, 1843), pp vii, 43, 46–9.

10   Davis to D. O. Madden, 3 Mar. 1843 (Duffy, *Thomas Davis*, p. 107).

11   *Nation*, 27 May 1843.

12   Thornton MacMahon (ed.), *The Casket of Irish Pearls* (Dublin, 1846), p. 63n.

13 Ibid.

14 Duffy, *Thomas Davis*, p. 108.

15 'The Green Book', *Nation*, 28 Sept. 1844.

16 *Nation*, 26 Oct. 1844.

17 Ibid.

18 'An Irish vampire', *Nation*, 22 Oct. 1842.

19 *Nation*, 4 Nov. 1843.

20 'The history of a hundred years, part I', *Nation*, 20 Nov. 1847.

21 'Propagandism', *Nation*, 18 Sept. 1843.

22 'Review of Thomas Moore's History of Ireland', *Nation*, 27 June 1846.

23 'Review of R. R. Madden, The Connexion between the Kingdom of Ireland and the Crown of England', *Nation*, 25 Oct. 1845.

24 'Review of *Dublin University Magazine*, Feb. 1847', *Nation*, 6 Feb. 1847.

25 See especially Joep Leerssen, 'Petrie: polymath and innovator', in Peter Murray (ed.), *George Petrie: The Rediscovery of Ireland's Past* (Cork & Kinsale, 2004), pp 7–11.

26 *Dublin Penny Journal*, 6 Apr. 1833.

27 Ibid., 8 Sept. 1832.

28 William Stokes, *The Life and Labours in Art and Archaeology of George Petrie* (London, 1868), pp 394–5.

29 Preface to *Dublin Penny Journal*, 30 June 1832.

30 Patricia Boyne, *John O'Donovan (1806–1861): A Biography* (Kilkenny, 1987), pp 51–4.

31 'Ecclesiastical antiquities of Ireland', *Nation*, 19 July 1845.

32 'Review of Charles Lever's St Patrick's Eve', *Nation*, 12 Apr. 1845.

33 [Thomas MacNevin], 'Second letter to a Connaught squire', *Nation*, 30 Sept. 1843.

34 'Gaelic literature', *Nation*, 6 Sept. 1845.

35 *Nation*, 16 Mar. 1844, 6 Apr. 1844; Gillian M. Doherty, *The Irish Ordnance Survey: History, Culture and Memory* (Dublin, 2006), pp 80, 86; J. H. Andrews, *A Paper Landscape: the Ordnance Survey in Nineteenth-Century Ireland* (Oxford, 1975), p. 142.

36 Doherty, *Irish Ordnance Survey*, p. 164, 184.

37 Ibid., pp 31–2.

38 'Survey of Ireland', *Nation*, 16 Mar. 1844 (see also *Nation*, 15 Oct. 1842).

39 Duffy, *Thomas Davis*, pp 147–8.

40 'Irish antiquities and Irish savages', *Nation*, 6 July 1844; 'Preservation of our historical monuments', *Nation*, 5 Dec. 1843.

41 John Hutchinson, *The Dynamics of Cultural Nationalism: The Gaelic Revival and the Creation of the Irish Nation State* (London, 1954), pp 94–6.

42 'Growth of an Irish nation', *Nation*, 12 July 1845.

43 'Review of *Dublin University Magazine*, Feb. 1847', *Nation*, 6 Feb. 1847.

44 'Irish literature and publication', *Nation*, 15 Apr. 1843.

45 Doherty, *Irish Ordnance Survey*, pp 152–5; 'Irish history – The Celtic Atheneum', *Nation*, 7 Mar. 1846.

46 'Review of Roderic O'Flaherty's *Chorographical description of H-Iar or West Connaught 1684 AD* ed. by James Hardiman', *Nation*, 21 Nov. 1846.

47 *Prospectus of the Irish Celtic Society* (1845) (RIA SR 12 I 15, no. 11); Damien Murray, *Romanticism, Nationalism and Irish Antiquarian Societies, 1840–80* (Maynooth, 2000), pp 65–7.

48 'The Irish Celtic Society', *Nation*, 13 Dec. 1845; 'Irish history – The Celtic Atheneum', *Nation*, 7 Mar. 1846.

49 Damien Murray, *Romanticism, Nationalism and Irish Antiquarian Societies, 1840–80* (Maynooth, 2000), p. 69.

50 John O'Donovan to Davis, 11 July 1845 (RIA MS 12 P 19 (12)); Duffy, *Thomas Davis*, pp 337–8; Doherty, *Irish Ordnance Survey*, p. 120. Davis also corresponded with the Cork antiquarian John Windele (1801–65), encouraging him to write a history of Cork – Davis to Windele, 22 Nov. 1843 (RIA, Windele MS 4/B/2/156).

51 On its significance see especially Bernadette Cunningham, '"An honour to the nation": publishing John O'Donovan's edition of the Annals of the Four Masters, 1848–56', in Martin Fanning and Raymond Gillespie (eds), *Print Culture and Intellectual Life in Ireland, 1660–1941* (Dublin, 2006), pp 116–42; idem., 'John O'Donovan's edition of the Annals of the Four Masters: An Irish classic', *European Studies*, 26 (2008), pp 129–49.

52 'Review of Prospectus of the Annals of the Four Masters by John O'Donovan', *Nation*, 2 Mar. 1844; 'Review of John O'Donovan's Annals of the Four Masters from 1171–1616', *Nation*, 29 Jan. 1848.

53 'Hy Fiachrach', *Nation*, 7 Sept. 1844.

54 Duffy, *Thomas Davis*, p. 340; Patricia Boyne, *John O'Donovan (1806–61): A Biography* (Kilkenny, 1987) p. 84.

55 *Nation*, 9 Nov. 1844; Bernadette Cunningham, 'John O'Donovan's edition of the Annals of the Four Masters: An Irish classic', *European Studies*, 26 (2008), p. 138.

56 'Irish annalists, part 1', *Nation*, 24 Oct. 1846.

57 'Irish annalists, part 2', *Nation*, 7 Nov. 1846.

58 Duffy, *Thomas Davis*, pp 87, 337–40.

59 Ibid., pp 352–3.

60 'India – her own and another's', *The Citizen or Dublin Monthly Magazine*, I, pp 255–63, 418–33; II, pp 120–9, 325–36; III, pp 83–95; 'Who are the Afghans? ibid., v, 439–52.

61 *Dublin Monthly Magazine*, I, p. 419.

62 'Sympathy', *Nation*, 25 Mar. 1843.

63 'Patience and propaganda', *Nation*, 9 Sept. 1843.

64 'Sketches of Polish history', *Nation*, 28 Mar. 1846; see also *Nation*, 4 Apr. 1846.

65 Michael J. Barry, 'Ireland as she was, as she is, and as she shall be', in *Repeal Prize Essays* (Dublin, 1845), p. 12.

66 'Our Scottish cousins', *Nation*, 3 Dec. 1842; 'The kirk of Scotland', *Nation*, 28 Jan. 1843; 'The fate of the kirk', *Nation*, 11 Mar. 1843.

67 'Repeal of the Scottish union', *Nation*, 18 Mar. 1843; 'Scotland our ally – her kirk and union', *Nation*, 26 Nov. 1842.

68 *Nation*, 12 Nov. 1842.

69 'How America became a nation', *Nation*, 1 May 1847.

70 Nicholas Mansergh, *Ireland in the Age of Reform and Revolution* (London, 1940), pp 46, 56–7; Kevin B. Nowlan, 'The Risorgimento and Ireland, 1820–48', in R. Dudley Edwards (ed.), *Ireland and the Italian Risorgimento* (Dublin, 1960), pp 24–5; Colin Barr, 'Giuseppe Mazzini and Irish nationalism, 1845–70', in C. A. Bayly and E. F. Biagini (eds), *Giuseppe Mazzini and the Globalisation of Democratic Nationalism* (Oxford, 2008) (Proceedings of the British Academy, no. 152), pp 125–44.

71 Eugene Kamenka (ed.), *Nationalism: The Nature and Evolution of an Idea* (London, 1976), p. 40.

72 Peter Alter, *Nationalism* (London, 1989), pp 59–64.

73 Robert B. Pynsent, 'Zabid Vysokomytsky: a Czech rebel historian of 1848–9', in Dennis Deletant & Harry Hanak (eds), *Historians as Nation Builders: Central and South East Europe* (London, 1988), pp 174–205.

74 'Irish history', *Nation*, 7 Mar. 1846; Duffy, *Young Ireland*, pp 166–7.

75 'National manuscripts', *Nation*, 31 July 1847.

76 'Irish history', *Nation*, 5 Apr. 1845.

77 Emery Edward Neff, *The Poetry of History: The Contribution of Literature and Literary Scholarship to the Writing of History since Voltaire* (New York, 1947), pp 119–20; Lionel Gossman, *Between History and Literature* (Cambridge, Mass., 1990), p. 99, 102.

78 *Nation*, 4 Nov. 1843; 3 Dec. 1843.

79 'A ballad history of Ireland', *Nation*, 30 Nov. 1844.

80 'Irish literature', *Nation*, 15 Mar. 1845.

81 Owen Dudley Edwards, '"True Thomas": Carlyle, Young Ireland and the legacy of millennialism', in David Sorensen and Rodger L. Tarr (eds), *The Carlyles at Home and Abroad* (Aldershot, 2006), pp 61–76.

82 Mitchel to Martin, 29 Nov. 1838 (William Dillon, *Life of John Mitchel* (London, 2 vols, 1888), I, p. 37).

83 Mitchel to Martin, *c.* May 1846 (William Dillon, *Life of John Mitchel* (London, 2 vols, 1888), I, p. 111); *Nation*, 10 Jan., 21 Mar. 1846.

84 Charles Gavan Duffy, *My Life in Two Hemispheres* (2 vols, New York, 1898), I, p. 52.

85 Roger Swift, 'Carlyle and Ireland', in D. George Boyce and Roger Swift (eds), *Problems and Perspectives in Irish History since 1800: Essays in Honour of Patrick Buckland* (Dublin, 2004), p. 135; John Morrow, 'Thomas Carlyle, "Young Ireland" and the "condition of Ireland question"', *The Historical Journal*, LI, no. 3 (2008), pp 643–67.

86 Charles Gavan Duffy, *Conversations with Carlyle* (London, 1896), p. 103.

87 J. A. Froude (ed.), *Letters and Memorials of Jane Welsh Carlyle* (London, 3 vols, 1883), i, 307.

88 Duffy, *Conversations with Carlyle*, p. 4, 23.

89 *Nation*, 10 Jan. 1846.

90 Joep Leerssen, '1798: The recurrence of violence and two conceptions of history', *The Irish Review*, 22 (Summer, 1998), p. 40.

91 Mitchel to Duffy, 22 Aug., 11 Sept. 1845 (NLI MS 5756/183, 191).

92 Thomas D'Arcy McGee, *A Memoir of the Life and Conquests of Art Mac Murrogh* (Dublin, 1847), p. 74.

93 Helen F. Mulvey, *Thomas Davis and Ireland: A Biographical Study* (Washington DC, 2003), pp 37–40; Patrick O'Neill, *Ireland and Germany: A Study in Literary Relations* (New York, 1985), pp 95–8.

94 O'Neill, *Ireland and Germany*, pp 103–4.

95 Eugene Kamenka (ed.), *Nationalism: The Nature and Evolution of an Idea* (London, 1976), p. 40.

96 Hans Kohn, *The Idea of Nationalism: A Study of its Origins and Background* (New York, 1944), p. 429; Kamenka (ed.), *Nationalism*, p. 25.

97 F. M. Barnard, *Herder's Social and Political Thought: From Enlightenment to Nationalism* (Oxford, 1965), pp 2–5.

THREE

WRITING HISTORY

1   [Mac], 'The Ulster Milesians: the O'Neills and O'Reillys No. 1', *Nation*, 7 Jan. 1843.

2   'Irish history', *Nation*, 5 Apr. 1845.

3   *The Citizen or Dublin Monthly Magazine*, vii (Jan.–Apr. 1843), pp 25–42, 75–90, 105–34, 170–201.

4   See Kevin B. Nowlan, *The Politics of Repeal: A Study of the Relations between Great Britain and Ireland, 1841–50* (London, 1965); Charles Gavan Duffy, *Young Ireland: A Fragment of Irish History 1840–1850* (London, 1880), pp 305–7.

5   Thomas Davis, *The Patriot Parliament of 1689* (London, 1893), pp xci–xcii.

6   Ibid., p. 70, 137.

7   Ibid., pp 52–3, 55–62.

8   Ibid., p. 62, 150.

9   Ibid., pp 149–51.

10 Ibid., pp xciii, 2.

11 Ibid., pp 38–9.

12 *Nation*, 12 July 1845.

13 Davis, *Patriot Parliament*, p. 39.

14 Thomas Davis, *Speeches of the Right Honourable John Philpot Curran* (Dublin, 1843); D. O. Madden, *The Select Speeches of the Right Hon. Henry Grattan* (Dublin, 1845); Thomas MacNevin, *The Speeches of the Right Honourable Richard Lalor Shiel MP* (Dublin, 1845).

15 For Davis's history notes see his papers at NLI MS 3199, RIA MS 12 P 15/15–17 and RIA MS 12 P 16.

16 'The individuality of a native literature', *Nation*, 21 Aug. 1847.

17 'Street ballads and popular poetry', in *The Voice of the Nation* (Dublin, 1844), pp 104–6 (this article does not appear to have been published in the *Nation*).

18 'The individuality of a native literature', *Nation*, 21 Aug. 1847.

19 Charles Gavan Duffy, *The Ballad Poetry of Ireland* (Dublin, 1845), p. 32, 38; Duffy, *Young Ireland*, pp 164–5.

20 M. J. Barry (ed.), *The Songs of Ireland* (Dublin, 1845), p. vii.

21 'Essay on Irish songs', *Nation*, 4 Jan. 1845; see also Duffy, *Ballad Poetry*, p. 38.

22 'Essay on Irish songs', *Nation*, 4 Jan. 1845.

23 For the influence of both the United Irishmen and Moore see especially Mary Helen Thuente, *The Harp Re-Strung: The United Irishmen and the Rise of Irish Literary Nationalism* (New York, 1994), pp 171–92.

24 'National Gallery 1: Thomas Moore', *Nation*, 29 Oct. 1842.

25 'Irish songs', *Nation*, 21 Dec. 1844.

26 'Irish literature and publication', *Nation*, 15 Apr. 1843.

27 *Nation*, 25 Mar. 1843; *Nation*, 28 Oct. 1843.

28 Duffy, *Young Ireland*, p. 181.

29 'Essay on Irish songs', *Nation*, 4 Jan. 1845.

30 Samuel Ferguson, 'Thomas Davis', *Dublin University Magazine*, xxix (Feb. 1847), p. 191.

31 John Mitchel, *The Last Conquest of Ireland (perhaps)* (Glasgow, 1861), p. 84.

32 'Ballad poetry of Ireland', The *Celt*, Aug. 1858, pp 285–7.

33 See, for example, Brigitte Anton, 'Women of the *Nation*', *History Ireland*, 1, no. 3 (autumn 1993), pp 34–5; and Jan Cannavan, 'Romantic revolutionary Irishwomen: women, Young Ireland and 1848', in Margaret Kelleher and James H. Murphy (eds), *Gender Perspectives in 19th Century Ireland* (Dublin, 1997), pp 212–20.

34 Jane Wilde, 'Thomas Moore', in *Notes on Men, Women and Books* (London, 1891), p. 221.

35 Duffy, *Ballad Poetry*, p. 29.

36 Charles Gavan Duffy, 'Personal memories of James Clarence Mangan', *Dublin Review*, 142 (1908), p. 286.

37 Mangan to Duffy, 10 Nov. 1846 (NLI MS 248, f. 9); Ellen Shannon-Mangan, *James Clarence Mangan: A Biography* (Dublin, 1996), p. 165; David Lloyd, N*ationalism and Minor Literature: James Clarence Mangan and the Emergence of Irish Cultural Nationalism* (Berkeley, 1987), p. 79.

38 NLI MS 138, Mangan MS no. 13 cited in Shannon-Mangan, *James Clarence Mangan*, p. 339.

39 NLI MS 138, Mangan MS no. 20; Mangan to Mitchel (*United Irishman*, 25 Mar. 1848).

40 C. P. Meehan (ed.), *Essays in Prose and Verse by J. Clarence Mangan* (Dublin and London, 1884); D. J. O'Donoghue (ed.), *Poems of James Clarence Mangan . . . introduced by John Mitchel* (Dublin, 1903); Charles Gavan Duffy, 'Personal memories of James Clarence Mangan', *Dublin Review*, 142 (1908), p. 278–94.

41 R. F. Foster, *Paddy and Mr Punch: Connections in Irish History* (London, 1993), p. 289.

42 *Nation*, 13 July 1844; 1 Apr. 1843; 28 Jan. 1843; 3 Feb. 1844.

43 'A ballad history of Ireland', *Nation*, 16 Nov. 1844.

44 Duffy, *Thomas Davis*, p. 200.

45 'A ballad history of Ireland', *Nation*, 30 Nov. 1844.

46 Ibid.

47 Ibid.,16 Nov. 1844.

48 *Nation*, 18 Jan. 1845; 15 Mar. 1845; 22 Mar. 1845; 3 May 1845.

49 Davis to William Smith O'Brien, *c.* June 1845 (Duffy, *Young Ireland*, p. 672).

50 *The Times*, 12 Dec. 1843.

51 Georges Denis Zimmerman, *Irish Political Street Ballads and Rebel Songs, 1780–1900* (Geneva, 1966), p. 80n.

52 Charles Gavan Duffy, *My Life in Two Hemispheres* (2 vols, New York, 1898), 1, pp 89–90; Duffy, *Young Ireland*, p. 285.

53 William Joseph O'Neill Daunt, *Eighty-Five Years of Irish History* (London, 1888), p. 221.

54 Duffy, *Young Ireland*, pp 164–5; 'Street ballads and popular poetry', in *The Voice of the Nation* (Dublin, 1844), p. 106.

55 Duffy, *Thomas Davis*, p. 95.

56 'Irish literature and publication', *Nation*, 15 Apr. 1843.

57 Davis to D. O. Maddyn, nd [*c.* 1843] (Duffy, *Young Ireland*, p. 289).

58 'Continental Literature', *Nation*, 3 Dec. 1843.

59 'Irish literature and publication', *Nation*, 15 Apr. 1843.

60 Robert H. Canary and Henry Kozicki (eds), *The Writing of History: Literary Form and Historical Understanding* (Madison, Wisconsin, 1978), p. 38.

61 Cited in J. R. Hale, *The Evolution of British Historiography* (London, 1967), p. 36.

62 Joep Leerssen, *National Thought in Europe: A Cultural History* (Amsterdam, 2006), pp 124–5.

63 'Irish historical romance', *Nation*, 3 May 1845; Duffy, *Thomas Davis*, p. 8.

64 'National Gallery 1: Thomas Moore', *Nation*, 29 Oct. 1842; 'Popular reading societies', ibid. 4 Mar. 1843; see also Joep Leerssen, *Remembrance and Imagination; Patterns in the Historical and Literary Representation of Ireland in the Nineteenth Century* (Cork, 1996), pp 85–6.

65 *Nation*, 10 June 1843; J. M. Hone, *Thomas Davis* (London, 1934), p. 80.

66 'Review of Charles Lever's *St Patrick's Eve*', *Nation*, 12 Apr. 1845.

67 Duffy, *Young Ireland*, pp 502–3; 'Review of Charles Lever's *St Patrick's Eve*', *Nation*, 12 Apr. 1845.

68 Duffy, *Young Ireland*, p. 505; 'Review of Charles Lever's *St Patrick's Eve*', *Nation*, 12 Apr. 1845; *Nation*, 12 Apr. 1845; Malcolm Brown, *The Politics of Irish Literature: From Thomas Davis to W. B. Yeats* (London, 1972), p. 65.

69 'Reviews', *Nation*, 2 Aug. 1845.

70 The *Celt*, May 1858, p. 114.

71 'Patience and propaganda', *Nation*, 9 Sept. 1843.

72 Duffy, *Thomas Davis*, p. 205; Davis's research notes are held in RIA MS 12 P 15–16.

73 Duffy, *Thomas Davis*, p. 208.

74 'Irish history', *Nation*, 5 Apr. 1845.

75 'Irish literature', *Nation*, 15 Mar. 1845; see also *Nation*, 15 Oct. 1842.

76 'Irish history', *Nation*, 5 Apr. 1845.

77 Ibid.

78 Charles Gavan Duffy to Smith O'Brien, nd (Charles Gavan Duffy, *Four Years of Irish History* (London, 1883), p. 64n).

79 'Review of the writings of Nicholas French', *Nation*, 14 Nov. 1846.

80 'James Duffy the publisher', *Irish Monthly*, XXIII (1895), pp 596–9; Rolf Loeber and Magda Stouthamer-Loeber, 'James Duffy and Catholic nationalism', in James H. Murphy (ed.), *The Oxford History of the Irish Book, vol. iv: The Irish Book in English 1800–1891* (Oxford, 2011), pp 115–21.

81 Preface to Thomas MacNevin, *The Confiscation of Ulster* (Dublin, 1847), p. 2.

82 T. F. O'Sullivan, *The Young Irelanders* (Tralee, 1944), p. 421.

83 'Repeal reading rooms', *Nation*, 14 Dec. 1844.

84 Thomas MacNevin, *History of the Volunteers of 1782* (Dublin, 1845), pp 38, 80,126–8.

85 Thomas MacNevin, *The Confiscation of Ulster in the Reign of James the First, commonly called the Ulster Plantation* (Dublin, 1846), p. 29, 151, 250.

86 C. P. Meehan, *History of the Confederation of Kilkenny* (Dublin, 1846), p. 1, 72.

87 'Notes on the Library of Ireland', Duffy, *Young Ireland*, pp 679–80; P. S. O'Hegarty, 'The "Library of Ireland" 1845–1847', in M. J. MacManus (ed.), *Thomas Davis and Young Ireland* (Dublin, 1945), pp 109–113.

88 Duffy, *Young Ireland*, p. 679; Duffy, *Four Years*, p. 59; 'Listing of the Library of Ireland', *Nation*, 5 July 1845.

89 Davis to John Mitchel, 7 July 1845 (Mitchel, *Last Conquest*, p. 88).

90 'Irish history', *Nation*, 5 Apr. 1845.

91 John Curry, *Historical and Critical Review of the Civil Wars in Ireland* (London, 1775); James MacGeoghegan, *History of Ireland, Ancient and Modern. Translated from the French by P. O'Kelly* (Dublin, 1844); Thomas Leland, *The History of Ireland* (Dublin, 1773); Sylvester O'Halloran, *A General History of Ireland* (Dublin, 1778); Francis Plowden, *An Historical Review of the State of Ireland* (London, 1803); Denis Taaffe, *An Impartial History of Ireland* (4 vols, Dublin, 1809–11).

92 Duffy, *Thomas Davis*, p. 335; Denis Gwynn, 'John E. Pigot and Thomas Davis', *Studies: An Irish Quarterly Review*, XXXVIII (1949), p. 156.

93 Duffy, *Four Years*, p. 224; The works of the National Library of Ireland were the subject of a highly critical article in the *Dublin University Magazine*, XXXIX (Jan. 1847) pp 80–90, which denounced their glorification of the 1798 Rebellion as 'most dangerous auxiliaries to the cause of disloyalty and sedition' and dismissed the entire series as 'treason made easy' (pp 81–2). In his *Irish Literature in English: The Romantic Period* (1789–1850) (Gerrards Cross, 1980), pp 146–7, Patrick Rafroidi erroneously attributes these publications to the *Nation*.

94 Davis to Pigot, July 1845, 'Letters of Thomas Davis', *Irish Monthly*, XVI (1888), p. 346; Davis to Mitchel, 7 July 1845 (Mitchel, *Last Conquest*, p. 88).

95 A. M. Sullivan, *The Story of Ireland* (Dublin, 1910), pp 236–7.

96 R. Barry O'Brien, *The Best Hundred Irish Books* (Dublin, 1886), p. 8.

97 Ibid., p. 45.

98 P. S. O'Hegarty, 'The "Library of Ireland" 1845–1847', in M. J. MacManus (ed.), *Thomas Duffy and Young Ireland* (Dublin, 1945), p. 110, 113.

FOUR
THE USES OF HISTORY

1 'Circular letter from the Dublin Society of United Irishmen' (30 Dec. 1791), in *The Report of the Secret Committee of the House of Commons* (Dublin, 1798), p. 94.

2 Charles Gavan Duffy, *Thomas Davis: The Memoirs of an Irish Patriot* (London, 1890), p. 70.

3 John Mitchel, *The Last Conquest of Ireland (perhaps)* (Glasgow, 1861), p. 84.

4 'The fate of history', *Nation*, 6 Nov. 1847.

5 'The lessons of history', *Nation*, 4 Nov. 1843.

6 Davis papers, NLI MS 3199.

7 Duffy, *Thomas Davis*, p. 137.

8 Charles Gavan Duffy, *My Life in Two Hemispheres* (2 vols, New York, 1898), I, p. 13.

9 'National monuments', *Nation*, 8 Nov. 1845.

10 David Dwan, *The Great Community: Culture and Nationalism in Ireland* (Dublin, 2008), pp 31–9, 58–61.

11 'United Irishmen'. *Nation*, 8 July 1843.

12 'National literature', *Nation*, 20 Sept. 1845.

13 'Irish scenery', *Nation*, 20 July 1844; 'A year's work', ibid., 14 Oct. 1843.

14 W. Torrens McCullagh, *On the Use and Study of History* (Dublin, 1842), p. 23, 25.

15 'The history of Ireland', *Nation*, 11 Nov. 1843.

16 'National art', *Nation*, 12 Aug. 1843; 'Hints for Irish historical paintings', ibid., 29 July 1843.

17 'Irish pictures', *Nation*, 19 Apr. 1845.

18 'Public monuments', in *The Voice of the Nation* (Dublin, 1844), p. 156; (a slightly different version of this article appears in 'Answers to Correspondents', *Nation*, 5 Aug. 1843).

19 'The red above the green', *Nation*, 17 Apr. 1847.

20 *Nation*, 18 Feb. 1843; Duffy, *Thomas Davis*, p. 137.

21 'National literature', *Nation*, 20 Sept. 1845.

22 'National manuscripts', *Nation*, 31 July 1847.

23 'Irish literature', *Nation*, 15 Mar. 1845.

24 '"Saxon views" of Irish history', *Nation*, 9 Jan. 1847.

25 'National monuments', *Nation*, 8 Nov. 1845; 'Saxon views of Irish history', *Nation*, 17 Apr. 1847.

26 Thomas MacNevin, *The History of the Volunteers of '82* (Dublin, 1846), p. 58; Charles Gavan Duffy, *Young Ireland: A Fragment of Irish History 1840–1850* (London, 1880), p. 85; Bernadette Cunningham, *The World of Geoffrey Keating: History, Myth and Religion in Seventeenth-Century Ireland* (Dublin, 2000), pp 114–16.

27 Thomas MacNevin, *The Confiscation of Ulster* (Dublin, 1846), p. 248.

28 'National monuments', *Nation*, 8 Nov. 1845.

29 'Old Ireland', *Nation*, 10 Sept. 1844; 'Popular fallacies about Irish history', *Nation*, 9 Jan. 1847.

30 Duffy, *Young Ireland*, p. 83.

31 'The Celts in Ireland', *Nation*, 8 June 1844; *Nation*, 29 May 1847; C. P. Meehan, *The Geraldines* (Dublin, 1847), p. ix.

32 'The study of Irish in Ireland', *Nation*, 14 Mar. 1846; 'Creed of the *Nation*', *Nation*, 29 Apr. 1848; 'National monuments', *Nation*, 8 Nov. 1845; 'Popular education', *Nation*, 26 July 1845.

33 MacNevin, *Confiscation*, pp 27, 57; see also *Nation*, 9 Nov. 1844.

34 'Irish history – Mr D'Alton', *Nation*, 22 Nov. 1845.

35 'An Irish vampire', *Nation*, 22 Oct. 1842.

36 John Mitchel, *The Life and Times of Aodh O'Neill* (Dublin, 1845), pp v–vi.

37 Oliver MacDonagh, *States of Mind: A Study of Anglo-Irish Conflict* (London, 1983), pp 9–10.

38 'The life and times of Henry Grattan', *The Citizen or Dublin Monthly Magazine*, IV, 53.

39 'The history of Ireland', *Nation*, 11 Nov. 1843.

40 'The lessons of history – Saxon, Norman and Irish', *Nation*, 16 Sept. 1843.

41 'Popular fallacies about Irish history', *Nation*, 9 Jan. 1847.

42 MacNevin, *Confiscation*, pp 21, 106, 109–10.

43 'Propagandism', *Nation*, 18 Sept. 1843.

44 Charles Rearick, *Beyond the Enlightenment: Historians and Folklore in Nineteenth-Century France* (Bloomington, In., 1974), p. 24.

45 'Irish history', *Nation*, 18 May 1844.

46 J. C. O'Callaghan, *History of the Irish Brigades in the Service of France* (Shannon, 1969), p. vi.

47 Herbert Butterfield, *Man on his Past* (Cambridge, 1969), p. 70.

48 Graham Gargett, 'Voltaire and Irish history', *Eighteenth-Century Ireland*, v (1990), pp 117–41.

49 MacNevin, *Confiscation*, p. 50.

50 'National literature', *Nation*, 20 Sept. 1845.

51 James Quinn, 'John Mitchel and the rejection of the nineteenth century', *Éire-Ireland*, XXXVIII, pts 3–4 (fall/winter 2003), pp 90–108.

52 John Mitchel, *Jail Journal, or Five Years in British Prisons* (New York, 1854), p. 20, 128n.

53 Ibid., p. 20, 29, 128n.

54 Ibid., pp 86–7.

55 'Misrepresentations of history', *Nation*, 9 Dec. 1843.

56 'Letter to the Duke of Wellington', *Nation*, 8 June 1844.

57 Mitchel, *Last Conquest*, p. 33.

58 'Review of the 'Battle of Moira' by John O'Donovan, *Nation*, 22 Oct. 1842; 'Illustrations of Irish history', *Nation*, 13 May 1843.

59   Thomas D'Arcy McGee, *A Memoir of the Life and Conquests of Art Mac Murrogh* [*sic*] (Dublin, 1847), p. xvii.

60   'Review of T. D. McGee, *Irish Writers of the Seventeenth Century*', *Nation*, 7 Feb. 1846.

61   'The battle of Fontenoy', *Nation*, 26 Apr. 1845.

62   'Pictorial history of Ireland', *Nation*, 18 Nov. 1843; 'The Brigade at Fontenoy 11 May 1745', *Nation*, 17 May 1845.

63   Thomas Bartlett, 'Ormuzd abroad . . . Ahriman at home: some early historians of the Wild Geese in French service, 1750–1950', in J. Conroy (ed.), *Franco-Irish Connections: Essays, Memoirs and Poems in Honour of Pierre Joannon* (Dublin, 2009), pp 15–30.

64   John Cornelius O'Callaghan, *The Green Book or Gleanings from the Writing Desk of a Literary Agitator* (Dublin, 1841), pp xvi–xvii, 209, 216.

65   'Review of *The Green Book*', *Nation*, 28 Sept. 1844.

66   'Illustrations of Irish history, no. iii', *Nation*, 22 Apr. 1843.

67   MacNevin, *Volunteers*, p. 155, 81.

68   D. J. O'Donoghue (ed.), *Essays, Literary and Historical by Thomas Davis* (Dundalk, 1914), p. 30.

69   'Irish biography', *Nation*, 27 Feb. 1847.

70   'The historical works of . . . Nicholas French', *Nation*, 26 Dec. 1846.

71   Duffy, *Young Ireland*, pp 67–8.

72   Duffy, *Thomas Davis*, pp 137–8.

73   Thomas D'Arcy McGee, *A Memoir of the Life and Conquests of Art Mac Murrogh* [*sic*] (Dublin, 1847), p. 133.

74   'Irish biography', *Nation*, 27 Feb. 1847.

75   *Nation*, 18 Mar. 1843.

76   *Nation*, 22 Apr. 1843.

77   'Irish biography', *Nation*, 27 Feb. 1847.

78   Charles Gavan Duffy, *Four Years of Irish History* (London, 1883), p. 63.

79   For the myth-making surrounding Sarsfield see Liam Irwin, 'Sarsfield: the man and the myth', in Bernadette Whelan (ed.), *The Last of the Great Wars* (Limerick, 1995), pp 108–26.

80   T. W. Moody, 'Irish history and Irish mythology', *Hermathena*, cxxiv (1978), p. 17.

81   Duffy, *Thomas Davis*, p. 137.

82   'No redress – no inquiry', *Nation*, 15 July 1843.

83   'The lessons of history – Saxon, Norman and Irish', *Nation*, 16 Sept. 1843.

84   'Divide and conquer', *Nation*, 4 Nov. 1843.

85   'The history of Ireland', *Nation*, 11 Nov. 1843.

86   Duffy, *Young Ireland*, p. 282.

87   MacNevin, *Volunteers*, p. 73.

88   C. P. Meehan, *The Confederation of Kilkenny* (Dublin, 1846); Thomas Davis, *The Patriot Parliament of 1689, with its Statutes, Votes and Proceedings*, ed. by Charles Gavan Duffy (Dublin, 1893); MacNevin, *Volunteers* (Dublin, 1845).

89   Benedict Anderson, *Imagined Communities: Reflections on the Origins and Spread of Nationalism* (1983; revised ed. London, 2006), p. 6, 36.

90   W. J. Fitzpatrick, *The Life of the Very Revd Thomas N. Burke* (2 vols, London, 1885), i, p. 71.

91   'The Celts in Ireland', *Nation*, 29 May 1847.

92   'National manuscripts', *Nation*, 31 July 1847.

93　See, for example, Julie M. Dugger, 'Black Ireland's race: Thomas Carlyle and the Young Ireland movement', *Victorian Studies*, XLVIII, no. 3 (spring 2006), pp 462–3.

94　'English morality', *Nation*, 24 Dec. 1842 (a toned-down version of this article appears as 'National distinctions', in *The Voice of the Nation* (Dublin, 1844), pp 116–18).

95　'Continental literature', *Nation*, 26 Nov. 1843.

96　'Ballad poetry of Ireland', *Nation*, 2 Aug. 1845.

97　'Letter to the Duke of Wellington', *Nation*, 8 June 1844.

98　'*Times* commissioner', *Nation*, 6 Sept. 1845.

99　Maureen Wall, 'The decline of the Irish language', in Brian Ó Cuív (ed.), *A View of the Irish Language* (Dublin, 1969), pp 81–90; P. Ó Loinsigh, 'The Irish language in the nineteenth century', *Oideas*, 14 (1975), pp 5–21; Garret FitzGerald, 'Estimates for baronies of minimum level of Irish-speaking among successive Decennial Cohorts: 1771–1781 to 1861–1871', *Proceedings of the Royal Irish Academy*, 84C (1984), p. 127; B. S. MacAodha, 'Aspects of the linguistic geography of Ireland in the early nineteenth century', *Studia Celtica*, 20/21 (1985–6), pp 205–20.

100　K. R. Minogue, *Nationalism* (London, 1969), pp 60–1.

101　Gearóid Ó Tuathaigh, 'The state, sentiment and the politics of language', in Bruce Stewart (ed.), *Hearts and Minds: Irish Culture and Society under the Act of Union* (Gerrards Cross, 2002), pp 76–8.

102　'Our national language', *Nation*, 1 Apr. 1843, p. 394.

103　'The Irish language', *Nation*, 30 Dec. 1843.

104　Denny Lane, 'The Irish accent in English literature', *Irish Monthly*, XXI (Mar. 1893), pp 153–6.

105　Duffy, *Young Ireland*, p. 561.

106　Ibid., p. 563.

107　'Report of the education commissioners', *Nation*, 28 Nov. 1846.

108　Charles Gavan Duffy, *Ballad Poetry* (1866), p. 24; Denis Florence MacCarthy (ed.), *The Book of Irish Ballads* (Dublin, 1846), p. 23; 'The individuality of a native literature', *Nation*, 21 Aug. 1847.

109　Charles Gavan Duffy, *Ballad Poetry* (1866), pp 24–6.

110　P. S. O'Hegarty, *A History of Ireland under the Union 1801–1922* (London, 1952), p. 628.

111　Perhaps best expressed by Thomas Davis in his 'Orange and Green will carry the day', *Nation*, 14 Dec. 1844; see also 'A nation', *Nation*, 20 July 1844, and 'Celts and Saxons', *Nation*, 13 Apr. 1844.

112　Mitchel, *Aodh O'Neill*, p. xi.

113　'The betrayed Protestants', *Nation*, 25 Jan. 1845.

114　'The Orangemen of Ireland', *Nation*, 14 June 1845.

115　'Orange anniversaries', *Nation*, 29 June 1844.

116　'Twelfth of August', *Nation*, 9 Aug. 1845.

117　'Irish history – The Celtic Athenaeum', *Nation*, 7 Mar. 1846.

118　'Irish sedition', *Nation*, 9 Sept. 1843.

119　Samuel Ferguson, 'The Annals of the Four Masters', *Dublin University Magazine*, XXXI (1848), p. 361.

120　Lady Ferguson, *Sir Samuel Ferguson in the Ireland of his Day* (2 vols, London), I, pp 38–45; Eve Patten, *Samuel Ferguson and the Culture of Nineteenth-Century Ireland* (Dublin, 2004), pp 40–51.

121　'Our Protestant fellow citizens', *Nation*, 13 May 1848; 'Protestant Repeal Association', *Nation*, 3 June 1848.

122　Eve Patten, *Samuel Ferguson and the Culture of Nineteenth-Century Ireland* (Dublin, 2004), p. 179.

123 'Review of the *Dublin University Magazine* for February', *Nation*, 6 Feb. 1847.

124 Duffy, *Thomas Davis*, pp 352–3.

125 W. J. O'Neill Daunt, *Eighty-Five Years of Irish History* (London, 1888), p. 226.

126 D. O. Madden, *Ireland and its Rulers since 1829* (3 vols, London, 1843), p. 230.

127 'Review of McGee, *Irish Writers of the Seventeenth Century*', *Nation*, 7 Feb. 1846.

128 *Irish American*, 27 Mar. 1852.

FIVE

MAKING HISTORY

1 See *Reports of the Parliamentary Committee of the Loyal National Repeal Association of Ireland* (3 vols, Dublin, 1844–6).

2 'Slander and coercion', *Nation*, 21 Mar. 1846.

3 Charles Gavan Duffy, *Young Ireland: A Fragment of Irish History* (London, 1880), p. 65.

4 Duffy, *Young Ireland*, p. 163, 165.

5 *Nation*, 17 June 1843.

6 *Nation*, 20 Jan. 1844.

7 Duffy, *Young Ireland*, p. 383.

8 *Nation*, 7 Sept. 1844.

9 Kevin B. Nowlan, *The Politics of Repeal* (London, 1964), pp 57–8.

10 Charles Gavan Duffy, *Thomas Davis: The Memoirs of an Irish Patriot* (London, 1890), p. 187.

11 'The *Nation* – Repeal reading rooms', *Nation*, 8 Aug. 1846; Duffy, *Young Ireland*, pp 500–1.

12 Duffy, *Young Ireland*, pp 287–8.

13 Charlotte Kelly, 'The '82 club', *Studies: An Irish Quarterly Review*, XXXIII (1944), p. 257.

14 'Onward again', *Nation*, 11 Jan. 1845; see also *Nation*, 18 Jan. 1845.

15 Kelly, 'The '82 club', *Studies* XXXIII (1944), pp 260–2; by June 1846 the *Nation* was complaining of the club's inaction ('Irish music', *Nation*, 27 June 1846). On its annoyance with O'Connell see T. M. Ray to O'Connell, 20 June 1846 (M. R. O'Connell (ed.), *O'Connell Correspondence*, VIII, p. 53).

16 Oliver MacDonagh, *The Life of Daniel O'Connell 1775–1847* (London, 1991), pp 54–5, 63, 94; C. J. Woods, 'Historical revision: was O'Connell a United Irishman?', *Irish Historical Studies*, XXXV (2006), pp 173–83.

17 *Nation*, 8 July 1843 and 25 July 1845. See especially Sean Ryder, 'Speaking of '98: Young Ireland and republican memory', *Éire-Ireland*, 34: 2 (1999), pp 51–69; and idem, 'Young Ireland and the 1798 rebellion', in L. M. Geary (ed.), *Rebellion and Remembrance in Modern Ireland* (Dublin, 2001), pp 135–47.

18 *Nation*, 8 July 1843.

19 Ibid.

20 See G. K. Peatling, 'Who fears to speak of politics? John Kells Ingram and hypothetical nationalism', *Irish Historical Studies*, XXXI (1998–9), pp 202–21.

21 Ryder, 'Young Ireland and the 1798 rebellion', pp 135–8.

22 Ryder, 'Speaking of '98', p. 65, 68.

23 *Nation*, 27 Sept. 1845.

24 NLI MS 1791/24–7; *Nation*, 17 Dec. 1842.

25 Marianne Elliott, *Wolfe Tone: Prophet of Irish Independence* (Yale, 1989), pp 413–4.

26 'Ninety-eight', *Nation*, 28 Sept. 1844.

27 *Nation*, 23 Sept. 1843.

28 'Ninety-eight', *Nation*, 28 Sept. 1844.

29 'Beware of the Whigs', *Nation*, 30 May 1846; 'Look out for the Whigs', *Nation*, 13 June 1846.

30 *Nation*, 25 July 1845.

31 Ibid., 14 Feb. 1846.

32 *United Irishmen*, 12 Feb. 1848.

33 *Nation*, 17 May 1845.

34 See Denis Gwynn, *O'Connell, Davis and the Colleges Bill* (Cork, 1948); Donal Kerr, *Peel, Priests and Politics* (Oxford, 1982), pp 312–14.

35 Gwynn, *O'Connell, Davis and the Colleges Bill*, p. 68.

36 Duffy, *Thomas Davis*, pp 269–70.

37 Ibid., p. 318.

38 Charles Gavan Duffy, *My Life in Two Hemispheres* (2 vols, New York, 1898), I, p. 124.

39 Brendan Ó Cathaoir, *John Blake Dillon: Young Irelander* (Dublin, 1990), p. 30; for a list of chapters and the introductory chapter from Davis's proposed work on Tone, see Duffy, *Young Ireland*, pp 680–1.

40 [Matthew Russell], 'Contributions to Irish biographies: John Edward Pigot', *Irish Monthly*, XXIV (May 1896), p. 236.

41 Duffy, *Thomas Davis*, p. 319; RIA, Duffy papers, 12 P 15 (16–17).

42 Mitchel to Martin, 21 June 1844 (William Dillon, *Life of John Mitchel* (London, 1888), I, pp 53–4).

43 *Nation*, 22 Nov. 1845.

44 Charles Gavan Duffy, *Four Years of Irish History, 1845–9* (London, 1883), pp 117–18.

45 *Nation*, 18 July 1846. Mitchel was stretching things a little in describing his father as a United Irishman. As a boy his father had accompanied a party of United Irishmen with a cart of ammunition and was made to swear the United oath before being allowed to leave (James Quinn, *John Mitchel* (Dublin, 2008), p. 3).

46 *Nation*, 18, 25 July, 1 Aug. 1846.

47 'The road before us', *Nation*, 1 Aug. 1846.

48 *Nation*, 31 Oct., 7 Nov. 1846.

49 'The *Nation* – Repeal reading rooms', *Nation*, 8 Aug. 1846.

50 Duffy, *My Life*, I, p. 175.

51 'Popular fallacies about Irish history', *Nation*, 9 Jan. 1847.

52 Irish Confederation minute books (RIA MS 23 H 43).

53 'Confederate clubs', *Nation*, 10 July 1847.

54 'The use and capacity of Confederate clubs', *Nation*, 25 Sept. 1847.

55 Duffy, *Four Years*, p. 256.

56 McGee to Duffy, 31 Oct. 1846, Duffy papers (RIA MS 12 P 19).

57 'Answers to correspondents', *Nation*, 1 May 1847.

58 Duffy, *Four Years*, pp 453–4.

59 Ibid., p. 441.

60 J. F. Lalor, 'A new nation', *Nation*, 24 Apr. 1847; idem, 'Tenants' right and landlord law', ibid., 15 May 1847.

61 Lalor, 'A new nation', *Nation*, 24 Apr. 1847; *Irish Felon*, 26 June, 1 July 1848; the letter published on 1 July 1848 had been sent as a private letter to Mitchel in January 1847.

62 *Nation*, 16 Sept., 2 Oct., 20, 27 Nov. 1847.

63 Mitchel to Lalor, 4 Jan. 1848 (L. Fogarty, *James Fintan Lalor* (Dublin, 1918), pp 120–23).

64 *Nation*, 5 Feb. 1848; see also Robert Sloan, *William Smith O'Brien and the Young Ireland Rebellion of 1848* (Dublin, 2000), p. 206.

65 *Nation*, 5 Feb. 1848.

66 John Mitchel, *The Last Conquest of Ireland (perhaps)* (Glasgow, 1861), p. 159.

67 *United Irishman*, 4, 25 Mar. 1848.

68 Ibid.

69 'The union that is strength', *Nation*, 10 June 1848.

70 'To-day in Ireland', *Nation*, 18 Mar. 1848.

71 'Indecision – a lesson from our own history', *Nation*, 22 Jan. 1848.

72 *United Irishman*, 13 May 1848.

73 'Female education', *Nation*, 24 Apr. 1847.

74 'The road before us', *Nation*, 1 Aug. 1846.

75 'Answers to correspondents', *Nation*, 13 May 1848, p. 312.

76 Sean Ryder, 'Gender and the discourse of "Young Ireland" nationalism', in Timothy P. Foley *et al* (eds), *Gender and Colonialism* (Galway, 1995), p. 219.

77 Duffy, *My Life*, 1, p. 269; Mitchel too described the struggle on the *Nation* as one between Girondists and Montagnards (John Mitchel, *Jail Journal, or Five Years in British Prisons* (New York, 1854), p. 7).

78 Mitchel, *Last Conquest*, p. 187.

79 *Irish Felon*, 24 June 1848.

80 John O'Donovan to Daniel McCarthy, 2 June 1848 (NLI O'Donovan correspondence MS 132); Dillon, *Life of Mitchel*. 1, p. 320; W. J. Lowe, 'The Chartists and the Irish Confederates: Lancashire, 1848', *Irish Historical Studies*, XXIV: 94 (Nov. 1984), p. 179; *Nation*, 27 May, 17 June 1848.

81 Robert Sloan, *William Smith O'Brien and the Young Ireland Rebellion of 1848* (Dublin, 2000), p. 11.

82 O'Brien memorandum, O'Brien papers, NLI MS 449.

83 Ibid.

84 Gearóid Ó Tuathaigh, *Ireland Before the Famine 1798–1848* (Dublin, 1972), p. 187.

85 Justin McCarthy, *The Story of an Irishman* (London, 1904), p. 75.

86 TCD MS 6455/109 (presented to Adelaide Dillon) cited in Brendan Ó Cathaoir, *John Blake Dillon: Young Irelander* (Dublin, 1990), p. 103.

87 James M. Cahalan, *Great Hatred, Little Room: The Irish Historical Novel* (Dublin, 1983), p. 72, 78, 84.

88 Duffy, *Four Years*, pp 777–8.

89 Dillon to Adelaide Dillon, 1848 (Duffy, *My Life*, II, p. 3).

90 David A. Wilson, *Thomas D'Arcy McGee: Volume 1 Passion, Reason, and Politics 1825–1857* (Montreal, 2008), pp 234–6.

91 Cyril Pearl, *The Three Lives of Gavan Duffy* (Kensington, NSW, 1979), p. 132.

92 *Nation*, 8 Sept. 1849.

93 'The new *Nation*', parts 1 and 2, *Nation*, 1, 8 Sept. 1849.

94 *Nation*, 8 Sept. 1849.

95 Marie-Louise Legg, *Newspapers and Nationalism: The Irish Provincial Press 1850–1892* (Dublin, 1999), pp 23–4.

96 *Nation*, 18 Aug. 1855.

SIX

THE HISTORY OF THEIR OWN TIMES

1 Michael Doheny, *The Felon's Track (or History of the Attempted Outbreak in Ireland Embracing the Leading Events in the Irish Struggle from the Year 1843 to the Close of 1848)* (Dublin, 1918), p. xxvii.

2 Ibid., p. xxviii, 27, 29.

3 Ibid., pp 100–9, 118.

4 Ibid., pp 159–60.

5 Ibid., pp 170, 191–6.

6 Ibid., pp 287–8.

7 Sean Ryder, '"With a heroic life and a governing mind": nineteenth-century Irish nationalist autobiography', in Liam Harte (ed.), *Modern Irish Autobiography: Self, Nation and Spirit* (Basingstoke, 2007), p. 29.

8 John Mitchel, *Jail Journal, or Five Years in British Prisons* (New York, 1854), p. 3, 18, 49; p. 3 – 'God knoweth the heart'; p. 18 – 'I 'gin to be aweary of the sun'; p. 49 – 'Let him like good old Gloster (*sic*) "Shake patiently his great affliction off"'.

9 Mitchel, *Jail Journal*, p. xxvii.

10 See especially Ryder, 'With a heroic life and a governing mind', in Harte (ed.), *Modern Irish Autobiography*, pp 24–5.

11 Mitchel, *Jail Journal*, pp 75–6.

12 Ibid., p. 60.

13 Ibid., pp 86–7.

14 Ibid., p. 141.

15 Ibid., p. 145, 207.

16 W. B. Yeats, *Autobiographies*, ed. by William H. O'Donnell and Douglas N. Archibald (New York, 1999), pp 225–6.

17 R. Barry O'Brien, *The Best Hundred Irish Books* (Dublin, 1886), p. 28.

18 Jeremiah O'Donovan Rossa, *O'Donovan Rossa's Prison Life: Six Years in English Prisons* (New York, 1874); Michael Davitt, *Leaves from a Prison Diary; or, Lectures to a Solitary Audience* (London, 1885); Thomas Clarke, *Glimpses of an Irish Felon's Prison Life* (London and Dublin, 1922).

19 John Mitchel, *The Last Conquest of Ireland (Perhaps)* (Dublin, 2005), p. 144.

20 Patrick Maume (ed.), introduction to Mitchel, *Last Conquest*, pp 60–1.

21 Mitchel, *Last Conquest*, pp 136–7.

22 Ibid., p. 71.

23 Ibid., p. 92.

24 Ibid., p. 142.

25 Ibid., p. 157.

26 Ibid., pp 138–9.

27 Ibid., p. 218.

28 John Mitchel, *Life and Times of Aodh O'Neill* (Dublin, 1845), pp 221–2, 224–5.

29 Clare O'Halloran, 'Historical writings, 1690–1890', in Margaret Kelleher and Philip O'Leary (eds), *The Cambridge History of Irish Literature: volume 1 to 1890* (Cambridge, 2006), p. 619.

30 Mitchel, *Last Conquest*, p. 220.

31 Patrick Maume (ed.), Mitchel, *The Last Conquest*, p. xvi.

32 Ibid., pp 210–20.

33 Patrick O'Farrell, 'Whose reality? The Irish Famine in history and literature', *Historical Studies*, xx: 78 (Apr. 1982), p. 1.

34 Mitchel, *Last Conquest*, p. 219.

35 See James S. Donnelly Jr, *The Great Irish Potato Famine* (Stroud, 2002), pp 217–19; idem, 'The Great Famine: its interpreters, old and new', *History Ireland*, 1: 3 (autumn 1993), pp 27–33.

36 W. J. O'Neill Daunt, *Ireland and her Agitators* (Dublin, 1867), p. 231.

37 P. S. O'Hegarty, *John Mitchel: An Appreciation: With Some Account of Young Ireland* (Dublin, 1917), p. 128.

38 Graham Davis, 'The historiography of the Irish Famine', in Patrick O'Sullivan (ed.), *The Meaning of the Famine* (London and Washington, 1996), p. 17.

39 Christopher Morash, 'Making memories: the literature of the Irish Famine', in Patrick O'Sullivan (ed.), *The Meaning of the Famine* (London and Washington, 1996), pp 40–53; Melissa Fegan, *Literature and the Irish Famine 1845–1919* (Oxford, 2002), pp 10–34.

40 Charles Gavan Duffy, *Young Ireland: A Fragment of Irish History* (London, 1880); idem, *Four Years of Irish History* (London, 1883); idem, *The League of North and South: An Episode in Irish History 1850–1854* (London, 1886); Duffy's autobiographical *My Life in Two Hemispheres* (2 vols, New York, 1898) also gives a historical overview of these years.

41 'Notes by Duffy on the Rising of 1641', *c.* 1879 (NLI MS 4193–98).

42 Duffy to John O'Hagan (Charles Gavan Duffy, *My Life in Two Hemispheres* (2 vols, New York, 1898), 11, pp 377–8).

43 Duffy, *My Life*, 1, pp 2–3; Duffy, *Young Ireland*, p. iv.

44 Duffy, *Young Ireland*, p. iv.

45 Ibid., p. iii; Duffy to John O'Hagan, *c.* 1878 (Duffy, *My Life*, 11, p. 378).

46 Duffy, *Young Ireland*, p. 731.

47 Duffy, *Four Years*, pp 2–3.

48 Ibid., p. 397.

49 Ibid., pp 397–400.

50 Duffy, *Young Ireland*, pp 21–3, 366–8, 530–1, 708–9; Duffy, *Four Years*, pp 36, 40, 212, 258–62; see also Davis to Smith O'Brien, 26 July 1845 (NLI Smith O'Brien papers, 435: 1371).

51 Duffy, *My Life*, 11, p. 366.

52 W. E. H. Lecky, *Leaders of Public Opinion in Ireland* (2 vols, London, 1912), 11, p 304.

53 Duffy, *Young Ireland*, p. 367.

54 Ibid., p. 381.

55 Angus MacIntyre, *The Liberator: Daniel O'Connell and the Irish Party, 1830–47* (London, 1965), p. 267n.

56 Kevin B. Nowlan, *Charles Gavan Duffy and the Repeal Movement* (NUI, 1963), p. 9.

57 Ibid., pp 9–10.

58 Duffy, *Four Years*, pp 1–2; idem, *My Life*, i, 145, 169.

59 Duffy, *My Life*, I, p. 169.

60 Duffy, *Four Years*, p. 391.

61 Ibid., pp 353–6.

62 Nowlan, *Charles Gavan Duffy and the Repeal Movement*, p. 4, 9, 14; idem, *The Politics of Repeal* (London, 1965), p. III.

63 Denis Gwynn, 'Young Ireland', in Michael Tierney (ed.), *Daniel O'Connell: Nine Centenary Essays* (Dublin, 1949), pp 173–5.

64 Denis Gwynn, 'O'Connell, Davis and the Colleges Bill', *Irish Ecclesiastical Record*, 5th ser., LXIX (July, 1947), p. 561.

65 Gwynn, 'Young Ireland', in Tierney (ed.), *Daniel O'Connell*, p. 171.

66 'Smith O'Brien', *Nation*, 30 May 1846.

67 Duffy, *Four Years*, p. 500.

68 Ibid., pp 510–15.

69 Nowlan, *Charles Gavan Duffy and the Repeal Movement*, p. 18.

70 Duffy, *Four Years*, pp 493–4, 509–10, 516.

71 Ibid., p. 491.

72 See for example Duffy's account in an appendix to his *League of North and South*, pp 387–400.

73 W. B. Yeats, *Autobiographies*, ed. William H. O'Donnell and Douglas N. Archibald (New York, 1999), pp 225–6.

74 Duffy, *Four Years*, pp 57–8, 441.

75 Ibid., p. 689.

76 Ibid., p. 689.

77 Ibid., p. 778.

78 Ibid., p. vii.

79 Duffy, *Young Ireland*, p. 709.

80 Charles Gavan Duffy, *Thomas Davis: The Memoirs of an Irish Patriot, 1840–1846* (London, 1890); idem, *Short Life of Thomas Davis 1840–1846* (London, 1896).

81 Charles Gavan Duffy, *The Ballad Poetry of Ireland* (Dublin, 1866), p. 12.

82 Nowlan, *Charles Gavan Duffy and the Repeal Movement*, p. 7.

83 Brinsley MacNamara, 'Charles Gavan Duffy', in M. J. MacManus (ed.), *Thomas Duffy and Young Ireland* (Dublin, 1945), p. 38.

84 Nowlan, *Charles Gavan Duffy and the Repeal Movement*, p. 4.

85 Shane Leslie, 'Irish leaders', in Joseph Dunn and Peter Lennon (eds), *The Glories of Ireland* (Washington DC, 1914), p. 158.

86 P. S. O'Hegarty, 'The "Library of Ireland" 1845–1847', in M. J. MacManus (ed.), *Thomas Duffy and Young Ireland* (Dublin, 1945), p. 109.

87 Duffy, *My Life*, I, pp 251, 314–15.

88 Ibid., p. 316.

89 Duffy, *League of North and South*, p. 381; idem, *Four Years*, p. 767; idem, *My Life*, I, p. 251.

90 Duffy, *League of North and South*, p. vii.

91 Ibid., p. vii.

92 Ibid., pp viii–ix, 376.

93 See Donal McCartney, 'James Anthony Froude and Ireland: a historiographical controversy of the nineteenth century', in T. D. Williams (ed.), *Historical Studies*, VIII (1971), pp 171–90;

Eileen Reilly, 'J. A. Froude's use of history and his Irish prescription', in Lawrence W. McBride (ed.), *Reading Irish Histories: Texts, Contexts, and Memory in Modern Ireland* (Dublin, 2003) pp 140–55; and especially Ciaran Brady, *James Anthony Froude: An Intellectual Biography of a Victorian Prophet* (Oxford, 2013), pp 262–97.

94 Duffy, *Young Ireland*, pp iii–iv.

95 Ibid., p. 79.

96 Ibid., p. 81.

97 Malcolm Brown, *The Politics of Irish Literature, from Thomas Davis to W. B. Yeats* (London, 1972), p. 15.

98 Thomas Clarke Luby, Robert F. Walsh and Jeremiah C. Curtin, *The Story of Ireland's Struggle for Self-Government with the Lives and Times of Her Great Leaders* (New York, 1893), pp 540–1.

SEVEN

CONTINUITIES: FROM THE CELTIC UNION TO GRIFFITH'S 'BALLAD HISTORY'

1 *Prospectus of the Celtic Union* (Dublin, 1854) (copy in The *Celt*, 2nd ser. (1858) in RIA Library). For Cane see Tony Patterson, 'Robert Cane and Young Ireland', *Old Kilkenny Review: Journal of the Kilkenny Archaeological Society*, 1 (1998), pp 67–82.

2 R. V. Comerford, *Charles Kickham: A Study in Irish Nationalism and Literature* (Dublin, 1979), p. 44.

3 *Celt*, 1 Aug. 1857.

4 *Irishman: A Weekly Journal of Irish National Politics and Literature*, 17 July 1858.

5 *Irish Harp: A Monthly Magazine of National and General Literature* (Mar. 1863), p. 1.

6 Ibid., p. 3.

7 Charles Gavan Duffy, *Young Ireland: A Fragment of Irish History 1840–1850* (London, 1880), p. 667.

8 Cited in T. F. O'Sullivan, *The Young Irelanders* (Tralee, 1940), p. 4.

9 *Irish People*, 19 Dec. 1863.

10 See for example '1798 in Wexford', *Irish People*, 5, 12 Dec. 1863; 'Michael Dwyer: the insurgent captain of the Wicklow Mountains', ibid., 30 Jan. 1864; 'Trials of prisoners in '98', ibid., 6 Feb. 1864; 'A glance at '98', ibid., 24 June 1865.

11 'Liberty or destruction', *Irish People*, 23 Jan. 1864.

12 E. R. R. Green, 'The beginnings of Fenianism', in T. W. Moody (ed.), *The Fenian Movement* (Dublin, 1968), pp 11–22; Owen McGee, *The IRB: The Irish Republican Brotherhood, from the Land League to Sinn Féin* (Dublin, 2005), pp 18–27; John O'Leary, *Recollections of Fenians and Fenianism* (2 vols, London, 1896), 1, pp 2–3, 50–1, 79; Jeremiah O'Donovan Rossa, *Rossa's Recollections, 1838 to 1898: Memoirs of an Irish Revolutionary* (New York, 1898), p. 172; T. D. Sullivan, *Recollections of Troubled Times in Irish Politics* (Dublin, 1905), pp 6, 128.

13 John O'Leary, *Recollections of Fenians and Fenianism* (2 vols, London, 1896), 1, pp 2–3, 50.

14 John Devoy, *Recollections of an Irish Rebel* (New York, 1929), pp 39, 290, 378; William O'Brien, *Recollections* (London, 1905), p. 56; John Denvir, *The Life Story of an Old Rebel* (Dublin, 1910), p. 37.

15 T. C. Luby, *Illustrious Irishmen* (New York, 1878), pp iii–iv.

16   John Denvir, *The Life Story of an Old Rebel* (Dublin, 1910), p. 137.

17   Elizabeth Tilley, 'Periodicals', in James H. Murphy (ed.), *The Oxford History of the Irish Book, vol. iv: The Irish Book in English 1800–1891* (Oxford, 2011), pp 166–70; Charles Benson, 'The Dublin book trade', in ibid., p. 36.

18   E. W. McFarland, *John Ferguson 1836–1906: Irish Issues in Scottish Politics* (East Linton, East Lothian, 2003), pp 20–5, 54–5, 279. This point is made by Patrick Maume in his introduction to Mitchel's *Last Conquest* (2005), p. xxiv.

19   Thomas N. Brown, *Irish American Nationalism* (Philadelphia and New York, 1966), pp 17–21.

20   Paul A. Townend, '"Academies of Nationality": the reading room and Irish national movements, 1838–1905', in Lawrence W. McBride (ed.), *Reading Irish Histories: Texts, Contexts and Memory in Modern Ireland* (Dublin, 2003), p. 31.

21   Martin J. Burke, 'Irish-American publishing', in James H. Murphy (ed.), *The Oxford History of the Irish Book, vol. iv: The Irish Book in English 1800–1891* (Oxford, 2011), pp 106–10.

22   David A. Wilson, *Thomas D'Arcy McGee: Volume 1: Passion, Reason, and Politics 1825–1857* (Montreal & Kingston, 2008), pp 274–5.

23   Ibid., pp 308–9.

24   Thomas D'Arcy McGee, *A Popular History of Ireland, from the Earliest Times to the Emancipation of the Catholics* (2 vols, New York, 1864), 11, p. 597.

25   Ibid., 11, pp 680, 699, 726–7.

26   A. M. Sullivan to Charles Gavan Duffy, 28 May 1869 (Duffy Correspondence, NLI MS 10, 489).

27   Wilson, *Thomas D'Arcy McGee*, pp 184–5.

28   'The history of Ireland', *Nation*, 11 Nov. 1843.

29   John Mitchel, *The History of Ireland from the Treaty of Limerick to the Present Time* (2 vols, Dublin, 1869), 1, p. viii.

30   Ibid., 1, pp vii–viii.

31   Ibid., 1, p. 14.

32   Ibid., 1, pp 26–7, 40, 42.

33   Ibid., 1, pp vii–viii.

34   J. Pope-Hennessy, 'What do the Irish read?', *Nineteenth Century*, xv (Jan.–June 1884), pp 926–7.

35   John Vincent (ed.), *The Diaries of Edward Henry Stanley, 15th Earl of Derby (1826–1893) between 1878 and 1893: A Selection* (Oxford, 2003), p. 864 (cited in Maume, *Last Conquest*, p. xxv).

36   P. S. O'Hegarty, *John Mitchel: An Appreciation: With Some Account of Young Ireland* (Dublin, 1917), p. 127.

37   Statement of Patrick Lyons, Bureau of Military History, WS 1645, p. 1.

38   Mitchel, *History of Ireland*, 1, pp 180–1.

39   Ibid., 11, p. 96.

40   P. S. O'Hegarty, 'The "Library of Ireland" 1845–1847', in M. J. MacManus (ed.), *Thomas Duffy and Young Ireland* (Dublin, 1945), p. 110.

41   Enda Delaney, 'Narratives of exile' in T. Dooley (ed.), *Ireland's Polemical Past: Views of Irish History in Honour of R. V. Comerford* (Dublin, 2010), p. 105.

42   'National education – Intermediate schools', *Irishman*, 4 Sept. 1858.

43   Lawrence W. McBride, 'Young readers and the learning and teaching of Irish history', idem (ed.), *Reading Irish Histories*, pp 86–8.

44 Ibid., p. 105, 107.

45 *Young Ireland*, 5, 12, 19, 26 June 1875.

46 A. M. Sullivan to Charles Gavan Duffy, 10 May 1863 (Duffy Correspondence, NLI MS 10, 489).

47 Joep Leerssen, *Remembrance and Imagination: Patterns in the Historical and Literary Representation of Ireland in the Nineteenth Century* (Cork, 1996), pp 151–2.

48 A. M. Sullivan, *The Story of Ireland* (Dublin, 1867), pp 6–7.

49 See especially R. F. Foster, 'The story of Ireland', in idem, *The Irish Story: Telling Tales and Making it up in Ireland* (Oxford, 2002), pp 1–22.

50 Sullivan, *Story of Ireland*, p. 615, 617.

51 A. M. Sullivan to Charles Gavan Duffy, 28 May 1869 (Duffy Correspondence, NLI MS 10, 489); Mary C. Bromage, 'Image of nationhood', *Éire-Ireland*, III: 3 (Fall 1968), p. 13.

52 J. J. Lee, *The Modernisation of Irish Society* (Dublin, 1973), p. 13; Marie-Louise Legg, *Newspapers and Nationalism: The Irish Provincial Press 1850–1892* (Dublin, 1999), pp 44–6.

53 J. Pope-Hennessy, 'What do the Irish read?', *Nineteenth Century*, xv (Jan.–June 1884), pp 925–6.

54 Ibid., p. 926.

55 Ibid., p. 926, 930.

56 On the Young Ireland societies of the 1880s, see M. J. Kelly, *The Fenian Ideal and Irish Nationalism 1882–1916* (Woodbridge, 2006), pp 16–31.

57 *Nation*, 2 Apr. 1881. For its discussions see Young Ireland Society Minute Books (1881–4), NLI MS 16095.

58 *Dublin Evening Telegraph*, 7 Jan. 1884.

59 Brian Maye, *Arthur Griffith* (Dublin, 1997), p. 13.

60 John O'Leary, *Young Ireland: The Old and the New* (Dublin, 1885), p. 7, 11, 13.

61 R. F. Foster, *W. B. Yeats: A Life: I: the Apprentice Mage 1865–1914* (Oxford, 1997), p. 44.

62 W. B. Yeats, *Autobiographies*, William H. O'Donnell and Douglas N. Archibald (eds) (New York, 1999), p. 173.

63 *Poems and Ballads of Young Ireland* (Dublin, 1888).

64 *Freeman's Journal*, 6 Feb. 1892.

65 Foster, *Yeats*, I, pp 120–1.

66 Ibid., I, p. 118.

67 Charles Gavan Duffy, *The Revival of Irish Literature* (London, 1893), p. 10.

68 Charles Gavan Duffy, *Four Years of Irish History, 1845–9* (London, 1883),, pp 778–9.

69 Duffy, *The Revival of Irish Literature*, pp 24–5.

70 See Foster, *Yeats*, I, pp 118–24.

71 Yeats, *Autobiographies*, pp 184–6.

72 Thomas Davis, *The Patriot Parliament of 1689* (London, 1893), p. viii.

73 Yeats, *Autobiographies*, pp 184–6; see also a letter from Yeats to the editor of *United Ireland*, 1 Sept. 1894.

74 Martin MacDermott (ed.), *The New Spirit of the Nation* (London, 1894), p. viii.

75 Roger Casement, 'The romance of Irish history', in Joseph Dunn and Peter Lennon (eds), *The Glories of Ireland* (Washington DC, 1914), pp 1–9.

76 'Ballad History of Ireland II', *United Irishman*, 4 Jan. 1904.

77 'Ballad History of Ireland XXII, XXIII, XXVI, LIII, LIV', *United Irishman*, 4, 11 June, 1904; 2 July 1904; 14, 21 Jan. 1905.

78 'Ballad History of Ireland XCIX', *United Irishman*, 2 Dec. 1905.

79 *Nation*, 1 Sept. 1849.

EIGHT
THE LEGACY OF YOUNG IRELAND'S WRITINGS

1 A. M. Sullivan, *New Ireland: Political Sketches and Personal Reminiscences* (London, 1878), p. 170.

2 Justin McCarthy, *Ireland and Her Story* (London, 1903), pp 158–69.

3 Richard Barry O'Brien, *The Best Hundred Irish Books* (Dublin, 1886), p. 45.

4 Ibid., p. 8; this listing was first published in the *Freeman's Journal*, 23 Mar. 1886.

5 O'Brien, *The Best Hundred Irish Books*, p. 16.

6 William Rooney, *Prose Writings* (Dublin, [1909]), pp 62, 67, 90–2, 167–77, 272–6.

7 George A. Lyons, *Some Recollections of Griffith and his Times* (Dublin, 1923), pp 3–4.

8 Donal McCartney, 'The political use of history in the work of Arthur Griffith', *Journal of Contemporary History*, VIII: 1 (1973), p. 4, 8.

9 Arthur Griffith (ed.), *Thomas Davis: The Thinker and Teacher* (Dublin, 1916), pp xi–xiii.

10 Brian Maye, *Arthur Griffith* (Dublin, 1997), p. 357; Padraic Colum, *Arthur Griffith* (Dublin, 1959), p. 46; P. S. O'Hegarty, *A History of Ireland under the Union 1801–1922* (London, 1952), p. 117; Patrick Maume, 'Young Ireland, Arthur Griffith, and republican ideology: the question of continuity', *Éire-Ireland*, XXXIV: 2 (summer 1999), pp 155–74.

11 Michael J. Lennon, 'Griffith of Dublin' [typescript], Chapter 2, p. 3 (NLI MS 22, 293).

12 F. S. L. Lyons, *John Dillon: A biography* (London, 1968), p. 16; Terence Denman, *A Lonely Grave: The Life and Death of William Redmond* (Dublin, 1995), pp 22–3; Frank Callanan, *T. M. Healy* (Cork, 1996), pp 14, 82–3, 383.

13 Anna Kinsella, '1798 claimed for the Catholics: Father Kavanagh, Fenians and the centenary celebrations', in Dáire Keogh and Nicholas Furlong (eds), *The Mighty Wave: The 1798 Rebellion in Wexford* (Dublin, 1996), pp 151–3.

14 *Irish Freedom*, July 1911.

15 O'Hegarty, *A History of Ireland under the Union*, p. 628.

16 Ibid., p. 378.

17 'The north began', *An Claidheamh Soluis*, 1 Nov. 1913; Davis's 'Song of the Volunteers of 1782' was originally published in the *Nation*, 13 May 1843.

18 Johann A. Norsstedt, *Thomas MacDonagh: A Critical Biography* (Charlottesville, Va., 1980), pp 35–6.

19 Roger Casement, *Some Poems of Roger Casement* (Dublin, 1918), pp 15–20, 22–4; Roger Casement, 'The romance of Irish history', in Joseph Dunn and Peter Lennon (eds), *The Glories of Ireland* (Washington DC, 1914), pp 1–9. For the influence of Irish history on Casement, see also Margaret O'Callaghan, '"With the eyes of another race, of a people once hunted themselves": Casement, colonialism and a remembered past', in D. George Boyce and Alan O'Day (eds), *Ireland in Transition* (London, 2004), pp 165–6.

20 Casement to Alice Stopford Green, 1906 (cited in Séamus Ó Cléirigh, *Casement and the Irish Language, Culture and History* (Dublin, 1977), p. 10; Brian Inglis, *Roger Casement* (London, 1973), p. 142, 149.

21 *Irish Volunteer*, 8 Sept. 1914.

22 Cahir Davitt, Bureau of Military History (BMH), WS 993, p. 1; Kevin O'Shiel, BMH, WS 1770 p. 67; Sean O'Neill, BMH, WS 1219, p. 1, 33; Eamon Broy, BMH, WS 1280, p. 9; Sean Ó Ceallaigh, BMH, WS 1476, p. 1; Michael McCormick, BMH, WS 1503, p. 1; Thomas Reidy, BMH, WS 1555, p. 1; Patrick Lyons, BMH, WS 1645, p. 1; Thomas Hevey, BMH, WS, p. 4.

23 Peter Hart, *The IRA and its Enemies: Violence and Community in Cork, 1916–1923* (Oxford, 1998), p. 207.

24 Tom Barry, *Guerilla Days in Ireland* (Dublin, 1949), p. 3.

25 Ernie O'Malley, *On Another Man's Wound* (Dublin, rev. ed. 2002), pp 42–3, 48.

26 'Prospectus of Scoil Éanna', in S. P. Ó Buachalla (ed.), *A Significant Irish Educationalist: The Educational Writings of P. H. Pearse* (Dublin & Cork, 1980), p. 319.

27 'Irish history', *An Claidheamh Soluis*, 13 Jul 1907; Desmond Ryan, 'The man called Pearse' in Desmond Ryan (ed.), *Collected Works of Padraic H. Pearse* (Dublin, 1917–22), p. 135, 227.

28 Elaine Sisson, *Pearse's Patriots: St Enda's and the Cult of Boyhood* (Cork, 2004), 19–21; R. F. Foster, 'History and the Irish question', in Ciaran Brady (ed.), *Interpreting Irish History: The Debate on Historical Revisionism* (Dublin, 1994), p. 137; Gregory Castle, 'Nobler forms: Standish James O'Grady's *History of Ireland* and the Irish Literary Revival', in Lawrence W. McBride (ed.), *Reading Irish Histories: Texts, Contexts, and Memory in Modern Ireland* (Dublin, 2003), pp 156–77.

29 'Robert Emmet and the Ireland of today' (New York, 2 Mar. 1914), in Ryan (ed.), *Collected Works of Padraic H. Pearse*, p. 66).

30 Pearse, 'Ghosts' (*Political Writings*, p. 230).

31 James Quinn, 'Patrick Pearse and the reproach of history', in Roisín Higgins and Regina Uí Chollatáin (eds), *The Life and After-Life of P. H. Pearse – Pádraic Mac Piarais: Saol agus Oidhreacht* (Dublin, 2009), pp 99–110.

32 Donal McCartney, *W. E. H. Lecky, Historian and Politician 1838–1903* (Dublin, 1994), p. 9, 57; 'Thoughts on history' in W. E. H. Lecky, *Historical and Political Essays* (London, 1910), pp 2–3; *A Memoir of the Rt Hon. William Edward Hartpole Lecky*, by his wife (London, 1909), p. 13; Helen F. Mulvey, 'The historian Lecky: opponent of Irish Home Rule', *Victorian Studies*, I: 4 (June 1958), pp 341–2.

33 Anne Wyatt, 'Froude, Lecky and the "humblest Irishman"', *Irish Historical Studies*, xix: 75 (Mar. 1975), pp 273–6.

34 'The political value of history', in W. E. H. Lecky, *Historical and Political Essays* (London, 1910), p. 22; 'Ireland in the light of history' in ibid., p. 62.

35 R. Barry O'Brien, *The Best Hundred Irish Books* (Dublin, 1886), p. 45.

36 Ibid., p. 53.

37 John Eglinton, 'The de-Davisisation of Irish literature', in *Bards and Saints* (Dublin, 1906), p. 36, 42, 43.

38 'An Irish poet', Dublin *Daily Express*, 11 Dec. 1902.

39 W. B. Yeats, *Autobiographies*, ed. by William H. O'Donnell and Douglas N. Archibald (New York, 1999), pp 172–3.

40 R. F. Foster, 'Oisin comes home: Yeats as inheritor', idem, *Words Alone: Yeats and his Inheritances* (Oxford, 2011), p. 142.

41 Yeats, *Autobiographies*, pp 187, 224–5, 296.

42 'Journal no. 94', 12 Mar. [1909], Yeats, *Autobiographies*, p. 364.

43 Eoin MacNeill, 'Some notes on our national literature', *New Ireland Review*, I (May 1894), p. 149.

44 Douglas Hyde, 'The necessity for de-Anglicising Ireland', in Douglas Hyde (ed.), *Language, Lore and Lyrics: Essays and Lectures* (Dublin, 1986), p. 131.

45 D. P. Moran, *The Philosophy of Irish Ireland* (Dublin, 1905), p. 43, 102.

46 Donal McCartney, 'The political use of history in the work of Arthur Griffith', *Journal of Contemporary History*, VIII: 1 (1973), pp 16–17.

47 Patrick Maume, *The Long Gestation: Irish Nationalist Life, 1891–1918* (Dublin, 1999), p. 220.

48 Stephen J. Brown, *Poetry of Irish History* (Dublin, 1927), p. xv.

49 M. J. MacManus (ed.), *Thomas Duffy and Young Ireland* (Dublin, 1945), p. vii.

50 John Coolahan, 'Perceptions of Ireland and its past in nineteenth-century national school textbooks', in Terence Dooley (ed.), *Ireland's Polemical Past: Views of Irish History in Honour of R. V. Comerford* (Dublin, 2010), pp 81–4; Janet Nolan, 'Unintended consequences: the national schools and Irish women's mobility in the late nineteenth and early twentieth centuries', in D. George Boyce and Alan O'Day (eds), *Ireland in Transition* (London, 2004), p. 182.

51 See, for example, the attack on Professor Teegan of Marlboro St Teacher Training College for his unflattering remarks about Patrick Sarsfield whom he allegedly described as 'a coward and a renegade', *Irish Freedom*, Apr. 1911, p. 2.

52 'The teaching of history in Irish schools', *An Claidheamh Soluis* (supplement), 28 Oct. 1911.

53 Francis T. Holohan, 'History teaching in the Free State 1922–1935', *History Ireland*, 11: 4 (winter 1994) pp 53–6.

54 'The teaching of history in Irish schools', *An Claidheamh Soluis* (supplement), 28 Oct. 1911.

55 Department of Education, *Notes for Teachers: History* (Dublin, 1934), p. 3.

56 Ibid., p. 5, 6, 24 and appendix.

57 Edmund Curtis, 'Irish history and its popular versions' in the *Irish Rosary*, XXIX (May 1925), pp 321–3.

58 Sean O'Faolain, 'The plain people of Ireland', in the *Bell*, VII: 1 (1943), p. 6.

59 *Irish Historical Studies*, I: 1 (March, 1938), p. 1.

60 Patrick Maume, *The Long Gestation: Irish Nationalist Life, 1891–1918* (Dublin, 1999), p. 220.

61 D. G. Boyce, *Nationalism in Ireland* (2nd edn, London, 1991), p. 392.

62 Kenneth Milne, *New Approaches to the Teaching of Irish History* (London, 1979), pp 18–19, 24–5, 43–7.

63 Brendan Bradshaw, 'Nationalism and historical scholarship in modern Ireland', *Irish Historical Studies*, XXVI: 104 (Nov., 1989), p. 341, 350.

64 Ibid., p. 341.

65 Martin Mansergh (ed.), *The Spirit of the Nation: The Speeches and Statements of Charles J. Haughey (1957–1986)* (Cork, 1986).

Biographical Notes

—

Barante, Amable (1782–1866), French administrator and historian, was educated at the École Polytechnique and rose through Napoleon's administration to become prefect of Vendée (1809). A senior official and peer (1819) under the Bourbons, he used his position to promote liberal reforms. After the revolution of 1830, he became ambassador at Turin (1830) and St Petersburg (1835). His major historical work was *Histoire des ducs de Bourgogne* (1824–8), which was admired for its colourful and fast-moving narrative, but criticised for lacking critical discernment and careful scholarship. He also wrote *Histoire de la Convention Nationale* (1851–3), *Histoire du Directoire de la République Française* (1855) and biographies of Joan of Arc and other French historical figures.

Barry, Michael Joseph (1817–89), journalist and poet, was born in Cork city and educated at Carlow College. He practised law and contributed poetry to the *Dublin University Magazine*. A regular at the College Historical Society at TCD, he became a friend of Thomas Davis and contributed to the *Nation*. He joined the Repeal Association in 1843 and won first prize in the association's essay competition with *Ireland, as She Was, as She Is, and as She Shall Be* (1845) which argued the case for Irish self-government. He compiled *Songs of Ireland* (1845) for the Library of Ireland, one of the series' most successful publications. A founding member of the Irish Confederation in 1847, he founded a Confederate Club in Cork and encouraged it to arm in defence of Ireland's rights. He took over the *Southern Reporter* in Cork in 1847 and used it to condemn the inadequacy of the government's famine relief policies and welcome the overthrow of the French monarchy in February 1848. Disillusioned by the poor popular response to the Confederation's call to arms in 1848, he concluded that Ireland should reconcile itself to union with Britain. He was an enthusiastic supporter of the Crimean War (1854–6) and served as divisional police magistrate for Dublin (1871).

Betham, William (1779–1853), archivist and antiquarian, was born in Suffolk and apprenticed to a printer. In 1805 he became deputy keeper of records at Dublin Castle, and until his death was a leading figure in Irish antiquarianism and public life. He developed some speculative theories on Irish antiquities and linguistic theory, claiming in his *Etruria Celtica* (1842) that both Etruscan and Irish were derived from Phoenician. His claim that Irish round towers were also Phoenician in origin was comprehensively refuted by the work of George Petrie, although Betham refuse to accept Petrie's findings. In addition to his important work in the archives, he collected and preserved many valuable Irish medieval manuscripts, including the Book of Armagh and the Cathach of Colm Cille.

Bindon, Samuel Henry (1811–79), lawyer, antiquary and politician, was born in Waterpark, County Clare, educated at Trinity College Dublin (TCD), and called to the Irish bar (1838). At Trinity he met several of the Young Irelanders and formed a loose attachment with the group, editing and writing an introduction to *The Historical Works of the Rt Rev. Nicholas French DD* (1846) for the Library of Ireland. He also became a member of the Celtic Society and the Irish Archaeological Society. In 1850 he served as secretary of the council of the Tenant League. After the League's collapse, he emigrated to Australia in 1855. Elected to Victoria's legislative assembly in 1864, he was appointed minister for justice (1866–8) and a county a county court judge (1869). He was a strong advocate of economic development and technical education, and published *Industrial Instruction in Europe and Australia* (1872).

Brenan, Joseph (1828–57), journalist and poet, was born and educated in Cork city. He joined the Cork Historical Society, edited its *Cork Magazine* (1847–8) and contributed articles and verse to the *Nation* and *United Irishman*. He identified with the militant policies of John Mitchel and James Fintan Lalor and called for immediate insurrection in the *Irish Felon* of June and July 1848. Arrested and imprisoned until March 1849, on his release he edited the *Irishman* and joined a revolutionary secret society which mounted an unsuccessful attack on a police barracks in Cappoquin, County Waterford, in September 1849. Fleeing to New York, he worked as a journalist and continued to write nationalist verse. In America he became an enthusiastic supporter of the Southern states, writing *Ballads of the Young South* (1857) and founding and editing the New Orleans *Daily Times* to assert the concept of states' rights.

Callan, Margaret ('Thornton MacMahon') (*c.*1817–*c.*1883), writer and teacher, was born in Newry, County Down. She was a sister of the nationalist journalist Terence MacMahon Hughes and a cousin and sister-in-law of Charles Gavan Duffy. In 1835 she established a boarding school for girls in Blackrock, County Dublin, that sought to inspire its pupils with the ideals of Young Ireland, and taught there until she married John B. Callan, MD and occasional contributor to the *Nation*. She also contributed to the *Nation* and under the pseudonym Thornton MacMahon edited *The Casket of Irish Pearls* (1846), a collection of Irish verse and prose for the Library of Ireland. When Duffy was arrested in July 1848, she and Jane Francesca Elgee assumed editorial control of the *Nation*. Callan and her family emigrated to Australia in 1856.

Camden, William (1551–1623), English historian, was born in London and educated at Oxford. From 1571 to 1600 he travelled through England collecting antiquarian materials which he used in his wide-ranging *Britannia* (1586). He was a founder of the first Society of Antiquaries *c.*1585. Among his many historical collections were the *Annals of Elizabeth I's Reign* (1615–25), which was heavily criticised by Irish historians for its anti-Irish bias.

Campion, John Thomas (1814–98), writer and physician, was born and educated in Kilkenny. While studying medicine in Dublin, he contributed articles and verse to the *Nation, United Irishman, Irish Felon* and *Duffy's Fireside Magazine*. His 'Sketches' appeared in the *Celt* – the magazine of the Kilkenny-based Celtic Union founded in 1853 – and in 1858 he became the magazine's editor, dedicated to ensuring that it was 'national, Catholic, interesting and progressive'. After the demise of the *Celt* in 1859, he became MD (1860) and practised medicine in Dublin, but continued to contribute to nationalist periodicals, including the *Irish People*. He wrote the novel *Alice: A Historical Romance of the Crusaders in Ireland* (1862) for the Celtic Union, and published other historical fiction such as *Adventures of Michael Dwyer* (1856) and *The Last Struggles of the Irish Sea Smugglers* (1869).

Cane, Robert (1807–58), historian and physician, was born and educated in Kilkenny city. He and graduated MD from Glasgow University (1842) and practised medicine in Dublin and Kilkenny. A leading repealer in Kilkenny, he was elected mayor of the city in 1844 and 1849. He admired the Young Irelanders and after the split of 1846 tried to mediate between them and the O'Connellites. Although an active member of the Irish Confederation, he believed the rising of 1848 was doomed to failure and refused to participate. In 1849 he became the first treasurer of the Kilkenny Archaeological Society and in 1853 founded the Celtic Union, a nationalist literary and political society, and edited its magazine, the *Celt*, in 1857. He contributed articles to the *Celt*, the *Nation*, and various antiquarian journals, and wrote an uncompleted *History of the Williamite and Jacobite Wars in Ireland* (1859) which was published posthumously by the Celtic Union.

Carew, Sir George (1555–1629), nobleman, soldier and antiquarian, was born in Devon and educated at Oxford. He served as a soldier and administrator in Ireland at various times from 1575 to 1611, and as provincial president of Munster (1600–3) was noted for his brutal suppression of Catholic forces during the Nine Years' War. He built up a major collections of papers related to Ireland, which were used by his natural son Sir Thomas Stafford to publish *Pacata Hibernia* (1633), an account of the Munster campaign which sought to promote his father's reputation at the expense of Lord Deputy Mountjoy.

Carleton, William (1794–1869), novelist, was born near Clogher, County Tyrone, and educated locally. For a time he lived in poverty as a wandering teacher and scholar until in 1828 he met the writer Revd Caesar Otway who encouraged him to write and convert to Protestantism (1828). Carleton came to public attention with *Traits and Stories of the Irish Peasantry* (1830), a collection of vivid sketches of Irish rural life. His novels *Fardorougha the Miser* (1839) and *Valentine M'Clutchy* (1845) also enjoyed success. Thomas Davis admired his work and encouraged him to write three novels for the Library of Ireland: *Rody the Rover, or the Ribbonman* (1845), *Parra Sastha* (1845), and *Art Maguire* (1845). The Famine prompted some of his best-known fiction: *The Black Prophet* (1847), *The Emigrants of Ahadarra* (1848) and *The Tithe Proctor* (1849), in which he stressed the complexity of Ireland's social problems. His later work became increasingly conventional and sentimental. Always uneasy about the nationalist politics of Young Ireland, he distanced himself from the movement after the failure of the 1848 insurrection and opposed the repeal of the union.

Carlyle, Thomas (1795–1881), essayist and historian, was born in Ecclefechan, Scotland, and educated at Edinburgh University. One of the most prominent intellectuals of his day, he combined the discipline and asceticism of his Calvinist background with the emotionalism of German romanticism to forge an idiosyncratic and highly-charged philosophy, expressed in numerous essays and books such as *Signs of the Times* (1829), *Sartor Resartus* (1838) and *On Heroes, Hero-Worship and the Heroic in History* (1841). His colourful and dramatic account of the French Revolution (1837) was one of the one of the most widely read and influential histories of the time. In works such as *Chartism* (1839) and *Past and Present* (1843) he denounced unrestrained capitalism and industrialism claiming that they had destroyed the social bonds that had previously held society together and replaced them with a soulless commercialism. Such ideas proved highly attractive to the romantic idealists of Young Ireland, most of whom were avid readers of his work, despite Carlyle's contempt for the Irish masses and his belief that Irish nationalism was provincial and misguided.

Cobbett, William (1763–1835), essayist and politician, was born in Farnham, Surrey. After serving as a soldier (1783–91), he worked as a publisher in France and the US, returning to London in 1800 to become a journalist, publishing *Cobbett's Weekly Political Register* from 1802. Although a staunch anti-Jacobin, from 1804 he became increasingly critical of government policies and railed against the 'Old Corruption' that underpinned aristocratic power. In *Rural Rides* (1830), written on his travels around England, he denounced the changes wrought by industrialism capitalism, especially the erosion of the independence of small farmers and artisans, and the destruction of rural communities.

Curry, John (1710–80), Catholic activist and historian, was born in Dublin and educated as a physician in France. On his return to Dublin he practised his profession successfully and published some medical works. A founder of the Catholic Committee in 1760, he played a central role in directing its affairs and with Charles O'Conor wrote a series of pamphlets advocating relief for Catholics from the penal laws. His *Historical Memoirs of the Irish Rebellion* (1758) and *Review of the Civil Wars in Ireland* (1775) presented Irish history from a Catholic point of view and challenged exaggerated claims about the massacres of Protestant civilians in 1641. They remained popular with Catholics well into the nineteenth century.

Davies, Sir John (1569–1626), lawyer and poet, was born in Wiltshire and educated at Oxford. Appointed solicitor general (1603–6) and attorney general (1606–19) for Ireland, he was a keen observer of the condition of the country in the aftermath of the Nine Years' War and wrote *Discovery of the True Cause Why Ireland Was Never Entirely Subdued* (1612). Davies claimed that prior to the introduction of English law in Ireland in the reign of James 1, English settlers had been seduced by Irish customs and their colonies had become degenerate. Only with the extension of royal power and common law could ethnic division and lordly tyranny be abolished, and the kingdom transformed into a true commonwealth for the benefit of all. Davies's *Reports of Cases* (1615) was a rich repository of Irish legal and antiquarian information.

Davis, Thomas Osborne (1814–45), journalist and poet, was born in Mallow, County Cork, and educated at TCD. In an address to the Historical Society at TCD in 1840 he pleaded with his fellow students to take up the study of Irish history. A founder of the *Nation* in 1842, he wrote much of the paper's most memorable articles and poetry and these formed the core of Young Ireland anthologies. He wrote and edited several works of history, including an account of the Jacobite parliament of 1689 (1843) and a collection of the speeches of John Philpot Curran (1843). Davis was the driving force behind the decision to publish the Library of Ireland series of works in history, verse and fiction, to lay the foundations for an Irish national literature. Acknowledged as the leader of the Young Ireland group within the Repeal Association, he pursued his work with an energy and zeal that galvanised those around him. Deeply committed to Irish independence and national fraternity, he clashed sharply with Daniel O'Connell on federalism and non-denominational university education. His early death deprived Young Ireland of its most talented and inspirational leader. Most of his writings were published or re-published by colleagues and admirers after his death and influenced generations of Irish nationalists.

Denvir, John (1834–1916), Fenian, author and publisher, was born in County Antrim and raised in Liverpool, where he was educated by the Christian Brothers. Sworn into the IRB in Liverpool in 1866, he served as an organiser with various Irish bodies in England. He founded a printing and publishing business in Liverpool, which produced newspapers such as the *United Irishman* (1875–8), the organ of the Home Rule Confederation of Great Britain. From 1870 he also published the 'Illustrated Irish Penny Library' series of volumes of Irish poetry, drama, history, biography and fiction, written by a variety of authors, including himself under the pseudonym 'Slieve Donard', that proved very popular among the Irish community in Britain. He also wrote *The Irish in Britain* (1892), the novels *The Brandons* (1903) and *Olaf the Dane* (1908), and his memoirs, *The Life Story of an Old Rebel* (1910).

Dillon, John Blake (1816–66), nationalist and journalist, was born in Ballaghaderreen, County Roscommon, and educated at TCD where he became a close friend of Thomas Davis. Like Davis he was elected president of the Historical Society at TCD and in 1841 gave a stirring address encouraging its members to reclaim their past. A founder of the *Nation* in 1842, he contributed some articles on the land question, but wrote little on historical topics. He took part in the unsuccessful rising of 1848, and after its failure concluded that Young Ireland's efforts to use history and culture to create a sense of Irish nationality had failed. After practising law in New York (1848–55), he returned to Ireland and in 1865 became MP for Tipperary and secretary of the National Association of Ireland, a constitutional organisation sponsored by Archbishop Paul Cullen. His son John Dillon (1851–1927) was a leading nationalist parliamentarian and promoter of the legacy of Young Ireland.

Doheny, Michael (1805–63), author and lawyer, was born on a small farm near Fethard, County Tipperary, and was largely self-educated. He practised law and associated with the Young Ireland group in the Repeal Association. He wrote occasionally for the *Nation* and contributed the *History of the American Revolution* (1846) to the Library of Ireland, although his age and social background meant that he was somewhat detached from the Young Ireland leadership. Disapproving of Daniel O'Connell's moderate constitutionalism, he was attracted to James Fintan Lalor's revolutionary agrarianism and attempted to organise the peasantry in County Tipperary in July 1848. On the run for two months, he eventually reached safety in New York. He recorded his opinions and adventures in *The Felon's Track* (1849). A founder of the Emmet Monument Association in New York in 1856, he also helped in the founding of the Fenian Brotherhood in 1859.

Downing, Ellen Mary Patrick (1828–69), poet, was born in Cork, and composed poetry from an early age. A member of the Cork Historical Society, she contributed verse to the *Nation* (1845–7) using the pseudonyms 'Mary' or her initials 'E. M. P. D'. After the split in the Irish Confederation in January 1848 she wrote for Mitchel's radical *United Irishman*. In October 1849 she began her novitiate in the North Presentation Convent, Cork, but left after 18 months owing to ill health. Her religious poetry was collected and edited as *Voices from the Heart* (1868) by John Pius Leahy, Bishop of Dromore, who also edited her unpublished *Novenas and Meditations* (1879) and *Poems for Children* (1881). Her work featured strongly in nationalist anthologies.

Duffy, Sir Charles Gavan (1816–1903), journalist and historian, was born in Monaghan and largely self-educated. After working as a journalist in Dublin and Belfast, he founded the *Nation* with Thomas Davis and John Blake Dillon in 1842. In addition to editing the paper, Duffy contributed some articles and verse and compiled the best-selling *Ballad Poetry of Ireland* (1845). His business sense and organisational talents complemented Davis's inspirational qualities and between them they guided the fortunes of Young Ireland. After the death of Davis in 1845, Duffy recruited young journalists to carry on Davis's work and, despite several bouts of ill health, continued to devote himself to the *Nation* and its educational mission. Wary of the militancy of colleagues such as John Mitchel, in 1847 he committed the Irish Confederation to constitutional politics, but during the revolutionary year of 1848 he flirted with the language of insurrection and was arrested and imprisoned until April 1849. On his release he revived the *Nation* and founded the Tenant League to pursue agrarian reform in alliance with the Independent Irish Party at Westminster. Elected MP for New Ross (1852–5), he became disillusioned with Irish politics and emigrated to Australia in 1855. He was premier of Victoria (1871–2), was knighted in 1873, and became speaker of the assembly (1876–80). He retired to the south of France in 1880 and devoted himself to writing, publishing a two-part history of the Young Ireland movement (1880 and 1883), a life of Davis (1892) and an autobiography (1898). During the 1890s he took an active part in Irish cultural societies and strongly encouraged them to continue the work of Young Ireland.

Duffy, James (1809–71), publisher, was born in County Monaghan and educated in a local hedge school. After working as a pedlar, he formed a publishing firm in Dublin in the 1830s that concentrated on cheap Catholic devotional books and his business thrived. He was chosen by Charles Gavan Duffy (no relation) to reprint *The Spirit of the Nation* when the *Nation*'s presses could not cope with the demand, and to publish the Library of Ireland series (1845–8). He later published several popular Catholic journals designed for family reading that combined literature, history and religion. Publishing nationalist histories became his core business after the Famine, and his ability to produce and distribute books cheaply made him the most important Irish nationalist publisher of the nineteenth century. The firm was taken over by his sons after his death and continued in existence until 1980.

Ferguson, Sir Samuel (1810–86), poet and antiquarian, was born in Belfast and educated at the Belfast Academical Institution and TCD. Called to the bar in 1838, he devoted much of his time to antiquarian research, translating texts from Irish and writing poetry. He was a regular contributor to the *Dublin University Magazine*, distinguishing himself in 1834 with a severe review of James Hardiman's *Irish Minstrelsy* (1831) in which he denounced its narrow nationalism. Although he admired Thomas Davis's cultural and educational endeavours, he kept his distance from nationalist politics and never wrote for the *Nation*; his verse did, however, appear in some anthologies published by Young Irelanders. His anger at the government's inadequate efforts to relieve the Famine led him to found the Protestant Repeal Association in 1848, but he reverted to unionism soon after that year's insurrection. Ferguson attempted to create a distinctive Irish poetry in English, and his collected poems, many based on the Irish mythological cycles, were published as *Lays of the Western Gael* (1865). In 1867 he was appointed deputy keeper of public records in Ireland, was knighted for this work in 1878, and became president of the RIA in 1882.

Frazer, John de Jean (1803/4–52), poet, was born in Birr, County Offaly, and apprenticed to a cabinet maker. While earning his living as a craftsman in Dublin in the 1830s and 1840s, he contributed verse to a variety of journals including the *Dublin University Magazine*, the *Pilot*, the *Nation*, the *Irish Felon* and the *Irish Tribune*. He published a collection of nationalist verse, *Poems for the People* (1845) and another in 1851 drawn largely from his contributions to the *Nation*.

French, Nicholas (1604–78), Catholic bishop of Ferns and Confederate politician, was born in Wexford and educated mostly in Louvain. A strong supporter of the Irish Confederate Catholics in the 1640s, he opposed the first Ormond peace but accepted the second (1648). By 1650 he regretted his support for Ormond and went to the Continent, where he wrote a series of political tracts in which he denounced Ormond and the Restoration regime: *A Narrative of the Earl of Clarendon's Settlement and Sale of Ireland* (1668), *The Bleeding Iphigenia* (1674) and *The Unkinde Desertor of Loyall Men and True Frinds* (1676). All three were originally published in Louvain and republished in Dublin in 1846 in cheap editions as part of Young Ireland's efforts to make classic historical texts available to the general public.

Froude, James Anthony (1818–94), historian, was born in Devon, and educated at Westminster College and Oriel College, Oxford. In the 1840s he was a regular visitor to Ireland and did some historical research on Irish saints. He was best known for his *History of England from the Fall of Wolsey to the Defeat of the Spanish Armada* (12 vols, 1856–70), which was highly-opinionated and not always accurate, but gave an insight into muscular English Protestantism that remains valuable to cultural and religious historians. He acted as the literary executor of his friend Thomas Carlyle, and published an Irish historical novel, *The Two Chiefs of Dunboy* (1889). His main contribution to Irish historiography was *The English in Ireland in the Eighteenth Century* (1872) in which he argued that eighteenth-century Irish society was underdeveloped and lawless because it was not ruled firmly enough, that the Irish were not suited for self-government, and should be ruled in the same way as the inhabitants of India. Many of the effects of the book were unintended: Irish nationalists cited his condemnations of Ireland's ills to support their own claims of British mismanagement, while his polemical exaggerations prompted spirited responses from liberal and nationalist writers.

Giraldus Cambrensis (Gerald of Wales) (*c.*1146–*c.*1223), Cambro-Norman cleric and historian, who was educated at Gloucester and Paris. Twice in the 1180s he visited Ireland, where several of his relatives had seized land after the Norman invasion of 1169–70, to collect material for his *Topographia Hiberniae* (The Topography of Ireland) (1187) and *Expugnatio Hibernica* (The Conquest of Ireland) (1188). Both works were intended to justify the invasion, and portrayed the Irish (often in lurid detail) as primitive, barbaric and more pagan than Christian. Some subsequent English commentators recycled his arguments to denigrate the native Irish and justify conquest and expropriation, and he became the prime source for defenders of Gaelic Ireland to refute.

Hallam, Henry (1777–1859), historian, was born in Windsor and educated at Eton and Christ Church, Oxford. He was a leading contributor to the Whig periodical, the *Edinburgh Review*. Among his major works was *The Constitutional History of England from the Accession of Henry VII* *to the Death of George II* (1827), which gave some consideration to Irish affairs. His approach was that of a moderate Whig, and he was critical of the Tory defence of the Stuarts in David Hume's *History of England.*

Hardiman, James (1782–1855), historian and librarian, was born in County Mayo, and educated in Galway and Dublin. He worked for the Public Record Office in Dublin (1811–30) and published several significant works: *History of the Town and County of Galway* (1820), *Annals of Innisfallen* (1822), *Irish Minstrelsy: or, Bardic Remains of Ireland* (1831), several collections of documents for the Irish Record Commission, and an edition of Roderic O'Flaherty's *A Chorographical Description of West or h-Iar Connacht* (1684) for the Irish Archaeological Society in 1846. *Irish Minstrelsy*, a collection of translated Gaelic poetry from all periods, was one of the most significant works of the 1830s: it drew on oral and manuscript sources, and argued that Ireland had a native literature that could rival those of classical Greece and Rome. A founder member of the Irish Archaeological Society (1840) and the Celtic Society (1846), Hardiman was appointed librarian of Queen's College Galway in 1849.

Hay, Edward (1761?–1826), Catholic activist and historian, was born in Enniscorthy, County Wexford, and educated in France and Germany. He was a delegate for County Wexford at the Catholic Convention of 1792 and one of those who presented a petition for Catholic relief to Lord Lieutenant Fitzwilliam in 1795. His social prominence in Wexford gave him some authority with rebel forces in 1798, and after the rebellion he was tried and acquitted on charges of treason. He published his *History of the Insurrection of the County of Wexford AD 1798* (1803) to defend the behaviour of his co-religionists and counter loyalist claims that he had been directly involved in the rebellion. It argued that Catholics had been the victims rather than the instigators of sectarian violence and had taken up arms only to defend themselves. For the remainder of his life he continued to agitate for Catholic emancipation. In 1847 the Young Irelanders re-published his account of the 1798 Rebellion for the Library of Ireland.

Holland, Denis (1826–72), journalist, was born and educated in Cork city. He left Queen's College Cork to become a journalist on the *Cork Southern Reporter*. The collapse of the repeal movement and the devastation caused by the Famine led him to adopt the militant views of John Mitchel, and in 1849 he took part in an abortive revolutionary conspiracy led by James Fintan Lalor. In 1852 he moved to Belfast to become editor of the *Northern Whig* and in 1857 left to establish the nationalist *Ulsterman*. This was replaced in 1858 by the *Irishman* which Holland claimed was more in keeping with the original nationalist ideals of the *Nation* than the paper edited by A. M. Sullivan. Legal tussles with Sullivan cost him heavily and in 1863 he emigrated to London and four years later to America, continuing to contribute to Irish nationalist papers. He wrote some historical fiction, most notably *Donal Dun O'Byrne: A Tale of the Rising in Wexford in 1798* (1869).

Hudson, William Elliott (1796–1853), lawyer and antiquarian, was born in Dublin and educated at TCD and King's Inns, Dublin. He became a successful barrister and by the 1840s was sympathetic to the repeal movement. When he relaunched the *Citizen* in 1842 as the *Dublin Monthly Magazine*, he invited Thomas Davis, a close friend, to contribute several articles. He also financed the publication of *The Spirit of the Nation* (1843), and composed tunes for some of its songs. On his deathbed, Davis is said to have described him as the best man and best Irishman he had ever known. He was a founding member of the Irish Archaeological Society in 1840, and of the Ossianic Society, established in 1853 to preserve and publish early Irish texts.

Hughes, Terence MacMahon (1812–49), journalist and poet, was born and educated in Newry, County Down, where he developed a command of several European languages. He wrote the satirical political works *Irish Stew* (1836) and *The Biliad* (1846) and worked with Charles Gavan Duffy (later his brother-in-law) on the *Belfast Vindicator*. Duffy enlisted him to work on the *Nation* and he regularly contributed verse to the paper (1842–3). Afterwards he was Spanish correspondent for the *Morning Chronicle* and *Times*, and travelled through Iberia writing several works on Spain, Portugal and Madeira.

Hume, David (1711–76), philosopher and historian, was born and educated in Edinburgh. His main philosophical works, *Treatise of Human Nature* (1739–40) and the *Enquiry Concerning Human Understanding* (1748), followed John Locke's example in assessing the nature and limits of human knowledge. He was also a political essayist and historian of note and his *History of England* (1754–62) enjoyed great success. His style was generally judicious and balanced, and his work evinced scepticism of simple moral and political stances and a distaste for religious fanaticism. He was much criticised by Irish Catholic historians for his portrayal of Catholicism as barbarous superstition and his uncritical repetition of Sir John Temple's account of the massacres of Protestants in 1641.

Ingram, John Kells (1823–1907), economist, poet and academic, was born in County Donegal and educated in Newry and at TCD. He became a fellow of TCD in 1846 and was a prominent figure in the college for over 50 years: he was professor of oratory (1852–66), of English literature (1855–66), regius professor of Greek (1866–77), librarian (1879–87), senior lecturer (1886–93), registrar (1893–6) and vice-provost (1898–9). In 1873 he founded the college journal *Hermathena*. Although not regarded as having any significant nationalist sympathies, in 1843 he contributed 'The memory of the dead' to the *Nation* in praise of the United Irishmen; it became one of Young Ireland's most enduringly popular songs. His reputation as an economist rests largely on his internationally successful *History of Political Economy* (1888). He was president of the RIA (1892–6). He continued to write poetry throughout his life and proudly acknowledged his authorship of 'The memory' with the publication of his *Sonnets and Other Poems* in 1900.

Irwin, Thomas Caulfield (1823–92), poet, was born in Warrenpoint, County Down. After studying medicine and travelling widely he returned to Ireland (*c.*1853) and contributed patriotic verse to the *Nation*; he also write for the *Dublin University Magazine* and the *Shamrock*. His *Versicles* (1856), containing much of his best poetry, was published by the Celtic Union. Other collections included *Poems* (1866), *Irish Poems and Legends* (1869), *Songs and Romances* (1878) and *Poems, Sketches, and Songs* (1889).

Keating, Geoffrey (*c.*1580–1644), historian and Catholic priest, was born in south County Tipperary, and educated locally and on the Continent. He is best known for his narrative history of Ireland 'Foras Feasa ar Éirinn' (Compendium of wisdom about Ireland) (*c.*1634) which was widely circulated in manuscript and in English and Latin translations. Some commentators criticised him as too credulous, since he incorporated in his history some fabulous tales of mythical peoples who were among the supposed ancestors of the Irish, but he did this deliberately to establish the antiquity of Irish civilisation and the learning, piety and courage of its people. His work also sought to bind together all those who were Irish born and Catholic, helping to establish the concept of Ireland as a Gaelic nation into which the Old English had been absorbed. Although it dealt only with the period up to the Norman invasion of 1169–70, its polemical introduction was much used by later historians to refute the arguments of hostile writers such as Giraldus Cambrensis and Edmund Spenser.

Keegan, John (1816–49), poet, was born and educated in County Laois. He contributed verse to several journals including the *Dublin University Magazine*, the *Irish Penny Journal*, the *Tipperary Vindicator*, the *Nation*, the *Irishman*, the *Cork Magazine* and the *Irish National Magazine*. He seems to have worked briefly as clerk on a famine relief committee and this influenced some of his best known work such as 'To the cholera' (1848). His *Legends and Poems of the Irish Peasantry* was published in 1907 and his *Selected Poems* in 1999.

Kelly, Mary Anne ('Eva') (1830–1910), poet, was born in Headford, County Galway, and educated at home by a governess. An enthusiastic reader of the *Nation*, she contributed verse to the paper from December 1844, most of her work appearing under the name 'Eva'. Her work also appeared in the short-lived militant papers of 1848, the *United Irishman*, the *Irish Felon* and the *Irishman*. She became engaged to the Young Irelander Kevin Izod O'Doherty, who was transported to Tasmania, and her devotion to him caught the public imagination. She continued to contribute to the *Nation*, becoming one of its best-known writers as 'Eva of the *Nation*'. After their marriage in 1855, she and O'Doherty emigrated to Australia, where she contributed poetry to the *Sydney Freeman's Journal*. *Poems by Eva of the Nation* (1877) was published in San Francisco and just before her death her collected poems were published in Dublin (1909).

Kelly, Matthew (1814–58), priest and historian, was born and educated in Kilkenny and at Maynooth College. Appointed professor of philosophy at the Irish College in Paris in 1839, he became professor of English and French (1841–57) and ecclesiastical history (1857–8) at Maynooth. He was a founder member of the Celtic Society, for which he translated and edited John Lynch's *Cambrensis Eversus* (1848–51). A frequent contributor to the *Dublin Review* (1842–55), he also published the *Apologia pro Hibernia* of the sixteenth-century Jesuit priest Stephen White (1849), the *Historiae Catholicae Iberniae Compendium* of Philip O'Sullivan Beare (1850) and the *Calendar of Irish Saints: The Martyrology of Tallagh* (1857).

Lalor, James Fintan (1807–49), journalist and agrarian reformer, was born in County Laois. His health impaired by a childhood injury, he had only a year's formal education at Carlow College. His father Patrick Lalor was a prominent repealer but, in the midst of the devastation of the Famine, James regarded land reform as infinitely more important than repeal of the union. In 1847 he set out his ideas in a series of letters to the *Nation*, calling for a land settlement which would secure the position of tenant farmers and, failing this, for tenants to embark on a nationwide rent strike. His ideas frightened moderates in the Irish Confederation but appealed to militants such as John Mitchel. In June 1848 he contributed further articles advocating peasant proprietorship to the radical *Irish Felon* and was briefly imprisoned. On his release he became involved with a new revolutionary secret society, but its attempts to mount an insurrection in September 1849 collapsed and he died soon afterwards. Although they made occasional appeals to the past, his writings had little in common with the romantic, celebratory history of Young Ireland.

Lane, Denny (1818–95), poet and businessman, was born in Cork and educated locally and at TCD. At the College Historical Society he became a good friend of Thomas Davis, and contributed verse occasionally to the *Nation*, usually under the name 'Donall na Glanna'. He was active in organising Confederate clubs in Cork and was briefly imprisoned after the attempted insurrection of 1848. On his release he devoted himself to developing Cork's industries and infrastructure, inspired by Young Ireland ideals of national self-sufficiency. A member and president (1885) of the Cork Literary and Scientific Society and a foundation vice-president of the Cork Historical and Archaeological Society (1891), he wrote an introduction to the first number of the latter's journal on the importance of history to the Irish people, and paid tribute to the idealism of Davis and the Young Irelanders in a published address to the National Literary Society (1893).

Lawless, John (1773–1837), lawyer and journalist, was born in Dublin. He was an associate of Robert Emmet and came under suspicion after the insurrection of 1803. Known as 'Honest Jack' for his forthright and democratic opinions and defence of democratic ideals, he founded the *Ulster Register* (Belfast), a political and literary magazine (1816–18) and another weekly newspaper, the *Irishman* (1819–25). In *A Compendium of the History of Ireland from the Earliest Period to the Reign of George I* (1814), he deliberately passed over the earliest ages as being more useful to 'the curious antiquarian than to the practical politician' and concentrated on 'our modern history' which consisted of 'the recorded sufferings of Ireland'. His work relied heavily on Denis Taaffe's *An Impartial History of Ireland* (1809–11).

Lecky, William Edward Hartpole (1838–1903), historian, was born in Dublin and educated in TCD (1856–60). His first book *Leaders of Public Opinion in Ireland* (1861) looked nostalgically to the aristocratic patriotism of Henry Grattan and lamented that the landed classes had ceded political leadership to the Catholic clergy. His *Spirit of Rationalism in Europe* (1865) and *History of European Morals from Augustus to Charlemagne* (1869) were positivist-influenced studies into the new sociological history of ideas. Lecky's major work, *A History of England in the Eighteenth Century* (1878–90), was praised for its impartiality, judiciousness and liberal sympathies. This work included his influential treatment of Ireland in the same period, which was later published separately (5 vols, 1892). His refutation of Froude, understanding of Irish grievances and praise of Grattan's parliament were all welcomed by Irish nationalists, who used his findings to argue the case for Irish self-government. Lecky regarded this as a gross distortion of his work. Although sympathetic to some aspects of Irish nationalism in his youth, he opposed Home Rule for Ireland and regarded Parnell and his party as unprincipled demagogues with no respect for property or the rule of law. As MP for TCD (1895–1902), he was a staunch defender of the union with Britain.

Ledwich, Edward (1738–1823), Church of Ireland clergyman and antiquarian, was born in Dublin and educated at TCD. Ledwich strongly opposed Charles Vallancey's views on ancient Irish history, particularly his claims about the Phoenician origins of the Irish people. Convinced that the Irish originated in Scandinavian and had lived in barbarism until the arrival of English colonists, he dismissed claims that Ireland had an indigenous culture of any value. He published

The Antiquities of Ireland (1790) which cast doubt on the authenticity of many native Irish texts, the lives of Irish saints, and, most notoriously, even on the existence of St Patrick himself. Subsequent scholars such as George Petrie criticised his religious bias and factual errors, and nineteenth-century nationalist historians devoted considerable effort to refuting his claims, especially those on Irish origins and the denial of the existence of Ireland's national saint.

Leland, Thomas (1722–85), Church of Ireland clergyman, classicist and historian, was born in Dublin. Educated at TCD, he became professor of oratory and history (1761–2) and of oratory alone (1762–81); he was also librarian (from 1768). His translation of the *Orations of Demosthenes* (1754–70) was regularly reprinted and provided a model for the Anglo-Irish tradition of parliamentary oratory; he also wrote several works of classical history. He was persuaded by Charles O'Conor and Edmund Burke to write a *History of Ireland from the Invasion of Henry II* (3 vols, 1773; repr. 1814). This was a more balanced work than previous Protestant histories (and alienated some Protestant readers), but its treatment of the 1641 Rebellion dismayed liberal Catholics such as O'Conor, and encouraged John Curry to publish his *Historical and Critical Review of the Civil Wars in Ireland* (1775) to challenge some of Leland's claims. His scholarship and relative impartiality ensured his work was read into the nineteenth century.

Luby, Thomas Clarke (1822–1901), Fenian and historian, was born in Dublin and educated at TCD. Influenced by the Young Ireland movement, he participated in unsuccessful armed actions in County Meath in July 1848 and around Cashel in September 1849, and was briefly imprisoned. He was a founder member of the IRB in 1858 and became the owner and sub-editor of its paper, the *Irish People*, in 1863, which was often critical of the timidity and revolutionary incompetence of Young Ireland. After the paper's suppression in 1865, he was found guilty of treason-felony and sentenced to 20 years' penal servitude. Released on amnesty in 1871, he settled in New York city and became a mainstay of the Fenian Brotherhood. He admired the literary efforts of Young Ireland, and sought to emulate them in works such as *The Lives and Times of Illustrious and Representative Irishmen* (1878) and *The Story of Ireland's Struggle for Self-Government* (1893).

Lynch, John (*c.*1599–1677), Catholic priest and historian, was born in Galway city and educated there and on the Continent. Appointed archdeacon of Tuam in 1631, he supported the Confederation of Kilkenny in the 1640s, but strongly opposed the papal legate Archbishop Rinuccini, declaring his loyalty to the English crown rather than Rome. After the surrender of Galway in 1652, he lived in exile in France. His most famous works were: *Cambrensis Eversus* (1662) which followed up Keating's attack on Cambrensis, and *Alithinologia*, a defence of pro-Ormond Confederates. Lynch defended the Old English settlers, praising their dedication to their religion and their king, and censured the Gaelic Irish as selfish and undisciplined. He also translated Keating's *Foras Feasa ar Éirinn* into Latin. His works, especially *Cambrensis Eversus*, were much quoted by Irish Catholic historians from the eighteenth century onwards. An edition of *Cambrensis* by Matthew Kelly and Lynch's *Pii Antistitis Icon* (1669), a life of Bishop Francis Kirwan of Killala translated from Latin to English by C. P. Meehan, were published in Dublin in 1848.

Macaulay, Thomas Babington (1800–59), politician and historian, was born in Leicestershire and educated at Cambridge. A Whig MP, he served as secretary at war (1839–41) and paymaster general (1846–8), and drafted India's penal code. He published the highly-successful *Lays of*

Ancient Rome in 1842 and was a regular contributor to the *Edinburgh Review*. His dramatic *History of England* (5 vols, 1849–61) traced the political, moral and intellectual progress of England through the seventeenth century and was the foundation text of the Whig interpretation of history.

McCann, Michael Joseph (1820–83), poet and journalist, was born in Galway and educated at St Jarlath's College, Tuam. While teaching at St Jarlath's, he contributed verse to the *Nation*, most notably 'O'Donnell Aboo' (28 Jan. 1843), one of Young Ireland's most enduring war songs. In 1859 he launched the *Harp* (Mar.–Oct. 1859), a monthly magazine published in Cork, which featured articles on Irish history, antiquities and literature. He revived it as the *Irish Harp* (Mar. 1863–Feb. 1864), but it had little success and soon afterwards he moved to America and then London.

MacCarthy, Denis Florence (1817–82), poet, was born in Dublin and educated at TCD, where he met Davis through the College Historical Society. He contributed verse to several Irish journals, including the *Dublin Weekly Satirist, Dublin Evening Packet, Dublin University Magazine, Irish Catholic Magazine, Irish Monthly* and the *Nation*. Much of his verse was based on historical research and stressed the cultural sophistication of Gaelic civilisation. In 1846 he edited *The Book of Irish Ballads* and *The Poets and Dramatists of Ireland* for the Library of Ireland. Although he wrote some rousingly nationalistic verse, his attachment to Young Ireland was more personal than political and he played no part in the insurrection of 1848. He published several successful collections of poems in the 1850s, and was regarded by many nationalists as Ireland's poet laureate.

McCullagh (Torrens), William Torrens (1813–94), writer and reformer, was born in County Dublin and educated at TCD, where he was president of the College Historical Society and a friend of Davis and Dillon. More inclined to liberalism than nationalism, he worked for the government commission on poor relief (1833–5) and was a founder of the first Mechanics' Institute in Dublin (1842). He delivered a series of lectures on history to the institute, published as *The Use and Study of History* (1842), a work admired by the Young Irelanders. He was a member of the Celtic Atheneum, the Anti-Corn-Law League, and the Tenant League. As an independent liberal MP for Dundalk (1847–52), Great Yarmouth (1857–65) and Finsbury (1865–85), he advocated social reforms, and published widely on history, politics and social issues.

McGee, Thomas D'Arcy (1825–68), journalist, politician and historian, was born in Carlingford, County Louth, and educated in Wexford. He emigrated to the USA in 1842 and became editor of the *Boston Pilot* within two years. He returned to Ireland in 1845 and became one of the *Nation*'s most prolific contributors, publishing *The Poets and Dramatists of Ireland* (1846) and the *Life and Conquests of Art MacMurrogh* (1847) for the Library of Ireland. From June 1847 he was secretary of the Irish Confederation and supported the decision to take up arms in July 1848. He fled to America after the Rising's failure and founded several newspapers which promoted Irish interests. Supporting moderate constitutional politics, he was bitterly attacked by former colleagues. He published *A History of Irish Settlers in North America* (1851), *A History of the Attempts to Establish the Protestant Reformation in Ireland* (1853), and *A Popular History of Ireland, from the Earliest Times to the Emancipation of the Catholics* (1864), all of which sold well and were marked by his nationalism and Catholicism. Moving to Montreal in 1857, he took a leading part in promoting Canadian federation and urged that Ireland should emulate Canada by seeking self-government within the British empire rather than the independent republic advocated by the Fenians. After condemning Fenian raids on Canada, he was assassinated in Ottawa.

MacGeoghegan, James (1702–64), Catholic priest and historian, was born in County Westmeath and educated for the priesthood in France, where he became an administrator of the Irish College in Paris and chaplain to the Irish Brigade in the French army. His *Histoire de l'Irlande, Ancienne et Moderne, Tiré des Monuments les Plus Authentiques* (3 vols, Paris, 1758–62) covered Irish history from the earliest times to the Treaty of Limerick of 1691. Dedicated to the Irish Brigade, it was strongly Jacobite in its sympathies, asserting the legitimacy of the Stuarts while denouncing the brutality of successive English governments in Ireland and insisting on Ireland's status as a separate kingdom. Available in English translation from 1831–2, it was popular among nineteenth-century nationalists for its detailing of the oppression suffered by Irish Catholics and its spirited defence of their culture, courage and piety.

MacNevin, Thomas (1814–48), journalist and historian, was born in Dublin and educated at TCD, where he was a friend of Davis and auditor and president of the College Historical Society. He became a regular contributor to the *Nation* and a leading spokesman for Young Ireland in the Repeal Association. One of the *Nation*'s most prolific writers, he edited *The Leading State Trials of Ireland from . . . 1794 to 1803* (1844) and *The Speeches of the Right Honourable Richard Lalor Sheil MP* (1845), and wrote *The History of the Volunteers of 1782* (1845) and *The Confiscation of Ulster* (1846) for the Library of Ireland. Although they were acknowledged as competent works, some colleagues observed that they failed to match his sparkling intellect in conversation. Devastated by Davis's death, he decided he could best honour his memory by carrying on his work and writing a history of Ireland from the earliest times. His failure to complete the task contributed to a mental breakdown in 1846 and he died soon afterwards.

Madden (Maddyn), Daniel Owen (1815–59), writer, was born in Mallow, County Cork, and educated locally. He enrolled at the King's Inns in 1838 and became an active member of the College Historical Society at TCD where he befriended Davis, despite not sharing his nationalist views. He admired the British empire, opposed repeal of the union, and in about 1842 converted from Catholicism to Protestantism and emigrated to London. His *Ireland and its Rulers since 1829* (1844) contrasted Davis's idealism with O'Connell's venality and coined the term Young Ireland for the *Nation* group. He wrote a memoir of Henry Grattan (1846), a volume of Grattan's speeches and the *Age of Pitt and Fox* (1846), which was severely reviewed in the *Nation* for its imperialist sympathies. Madden returned to Ireland in 1857 as a correspondent for the *Daily News* and devoted himself to historical research, publishing *The Chiefs of Parties, Past and Present* (1859).

Madden, Richard Robert (R. R.) (1798–1886), historian and government official, was born and educated in Dublin. During the 1820s and early 1830s he practised medicine on the Continent, in the Middle East and in the West Indies, and became a leading figure in the international Anti-Slavery Society. His *Travels in Turkey, Egypt, Nubia and Palestine* (1829) established him as a travel writer. After meeting the elderly United Irishman William James MacNevin in New York in 1835 he was persuaded to write a history of the United movement and diligently researched the topic for the next six years. In 1842 he produced the first volume of *The United Irishmen, Their Lives and Times* (7 volumes, 1842–6); four more volumes were added (1857–60) and the work was subsequently published in several different series and editions. It provided over 50 biographies of United Irishmen, and sought to rehabilitate their reputation by explaining the rebellion as the inevitable consequence of oppressive government. Although rather rambling and disorganised, his work was highly influential in its portrayal of the United men and helped establish their reputation as noble and courageous patriots. After Madden's death, C. P. Meehan published some of his research and poetry as *Literary Remains of the United Irishmen* (1887).

Mangan, James Clarence (1803–49), poet, was born in Dublin and educated locally. At 15 he was apprenticed to a scrivener and afterwards worked as a legal copyist. He contributed to various periodicals such as the *Comet*, the *Dublin Satirist*, and the *Dublin Penny Journal*. From 1835 he contributed translations of modern German romantic poetry to the *Dublin University Magazine (DUM)*, later collected as a *German Anthology* (1845); he also contributed a series of oriental translations from 1837. He was employed as a copyist by the Ordnance Survey (1838–41) and in the library of TCD (1842–6). Eccentric in his habits and dress, morbidly shy and melancholic, he lived a solitary life and sought solace in alcohol and opium. He wrote some of the *Nation*'s most powerful verse, evoking Ireland as a desolate wasteland during the Famine, and was commissioned to write a volume called 'Echoes of Foreign Song' for the Library of Ireland, but never completed it. In 1847 he began an *Anthologia Hibernica* in the *DUM*, a series of translations of Jacobite poetry with the scholar and publisher John O'Daly (Mangan's knowledge of Irish was cursory), later published as *The Poets and Poetry of Munster* (1849). Mangan was too protean and idiosyncratic to subsume himself to the demands and discipline of any party and his affiliation to Young Ireland was sporadic, but after his death it was mainly Young Irelanders such as Mitchel, Duffy and Meehan who championed his work and promoted his reputation.

Meagher, Thomas Francis (1823–67), nationalist, was born into a prosperous merchant family in Waterford and educated by the Jesuits at Clongowes Wood, County Kildare, and Stonyhurst, Lancashire. Soon after his return to Ireland in 1843 he attached himself to the Young Ireland group and wrote some minor articles for the *Nation*. He was commissioned to write 'The Williamite Wars' and 'Orators of the Irish Parliament' for the Library of Ireland, but did not complete either of them. His impassioned speech against O'Connell's peace resolutions in July 1846 led William Makepeace Thackeray to give him the sarcastic nickname 'Meagher of the Sword'. A founder of the Irish Confederation in 1847, the following year he was one of three delegates chosen to carry a congratulatory address to the new French republic and returned with a green, white and orange tricolour. For his part in the attempted rising of 1848 he was transported to Tasmania but escaped to New York in 1852, where he became a prominent journalist, lawyer and public speaker, publishing *Speeches on Ireland* (1853). In 1861 he organised an Irish brigade to fight for the North in the civil war and became a brigadier-general, serving with distinction in some of the war's bloodiest battles. Appointed acting governor of Montana territory after the war, he fell overboard while on an official tour and drowned in the Missouri.

Meehan, Charles Patrick (1812–90), priest and historian, was born in Dublin and educated in a Longford hedge school and the Irish College in Rome. An excellent preacher and a strong advocate of temperance and Irish self-government, he was attracted by the nationalist ideals of Young Ireland, contributing occasionally to the *Nation* and defending the Young Irelanders from accusations of irreligion. He wrote *The Confederation of Kilkenny* (1846) and a translation of Daniel O'Daly's *The Geraldines, Earls of Desmond, and the Persecution of the Irish Catholics* (1847) for the Library of Ireland. Despite the disapproval of the hierarchy, he was one of the few Catholic priests active in the Irish Confederation (1847–8). A diligent scholar, he was elected MRIA

(1865) and continued to write Irish history after the demise of the Library of Ireland with works such as *The Fate and Fortunes of Hugh O'Neill . . . and Rory O'Donel* (1868) and *The Rise and Fall of the Irish Franciscan Monasteries* (1869). He edited a new edition of *The Spirit of the Nation* (1882), published selections of Mangan's poetry in *The Poets and Poetry of Munster* (1883) (with an important biographical memoir), and re-edited *Literary Remains of the United Irishmen* (1887) to include manuscript material by R. R. Madden.

Michelet, Jules (1798–1874), historian, was born and educated in Paris. He taught history at the École Normale Supérieure and in 1831 published *Introduction á L'Histoire Universelle*. That year he was appointed head of the historical section in the French Record Office, which provided ready access to the sources used for his magnum opus *Histoire de France*; the first six volumes (1833–43) portrayed the emergence of France as a nation in the Middle Ages. In 1847 he interrupted this to write his vivid and impassioned *Histoire de la Revolution Française* (7 vols, 1847–53), which exhibited to the full his lively imagination and strong political and religious prejudices. His work was widely read by romantic historians throughout Europe, who often tried to emulate his declamatory, opinionated style. He welcomed the revolution of 1848, but refused allegiance to the Second Empire and lost his official positions. He then resumed the writing of the *Histoire de France* from the Renaissance to the eve of the 1789 Revolution, published in another 11 volumes (1855–67).

Mitchel, John (1815–75), journalist and author, was born in County Derry and educated in Newry and at TCD. While working as a solicitor in County Down, he became attracted to the nationalist ideals of Young Ireland and contributed occasionally to the *Nation*, writing the *Life of Aodh O'Neill* (1845) for the Library of Ireland. After the death of Davis he was recruited as assistant editor of the *Nation* in 1845. As Famine conditions worsened, he introduced an increasingly strident note to the paper and spoke strongly against O'Connell's peace resolutions in July 1846. He disagreed with his colleagues in the Irish Confederation over their adherence to constitutional methods and resigned from the *Nation* to publish in February 1848 his own militant paper, the *United Irishman*, which openly advocated armed revolution. Arrested on charges of treason-felony, he was sentenced to 14 years' transportation, an experience he recorded in his *Jail Journal* (1854); its defiance and bitterness towards English rule made it a seminal text of Irish nationalism. He escaped from Tasmania in 1853 and went to New York, where he founded the *Citizen* newspaper and became involved in controversy because of his support for slavery. Moving to Tennessee, he wrote *The Last Conquest of Ireland (Perhaps)* (1860), which accused the British government of deliberately using famine to undermine Ireland's aspirations to independence. He supported the Confederate States during the Civil War, after which he was briefly imprisoned. While living in New York, he wrote a *History of Ireland from the Treaty of Limerick* (1867) which became a standard nationalist account, and *The Crusade of the Period* (1873), attacking the anti-Irish views of J. A. Froude.

Moore, Thomas (1779–1852), poet and historian, was born in Dublin and educated in TCD. At Trinity in the 1790s he associated with United Irishmen and was sympathetic to their ideals. In 1800 he published his *Odes of Anacreon* which marked him out as a poet of promise. From 1807 to 1834 he published the ten volumes of his *Irish Melodies*, which he regarded as the texts to Ireland's national music, and added to them six volumes of his *National Airs* (1818–24). Some nationalists found his songs of longing and loss rather defeatist but they were immensely popular and established him as the national lyric poet of Ireland. His political sympathies were evident in his novel, *Memoirs of Captain Rock* (1824), which portrayed Irish history as an unending cycle of oppression and revolt. Moore was a biographer of note, publishing lives of Richard Brinsley Sheridan (1825), Byron (1830) and Lord Edward FitzGerald (1831). He spent many years researching a *History of Ireland* (4 vols, 1835–46) but its reception was mixed: it was not learned enough for scholars nor popular enough for the general public, and was severely reviewed by the *Nation*. Moore's poetry showed the capacity of historical verse to evoke patriotic emotions and though some later nationalist writers disparaged his drawing-room patriotism, few matched the power of his romantic lyricism.

Moryson, Fynes (1566–1630), writer and official, was born in Lincolnshire and educated at Cambridge. After travelling widely on the Continent, he accompanied Lord Deputy Mountjoy to Ireland in 1600 to write a journal of his Irish campaign and became his private secretary. He took part in the siege of Kinsale in 1601 and left Ireland in 1602, returning briefly in 1613. His account of his travels, *An Itinerary* (1617), made considerable use of official documents and correspondence to praise Mountjoy as a great soldier and statesman. Moryson denounced the native Irish as barbarians and approved of Mountjoy's severe methods during the Nine Years' War. The part concerning Ireland was reprinted as *An History of Ireland from the Year 1599 to 1603* (2 vols, Dublin, 1735).

Musgrave, Sir Richard (1746–1818), writer and MP, was born in County Waterford and educated at Oxford. He became MP for Lismore in 1778 and received a baronetcy for supporting the government. Active in supressing agrarian disturbances, during the 1790s he warned of the dangers of domestic rebellion and French invasion. In 1801 he published *Memoirs of the Different Rebellions in Ireland*, which largely ignored the political motivation of the United Irishmen and denounced the 1798 Rebellion as a bloodthirsty pogrom led by Catholic priests. His work was warmly welcomed by hardline Protestants but much criticised by Catholic and liberal writers such as Francis Plowden.

O'Brien, William Smith (1803–64), politician, was born into a Protestant landed family at Dromoland, County Clare, and educated at Harrow and Cambridge. He entered parliament as Conservative MP for Ennis (1825–31) and County Limerick (1835–49), but by 1843 had become a repealer. He identified with the Young Ireland group, but his age and political caution led him half in jest to describe himself as 'Middle-Aged Ireland'. O'Brien had great pride in his Gaelic Irish ancestry (especially his descent from Brian Boru) and strongly supported the educational efforts of the *Nation*, reading Irish history and making a sustained attempt to learn Irish, although his main efforts were devoted to writing well-researched reports for the Repeal Association's parliamentary committee. He led the secession from the Repeal Association in 1846, and was the leading figure in the Irish Confederation founded the following year; he was its only member elected to parliament in 1847. After the suspension of habeas corpus in July 1848, he committed the Confederates to armed rebellion but their efforts fizzled out after a skirmish at Ballingarry, County Tipperary. Arrested, he was convicted of high treason and transported for life to Tasmania. He was pardoned in 1854 and returned to Ireland two years later, writing occasionally on political issues but avoiding participation in public life.

O'Callaghan, John Cornelius (1805–83), journalist and historian, was born in Dublin and educated at Clongowes Wood College. He contributed to the *Comet* and the *Irish Monthly Magazine* and published the *Green Book* (1840), a collection of writing intended to vindicate the courage and fighting ability of the Irish. Its popularity led to his association with the *Nation*, to which he regularly contributed articles and verse. He designed the membership cards of the Repeal Association and wrote *The Irish in the English Army and Navy* (1843). His habit of talking incessantly about Irish history amused even the Young Irelanders. His work culminated in the *History of the Irish Brigades in the Service of France* (8 vols, 1869), which did much to establish the importance of the Wild Geese in nationalist historiography; he also wrote *The Irish at Home and Abroad, at Limerick and Cremona* (1869). O'Callaghan combined exhaustive research and careful scholarship with a picturesque and panoramic historical style.

O'Connell, Daniel (1775–1847), politician and lawyer, was born near Cahirciveen, County Kerry and educated locally and in France, where he witnessed violent scenes during the revolution in the early 1790s. He was called to the Irish bar in 1798, and soon built up a thriving practice. The 1798 Rebellion confirmed his horror of political violence. He strongly opposed the act of union and led a group of Catholic radicals who agitated for Catholic emancipation. In 1823 he founded the Catholic Association to harness the Irish masses behind the emancipation campaign and his efforts bore fruit in 1829. Regarded with awe as 'the Liberator', he was the undisputed leader of Catholic Ireland. After agitating for repeal of the union in the early 1830s, he settled for ameliorative reforms from the Whig ministry. Disappointed with their results, he renewed the campaign for legislative independence by founding the Repeal Association in 1840, to which he welcomed the accession of the energetic and articulate *Nation* group. He wrote *A Memoir of Ireland: Native and Saxon* (1843) which detailed the historic wrongs to which Ireland had been subjected and argued that repeal of the union was the only solution to the country's ills. In general though, O'Connell attached far less importance than the *Nation* to the propagation of Irish history and his failure to provide adequate funds for the Repeal Association's readings rooms caused some resentment. Tensions also emerged over political tactics, denominational education and the *Nation*'s celebration of Ireland's martial tradition, and in July 1846 the Young Irelanders seceded from the Repeal Association. Weakened by illness and appalled by the misery of the Great Famine, he passed the leadership of the association over to his son John O'Connell (1810–58) and died soon afterwards.

O'Conor, Charles (1710–91), Catholic activist and antiquarian, was the son of a Catholic landowner of Belanagare, County Roscommon, and a lineal descendant of Rory O'Connor, the last high king of Ireland. He was educated by Irish Catholic clergy in Sligo and Killala. An accomplished Gaelic scholar, he used his researches in old manuscripts to write *Dissertations on the Antient History of Ireland* (1753) (published anonymously). Intended to rebut the work of hostile English and Protestant observers, it described a politically stable, legally sophisticated and culturally advanced civilisation of eastern origin in pre-Christian Ireland. O'Conor posited a continuous golden age that was ruptured by the greed and venality of the Norman invaders and eventually destroyed by the oppressive policies of successive English governments. His writing of history was linked directly to his efforts to seek relief for Catholics from the penal laws. A founder of the Catholic Committee, he wrote several pamphlets arguing that such laws were politically and economically counter-productive. He wrote of religious matters in a cautious, secular manner, tinged with the scepticism of the Enlightenment and mindful of the pragmatic politics of seeking Catholic relief in a Protestant state.

O'Conor, Matthew (1773–1844), historian and lawyer, was the grandson of Charles O'Conor of Belanagare, County Roscommon. While practising as a barrister in Dublin he wrote *The History of the Irish Catholics from the Settlement in 1691, with a View of the State of Ireland from the Invasion of Henry II to the Revolution* (1813), which focused on the period since 1691, especially on violations of the Treaty of Limerick. His work showed an assertiveness lacking in most eighteenth-century Irish Catholic history. Towards the end of his life he began working on a history of the Irish Brigade, published a year after his death in May 1844 as *Military History of the Irish Nation; Comprising Memoirs of the Irish Brigade in the Service of France* (1845).

O'Curry, Eugene (Eoghan) (1796–1862), historian and Irish scholar, was born near Kilkee, County Clare, and educated in a home much frequented by scholars and poets. While working for the Ordnance Survey (1835–42), he collaborated with colleagues such as George Petrie and John O'Donovan and gained useful antiquarian experience. He was later employed to copy and translate Irish manuscripts by various institutions such as the British Museum, the Royal Irish Academy and Trinity College Dublin, making Irish language sources accessible to the wider academic community, and was a founder of the Irish Archaeological Society (1840). In 1854 he was appointed professor of Irish history and archaeology in the newly-founded Catholic University, and later published his lectures, which provided the basis for subsequent scholarly studies into ancient Irish history.

O'Daly, Daniel (Dominic de Rosario) (1595–1662), Dominican priest and historian, was born near Castleisland, County Kerry and educated at Burgos and Bordeaux, before returning to Ireland as a fugitive priest. From the late 1620s he served as a diplomat on the Continent on behalf of the Dominican order and the kings of Portugal. In 1655 he published (in Latin) a history of the Geraldines, together with an account of the religious persecutions in Ireland during his lifetime. This listed the penal enactments of the period and gave brief biographical notes on 20 Dominican friars known to him personally who were martyred in Ireland. It was translated into French by Abbé Joubert (1697) and English by C. P. Meehan (1847), in an edition published by the Library of Ireland.

O'Donovan, John (1806–61), antiquarian and scholar, was born in Atateemore, County Kilkenny, and educated locally and at Hunt's Academy, Waterford. After working under James Hardiman in the Irish Record Office (1827–30), he was employed by the Ordnance Survey (1830–42), and listed over 60,000 Irish placenames and made significant contributions to the topographical memoirs that were intended to accompany the finished maps. Working on the Survey brought him into contact with George Petrie, who formed a high opinion of his scholarly abilities, and he contributed several essays to the *Dublin Penny Journal* in 1832–3. A founder of the Irish Archaeological Society (1840), O'Donovan was awarded the RIA's Cunningam medal (1848) and appointed professor of Celtic languages in Queen's College Belfast (1849). His major publications, such as the *Grammar of the Irish Language* (1845), *The Annals of Ireland* (1846) and *Annála Ríoghachta Éireann* (7 vols, 1848–56), were among the most significant Irish scholarly works of the nineteenth century.

O'Grady, Standish James (1846–1928), novelist and historian, was born in Castletownbere, County Cork, and educated at Tipperary Grammar School and TCD. His interest in Irish history aroused by works such as O'Halloran's *History of Ireland* (1775) and O'Curry's *Manners and Customs of the Ancient Irish* (1873), he published *The History of Ireland: Heroic Period* (2 vols, 1878–81), *Early Bardic Literature of Ireland* (1879) and *Cuculain: An Epic* (1882), and wrote a series of novels based on Irish history and mythology. He was especially interested in the Elizabethan wars in Ireland, and contributed *The Bog of Stars: And Other Stories and Sketches of Elizabethan Ireland* (1893) to the New Irish Library; he also wrote historical novels about Red Hugh O'Donnell. Strongly influenced by Carlylean notions of hero worship, he saluted the valour of Irish resistance to English incursions, but believed that the Tudor conquest was a necessary step in Ireland's progress and never lamented Irish defeats. His idiosyncratic political views led Lady Gregory to call him a 'Fenian Unionist'. He edited and wrote most of the *All-Ireland Review* (1900–7) and contributed to other journals such as the *Irish Peasant* and the *New Age*. His evocation of Ireland's heroic past contributed significantly to the literary revival of the 1890s.

O'Hagan, John (1822–90), writer and lawyer, was born in Newry, County Down, and educated locally and at TCD, where he met Davis and Dillon through the College Historical Society. He contributed some notable verse such as 'Ourselves alone' and 'The union' to the *Nation*, but after 1843 concentrated on his legal career, and was appointed QC (1865) and judicial commissioner with the Irish Land Commission (1881–90). He contributed verse and reviews to various periodicals and some of his work was featured in the *Treasury of Irish Poetry* (1900). In the *Contemporary Review* (Oct. 1890) he maintained that Davis would have readily accepted home rule and opposed 'the blind, levelling, envious, anarchic forces which are the awful menace of our time'.

O'Halloran, Sylvester (1728–1807), Catholic surgeon and antiquary, was born in Limerick and studied in London and on the Continent. He published *An Introduction to the Study of the Antiquities of Ireland* (1770), *Ierne Defended* (1774) and *A General History of Ireland* (1775) to rebut arguments that the Gaelic Irish were a people without culture or nobility before the Norman invasion. His assertion of Irish national pride was attractive to liberal-minded Irish Patriots who supported legislative independence, but offended some Protestant scholars such as Edward Ledwich who saw it as a form of Catholic triumphalism. His praise of Irish culture and emphasis on the military and heroic aspects of Gaelic Ireland chimed with the outlook of nineteenth-century nationalists and his *History of Ireland* greatly influenced romantic writers and went through several editions (1803, 1819, 1820).

O'Hegarty, Patrick Sarsfield 'P. S.' (1879–1955), writer and civil servant, was born in Carrignavar, County Cork, and educated by the Christian Brothers in Cork city. While working for the Post Office in London, he joined the IRB and the Gaelic League and contributed to the IRB journal, *Irish Freedom* (1910–14). In 1922 he became secretary of the Department of Posts and Telegraphs. A great admirer of Young Ireland's historical writings, he was one of the separatist movement's most effective propagandists. His writings such as *John Mitchel: An Appreciation, with Some Account of Young Ireland* (1917), *Indestructible Nation* (1918), *The Victory of Sinn Féin* (1924) and *A History of Ireland under the Union* (1952) were strongly influenced by Young Ireland's nationalist determinism.

O'Leary, John (1830–1907), Fenian and journalist, was born in County Tipperary and educated at TCD and the Queen's Colleges of Cork and Galway. He took part in the 1848 insurrection, and a further conspiracy in 1849, and in 1858 joined the IRB. In 1863 he was appointed editor of the IRB journal, the *Irish People*, and was also a regular contributor. Arrested in 1865, he served six years in prison until pardoned in 1871 and then lived in exile in Paris until allowed return to Ireland in 1885. Much admired by young nationalists for his personal integrity and uncompromising views, he introduced many of them to the writings of Young Ireland, and was a leading figure in nationalist literary and political societies until his death. He published his memoirs as *Recollections of Fenians and Fenianism* (1896).

O'Neill Daunt, William Joseph 'W. J.' (1807–94), politician and writer, was born in Tullamore and reared on his father's estate in Ballineen, County Cork. A convert to Catholicism, he was secretary to Daniel O'Connell and a founder member of the Repeal Association in 1840. He was a prolific writer of nationalist history, his works including *Catechism of the History of Ireland* (1844), *Ireland and Her Agitators* (1845), *Personal Recollections of the Late Daniel O'Connell* (1848) and *Eighty-Five Years of Irish History* (1886). He also wrote several historical novels under the pseudonym 'Denis Ignatius Moriarty'. During the 1870s he strongly supported home rule and served as secretary of the Home Government Association in 1873.

O'Sullivan Beare, Philip (1590–1636) historian and polemicist, was born on Dursey Island, County Cork, and educated at the University of Santiago de Compostela. In the latter 1610s he petitioned Philip III to invade Ireland, and worked on his *Historiae Catholicae Iberniae Compendium* (1621) ('Compendium of the history of catholic Ireland'), which defended Ireland from critics such as Giraldus Cambrensis, and claimed it was a land of piety and learning until conquered by heretics, who cruelly persecuted its people. To enlist Spanish support he invoked providence and prophecy and stressed the cultural and religious links between Ireland and Spain, including the myth of Irish descent from King Miletius. The work gives pride of place to the heroic deeds of the O'Sullivans in the Nine Years' War, notably the stubborn defence of Dunboy Castle and the gruelling winter march to Leitrim after the defeat at Kinsale. He also wrote a hagiographies of St Patrick and St Mochua, and an account of Irish flora and fauna in *Zoilomastix* (1625).

Palacký, František (1798–1875), Czech historian and politician, was born in Hodslavice, Moravia, and educated in Bratislava. In 1823 he settled in Prague and became editor of the journal of the Bohemian museum, in which he published articles on aesthetics and the Czech language. His major work was the *History of the Czech Nation in Bohemia and Moravia* (5 vols, 1836–67), which stressed Slav resistance to German influence, especially the Czech national and religious struggle during the Hussite period. Palacký wrote it in the hope that an awareness of centuries of struggle against foreign invaders would restore a sense of national identity and advance the campaign for Czech independence, and it became one of Czech nationalism's most influential works. He supported Austro-Slavic proposals for an Austrian federation of national groups with equal rights, and was chairman of the Prague Slavic Congress in 1848. After the collapse of the revolutions of 1848, he retired from active politics until his election as a deputy to the Reichsrat in 1861. In his *Idea of the Austrian State* (1865), he proposed the federation of Austria based on the historic provinces of the Habsburg Empire rather than nationalities. His bitter attacks on the establishment of the dual monarchy of Austria-Hungary in 1867 were under-pinned by his historical learning.

Petrie, George (1790–1866), artist and antiquarian, was born in Dublin and studied at the Dublin Society's drawing school. A talented landscape artist, he was elected to the RHA (1828). He wrote numerous antiquarian articles for the *Dublin Penny Journal* from 1832, and edited the *Irish Penny Journal* (1840–1). Working for the Topographical Section of the Ordnance Survey (1833–9), he rigorously investigated Ireland's historic remains and co-ordinated the field work of scholars such as John O'Donovan and Eoghan O'Curry. He invigorated the antiquarian research of the RIA, and was a leading figure in collecting the valuable manuscripts and artefacts which formed the core of its collections. His 'Essay on the Round Towers of Ireland' (1833), subsequently published in his *Ecclesiastical Architecture of Ireland* (1845), definitively established the towers' monastic origins and was a milestone in the development of Irish antiquarianism. He also collected many traditional Irish airs, published as *The Ancient Music of Ireland* (1855). His national enthusiasm was cultural rather than political, but his untiring efforts to preserve and record Ireland's past won him admiration from all quarters.

Pigot, John Edward (1822–71), was born in County Cork and educated at TCD, where he was part of the College Historical Society group that centred on Davis. He contributed occasional articles and verse to the *Nation* in 1842–3, and also collected traditional airs. From 1843 he concentrated on his legal education in London, but returned to Ireland in 1847 and joined the Irish Confederation. Because of illness he played no part in the events of 1848. Afterwards he was chiefly concerned with cultural matters, playing a central role in the Society for the Preservation and Publication of the Melodies of Ireland (1851), supporting efforts to revive the Irish language and becoming a founding member of the National Gallery of Ireland (1864). In 1858 he and Denis Holland launched the *Irishman* newspaper to carry on the work of Young Ireland.

Plowden, Francis (1749–1829), was born in Shropshire and educated by the Jesuits in France, becoming master of their college in Bruges. After the suppression of the Jesuits in 1773 he returned to England and became a lawyer. Attached to the Whig interest, he was encouraged by the government of Henry Addington (1801–4) to publish *An Historical Review of the State of Ireland from the Invasion of that Country under Henry II to its Union with Great Britain* (2 vols, London, 1803) to reconcile Catholic opinion in Ireland to the union with Britain. He also sought to discredit Musgrave's claims that the 1798 Rebellion had been a Catholic conspiracy, and further contradicted him with *Preface to the Historical Review* (1804) and *An Historical Letter to Sir Richard Musgrave* (1805). Greater involvement with Irish affairs made Plowden increasingly hostile to Orangeism and led him to produce a denunciatory pamphlet, *An Historical Disquisition Concerning the Rise, Progress, Nature and Effects of the Orange Societies in Ireland* (1810). This formed the introduction to *The History of Ireland from its Union with Great Britain in January 1801 to October 1810* (3 vols, Dublin, 1811). As one of the few available histories of Ireland sympathetic to Catholics, his *Historical Review of the State of Ireland* was popular with nineteenth-century nationalists.

Prendergast, John Patrick (1808–94), barrister and historian, was born in Dublin and educated at TCD. Called to the bar in 1830, he practised for 20 years on the Leinster circuit. In 1863 he published *The Cromwellian Settlement of Ireland*, among the earliest attempts to write a work of Irish history based on extensive archival research. He helped catalogue the Carte papers in the Bodleian Library, Oxford, and regularly contributed articles to the Kilkenny Archaeological Society Journal. He published a refutation of Froude's *The English in Ireland* in the *Nation* (1872–4), which was much admired by nationalists and was drawn on heavily by John Mitchel in his own challenge to Froude. In 1887 he published *Ireland from the Restoration to the Revolution*, based on his diligent research in the archives. Liberal in his politics, he had some sympathy for Irish nationalism, but this declined with the rise of the more militant home rule movement in the later 1870s.

Reilly, Thomas Devin (1824–54), journalist, was born in Monaghan and educated locally and in Dublin. He joined the staff of the *Nation* in April 1846 and was assigned the titles 'The Penal Days' and 'Biographies of the United Irishmen' for the Library of Ireland, but completed neither. While working for the *Nation*, he became a close friend and ally of John Mitchel, supporting him in his battles with moderates in the Irish Confederation. When in February 1848 Mitchel set up his own paper, the *United Irishman*, Reilly contributed some of its most militant articles. After the *United Irishman* was suppressed, Reilly and others founded the *Irish Felon* to carry on its work. He pressed strongly for insurrection in 1848 and afterwards escaped to the US, founding the *People* in New York and working for several other periodicals, in which he continued to denounce British imperialism.

Rooney, William (1873–1901), journalist and poet, was born in Dublin and educated by the Christian Brothers, leaving school at 14 to become a railway clerk. Deeply interested in Irish history and culture, he immersed himself in the works of Young Ireland and modelled himself on Thomas Davis. A leading figure in several nationalist cultural societies in the 1880s and 1890s, he regularly contributed articles and verse to nationalist periodicals such as *United Ireland*, *Shamrock* and *The Shan Van Vocht*. In 1899 he and his close friend Arthur Griffith founded the *United Irishman* newspaper, with Rooney writing most of its content until his death in 1901. His writings played an important role in bringing the ideals of Young Ireland to a new generation.

Savage, John (1828–88), was born and educated in Dublin. Attracted to the republican ideals of John Mitchel, he helped found the *Irish Tribune* in June 1848 to carry on his work. After leading a failed attack on a police barracks, Savage escaped to America where he worked as a journalist. In 1850 he wrote *Lays of the Fatherland*, a collection of nationalist ballads. He edited and wrote historical chapters for Meagher's *Speeches on Ireland* (1853) and published a history of Irish republicanism entitled *'98 and '48* (1856). He fought with the Union's Irish Brigade in the civil war and became president of the Fenian Brotherhood in 1867. His *Poems Lyrical, Dramatic and Romantic* was published in 1867 and his *Fenian Heroes and Martyrs* in 1868.

Scott, Sir Walter (1771–1832), poet and novelist, was born and educated in Edinburgh. He published several volumes of poems, notably *Minstrelsy of the Scottish Border* (1802), and contributed regularly to the *Edinburgh Review*, but from 1814 devoted himself to writing historical novels, including *Waverly* (1814), *Rob Roy* (1817), *The Heart of Midlothian* (1818) and *Ivanhoe* (1819), inspired by contemporary interest in national identity, folk culture and medieval literature. He also wrote a *History of Scotland* (1829–30), but it was his prose fiction that was his greatest achievement in illuminating the past. Scott became the most successful writer of his day, and his best-selling works brought Scotland's history to life for eager readers across Europe. Among these were the Young Irelanders, who hoped that one of their number might dramatise the Irish past in the same way.

Spenser, Edmund (1552–99), poet and administrator, was born in London. He probably first came to Ireland in 1580 as secretary to the lord deputy, Sir Arthur Grey, who suppressed the Desmond rebellion with great severity. During the Munster plantation he obtained an estate at Kilcolman, north County Cork, where his conflicts with Old English settlers fuelled his hatred for this class. While there he completed *The Faerie Queene* (1590–96) which has been interpreted as an allegorical demand for more forceful policies in Ireland. His *A View of the Present State of Ireland* (written *c*.1595, but only published in 1633 in an abridged version by James Ware) drew a sharp line between English civilisation and Irish barbarism. It advocated the reintroduction of Grey's draconian policies to complete the conquest of Ireland, claiming that the Irish were descended from the Scythians and therefore naturally savage, and argued that native Irish learning was fabricated and that the Catholic Old English who had adopted Gaelic customs had become even more degenerate than the natives. Spenser died in poverty in London after being driven off his Irish estates in October 1598.

Sullivan, Alexander Martin (1830–84), journalist and politician, was born in Bantry, County Cork, and educated locally. He joined the staff of the *Nation* in 1855 and became proprietor and editor in 1858; he also produced a series of ancillary nationalist publications. Under his editorship the paper largely equated nationalism with Catholicism. An admirer of moderate Young Irelanders such as O'Brien and Duffy, he supported constitutional agitation and opposed the Fenians, who labelled him a traitor and disrupted his meetings. Relations improved somewhat when he was briefly imprisoned for condemnation of the executions of the 'Manchester Martyrs' in 1867. With his brothers he edited *Speeches from the Dock* (1867) an account of the trials of rebels from 1798 to 1867, culminating in his own trial. His *Story of Ireland* (1867) was inspired by the Young Ireland project of writing patriotic popular history and became a bestseller. He served as Home Rule MP for County Louth (1874–80) and County Meath (1880–1). In 1876 he handed the *Nation* over to his older brother Timothy Daniel Sullivan (1827–1914), author of 'God Save Ireland' and several volumes of poetry including *Green Leaves* (1868), *Lays of the Land League* (1887) and *Poems* (1888).

Supple, Gerald Henry (1823–98), journalist and poet, was born in Cork city. A member of the Young Ireland Irish Confederation, he contributed patriotic verse to the *Nation* from 1847 to 1851. His poetry featured in several nationalist collections and in 1856 his *History of the Invasion of Ireland by the Anglo-Normans* was published by the Celtic Union. In 1857 he left for Australia where he became a journalist. Sentenced to life imprisonment in 1870 after mistakenly shooting dead a police detective, he was released on compassionate grounds in 1878 and spent the remainder of his life in Auckland, New Zealand.

Taaffe, Denis (1743–1813), priest and writer, was born in Termonfeckin, County Louth, and educated for the priesthood in France and Bohemia. Returning to Ireland in 1786, he was deprived of his priestly functions owing to his dissolute lifestyle and dalliance with Protestantism. From then on he earned a living as a writer and language teacher. During the 1790s he supported the

United Irishmen and wrote a pamphlet denouncing the act of union. Commissioned by leading Catholics to write a history of Ireland, he published *An Impartial History of Ireland, from the Period of the English Invasion to the Present Time* (4 vols, 1809–11). Relying heavily on Plowden's *Historical Review of the State of Ireland* (1803), it highlighted the sufferings of Irish Catholics and argued that their loyalty to the British crown had been poorly rewarded.

Taylor, John Francis (1853–1902), lawyer and journalist, was born and educated in Castlerea, County Roscommon. He was probably a member of the IRB in his youth, and retained a lifelong attachment to nationalist separatism. Called to the bar (1882), he became a QC in 1892. He wrote for several periodicals and was Dublin correspondent of the *Manchester Guardian*. A powerful orator, he was a prominent member of various nationalist and cultural societies and delivered an address on the 'Parliaments of Ireland' to the Young Ireland Society in January 1886. Thomas Carlyle and John Mitchel were abiding influences on his oratory and writings. He contributed *Owen Roe O'Neill* (1896) to the New Irish Library. Like Duffy, he earned the enmity of W. B. Yeats by using the venture as a means of propagating popular history in the Young Ireland style.

Temple, Sir John (1600–77), was born in Dublin and educated at TCD. In the early 1630s he entered the service of Charles I, acting as quartermaster of Dublin during the insurrection of 1641, but was accused of defrauding the king and was imprisoned in Dublin in 1643. Released after a year, he went to London, where he urged parliament to subdue Ireland without negotiating with either the Catholic Confederates or Ormond's royalists. To substantiate his case he produced *The Irish Rebellion* (1646), which drew on the sworn depositions of Protestant witnesses to highlight the massacres of Protestant civilians in 1641 and the universal complicity of Catholics in the rebellion. Its lurid claims contributed significantly to the severity of reprisals during the Cromwellian campaign of 1649–52. It was republished in 1679 and frequently afterwards, strongly fuelling anti-Catholic passions.

Thierry, Augustin (1795–1856), historian, was born in Blois in central France and educated locally and in Paris. An admirer of the liberal ideals of the French revolution, he was deeply influenced by the utopian socialist Saint-Simon and in 1814 became his secretary. Impressed by the writings of Sir Walter Scott, he sought to infuse the writing of history with some of the drama and picturesque scenes that Scott brought to fiction. He also pioneered the collection, publication and analysis of primary sources, especially for medieval French history, which assisted with his own research on the medieval German invasions of France, the formation of medieval communes and the gradual ascent of nations towards liberal and representative government. He was sceptical of conservative founding myths and urged historians to consult original materials rather than relying on later accounts by church or court propagandists. His most significant contribution to the Romantic revival of medieval history was the *History of the Conquest of England by the Normans* (3 vols, 1825). Its colourful and dramatic style, admiration for Irish resistance to the Norman conquest and general sympathy for the oppressed made it a favourite of the Young Irelanders, who praised Thierry above all other historians.

Todhunter, John (1839–1916), writer and physician, was born in Dublin and studied medicine at TCD, Paris and Vienna. On his return to Dublin in 1870, he practised medicine at Cork St fever hospital and lectured in English at Alexandra College until settling in London in 1874 and devoting himself to writing poems, plays and literary criticism. Influenced by the work of Standish James O'Grady, he became inspired by the mythical history of Ireland and published *The Banshee and Other Poems* (1888) and *Three Bardic Irish Tales* (1896). With W. B. Yeats he was a founder of the Irish Literary Society (1892), and wrote a *Life of Patrick Sarsfield* (1895) for the society's New Irish Library. His poems and plays on Irish themes had little public success but were significant in helping to alert Yeats to the possibilities of poetic drama.

Vallancey, Charles (1725?–1812), military engineer and antiquary, may have been born in Windsor or Flanders, and educated at Eton. Commissioned ensign in the British army Corps of Engineers in 1746, he was posted to Cork in the 1750s, and in 1761 became major of engineers and moved to Dublin. He worked on a military survey of Ireland (1776–96), probably the most elaborate cartographic project carried out in eighteenth-century Ireland. Alongside this work, he cultivated an interest in the Irish language, history and antiquities, was elected to the Dublin Society (1763) and was a founder member of the RIA (1785). His publications included *Collectanea de Rebus Hibernicis* (6 vols, 1770–1804), *Essay on the Antiquity of the Celtic Language* (1772), a *Grammar of the Irish Language* (1773) and *An Essay on the Primitive Inhabitants of Great Britain and Ireland* (1812). He is perhaps best remembered for his eccentric speculative theories on the Irish language, which he variously related to Arabic, Persian and Phoenician (among others), but his intention was to establish that Irish was an ancient tongue that deserved respect, and his Irish grammar encouraged others to study the language.

Varian, Elizabeth Willoughby (1821–96), was born in Ballymena, County Antrim, into a Protestant landed family. Under the name 'Finola' she published nationalist verse in the *Nation* and the *Irishman* in the 1850s. Her *Poems* (1851) featured historical verse such as 'The capture of Red O'Neill'. In 1871 she married the nationalist journalist and poet Ralph Varian (1820–86) who had included some of her poetry in the anthology *The Harp of Erin* (1869). She later published *Never Forsake the Ship, and Other Poems* (1874) and *The Political and National Poems of Finola* (1877), and was active in promoting land reform and home rule.

Walsh, Edward (1805–50), poet and translator, was born in Derry city and educated in hedge schools in County Cork. While a young man he worked as an itinerant hedge schoolmaster, and began writing for the *Dublin Penny Journal* in 1832. He became a national schoolteacher in Glantane, County Cork, but was dismissed in 1842 for writing a pro-repeal article in the *Nation*; he also contributed verse such as 'The defeat of Strongbow' and 'Song of the penal days' to the paper. With John O'Daly he collaborated in publishing the collections *Reliques of Irish Jacobite Poetry* (1844) and *Irish Popular Songs* (1847). He was appointed teacher at the prison on Spike Island but was dismissed in May 1848 for commiserating with John Mitchel after his conviction for treason-felony. Walsh's work had a significant influence on poets of the literary revival.

Williams, Richard D'Alton (1822–62), poet, was born in Dublin and educated at Tullabeg, County Offaly, and St Patrick's College, Carlow. From 1843, while studying medicine in Dublin, he became a regular contributor of ballads and war songs to the *Nation*. As the Famine worsened, his politics and verse became more extreme and he accused the British government of deliberate genocide. After Mitchel's *United Irishman* was suppressed he helped found the *Irish*

Tribune in June 1848, and was arrested on charges of treason-felony but was acquitted. Having completed his medical training in Edinburgh, he returned to Dublin and contributed verse to the *Nation* in 1851 that showed his disillusionment with nationalist politics. That year he emigrated to America. His verse remained popular and in 1894 P. A. Sillard published a complete collection, *The Poems of Richard D'Alton Williams*.

Wilde (née Elgee), Jane Francesca (1821–96), poet, was born in Dublin. A talented linguist, from 1846 she was contributing both prose (as 'John Fanshawe Ellis') and verse (as 'Speranza') to the *Nation*. During the Famine her verse evoked apocalyptic scenes and condemned the passivity of Irish landlords. When Duffy was arrested in 1848 she became leader-writer for the *Nation* and issued a stirring call to arms for the Young Irelanders. In 1851 she married the Dublin surgeon and polymath, William Wilde; their second child was the writer Oscar Wilde. Her collected *Poems* were published in 1864 by James Duffy. To the end of her life she remained proud of her links with Young Ireland and played a part in the literary revival, publishing her husband's unfinished *Ancient Legends, Mystic Charms and the Superstitions of Ireland* (1887) and *Ancient Cures, Charms and Usages of Ireland* (1890).

Wills, James (1790–1868), clergyman and biographer, was born in County Roscommon and educated at TCD. He contributed to various periodicals including *Blackwood's*, the *Dublin Penny Journal* and the *Dublin University Magazine*, briefly acting as editor of the latter in 1836. His most significant work was *Lives of Illustrious Irishmen* (6 vols, 1839–47), a historical compendium of Irish biography, which helped earn him the position of Donnellan lecturer at TCD (1855–6). It was later reissued with supplements by his son Freeman Wills as *The Irish Nation* (4 vols, 1871–5).

Bibliography

—

PRIMARY SOURCES

National Library Of Ireland
Thomas Davis papers, MS 138, 1791, 2644, 2798, 3199, 3228, 4571, 5935, 8075.
Press cuttings related to Thomas Davis 1847–1922, MS 14056.
Charles Gavan Duffy papers, MS 340, 2642, 4193–8, 4722, 5756–8, 5941, 8006, 8098, 10489.
Arthur Griffith papers, MS 22293.
Thomas Larcom papers, MS 7698, 7731.
James Clarence Mangan papers, MS 138.
John O'Donovan papers, MS 132.
William Smith O'Brien papers, MS 432–5, 441, 449.
Journals of W. J. O'Neill Daunt (1842–88), MS 3040–42.
T. D. Sullivan papers, MS 8237.
Young Ireland Society Minute Books (1881–4), MS 16095 and (1885–6) MS 19158.

National Archives of Ireland
Bureau of Military History Witness Statements.

Pearse Street Public Library, Dublin
Gilbert collection, R. R. Madden papers, MS 278.

Royal Irish Academy
Charles Gavan Duffy Papers, MS 12/P/15–18, 12/P/19.
John Windele papers, MS 4/B/2.
Irish Confederation minute books (RIA MS 23 H 43).

Trinity College Dublin
John Blake Dillon papers, MS 6355–8.

PRINTED PRIMARY SOURCES

'Circular letter from the Dublin Society of United Irishmen' (30 December 1791), in *The Report of the Secret Committee of the House of Commons* (Dublin, 1798).
Reports of the Commissioners of National Education in Ireland: From the Year 1834 to 1842 (Dublin, 1844).
Reports of the Commissioners of National Education in Ireland: From the Year 1834–60 (Dublin, 1851–61).

Reports of the Parliamentary Committee of the Loyal National Repeal Association of Ireland (3 vols, Dublin, 1844–6).

Froude, J. A. (ed.), *Letters and Memorials of Jane Welsh Carlyle* (London, 3 vols, 1883).

O'Connell, Maurice R. (ed.). The *Correspondence of Daniel O'Connell* (8 vols, Dublin, 1972–80).

Vincent, John (ed.). *The Diaries of Edward Henry Stanley, 15th Earl of Derby (1826–1893) between 1878 and 1893: A Selection* (Oxford, 2003).

NEWSPAPERS AND PERIODICALS

Belfast Vindicator (1839–42).

The Celt (1857–9).

The Citizen or Dublin Monthly Magazine (1839–43).

Dublin Evening Telegraph.

Dublin Penny Journal (1832–6).

Dublin University Magazine.

Freeman's Journal.

The Harp (1859).

Irish Felon (1848).

Irish Freedom (1910–14).

The Irish Harp (1863–4).

The Irishman (1849).

The Irishman (1858).

Irish Penny Journal (1840–1).

Irish People (1863–5).

Irish Tribune (1848).

Morning Register (1841).

The Nation (1842–8, 1849–91).

Sinn Féin (1906–1914).

United Irishman (1848).

United Irishman (1899–1906).

Young Ireland: An Irish Magazine of Entertainment and Instruction (1875–91).

YOUNG IRELAND HISTORICAL WRITINGS

Barry, Michael J. 'Ireland as she was, as she is, and as she shall be', in *Essays on the Repeal of the Union* (Dublin, 1845), pp 1–112.

_____. (ed.), *The Songs of Ireland* (Dublin, 1845).

Bindon, Samuel Henry (ed.). *The Historical Works of the Rt Rev. Nicholas French DD* (Dublin, 1846).

Cane, Robert. *History of the Williamite and Jacobite wars in Ireland: From their Origin to the Capture of Athlone* (Dublin, 1859).

Davis, Thomas. *The Reform of the Lords: By a Graduate of the Dublin University* (Dublin, 1837).

_____. *An Address Read Before the Historical Society, Dublin, June 1840* (Dublin, 1840).

_____. 'The life and times of Henry Grattan', *The Citizen or Dublin Monthly Magazine* (Nov. 1839–May 1840), I, pp 154–65; (July–Dec. 1841), IV, pp 53–63, 145–51.

_____. India – her own and another's', ibid., (Nov. 1839–May 1840), I, pp 245–53, 418–33; (June–Dec. 1840), II, pp 120–9, 325–36; (Jan.–June 1841), III, pp 83–95.

_____. 'Who are the Afghans? And why should Irishmen fight with them?' ibid., (Jan.–June 1842), V, pp 439–52.

_____. 'The Irish parliament of James II', ibid., (Jan.–Apr. 1843), VII, pp 25–42, 75–90, 105–34, 170–82, 182–201.

_____. (ed.). *Speeches of the Right Honourable John Philpot Curran* (Dublin, 1843).

_____. *The Life of the Right Hon. J. P. Curran. And a Memoir of the Life of the Rt. Hon. Henry Grattan, by D. O. Madden* (Dublin, 1846).

_____. *Literary and Historical Essays* (1846) (edited by C. G. Duffy).

_____. *The Poems of Thomas Davis: Now First Collected with Notes and Historical Illustrations* (Dublin, 1846) (edited by Thomas Wallis).

_____. *Letters of a Protestant on Repeal* (Dublin, 1847) (edited by Thomas F. Meagher).

_____. *Prose Writings of Thomas Davis* (London, 1890) (edited with an introduction by T. W. Rolleston).

_____. *The Patriot Parliament of 1689, with its Statutes, Votes and Proceedings* (London, 1893) (edited by C. G. Duffy).

_____. *National and Other Poems* (Dublin, 1907).

_____. *Essays Literary and Historical, Centenary Edition . . . with preface, notes . . . by D. J. O'Donoghue* (Dundalk, 1914).

_____. *Thomas Davis, Selections from his Prose and Poetry* (London, 1914) (edited with an introduction by T. W. Rolleston).

_____. *Essays and Poems with a Centenary Memoir 1845–1945* (Dublin, 1945).

Duffy, Charles Gavan. *The Ballad Poetry of Ireland* (Dublin, 1846).

_____. *Young Ireland: A Fragment of Irish History* (London, 1880).

_____. *Four Years of Irish History* (London, 1883).

_____. *The League of North and South: An Episode in Irish History 1850–1854* (London, 1886).

_____. *Thomas Davis: The Memoirs of an Irish Patriot, 1840–1846* (London, 1890).

_____. *The Revival of Irish Literature* (London, 1894).

_____. *Short Life of Thomas Davis* (London, 1896).

_____. *Conversations and Correspondence with Thomas Carlyle* (New York, 1892).

_____. *My Life in Two Hemispheres* (2 vols, New York, 1898).

_____. 'Personal memories of James Clarence Mangan', *Dublin Review*, CXLII (1908), pp 278–94.

Doheny, Michael. *The History of the American Revolution* (Dublin, 1846).

_____. *The Felon's Track: Or History of the Late Attempted Outbreak in Ireland* (New York, 1849).

MacCarthy, Denis Florence. *The Poets and Dramatists of Ireland* (Dublin, 1846).

_____. *The Book of Irish Ballads* (Dublin, 1846).

McGee, Thomas D'Arcy. *Historical Sketches of O'Connell and his Friends* (Boston, 1844).

_____. *The Irish Writers of the Seventeenth Century* (Dublin, 1846).

_____. *A Memoir of the Life and Conquests of Art MacMurrogh: King of Leinster from AD 1377 to AD 1417: With Some Notices of the Leinster Wars of 14th Century* (Dublin, 1847).

_____. *Memoir of Charles Gavan Duffy, Esq. as a Student, Journalist, and Organizer: With Selections From his Poems and Essays* (Dublin, 1849).

_____. *History of the Irish Settlers in North America* (Boston, 1851).

_____. *A History of the Attempts to Establish the Protestant Reformation in Ireland* (Boston, 1853).

_____. *A Popular History of Ireland, from the Earliest Times to the Emancipation of the Catholics* (Montreal, 1863).

_____. *Poems of Thomas D'Arcy McGee* (New York, 1869).

MacMahon, Thornton (ed.), *The Casket of Irish Pearls* (Dublin, 1846).

MacNevin, Thomas. *Address Delivered Before the College Historical Society, Dublin . . . 1836–7* (Dublin, 1836).

_____. *A Letter to the Rt. Hon., the Earl of Roden, K. P. on the Nature and Causes of Crime in Ireland* (London, 1838).

_____. *The Speeches of the Right Honourable Richard Lalor Shiel MP* (Dublin, 1845).

_____. *The History of the Volunteers of 1782* (Dublin, 1845).

_____. *The Confiscation of Ulster in the Reign of James the First, Commonly called the Ulster Plantation* (Dublin, 1846).

_____. *Characters of Great Men and the Duties of Patriotism* (Dublin, 1846).

Meehan, Charles Patrick. *The Confederation of Kilkenny* (Dublin, 1846).

_____. *The Fate and Fortunes of Hugh O'Neill, Earl of Tyrone, and Rory O'Donel, Earl of Tyrconnel* (Dublin, 1868).

_____. *A Lecture on the Life and Times of Hugh Roe O'Donnell* (Dublin, 1869).

_____. *The Rise and Fall of the Irish Franciscan Monasteries and Memoirs of the Irish Hierarchy in the Seventeenth Century* (Dublin, 1869).

Mangan, James Clarence. *The Poets and Poetry of Munster* (Dublin, 1849) (edited by John O'Daly).

_____. *Essays in Prose and Verse* (Dublin and London, 1884) (edited by C. P. Meehan).

Mitchel, John. *Life and Times of Aodh O'Neill, Prince of Ulster* (Dublin, 1845).

_____. *Jail Journal, or Five Years in British Prisons* (New York, 1854).

_____. *The Last Conquest of Ireland (Perhaps)* (Dublin, 1861).

_____. *An Apology for the British Government in Ireland* (Dublin, 1861).

_____. *The History of Ireland from the Treaty of Limerick to the Present Time: Being a Continuation of the History of the Abbé Macgeoghegan* (New York, 1868).

_____. *The Crusade of the Period: And Last Conquest of Ireland (Perhaps)* (New York, 1873).

_____. *1641: Reply to the Falsification of History by James Anthony Froude, entitled 'The English in Ireland'* (Glasgow, 1873?).

O'Callaghan, John Cornelius. *The Green Book or Gleanings from the Writing Desk of a Literary Agitator* (Dublin, 1841).

_____. *History of the Irish Brigades in the Service of France* (8 vols, Dublin, 1854–69).

_____. *The Irish at Home and Abroad, at Limerick and Cremona* (Glasgow, 1869).

Supple, Gerald. *History of the Invasion of Ireland by the Anglo-Normans* (Dublin, 1856).

The Spirit of the Nation. By the Writers of the Nation *Newspaper* (Dublin, 1843).

The Voice of the Nation: A Manual of Nationality. By the Writers of the Nation *Newspaper* (Dublin, 1844).

PUBLISHED BY YOUNG IRELAND

Hay, Edward. *History of the Insurrection of 1798* (Dublin, 1847).

Lynch, John. *The Portrait of a Pious Bishop: Or The Life and Death of Most Rev. Francis Kirwan,*

Bishop of Killala, translated from the Latin of John Lynch (Dublin, 1848).

MacGeoghegan, James. *History of Ireland, Ancient and Modern. Translated from the French by P. O'Kelly* (Dublin, 1844).

O'Daly, Dominicus De Rosario. *The Geraldines, Earls of Desmond and the Persecution of the Irish Catholics. Translated from the original Latin, with notes and illustrations by Rev. C. P. Meehan* (Dublin, 1847).

OTHER HISTORIES

Curry, John. *A Brief Account . . . of the Irish Rebellion of 23 October 1641* (London, 1747).

____. *Historical Memoirs of the Irish Rebellion in the Year, 1641* (London, 1758).

____. *Historical and Critical Review of the Civil Wars in Ireland* (London, 1775; reprinted with additional material 1786 and 1810).

Lawless, John. *A Compendium of the History of Ireland from the Earliest Period to the Reign of George I* (Dublin, 1814).

Ledwich, Edward. *Antiquities of Ireland* (Dublin, 1790).

Leland, Thomas. *The History of Ireland: From the Invasion of Henry II. With a Preliminary Discourse on the Ancient State of that Kingdom* (Dublin, 1773).

Madden, R. R. *The United Irishmen, their Lives and Times* (7 vols, London, 1842–6; 4 vols, London, 1857–60).

O'Connell, Daniel. *A Memoir on Ireland, Native and Saxon* (Dublin, 1843).

O'Conor, Charles. *Dissertations on the Antient History of Ireland* (Dublin, 1753).

O'Conor, Matthew. *The History of the Irish Catholics from the Settlement in 1691, with a View of the State of Ireland from the Invasion of Henry II to the Revolution* (Dublin, 1813).

____. *Military History of the Irish Nation, Comprising a Memoir of the Irish Brigade in the Service of France* (Dublin, 1845).

O'Halloran, Sylvester. *A General History of Ireland, from the Earliest Accounts to the Close of the Twelfth Century* (Dublin, 1778).

O'Neill Daunt, William J. *A Catechism of the History of Ireland, Ancient and Modern* (Dublin, 1844).

Plowden, Francis. *An Historical Review of the State of Ireland, from the Invasion of that Country under Henry II, to its Union with Great Britain* (London, 1803).

Smiles, Samuel. *History of Ireland and the Irish People, under the Government of England* (London, 1844).

Taaffe, Denis. *An Impartial History of Ireland, from the Time of the English Invasion to the year 1810* (4 vols, Dublin, 1809–11).

Wyse, Thomas. *Historical Sketch of the Late Catholic Association of Ireland* (2 vols, London, 1829).

OTHER CONTEMPORARY PUBLICATIONS

Anon. *Poems and Ballads of Young Ireland* (Dublin, 1888).

Barrett, Richard. *History of the Irish Confederation* (Dublin, 1849).

Casement, Roger. *Some Poems of Roger Casement* (Dublin, 1918).

____. 'The romance of Irish history', in Joseph Dunn and Peter Lennon (eds), *The Glories of*

Ireland (Washington DC, 1914), pp 1–9.

Cavanagh, Michael. 'Joseph Brenan', *Young Ireland: An Irish Magazine of Entertainment and Instruction*, xi, no.s 25–9 (20 June–18 July 1885), pp 400–1, 417–20, 433–5, 448–9, 464–7.

Clarke, Thomas. *Glimpses of an Irish Felon's Prison Life* (London and Dublin, 1922).

Davitt, Michael. *Leaves from a Prison Diary; or, Lectures to a Solitary Audience* (London, 1885).

Denvir, John. *The Life Story of an Old Rebel* (Dublin, 1910).

Devoy, John. *Recollections of an Irish Rebel* (New York, 1929).

Dillon, William. *Life of John Mitchel* (London, 2 vols, 1888).

Eglinton, John. *Bards and Saints* (Dublin, 1906).

Fagan, William. *The Life and Times of Daniel O'Connell* (2 vols, Cork, 1847–8).

Ferguson, Lady. *Sir Samuel Ferguson in the Ireland of his Day* (2 vols, London, 1896).

Ferguson, Samuel. 'Thomas Davis', *Dublin University Magazine*, xxix (Feb. 1847), pp 190–9.

Fitzpatrick, W. J. *The Life of the Very Rev. Thomas N. Burke* (2 vols, London, 1885).

Griffith, Arthur (ed.). *Thomas Davis: The Thinker and Teacher* (Dublin, 1916).

____. (ed.). *Meagher of the Sword: Speeches of Thomas Francis Meagher in Ireland 1846–48* (Dublin, 1916).

Hickey, Michael. 'Nationality according to Thomas Davis', *New Ireland Review* (May 1898), pp 129–38; (June 1898), pp 206–15.

Hyde, Douglas. *The Story of Early Gaelic Literature* (London, 1895).

Lane, Denny. 'The Irish accent in English literature', *Irish Monthly*, xxi (Mar. 1893), pp 151–6.

Leslie, Shane 'Irish leaders', in Joseph Dunn and Peter Lennon (eds), *The Glories of Ireland* (Washington DC, 1914), pp 153–61.

Luby, Thomas Clarke, Walsh, Robert F. and Curtin, Jeremiah C., *The Story of Ireland's Struggle for Self-Government with the Lives and Times of Her Great Leaders* (New York, 1893).

Lyons, George A. *Some Recollections of Griffith and His Times* (Dublin, 1923).

McCarthy, Justin. *Ireland and Her Story* (London, 1903).

____. *The Story of an Irishman* (London, 1904).

McCullagh, William Torrens. *On the Use and Study of History* (Dublin, 1842).

MacDermott, Martin (ed.). *The New Spirit of the Nation* (London, 1894).

MacSweeney, Patrick M. *A Group of Nation Builders* (Dublin, 1913).

Madden, Daniel Owen. *Ireland and its Rulers since 1829* (3 vols, London, 1843–4).

____. *The Select Speeches of the Right Hon. Henry Grattan* (Dublin, 1845).

Moore, Thomas. *Memoirs of Captain Rock: The Celebrated Irish Chieftain with Some Account of his Ancestors* (London, 1824).

Moran, D. P. *The Philosophy of Irish Ireland* (Dublin, 1905).

Noonan, John D. 'The library of Thomas Davis', *Irish Book Lover*, v (Oct. 1913), pp 37–41.

O'Brien, R. Barry. *The Best Hundred Irish Books* (Dublin, 1886).

O'Brien, William. *Recollections* (London, 1905).

O'Connell, John (ed.). *The Life and Speeches of Daniel O'Connell* (2 vols, Dublin, 1846).

O'Donoghue, D. J. (ed.). *The Life and Writings of James Clarence Mangan* (Dublin, 1897).

____. *Poems of James Clarence Mangan . . . introduced by John Mitchel* (Dublin, 1903).

O'Donovan Rossa, Jeremiah. *O'Donovan Rossa's Prison Life: Six Years in English Prisons* (New York, 1874).

____. *Rossa's Recollections, 1838 to 1898: Memoirs of an Irish Revolutionary* (New York, 1898).

O'Grady, Standish James. *The Bog of Stars: And Other Stories and Sketches of Elizabethan Ireland* (London, 1893).

O'Hagan, John. 'Thomas Davis', *The Irish Monthly*, xix (Jan. 1891), pp 1–17.

____. 'Leinster and Munster in the summer of 1844', *Irish Monthly*, xl (1912), pp 454–70, 517–28, 580–90.

____. 'Ulster in the summer of 1845', *Irish Monthly*, xli (1913), pp 38–42, 103–6, 158–62, 289–90, 329–33, 398–400, 459–61, 487–9.

O'Leary, John. *Young Ireland: The Old and the New* (Dublin, 1885).

____. *Recollections of Fenians and Fenianism* (2 vols, London, 1896).

O'Neill Daunt, William Joseph. *Personal Reminiscences of the Late Daniel O'Connell MP* (2 vols, London 1848).

____. *Ireland and Her Agitators* (Dublin, 1867).

____. *Eighty-Five Years of Irish History* (London, 1888).

____. *A Life Spent in Ireland* (London 1896).

Pope-Hennessy, J. 'What do the Irish read?', *Nineteenth Century*, xv (Jan.–June 1884), pp 920–30.

Rolleston, T. W. 'Thomas Davis', *Irish Book Lover*, vi, 4 and 5 (Nov. and Dec. 1914), pp 50–2, 65–9.

Rooney, William. *Prose Writings* (Dublin, [1909]).

[Russell, Matthew]. 'James Duffy the publisher', *Irish Monthly*, xxiii (1895), pp 596–9.

____. 'Contributions to Irish biographies: John Edward Pigot', *Irish Monthly*, xxiv (1896), pp 225–37.

Ryan, Desmond. (ed.), *Collected Works of Padraic H. Pearse* (Dublin, 1917–22).

Stokes, William. *The Life and Labours in Art and Archaeology of George Petrie LL.D., MRIA* (London, 1868).

Sullivan, A. M. *The Story of Ireland* (Dublin, 1867).

____. *New Ireland: Political Sketches and Personal Reminiscences* (London, 1878).

Sullivan, T. D. *Recollections of Troubled Times in Irish Politics* (Dublin, 1905).

Taylor, , J. F. *Owen Roe O'Neill* (London, 1896).

Todhunter, John. *Life of Patrick Sarsfield: Earl of Lucan. With a Short Narrative of the Principal Events of the Jacobite War in Ireland* (London, 1895).

Wallis, Thomas. 'Thomas Davis', (3 essays) *Nation*, 20 Oct.–3 Nov. 1849.

Wilde, Jane. 'Thomas Moore', in ibid. *Notes on Men, Women and Books* (London, 1891), pp 221–30.

W. B. Yeats, *Autobiographies*, William H. O'Donnell and Douglas N. Archibald (eds) (New York, 1999).

SECONDARY SOURCES

Anon., 'The teaching of history in Irish schools', *Administration (Journal of the IPA)* (Winter, 1967), pp 268–85.

Abrams, M. H. *The Mirror and the Lamp: Romantic Theory and the Critical Tradition* (London, 1953).

Adams, J. R. R. *The Printed Word and the Common Man: Popular Culture in Ulster* (Belfast, 1987).

Akenson, Donald H. *The Irish Education Experiment: The National System of Education in the Nineteenth Century* (London, 1970).

Alter, Peter. *Nationalism* (London, 1989).

Anderson, Benedict. *Imagined Communities: Reflections on the Origins and Spread of Nationalism* (1983; revised edn London, 2006).

Andrews, J. H. *A Paper Landscape: The Ordnance Survey in Nineteenth-Century Ireland* (Oxford, 1975).

Anton, Brigitte. 'Women of the *Nation*', *History Ireland*, 1, no. 3 (autumn, 1993), pp 34–8.

Armstrong, J. A. *Nations before Nationalism* (Chapel Hill, 1982).

Athearn, Robert G. *Thomas Francis Meagher: An Irish Revolutionary in America* (Boulder, Colo., 1949).

Auchmuty, James J. *Irish Education, a Historical Survey* (London and Dublin, 1937).

——. *The Teaching of History* (Dublin, 1940).

Bann, Stephen. *The Clothing of Clio: A Study of the Representation of History in Nineteenth-Century Britain and France* (Cambridge, 1984).

Barnard, Frederick M. *Herder's Social and Political Thought: From Enlightenment to Nationalism* (Oxford, 1965).

Barnes, Margaret. 'Repeal Reading Rooms', *An Leabharlann: The Irish Library*, XXIII, no. 2 (1965), pp 53–7.

Barr, Colin. 'Giuseppe Mazzini and Irish nationalism, 1845–70', in C. A. Bayly and E. F. Biagini (eds), *Giuseppe Mazzini and the Globalisation of Democratic Nationalism* (Oxford, 2008) (*Proceedings of the British Academy*, no. 152), pp 125–44.

Barry, Tom. *Guerilla Days in Ireland* (Dublin, 1949).

Bartlett, Thomas. 'Ormuzd abroad . . . Ahriman at home: some early historians of the Wild Geese in French service, 1750–1950', in J. Conroy (ed.), *Franco-Irish Connections: Essays, Memoirs and Poems in Honour of Pierre Joannon* (Dublin, 2009), pp 15–30.

Benson, Charles 'The Dublin book trade', in James H. Murphy (ed.), *The Oxford History of the Irish Book, vol. iv: The Irish Book in English 1800–1891* (Oxford, 2011), pp 27–46.

Berman, David. 'David Hume on the 1641 Rebellion in Ireland', *Studies: An Irish Quarterly Review*, LXV (1976), pp 101–12.

Boyce, D. George. *Nationalism in Ireland* (London, 1982).

Boyne, Patricia. *John O'Donovan (1806–61): A Biography* (Kilkenny, 1987).

Bradley, J. F. *Czech Nationalism in the Nineteenth Century* (Boulder, Colo., 1984).

Bradshaw, Brendan. 'Nationalism and historical scholarship in modern Ireland', *Irish Historical Studies*, XXVI, no. 104 (Nov. 1989), pp 329–51.

Bromage, Mary C. 'Image of nationhood', *Éire-Ireland*, III, no. 3 (Fall 1968), pp 11–26.

Brown, Malcolm. *The Politics of Irish Literature: From Thomas Davis to W. B. Yeats* (London, 1972).

Brown, Stephen J. *Poetry of Irish History* (Dublin, 1927).

Brown, Terence and Hayley, Barbara (eds), *Samuel Ferguson: A Centenary Tribute* (Dublin, 1988).

Brown, Thomas N. *Irish American Nationalism* (Philadelphia and New York, 1966).

Buckley, Mary. 'John Mitchel, Ulster and Irish Nationality (1842–48)', *Studies: An Irish Quarterly Review*, LXV (1976), pp 30–44.

Burke, Martin J. 'Irish-American publishing', in James H. Murphy (ed.), *The Oxford History of the Irish Book, vol. iv: The Irish Book in English 1800–1891* (Oxford, 2011), pp 98–112.

Burns, R. E. 'The Irish penal code and some of its historians', *Review of Politics*, XXI (Jan. 1959), pp 276–99.

Cahalan, James M. *Great Hatred, Little Room: The Irish Historical Novel* (Dublin, 1983).

Cahill, Edward. 'English education in Ireland during the penal era (1691–1800)', *Irish Ecclesiastical Record*, 5th ser., LIV (Oct. 1962), pp 495–508.

Calder, Grace J. *George Petrie and the Ancient Music of Ireland* (Dublin, 1968).

Campbell, J. J. 'Primary and secondary education', in T. W. Moody and J. C. Beckett (eds), *Ulster since 1800, Second Series: A Social Survey* (London, 1957), pp 182–91.

Campbell, Mary. *Lady Morgan: The Life and Times of Sydney Owenson* (London, 1988).

Canary, Robert H. and Kozicki, Henry (eds). *The Writing of History: Literary Form and Historical Understanding* (Madison, Wis., 1978).

Cannavan, Jan. 'Romantic revolutionary Irishwomen: women, Young Ireland and 1848', in Margaret Kelleher and James H. Murphy (eds), *Gender Perspectives in 19th Century Ireland* (Dublin, 1997), pp 212–20.

Carey, V. P. 'John Derricke's Image of Irelande, Sir Henry Sidney and the massacre at Mullaghmast, 1578', *Irish Historical Studies*, XXXI, no. 123 (May, 1999), pp 305–27.

Castle, Gregory. 'Nobler forms: Standish James O'Grady's *History of Ireland* and the Irish Literary Revival', in Lawrence W. McBride (ed.), *Reading Irish Histories: Texts, Contexts, and Memory in Modern Ireland* (Dublin, 2003), pp 156–77.

Castleyn, Mary. *A History of Literacy and Libraries in Ireland* (Dublin, 1984).

Chadwick, E. M. *The Nationalists of Europe and the Growth National Ideologies* (Cambridge, 1945).

Clarke, Randall. 'The relations between O'Connell and the Young Irelanders', *Irish Historical Studies*, III, no. 9 (Mar. 1942), pp 18–30.

Coldrey, Barry. *Faith and Fatherland: The Christian Brothers and the Development of Irish Nationalism, 1828–1921* (Dublin, 1988).

Collins, Kevin. *The Cultural Conquest of Ireland* (Cork, 1990).

Colum, Padraic. *Arthur Griffith* (Dublin, 1959).

Comerford, R. V. *Charles Kickham: A Study in Irish Nationalism and Literature* (Dublin, 1979).

____. 'Nation , nationalism, and the Irish language', in Thomas E. Hachey and Lawrence J. McCaffrey (eds), *Perspectives on Irish Nationalism* (Lexington, 1989), pp 20–41.

____. *Ireland: Inventing the Nation* (London, 2003).

Concanon, Helena. *Irish History for Junior Grade Class: The Defence of our Gaelic Civilisation 1460–1660* (Dublin and Belfast, 1920).

Coolahan, John. *Irish Education: Its History and Structure* (Dublin, 1981).

____. 'Perceptions of Ireland and its past in nineteenth-century national school textbooks', in Terence Dooley (ed.), *Ireland's Polemical Past: Views of Irish History in Honour of R. V. Comerford* (Dublin, 2010), pp 69–87.

Corcoran, Timothy. *Education Systems in Ireland, from the Close of the Middle Ages* (Dublin, 1928).

____. *The Catholic Schools of Ireland, Primary, Secondary, University* (Dublin, 1931).

Corish, P. J. 'Two contemporary historians of the Confederation of Kilkenny: John Lynch and Richard O'Ferall', *Irish Historical Studies*, VIII, no. 31 (Mar. 1953), pp 217–36.

Corkery, Daniel. 'Davis and the national language', in M. J. MacManus (ed.), *Thomas Davis and Young Ireland* (Dublin, 1945), pp 14–23.

Cronin, John. *The Anglo-Irish Novel: vol. 1, the Nineteenth Century; vol. 2, 1900–1940* (Belfast, 1980, 1990).

Cronin, Maura. 'Memory, story, and balladry: 1798 and its place in popular memory in pre-Famine Ireland', in Laurence M. Geary (ed.), *Rebellion and Remembrance in Modern Ireland* (Dublin, 2001), pp 112–34.

Crooke, Elizabeth. *Politics, Archaeology and the Creation of a National Museum in Ireland* (Dublin, 2000).

Crowley, Tony. *The Politics of Language in Ireland 1366–1922: A Sourcebook* (London, 2000).

Cullen, L. M. 'The cultural basis of Irish nationalism', in Rosalind Mitchison (ed.), *The Roots of Nationalism: Studies in Northern Europe* (Edinburgh, 1980), pp 91–106.

Cunningham, Bernadette and Kennedy, Máire (eds). *The Experience of Reading: Irish Historical Perspectives* (Dublin, 1999).

Cunningham, Bernadette. *The World of Geoffrey Keating: History, Myth and Religion in Seventeenth-Century Ireland* (Dublin, 2000).

_____. '"An honour to the nation": publishing John O'Donovan's edition of the Annals of the Four Masters, 1848–56', in Martin Fanning and Raymond Gillespie (eds), *Print Culture and Intellectual Life in Ireland, 1660–1941* (Dublin, 2006), pp 116–42.

_____. 'John O'Donovan's edition of the Annals of the Four Masters: an Irish classic', *European Studies*, XXVI (2008), pp 129–49.

Curtis, Edmund. 'Irish history and its popular versions', *Irish Rosary*, XXIX (May 1925), pp 312–29.

Daly, Dominic. *The Young Douglas Hyde: The Dawn of the Irish Revolution and Renaissance, 1874–1893* (Dublin, 1974).

Daly, Mary E. and Dickson, David (eds). *The Origins of Popular Literacy in Ireland: Language Change and Educational Development 1700–1920* (Dublin, 1990).

Daly, Mary E. 'The development of the national schools system', in Art Cosgrove and Donal McCartney (eds), *Studies in Irish History: Presented to R. Dudley Edwards* (Dublin, 1979), pp 150–63.

Davis, Graham. 'The historiography of the Irish Famine', in Patrick O'Sullivan (ed.), *The Meaning of the Famine* (London and Washington, 1996), pp 15–39.

Davis, Richard. *The Young Ireland Movement* (Dublin, 1987).

Deane, Seamus (ed.). *The Field Day Anthology of Irish Writing* (3 vols, Derry, 1991).

_____. *Strange Country: Modernity and Nationhood in Irish Writing since 1790* (Oxford, 1997).

Delaney, Enda. 'Narratives of exile: Irish Catholic emigrants and the national past, 1850–1914', in T. Dooley (ed.), *Ireland's Polemical Past: Views of Irish History in honour of R. V. Comerford* (Dublin, 2010), pp 102–22.

Deutsch, K. W. *Nationalism and Social Communication: An Inquiry into the Foundations of Nationalism*, (2nd edn, Cambridge (Mass.), 1966).

Dillon, Myles. 'George Petrie, 1789–1866', *Studies: An Irish Quarterly Review*, LVI (1967), pp 266–76.

Doherty, Gillian M. *The Irish Ordnance Survey: History, Culture and Memory* (Dublin, 2006).

Donnachie, Ian and Whately, Christopher (eds). *The Manufacture of Scottish History* (Edinburgh, 1992).

Donnelly, James S. Jr, 'The Great Famine: its interpreters, old and new', *History Ireland*, 1, no. 3 (Autumn 1993), pp 27–33.

_____. *The Great Irish Potato Famine* (Stroud, 2002).

Dowling, P. J. *The Hedge Schools of Ireland* (Dublin and Cork, 1935).

_____. *A History of Irish Education: A Study in Conflicting Loyalties* (Cork, 1971).

Dugger, Julie M. 'Black Ireland's race: Thomas Carlyle and the Young Ireland movement', *Victorian Studies*, XLVIII, no. 3 (Spring, 2006), pp 461–85.

Dunleavy, J. E. and G. W. *Douglas Hyde: A Maker of Modern Ireland* (Berkeley, 1991).

Dunne, Tom (ed.). *The Writer as Witness: Literature as Historical Evidence, Historical Studies* (Irish Conference of Historians), XVI (Cork, 1987).

_____. 'Haunted by history: Irish romantic writing, 1800–1850', in Roy Porter and Miklaus Teich (eds), *Romanticism in National Contexts* (Cambridge, 1988), pp 68–91.

Durkacz, V. E. *The Decline of the Celtic Languages: A Study of Linguistic and Cultural Conflict in Scotland, Wales and Ireland from the Reformation to the Twentieth Century* (Edinburgh, 1983).

Dwan, David. *The Great Community: Culture and Nationalism in Ireland* (Dublin, 2008).

Eagleton, Terry. *Scholars and Rebels in Nineteenth-Century Ireland* (Oxford, 1999).

Edwards, Owen Dudley. '"True Thomas": Carlyle, Young Ireland and the legacy of millennialism', in David Sorensen and Rodger L. Tarr (eds), *The Carlyles at Home and Abroad* (Aldershot, 2006), pp 61–76.

Edwards, R. Dudley. 'The contribution of Young Ireland to the development of the national idea', in Séamus Pender (ed.), *Féilscríbhinn Torna: Essays and Studies Presented to Tadhg Ua Donnchadha* (Cork, 1947), pp 115–33.

Elliott, Marianne. *Wolfe Tone: Prophet of Irish Independence* (Yale, 1989).

English, Richard. *Irish Freedom: The History of Nationalism in Ireland* (London, 2006).

Fanning, Martin and Gillespie, Raymond (eds). *Print Culture and Intellectual Life in Ireland, 1660–1941* (Dublin, 2006).

Farren, Sean. *The Politics of Irish Education 1920–65* (Belfast, 1995).

Fegan, Melissa. *Literature and the Irish Famine 1845–1919* (Oxford, 2002).

FitzGerald, Garret. 'Estimates for baronies of minimum level of Irish-speaking among successive decennial cohorts: 1771–1781 to 1861–1871', *Proceedings of the Royal Irish Academy, Section C*, vol. 84, no. 3 (1984), pp 117–55.

Foster, R. F. 'History and the Irish question', *Transactions of the Royal Historical Society*, 5th ser., XXX (1983), pp 169–92.

_____. *W. B. Yeats: A Life: I: The Apprentice Mage 1865–1914* (Oxford, 1997).

_____. 'The story of Ireland', in idem., *The Irish Story: Telling Tales and Making it up in Ireland* (Oxford, 2002), pp 1–22.

_____. 'The first romantics: Young Irelands between Catholic emancipation and the Famine', in idem., *Words Alone: Yeats and his Inheritances* (Oxford, 2011), pp 45–90.

Gargett, Graham. 'Voltaire and Irish history', *Eighteenth-Century Ireland: Iris an Dá Chultúr*, v (1990), pp 117–41.

Gellner, Ernest. *Nations and Nationalism* (Oxford, 1983).

Geoghegan, Vincent. 'A Jacobite history: the Abbé MacGeoghegan's *History of Ireland*', *Eighteenth-Century Ireland: Iris an Dá Chultúr*, VI (1991), pp 37–56.

Goldring, Maurice. *Faith of our Fathers: The Formation of Irish Nationalist Ideology 1890–1920* (Dublin, 1982).

Goldstrom, J. M. 'Richard Whately and political economy in school books, 1883–80', *Irish Historical Studies*, XV, no. 58 (Sept. 1966), pp 131–46.

Gooch, G. P. *History and Historians in the Nineteenth Century*, (2nd edn, London, 1952).

Gossman, Lionel. *Augustin Thierry and Liberal Historiography* (Middletown, Conn., 1976).

_____. *Between History and Literature* (Cambridge, Mass., 1990).

Green, E. R. R. 'The beginnings of Fenianism', in T. W. Moody (ed.), *The Fenian Movement* (Dublin, 1968), pp 11–22.

Greenfield, Liah. *Nationalism: Five Roads to Modernity* (Cambridge, 1992).

Gwynn, Denis. 'William Smith O'Brien', *Studies: An Irish Quarterly Review*, xxxv (Dec. 1946), pp 448–58; ibid., xxxvii (Mar. 1948), pp 7–17, 149–60.

———. *O'Connell, Davis and the Colleges Bill* (Cork, 1948).

———. *Young Ireland and 1848* (Cork, 1949).

———. 'Denny Lane and Thomas Davis', *Studies: An Irish Quarterly Review*, xxxviii (1949), pp 15–28.

———. 'John E. Pigot and Thomas Davis', *Studies: An Irish Quarterly Review*, xxxviii (1949), pp 144–57.

———. 'Young Ireland', in Michael Tierney (ed.), *Daniel O'Connell: Nine Centenary Essays* (Dublin, 1949), pp 171–206.

Hale, J. R. *The Evolution of British Historiography* (London, 1967).

Hall, Wayne E. *Dialogues in the Margins: A Study of the* Dublin University Magazine (Gerrards Cross, 2000).

Hart, Peter. *The IRA and its Enemies: Violence and Community in Cork, 1916–1923* (Oxford, 1998).

Hastings, Adrian. *The Construction of Nationhood: Ethnicity, Religion and Nationalism* (Cambridge, 1997).

Hayes, C. J. H. *The Historical Evolution of Modern Nationalism* (New York 1931, reprint 1963).

———. *Nationalism: A Religion* (New York, 1960).

Hayley, Barbara. 'Irish periodicals from the union to the *Nation*', *Anglo-Irish Studies*, 11 (1976), pp 83–108.

———. 'A reading and thinking nation': periodicals as the voice of nineteenth-century Ireland', in Barbara Hayley and Enda McKay (eds), *Three Hundred Years of Irish Periodicals* (Dublin, 1987), pp 29–48.

Hennessey, J. Pope. 'What do the Irish read?', *Nineteenth Century*, 15 (June 1884), pp 920–32.

Hertz, Friedrich O. *Nationality in History and Politics* (Oxford, 1944).

Higgins, Roisín. 'The *Nation* reading rooms', in James H. Murphy (ed.), *The Oxford History of the Irish Book, vol. iv: The Irish Book in English 1800–1891* (Oxford, 2011), pp 262–73.

Hill, Jacqueline R. 'The intelligentsia and Irish nationalism in the 1840s', *Studia Hibernica*, xx (1980), pp 73–109.

———. 'Popery and Protestantism, civil religious liberty: the disputed lessons of Irish history, 1690–1812', *Past and Present*, 118 (1988), pp 96–129.

———. 'Politics and the writing of history: the impact of the 1690s and 1790s on Irish historiography', in D. George Boyce, Robert Ecclesshall and Vincent Geoghegan (eds), *Political Discourse in Seventeenth- and Eighteenth-Century Ireland* (London, 2001), pp 222–39.

Hindley, Reg. 'Irish in the nineteenth century: from collapse to the dawn of revival', in idem, *The Death of the Irish Language: A Qualified Obituary* (London, 1990), pp 13–20.

Hobsbawm, E. J. and Ranger, T. (eds). *The Invention of Tradition* (Cambridge, 1983).

Hobsbawm, E. J. *Nations and Nationalism Since 1788* (Cambridge, 1990).

Holohan, Francis T. 'History teaching in the Free State 1922–1935', *History Ireland*, 11, no. 4 (Winter 1994) pp 53–6.

Hone, J. M. *Thomas Davis* (London, 1934).

Hroch, Miroslav. *Social Pre-conditions of National Revival in Europe* (Cambridge, 1985).

Hutchinson, John. *The Dynamics of Cultural Nationalism; the Gaelic Revival and the Creation of the Irish Nation State* (London, 1954).

_____. *Modern Nationalism* (London, 1994).

Inglis, Brian. 'O'Connell and the Irish press, 1800–42', *Irish Historical Studies*, VIII, no. 29 (Mar. 1952), pp 1–28.

_____. *The Freedom of the Press in Ireland, 1784–1841* (London, 1954).

_____. 'The press', in R. B. McDowell (ed.), *Social Life in Ireland, 1800–1845* (Dublin, 1957).

Irwin, Liam. 'Sarsfield: the man and the myth', in Bernadette Whelan (ed.), *The Last of the Great Wars* (Limerick, 1995), pp 108–26.

Isaacs, Harold R. *Idols of the Tribe: Group Identity and Political Change* (New York, 1975).

Jones, Howard Mumford. *The Harp that Once: A Chronicle of the Life of Thomas Moore* (New York, 1937).

Kearns, Gerry. 'Time and some citizenship: nationalism and Thomas Davis', *Bullán: An Irish Studies Review*, v, no. 2 (2001), pp 23–54.

Kedourie, Elie. *Nationalism* (London, 1960).

Kelly, Charlotte. 'The '82 club', *Studies: An Irish Quarterly Review*, XXXIII (1944), pp 257–62.

Kelly, M. J. *The Fenian Ideal and Irish Nationalism, 1882–1916* (Woodbridge, 2006).

Kelly, Ronan. *Bard of Erin: The Life of Thomas Moore* (Dublin, 2008).

Kerr, Donal. *Peel, Priests and Politics* (Oxford, 1982).

Kerrigan, Colm. 'The social impact of the Irish temperance movement, 1839–45', *Irish Economic and Social History*, XIV (1987), pp 20–38.

_____. *Fr Mathew and the Irish Temperance Movement 1838–1849* (Cork, 1992).

Kidd, Colin. 'Gaelic antiquity and national identity in Enlightenment Ireland and Scotland', *English Historical Review*, 109 (1994), pp 1,197–1,214.

Kinealy, Christine. *Repeal and Revolution: 1848 in Ireland* (Manchester, 2009).

Kinsella, Anna. '1798 claimed for the Catholics: Father Kavanagh, Fenians and the centenary celebrations', in Dáire Keogh and Nicholas Furlong (eds), *The Mighty Wave: The 1798 Rebellion in Wexford* (Dublin, 1996), pp 139–55.

Kohn, Hans. *The Idea of Nationalism: A Study of its Origins and Background* (New York, 1944).

_____. 'Romanticism and the rise of nationalism', *Review of Politics*, 12 (1950) pp 443–72.

_____. *The Age of Nationalism* (New York, 1962).

_____. *Nationalism: Its Meaning and History* (London, 1965).

Langer, William L. *Political and Social Upheaval, 1832–1852* (New York, 1969).

Lebow, Ned. 'British historians and Irish history', *Éire-Ireland*, VIII, no. 4 (1973), pp 3–38.

Leerssen, Joep. *Mere Irish and Fíor-Ghael: Studies in the Idea of Irish Nationality, its Development and Literary Expression prior to the Nineteenth Century* (Amsterdam, 1986).

_____. 'Antiquarian research: patriotism to nationalism', in Cyril Byrne and Margaret Harry (ed.), *Talamh an Éisc: Canadian and Irish Essays* (Halifax, Nova Scotia, 1986), pp 71–83.

_____. '1798: The recurrence of violence and two conceptions of history', *The Irish Review*, 22 (Summer 1998), pp 37–45.

_____. *Remembrance and Imagination: Patterns in the Historical and Literary Representation of Ireland in the Nineteenth Century* (Cork, 1996).

_____. *Hidden Ireland: Public Sphere* (Galway, 2002).

_____. 'Irish cultural nationalism and its European context', in Bruce Stewart (ed.), *Hearts and Minds: Irish Culture and Society under the Act of Union* (Gerrards Cross, 2002), pp 170–87.

_____. 'Petrie: polymath and innovator', in Peter Murray (ed.), *George Petrie: The Rediscovery of Ireland's Past* (Cork & Kinsale, 2004), pp 7–11.

_____. *National Thought in Europe: A Cultural History* (Amsterdam, 2006).

Legg, Marie-Louise. *Newspapers and Nationalism: The Irish Provincial Press 1850–1892* (Dublin, 1999).

_____. 'Libraries', in James H. Murphy (ed.), *The Oxford History of the Irish Book, vol. iv: The Irish Book in English 1800–1891* (Oxford, 2011), pp 243–61.

Lewis, Bernard. *History – Remembered, Recovered, Invented* (Princeton, 1975).

Liechty, Joseph. 'Testing the depth of Catholic/Protestant enmity: the case of Thomas Leland's *History of Ireland*, 1773', *Archivium Hibernicum*, XLII (1987), pp 13–28.

Lloyd, David. *Nationalism and Minor Literature: James Clarence Mangan and the Emergence of Irish Cultural Nationalism* (Berkeley, 1987).

Loeber, Rolf and Magda Stouthamer-. 'James Duffy and Catholic nationalism', in James H. Murphy (ed.), *The Oxford History of the Irish Book, vol. iv: The Irish Book in English 1800–1891* (Oxford, 2011), pp 115–21.

Love, Walter. 'Charles O'Conor of Belanagare and Thomas Leland's "philosophical history of Ireland"', *Irish Historical Studies*, XIII, no. 49 (Mar. 1962), pp 1–25.

Lowe, W. J. 'The Chartists and the Irish Confederates: Lancashire, 1848', *Irish Historical Studies*, XXIV, no. 94 (Nov. 1984), pp 172–96.

Lyons, F. S. L. *Culture and Anarchy in Ireland, 1890–1939* (Oxford, 1979).

MacAodha, B. S. 'Aspects of the linguistic geography of Ireland in the early nineteenth century', *Studia Celtica*, 20/21 (1985–6), pp 205–20.

McBride, Lawrence W. (ed.). *Reading Irish Histories: Texts, Contexts and Memory in Modern Ireland* (Dublin, 2003).

_____. 'Young readers and the learning and teaching of Irish history', in idem. (ed.), *Reading Irish Histories: Texts, Contexts, and Memory in Modern Ireland* (Dublin, 2003), pp 80–117.

McCartney, Donal. 'The writing of Irish history, 1800–1830', in *Irish Historical Studies*, X, no. 40 (Sept. 1957), pp 347–62.

_____. 'James Anthony Froude and Ireland: a historiographical controversy of the nineteenth century', in T. Desmond Williams (ed.) *Historical Studies*, VIII (1971), pp 171–90.

_____. 'The political use of history in the work of Arthur Griffith', *Journal of Contemporary History*, VIII, no. 1 (1973), pp 3–19.

_____. *W. E. H. Lecky, Historian and Politician, 1838–1903* (Dublin, 1994).

McCormack, W. J. *Ascendancy and Tradition in Anglo-Irish Literary History from 1789 to 1929* (Oxford, 1985).

MacDonagh, Oliver. 'Ambiguity in nationalism – the case of Ireland', *Historical Studies* (University of Melbourne), XIX, 76 (Apr. 1981), pp 337–52.

_____. *States of Mind: A Study of Anglo-Irish Conflict* (London, 1983).

_____. Mandle, W. F. and Travers, P. (eds). *Irish Culture and Nationalism 1750–1950* (London, 1983).

MacDonagh, Oliver. *The Life of Daniel O'Connell 1775–1847* (London, 1991).

McFarland, E. W. *John Ferguson 1836–1906: Irish Issues in Scottish Politics* (East Linton, East Lothian, 2003).

McGee, Owen. *The IRB: The Irish Republican Brotherhood, from the Land League to Sinn Féin* (Dublin, 2005).

McGrath, Fergal. *Newman's University: Idea and Reality* (London, 1951).

McGrath, Kevin. 'Writers in the *Nation*, 1842–5', *Irish Historical Studies*, VI, no. 23 (Mar. 1949), pp 276–302.

McHugh, Roger. 'William Carleton: a portrait of the artist as propagandist', *Studies: An Irish Quarterly Review*, XXVII (1938), pp 47–62.

_____. 'Charles Lever', *Studies: An Irish Quarterly Review*, XXVII (1938), pp 247–60.

MacIntyrne, Angus. *The Liberator: Daniel O'Connell and the Irish Party, 1830–47* (London, 1965).

McManus, Antonia. *The Irish Hedge School and its Books* (Dublin, 2002).

MacNamara, Brinsley. 'Charles Gavan Duffy', in M. J. MacManus (ed.), *Thomas Davis and Young Ireland* (Dublin, 1945), pp 38–42.

Magee, Jack. *The Teaching of Irish History in Irish Schools* (Belfast, 1971).

Malcolm, Elizabeth. 'Temperance and Irish nationalism', in F. S. L. Lyons and R. A. J. Hawkins (eds), *Ireland Under the Union: Varieties of Tensions: Essays in Honour of T. W. Moody* (Oxford, 1980), pp 69–114.

_____. *'Ireland Sober; Ireland Free': Drink and Temperance in Nineteenth-Century Ireland* (Dublin, 1986).

Mandelbaum, Maurice. *History, Man and Reason: A Study in Nineteenth-Century Thought* (Baltimore, 1974).

Mangan, Ellen Shannon. *James Clarence Mangan: A Biography* (Dublin, 1996).

Mansergh, Nicholas. *Ireland in the Age of Reform and Revolution* (London, 1940).

Maume, Patrick. *The Long Gestation: Irish Nationalist Life, 1891–1918* (Dublin, 1999).

_____. 'Young Ireland, Arthur Griffith, and republican ideology: the question of continuity', *Éire-Ireland*, XXXIV, pt 2 (summer 1999), pp 155–74.

Maye, Brian. *Arthur Griffith* (Dublin, 1997).

Miller, David. *On Nationality* (Oxford, 1995).

Milne, Kenneth. *New Approaches to the Teaching of Irish History* (London, 1979).

Minogue, K. R. *Nationalism* (New York, 1967).

Molony, John N. *A Soul Came into Ireland: Thomas Davis 1814–1845* (Dublin, 1995).

Moody, T. W. *Thomas Davis, 1814–1845* (Dublin, 1945).

_____. 'Thomas Davis and the Irish nation', *Hermathena*, CIII (1966), pp 5–31.

_____. (ed.). *The Fenian Movement* (Dublin, 1968).

_____. 'Irish history and Irish mythology', *Hermathena*, CXXIV (1978), pp 7–24.

Moore, Margaret. *The Ethics of Nationalism* (Oxford, 2001).

Morash, Christopher. *Writing the Irish Famine* (Oxford, 1995).

_____. 'Making memories: the literature of the Irish Famine', in Patrick O'Sullivan (ed.), *The Meaning of the Famine* (London and Washington, 1996), pp 40–53.

Morley, Vincent. 'Views of the past in Irish vernacular literature, 1650–1850', in T. C. W. Blanning and Hagen Schulze (eds), *Unity and Diversity in European Culture* (Oxford, 2006) (*Proceedings of the British Academy*, 134), pp 171–98.

Morrow, John. 'Thomas Carlyle, "Young Ireland" and the "condition of Ireland question"', *The Historical Journal*, LI, no. 3 (2008), pp 643–67.

Mulvey, Helen F. 'Sir Charles Gavan Duffy: Young Irelander and imperial statesman', *Canadian Historical Review*, XXXIII (1952), pp 369–89.

_____. 'The historian Lecky: opponent of Irish home rule', *Victorian Studies*, I, no. 4 (June 1958), pp 337–51.

_____. *Thomas Davis and Ireland* (Washington, 2003).

Murphy, Maura. 'The ballad singer and the role of the seditious ballad in nineteenth- century Ireland: Dublin Castle's view', *Ulster Folklife*, XXV (1979), pp 79–102.

Murphy, Sean. 'Women and *The Nation*', *History Ireland*, I, no. 3 (Autumn, 1993), pp 34–8.

Murray, Damien. *Romanticism, Nationalism and Irish Antiquarian Societies, 1840–80* (Maynooth, 2000).

Murray, Peter. *George Petrie: The Rediscovery of Ireland's Past* (Cork & Kinsale, 2004).

Namier, L. B. *1848: The Revolution of the Intellectuals* (6th edn, Oxford, 1971).

Neff, Emery Edward. *The Poetry of History: The Contribution of Literature and Literary Scholarship to the Writing of History since Voltaire* (New York, 1947).

Nolan, Janet. 'Unintended consequences: the national schools and Irish women's mobility in the late nineteenth and early twentieth centuries', in D. George Boyce and Alan O'Day (eds), *Ireland in Transition* (London, 2004), pp 179–92.

Norsstedt, Johann A. *Thomas MacDonagh: A Critical Biography* (Charlottesville, Va., 1980).

Nowlan, Kevin B. 'Writings in connection with the Thomas Davis and Young Ireland centenary, 1945', *Irish Historical Studies*, v, no. 19 (Mar. 1947) pp 265–72.

_____. 'The Risorgimento and Ireland, 1820–48', in R. Dudley Edwards (ed.), *Ireland and the Italian Risorgimento* (Dublin, 1960), pp 19–30.

_____. 'The meaning of repeal in Irish history', in G. A Hayes-McCoy (ed.) *Historical Studies*, IV, (London, 1963), pp 1–17.

_____. *Charles Gavan Duffy and the Repeal Movement* (NUI, 1963).

_____. *The Politics of Repeal: A Study of the Relations between Great Britain and Ireland, 1841–50* (London, 1965).

Ó Broin, Leon. *Charles Gavan Duffy* (Dublin, 1967).

_____. *An Maidíneach, Staraí na hÉireannach Aontaithe* (Dublin, 1971).

Ó Buachalla, S. P. (ed.), *A Significant Irish Educationalist: The Educational Writings of P. H. Pearse* (Dublin & Cork, 1980).

O'Callaghan, Margaret. '"With the eyes of another race, of a people once hunted themselves": Casement, colonialism and a remembered past', in D. George Boyce and Alan O'Day (eds), *Ireland in Transition* (London, 2004), pp 159–75.

Ó Cathaoir, Brendan. *John Blake Dillon: Young Irelander* (Dublin, 1990).

Ó Ciosáin, Niall. *Print and Popular Culture in Ireland, 1750–1850* (London, 1997).

Ó Cléirigh, Séamus. *Casement and the Irish Language, Culture and History* (Dublin, 1977).

Ó Cuív, Brian. *A View of the Irish Language* (Dublin, 1969).

_____. 'Irish language and literature 1691–1845', in T. W. Moody and W. E. Vaughan (eds), *A New History of Ireland: Eighteenth-Century Ireland 1691–1800*, IV, pp 374–422.

_____. 'Irish language and literature 1845–1921', in W. E. Vaughan (ed.), *A New History of Ireland: Ireland under the Union, II: 1870–1921*, VI, pp 385–435.

O'Day, Alan (ed.), *Reactions to Irish Nationalism* (Dublin, 1987).

O'Driscoll, Robert. 'Ferguson and the idea of an Irish national literature', *Éire-Ireland*, VI, no. 1 (spring, 1971), pp 82–95.

_____. *An Ascendancy of the Heart: Ferguson and the Beginnings of Modern Irish Literature* (Dublin, 1976).

O'Faolain, Sean. 'The plain people of Ireland', *The Bell*, VII, no. 1 (1943), pp 1–7.

———. *King of the Beggars: A Life of Daniel O'Connell* (London, 1938).

O'Farrell, Patrick. 'Whose reality? the Irish Famine in history and literature', *Historical Studies* (University of Melbourne), XX, no. 78 (Apr. 1982), pp 1–13.

O'Halloran, Clare. *Partition and the Limits of Irish Nationalism: An Ideology Under Stress* (Dublin, 1987).

———. 'Irish re-creations of the Gaelic past: the challenge of Macpherson's Ossian', *Past and Present*, 124 (Aug. 1989), pp 69–95.

———. '"The Island of Saints and Scholars": views of the early church and sectarian politics in late eighteenth-century Ireland', *Eighteenth-Century Ireland: Iris an Dá Chultúr*, V (1990), pp 7–20.

———. *Golden Ages and Barbarous Nations: Antiquarian Debate and Cultural Politics in Ireland, 1760–1800* (Cork, 2004).

———. 'Historical writings, 1690–1890', in Margaret Kelleher and Philip O'Leary (eds), *The Cambridge History of Irish Literature* (2 vols, 2006), I, pp 599–632.

O'Hegarty, P. S. 'The "Library of Ireland" 1845–1847', in M. J. MacManus (ed.), *Thomas Davis and Young Ireland* (Dublin, 1945), pp 109–13.

———. *A History of Ireland under the Union 1801–1922* (London, 1952).

Ó Loinsigh, P. 'The Irish language in the nineteenth century', *Oideas*, 14 (1975), pp 5–21.

O'Malley, Ernie. *On Another Man's Wound* (Dublin, rev. edn 2002).

O'Neill, Patrick. *Ireland and Germany: A Study in Literary Relations* (New York, 1985).

O'Neill, Thomas P. 'Notes on Irish radical journals', *An Leabharlann: The Irish Library*, XII, no. 4 (Dec. 1954), pp 139–44.

Ó Raifeartaigh, T. 'Mixed Education and the Synod of Ulster', *Irish Historical Studies*, IX, no. 35 (Mar. 1955), pp 281–99.

O'Sullivan, T. F. *The Young Irelanders* (Tralee, 1944).

Ó Tuathaigh, Gearóid. *Ireland Before the Famine 1798–1848* (Dublin, 1972).

———. 'The state, sentiment and the politics of language', in Bruce Stewart (ed.), *Hearts and Minds: Irish Culture and Society under the Act of Union* (Gerrards Cross, 2002), pp 71–89.

Palmer, Norman D. 'Sir Robert Peel's "Select Irish library"', *Irish Historical Studies*, VI, no. 22 (Sept. 1948), pp 101–13.

Paseta, Senia. *Before the Revolution: Nationalism, Social Change and Ireland's Catholic Elite, 1879–1922* (Cork, 1999).

Patten, Eve. *Samuel Ferguson and the Culture of Nineteenth-Century Ireland* (Dublin, 2004).

Patterson, Tony. 'Robert Cane and Young Ireland', *Old Kilkenny Review: Journal of the Kilkenny Archaeological Society*, 1 (1998), pp 67–82.

Pearl, Cyril. *The Three Lives of Gavan Duffy* (Kensington, NSW, 1979).

Pearton, Maurice. 'Nicolae Iorga as historian and politician', in Dennis Deletant & Harry Hanak (eds), *Historians as Nation Builders: Central and South East Europe* (London, 1988), pp 157–73.

Peatling, G. K. 'Who fears to speak of politics? John Kells Ingram and hypothetical nationalism', *Irish Historical Studies*, XXXI, no. 122 (Nov. 1998), pp 202–21.

Plumb, J. H. *The Death of the Past* (London, 1969).

Pynsent, Robert B. 'Zabid Vysokomytsky: a Czech rebel historian of 1848–9', in Dennis Deletant & Harry Hanak (eds), *Historians as Nation Builders: Central and South East Europe* (London, 1988), pp 174–205.

Quinn, James. 'John Mitchel and the rejection of the Nineteenth Century', *Éire-Ireland*, XXXVIII, pts 3–4 (fall/winter 2003), pp 90–108.

____. 'Patrick Pearse and the reproach of history', in Roisín Higgins and Regina Uí Chollatáin (eds), *The Life and After-Life of P. H. Pearse – Pádraic Mac Piarais: Saol agus Oidhreacht* (Dublin, 2009), pp 99–110.

____. 'The IRB and Young Ireland: varieties of tension', in Fearghal McGarry and James McConnel (eds), *The Black Hand of Republicanism: Fenianism in Modern Ireland* (Dublin, 2009), pp 3–17.

____. 'Thomas Davis and the Patriot Parliament of 1689', in James Kelly, John McCafferty and Charles Ivar McGrath (eds), *People, Politics and Power: Essays on Irish History 1660–1850 in Honour of James I. McGuire* (Dublin, 2009), pp 190–202.

Rafroidi, Patrick. *Irish Literature in English: The Romantic Period* (1789–1850) (2 vols, Gerrards Cross, 1980).

Raftery, Joseph. 'George Petrie: a reassessment', *Proceedings of the Royal Irish Academy*, 72C (1972), pp 153–7.

Rearick, Charles. *Beyond the Enlightenment: Historians and Folklore in Nineteenth-Century France* (Bloomington, Ind., 1974).

Renan, Ernest.'What is a nation?' (1882), in Louis L. Snyder (ed.), *The Meaning of Nationalism* (Westport, Conn., 1968).

Rigney, Anne. *The Rhetoric of Historical Representation* (Cambridge, 1990).

Ryder, Seán. 'Gender and the discourse of Young Ireland cultural nationalism', in Timothy P. Foley *et al.* (eds), *Gender and Colonialism* (Galway, 1995), pp 210–24.

____. 'Speaking of '98: Young Ireland and republican memory', *Éire-Ireland*, XXXIV, no. 2 (1999), pp 51–69.

____. 'Young Ireland and the 1798 Rebellion', in Laurence M. Geary (ed.), *Rebellion and Remembrance in Modern Ireland* (Dublin, 2001), pp 135–47.

____. '"With a heroic life and a governing mind": nineteenth-century Irish nationalist autobiography', in Liam Harte (ed.), *Modern Irish Autobiography: Self, Nation and Spirit* (Basingstoke, 2007), pp 14–31.

Sadleir, Michael. *The Dublin University Magazine; Its History, Contents, and Bibliography* (Dublin, 1938).

Sanders, Charles Richard. *Carlyle's Friendships and Other Studies* (Durham, N.C., 1977).

Sayers, Stephen. 'Irish myth and Irish national consciousness', *Irish Studies Review*, XII, no. 3 (Dec. 2004), pp 271–82.

Schenk, Hans G. H. V. *The Mind of the European Romantics* (London, 1966).

Seton-Watson, Hugh. *Nations and States: An Enquiry into the Origins of Nations and the Politics of Nationalism* (London, 1977).

Shafer, Boyd C. *Nationalism: Myth and Reality* (New York, 1955).

____. *Faces of Nationalism: New Realities and Old Myths* (New York, 1972).

Shannon-Mangan, Ellen. *James Clarence Mangan: A Biography* (Dublin, 1996).

Sheehy, Jeanne. *The Rediscovery of Ireland's Past: The Celtic Revival 1830–1930* (London, 1980).

Sisson, Elaine. *Pearse's Patriots: St Enda's and the Cult of Boyhood* (Cork, 2004).

Sloan, Barry. 'The autobiographies of John Mitchel and Charles Gavan Duffy: a study in contrasts', *Éire-Ireland*, XXII, no. 2 (summer 1987), pp 27–38.

Sloan, Robert. 'O'Connell's liberal rivals in 1843', *Irish Historical Studies*, xxx, no. 117 (May 1996), pp 47–65.

Smith, Anthony D. *The Ethnic Origins of Nations* (Oxford, 1987).

——. *Nationalism and Modernism* (London, 1998).

——. *Myths and Memories of the Nation* (Oxford, 1999).

——. *The Nation in History* (Hanover, N. H., 2000).

——. *Nationalism: Theory, Ideology, History* (Cambridge, 2001).

——. *The Antiquity of Nations* (Cambridge, 2004).

Smithson, Rulon Nephi. *Augustin Thierry: Social and Political Consciousness in the Evolution of an Historical Method* (Genève, 1973).

Swift, Cathy. 'John O'Donovan and the framing of medieval Ireland', *Bullán*, 1 (1994), pp 91–103.

Swift, Roger. 'Carlyle and Ireland', in D. George Boyce and Roger Swift (eds), *Problems and Perspectives in Irish History Since 1800: Essays in Honour of Patrick Buckland* (Dublin, 2004), pp 117–46.

Thuente, Mary Helen. *W. B. Yeats and Irish Folklore* (Dublin, 1980).

——. *The Harp Re-strung: The United Irishmen and the Rise of Irish Literary Nationalism* (New York, 1994).

Tierney, Mark. 'Eugene O'Curry and the Irish tradition', *Studies: An Irish Quarterly Review*, LI (winter, 1962) pp 449–62.

Tierney, Michael. 'Thomas Davis: 1814–1845', *Studies: An Irish Quarterly Review*, xxxiv, no. 135 (1945), pp 300–10.

Tilley, Elizabeth. 'Periodicals', in James H. Murphy (ed.), *The Oxford History of the Irish Book, vol. iv: The Irish Book in English 1800–1891* (Oxford, 2011), pp 144–70.

Townend, Paul A. '"Academies of Nationality": the reading room and Irish national movements, 1838–1905', in Lawrence W. McBride (ed.), *Reading Irish Histories: Texts, Contexts and Memory in Modern Ireland* (Dublin, 2003), pp 19–39.

Vance, Norman. 'Celts, Carthaginians and constitutions: Anglo-Irish literary relations 1780–1820', *Irish Historical Studies*, xxii, no. 87 (Mar. 1981), pp 216–36.

——. *Irish literature: A Social History* (Oxford, 1990).

Wall, Maureen. 'The decline of the Irish language', in Brian Ó Cuív (ed.), *A View of the Irish Language* (Dublin, 1969), pp 81–90.

Whelan, Kevin. 'The United Irishmen, the enlightenment and popular culture', in David Dickson, Dáire Keogh and Kevin Whelan (eds), *The United Irishmen: Republicanism, Radicalism and Rebellion* (Dublin, 1993), pp 297–306.

White, Harry. *The Keeper's Recital: Music and Cultural History in Ireland, 1770–1970* (Cork, 1998).

White, Hayden. *Metahistory: The Historical Imagination in Nineteenth-Century Europe* (Baltimore, 1987).

——. *The Content of Form: Narrative Discourse and Historical Representation* (Baltimore and London, 1987).

Whyte, John H. *The Independent Irish Party 1850–9* (Oxford, 1958).

——. 'Daniel O'Connell and the repeal party', *Irish Historical Studies*, xi, no. 44 (Sept. 1959), pp 297–316.

Williams, Martin. 'Ancient history and revolutionary ideology in Ireland 1878–1916', in *Historical Journal*, xvi (1983), pp 307–10.

Wilson, David A. *Thomas D'Arcy McGee: Volume 1: Passion, Reason, and Politics 1825–1857* (Montreal and Kingston, 2008).

_____. *Thomas D'Arcy McGee: Volume 2: The Extreme Moderate 1857–1868* (Montreal & Kingston, 2011).

Woods, C. J. 'Tone's grave at Bodenstown: memorials and commemorations, 1798–1913', in Dorothea Siegmund-Schultze (ed.), *Irland: Gesellschaft und Kultur VI* (Halle, 1989), pp 138–48.

_____. 'Historical revision: was O'Connell a United Irishman?', *Irish Historical Studies*, xxxv, no. 138 (Nov. 2006), pp 173–83.

Wyatt, Anne. 'Froude, Lecky, and "the humblest Irishman"', *Irish Historical Studies*, xix, no. 75 (Mar. 1975), pp 261–85.

Zimmerman, Georges Denis. *Irish Political Street Ballads and Rebel Songs, 1780–1900* (Geneva, 1966).

REFERENCE WORKS

Boyd, Kelly (ed.). *Encyclopaedia of Historians and History Writing* (2 vols, London and Chicago, 1999).

Cannon, John *et al* (ed.). *The Blackwell Dictionary of Historians* (Oxford, 1988).

Connolly, S. J. (ed.) *The Oxford Companion to Irish History* (Oxford, 1998).

Gardiner, Juliet (ed.). The History Today: *Who's Who in British History* (London, 2000)

Hickey, D. J. and Doherty, J. E. (eds). *A New Dictionary of Irish History from 1800* (Dublin, 2003).

Loeber, Rolf and Magda Stouthamer- (eds). *A Guide to Irish Fiction, 1650–1900* (Dublin, 2006).

McGuire, James and Quinn, James (eds). The Royal Irish Academy's *Dictionary of Irish Biography from the Earliest Times to the Year 2002* (9 vols, Cambridge, 2009).

Matthew, H. C. G and Harrison, Brian (eds). *Oxford Dictionary of National Biography* (60 vols, Oxford, 2004).

Moody, T. W., Martin, F. X. and Byrne, F. J (eds). *A New History of Ireland, VIII: A Chronology of Irish History to 1976* (Oxford, 1982).

Welch, Robert (ed.). *The Oxford Companion to Irish Literature* (Oxford, 1996).

Index

—